T0190475

# Communications in Computer and Information Science     1240

*Commenced Publication in 2007*
Founding and Former Series Editors:
Simone Diniz Junqueira Barbosa, Phoebe Chen, Alfredo Cuzzocrea,
Xiaoyong Du, Orhun Kara, Ting Liu, Krishna M. Sivalingam,
Dominik Ślęzak, Takashi Washio, Xiaokang Yang, and Junsong Yuan

More information about this series at http://www.springer.com/series/7899

Arup Bhattacharjee · Samir Kr. Borgohain ·
Badal Soni · Gyanendra Verma ·
Xiao-Zhi Gao (Eds.)

# Machine Learning, Image Processing, Network Security and Data Sciences

Second International Conference, MIND 2020
Silchar, India, July 30–31, 2020
Proceedings, Part I

 Springer

*Editors*
Arup Bhattacharjee (iD)
National Institute of Technology Silchar
Silchar, India

Badal Soni (iD)
National Institute of Technology Silchar
Silchar, India

Xiao-Zhi Gao (iD)
University of Eastern Finland
Kuopio, Finland

Samir Kr. Borgohain (iD)
National Institute of Technology Silchar
Silchar, India

Gyanendra Verma (iD)
National Institute of Technology
Kurukshetra
Kurukshetra, India

ISSN 1865-0929          ISSN 1865-0937   (electronic)
Communications in Computer and Information Science
ISBN 978-981-15-6314-0          ISBN 978-981-15-6315-7   (eBook)
https://doi.org/10.1007/978-981-15-6315-7

This Springer imprint is published by the registered company Springer Nature Singapore Pte Ltd.
The registered company address is: 152 Beach Road, #21-01/04 Gateway East, Singapore 189721, Singapore

# Preface

It is our great honor and privilege to present the proceedings of the Second International Conference on Machine Learning, Image Processing, Network Security and Data Sciences (MIND 2020), organized by the National Institute of Technology Silchar, India, and held during July 30–31, 2020. This conference is the second in a series which focuses on Machine Learning, Image Processing, Network Security, and Data Sciences. The papers included in these proceedings present original ideas and up-to-date discussions and directions regarding topics of interest of the conference.

MIND 2020 provided a platform to the researchers, practitioners, and technologists to present and discuss state-of-the-art novelties, trends, issues, and challenges in the area of Machine Learning, Image Processing, Network Security, and Data Sciences. Organization of this conference was primarily motivated by the need to promote research through sharing of ideas, technology, and trends at all levels of the scientific and technical community. Another motivation was the need for a common platform for building a framework for development of solutions to unresolved issues and challenges in different areas of computer engineering and engineering. This edition, continuing the spirit of the previous conference in this series, depicts the most important requirements of the academia and industry: quality and value. This was substantiated by the 219 high-quality submissions which posed a great challenge in the review and selection process. Each submission was subjected to at least three reviews under a double-blind peer review process mechanism. Based on the review results and recommendations of the Program Committee, 83 papers were accepted for presentation at the main conference. This resulted in an acceptance rate lower than 38%. Due to the COVID-19 outbreak, the conference was organized in a virtual format instead of as an onsite event. Further, though initially the conference was planned to be organized during April 23–24, 2020, the outbreak compelled the organizers to postpone the conference till July 30–31, 2020.

Any event of this nature needs sufficient time, complete support, and wholehearted cooperation and support of all, for success. We thank all the authors for submitting and presenting their quality paper(s) to/at MIND 2020. We are extremely thankful to the reviewers, who have carried out the most important and critical part of any academic conference, the evaluation of each of the submitted papers assigned to them. We also express our gratitude to the TPC members for their immense support and motivation in making MIND 2020 a success. We sincerely thank all the chairs for their hard work without which the success of MIND 2020 would not have been possible. We are also grateful to our invited speakers for enlightening and motivating the participants of the conference. We also express our sincere gratitude towards our publication partner,

Springer, for trusting and guiding us. We are obliged to TEQIP-III and DST-SERB for officially sponsoring MIND 2020.

May 2020                                                    Arup Bhattacharjee

# Organization

## Executive Committee

### Patron

Sivaji Bandyopadhyay     National Institute of Technology Silchar, India

### Honorary Chair

Rajkumar Buyya     The University of Melbourne, Australia

### General Chairs

Arup Bhattacharjee     National Institute of Technology Silchar, India
Salah Bourennane     École centrale de Marseille, France

### Organizing Chairs

Samir Kr. Borgohain     National Institute of Technology Silchar, India
Badal Soni     National Institute of Technology Silchar, India

### Technical Program Chairs

Xiao-Zhi Gao     University of Eastern Finland, Finland
Ching-Hsien Hsu     Asia University, Taiwan
Suganya Devi K.     National Institute of Technology Silchar, India
Gyanendra Verma     National Institute of Technology Kurukshetra, India
Bidyut Kumar Patra     National Institute of Technology Rourkela, India

### Finance and Hospitality Chairs

Ujwala Baruah     National Institute of Technology Silchar, India
Pantha K. Nath     National Institute of Technology Silchar, India
Umakanta Majhi     National Institute of Technology Silchar, India

## Publication and Publicity Committee

### Publication Chairs

Shyamosree Pal     National Institute of Technology Silchar, India
Naresh Babu M.     National Institute of Technology Silchar, India
Rajesh Doriya     National Institute of Technology Raipur, India

### Publicity Chairs

Rajib Kumar Jha     IIT Patna, India
Chiranjoy Chattopadhyay     IIT Jodhpur, India

| Manish Okade | National Institute of Technology Rourkela, India |
| Poonam Sharma | National Institute of Technology Nagpur, India |
| Divya Kumar | National Institute of Technology Allahabad, India |
| Nabajyoti Medhi | Tezpur University, India |
| Sraban Kumar Mohanty | IIITDM Jabalpur, India |

## Steering Committee

| Rajkumar Buyya | The University of Melbourne and Manjrasoft, Australia |
| Awadhesh Kumar Singh | National Institute of Technology Kurukshetra, India |
| B. B. Gupta | National Institute of Technology Kurukshetra, India |
| Gyanendra Verma | National Institute of Technology Kurukshetra, India |
| Rajesh Doriya | National Institute of Technology Raipur, India |

## Technical Program Committee

| A. Chandrasekhar | IIT Dhanbad, India |
| A. Rajesh | Vellore Institute of Technology, India |
| A. Muthumari | University College of Engineering, Ramanathapuram, India |
| Aakanksha Sharaff | National Institute of Technology Raipur, India |
| Abdel Badi Salem | Ain Shams University, Egypt |
| Abdel-Hamid Ali Soliman | Staffordshire University, UK |
| Abdul Jalil M. Khalaf | University of Kufa, Iraq |
| Aditya Trivedi | IIITDM Gwalior, India |
| Alexander Gelbukh | National Polytechnic Institute, Mexico |
| Ali Jaoua | Qatar University, Qatar |
| Amr Ahmed | Google AI, UK |
| Anil Sao | IIT Mandi, India |
| Ankit Kumar Jain | National Institute of Technology Kurukshetra, India |
| Annappa | National Institute of Technology Karnataka, India |
| Anoop Patel | National Institute of Technology Kurukshetra, India |
| Anshul Verma | Banaras Hindu University, India |
| Antonina Dattolo | University of Udine, Italy |
| Anupam Shukla | IIITDM Gwalior, India |
| Aparajita Ojha | IIITDM Jabalpur, India |
| Ashish Ghosh | Indian Statistical Institute, India |
| Ashish Khare | University of Allahabad, India |
| Ashraf Hossain | National Institute of Technology Silchar, India |
| Atul Gupta | IIITDM Jabalpur, India |
| Awadhesh Kumar Singh | National Institute of Technology Kurukshetra, India |
| B. L. Velammal | Anna University, India |
| Balwinder Singh Sodhi | IIT Ropar, India |
| Basant Kumar | NIT Allahabad, India |
| Biswajit Purkayastha | National Institute of Technology Silchar, India |

| | |
|---|---|
| Bondu Venkateswarlu | Dayananda Sagar University, India |
| Brijesh Kumar Chaurasia | Indian Institute of Information Technology Lucknow, India |
| C. Bose | Anna University, India |
| C. Rani | Government College of Engineering, Salem, India |
| C. S. Sastry | IIT Hyderabad, India |
| Carlos Becker Westphall | University of Kentucky, USA |
| Ching-Hsien Hsu | Asia University, Taiwan |
| Chun-I Fan | National Sun Yat-sen University, Taiwan |
| Dalton Meitei Thounaojam | National Institute of Technology Silchar, India |
| David Klaus | University of Kassel, Germany |
| Davide Adami | University of Pisa, Italy |
| Davide Adami | Unipi, Italy |
| Debajyoti Choudhuri | National Institute of Technology Rourkela, India |
| Deep Gupta | National Institute of Technology Nagpur, India |
| Desineni Subbaram Naidu | University of Minnesota Duluth, USA |
| Dimitrios A. Karras | National and Kapodistrian University of Athens, Greece |
| Dinesh Vishwakarma | Delhi Technological University Delhi, India |
| Dipti Kapoor Sarmah | Utrecht University, The Netherlands |
| Eugénia Moreira Bernardino | Instituto Politécnico de Leiria, Portugal |
| Fateh Krim | Ferhat Abbas University of Setif, Algeria |
| Félix J. García Clemente | University in Murcia, Spain |
| G. Lavanya Devi | Andhra University, India |
| G. C. Nandi | IIIT Allahabad, India |
| G. Jaya Suma | JNTUK, University College of Engineering, India |
| Gaurav Varshney | Indian Institute of Technology Jammu, India |
| Gaurav Verma | National Institute of Technology Kurukshetra, India |
| Gautam Barua | IIIT Guwahati, India |
| Gyan Singh Yadav | Indian Institute of Information Technology Kota, India |
| H. K. Sardana | Central Scientific Instruments Organization (CSIR), India |
| Haimonti Dutta | State University of New York at Buffalo, USA |
| Ioannis Pitas | Aristotle University of Thessaloniki, Greece |
| Jalel Ben-Othman | CerraCap Ventures, France |
| Jayendra Kumar | Vellore Institute of Technology, India |
| John Jose | Indian Institute of Technology Guwahati, India |
| José Mario de Martino | Campinas State University, Brazil |
| Joseph Gladwin | SSN College of Engineering, India |
| Jukka K. Nurminen | University of Helsinki, Finland |
| Jupitara Hazarika | National Institute of Technology Silchar, India |
| K. K. Shukla | Indian Institute of Technology Banaras, India |
| K. Vivekanandan | Pondicherry Engineering College Puducherry, India |
| Kamran Arshad | Ajman University, UAE |
| Karthikeyan Subramanian | Sohar College of Applied Sciences, Oman |

| | |
|---|---|
| Klaus Moessner | University of Surrey, UK |
| Kolin Paul | Indian Institute of Technology Delhi, India |
| Kouichi Sakurai | National University Corporation Kyushu University, Japan |
| Koushlendra Kumar Singh | National Institute of Technology Jamshedpur, India |
| Krishn K. Mishra | NIT Allahabad, India |
| Kulwinder Singh | University of South Florida, USA |
| Laiphrakpam Dolendro Singh | National Institute of Technology Silchar, India |
| Latha Parthiban | Pondicherry University, India |
| Thomas D. Little | Boston University, USA |
| M. Sampath Kumar | Andhra University College of Engineering, India |
| Madhusudan Singh | Woosong University, South Korea |
| Mahalakshmi A. | Anna University, India |
| Mahendra Kumar Murmu | National Institute of Technology Kurukshetra, India |
| Malaya Dutta Borah | National Institute of Technology Silchar, India |
| Manjula Perkinian | Anna University, India |
| Manoj Kumar Singh | Banaras Hindu University, India |
| Mantosh Biswas | National Institute of Technology Kurukshetra, India |
| Marcelo S. Alencar | UFCG, Brazil |
| Marcelo Sampaio Alencar | Federal University of Campina Grande, Brazil |
| Mayank Dave | National Institute of Technology Kurukshetra, India |
| Mitul Kumar Ahirwal | National Institute of Technology Bhopal, India |
| Mohammed A. Qadeer | Aligarh Muslim University, India |
| Mohammed Bouhorma | Abdelmalek Essaâdi University, Morocco |
| Mullavisala Ravibabu | IIT Ropar, India |
| N. Malmurugan | Mahendra College of Engineering, India |
| N. Nasimuddin | Agency of Science Technology and Research, Singapore |
| Nabanita Adhikary | National Institute of Technology Silchar, India |
| Narendra Kohli | Harcourt Butler Technical University Kanpur, India |
| Navjot Singh | NIT Allahabad, India |
| Neminath Hubbali | Indian Institute of Technology Indore, India |
| Nidhi Gupta | Chinese Academy of Sciences, China |
| Nidul Sinha | National Institute of Technology Silchar, India. |
| Niharika Singh | UPES, India |
| Nityananda Sarma | Tezpur University, India |
| Niyati Baliyan | Indira Gandhi Delhi Technical University for Women, India |
| O. P. Vyas | IIT Allahabad, India |
| Onkar Krishna | NTT Coporation, Japan |
| P. V. Lakshmi | Gitam University, India |
| P. Ganesh Kumar | Anna University, India |
| P. Yogesh | Anna University, India |
| P. Sudhakar | Annamalai University, India |

| | |
|---|---|
| Pankaj Pratap Singh | Central Institute of Technology (CIT) Kokrajhar, India |
| Pao-Ann Hsiung | National Chung Cheng University, Taiwan |
| Paolo Crippa | Università Politecnica delle Marche, Italy |
| Partha Pakray | National Institute of Technology Silchar, India |
| Pascal Lorenz | University of Haute Alsace, France |
| Poonam Dhaka | University of Namibia, Namibia |
| Poonam Saini | PEC Chandigarh, CSE Punjab Engineering College, India |
| Prabir Kumar Biswas | IIT Kharagpur, India |
| Pradeep Singh | National Institute of Technology Raipur, India |
| Pradip K. Das | Indian Institute of Technology Guwahati, India |
| Prashant Giridhar Shambharkar | Delhi Technological University, Delhi |
| Pratik Chattopadhyay | Indian Institute of Technology (BHU), India |
| Pritee Khanna | IIITDM Jabalpur, India |
| R. Vasanth Kumar Mehta | SCSVMV University, India |
| R. Balasubramanian | Indian Institute of Technology Roorkee, India |
| R. Murugan | National Institute of Technology Silchar, India |
| Rajdeep Niyogi | IIT Roorkee, India |
| Rajesh Pandey | IIT BHU, India |
| Rajesh Prasad | IIT Delhi, India |
| Rajlaxmi Chouhan | Indian Institute of Technology Jodhpur, India |
| Rakesh Kumar Lenka | IIIT Bhubaneswar, India |
| Ram Bilas Pachori | Indian Institute of Technology Indore, India |
| Ranjay Hazra | National Institute of Technology Silchar, India |
| Ranjeet Kumar | Madanpalle Institute of Technology and Science, India |
| Ravi Panwar | Indian Institute of Information Technology, Design and Manufacturing, India |
| Rekh Ram Janghel | National Institute of Technology Raipur, India |
| S. Sridevi | Thiagarajar College of Engineering, India |
| Saber Abd-Allah | Beni Suef University, Egypt |
| Salah Bourennane | École centrale de Marseille, France |
| Samudra Vijaya K. | CLST, Indian Institute of Technology Guwahati, India |
| Sanasam Ranbir Singh | IIT Guwahati, India |
| Sanjaya Kumar Panda | Veer Surendra Sai University of Technology (VSSUT) Odisha, India |
| Santosh Rathore | National Institute of Technology Jalandhar, India |
| Saroj Kumar Biswas | National Institute of Technology Silchar, India |
| Saurabh Ranjan | Orange County, USA |
| Saurabh Tiwari | DAIICT Gandhinagar, India |
| Seetharaman K. | Annamalai University, India |
| Senthilkumar | Anna University, India |
| Shankar. K. | National Institute of Technology Silchar, India |
| Sugam K. Sharma | Iowa State University, USA |
| Shashi Shekhar Jha | Indian Institute of Technology Ropar, India |

| Sherif Rashad | Morehead State University, USA |
| Shitala Prasad | Nanyang Technological University, Singapore |
| Shivashankar B. Nair | Indian Institute of Technology Guwahati, India |
| Shuai Zhao | University of Missouri, USA |
| Shyamapada Mukherjee | National Institute of Technology Silchar, India |
| Simon Pietro Romano | University of Naples Federico, Italy |
| Soumen Bag | Indian Institute of Technology, Indian School of Mines, Dhanbad, India |
| Srinivas Koppu | Vellore Institute of Technology, India |
| Srinivas Pinisetty | IIT Bhubaneswar, India |
| Sriparna Saha | IIT Patna, India |
| Subhash Bhalla | University of Aizu, Japan |
| Subhrakanta Panda | BITS-PILANI Hyderabad, India |
| Sudarsan Sahoo | National Institute of Technology Silchar, India |
| Sudhir Kumar | IIT Patna, India |
| Sudipta Mukhopadhyay | Indian Institute of Technology Kharagpur, India |
| Sukumar Nandi | Indian Institute of Technology Guwahati, India |
| Suneeta Agarwal | MNNIT Allahabad, India |
| Swati Vipsita | IIIT Bhubaneswar, India |
| Syed Taqi Ali | Visvesvaraya National Institute of Technology Nagpur, India |
| T. G. Vasista | Mizan Tepi University, Ethiopia |
| Thanikaiselvan V. | Vellore Institute of Technology, India |
| Thoudam Doren Singh | National Institute of Technology Silchar, India |
| Tomasz Rak | Rzeszow University of Technology, Poland |
| Tracy Liu | AT&LABS, USA |
| Tripti Goel | National Institute of Technology Silchar, India |
| Uma Shanker Tiwary | IIIT Allahabad, India |
| Umashankar Subramaniam | Prince Sultan University, Saudi Arabia |
| Utpal Sharma | Tezpur University, India |
| V. Balaji | KCG College of Technology, India |
| V. M. Senthilkumar | Malla Reddy College of Engineering and Technology, India |
| V. Ramalingam | Annamalai University, India |
| Veenu Mangat | Panjab University, India |
| Venkateswari Palanisami | Sengunthar Engineering College, India |
| Vijay Bhaskar Semwal | Maulana Azad National Institute of Technology Bhopal, India |
| Vikram Singh | National Institute of Technology Kurukshetra, India |
| Viranjay M. Srivastava | University of KwaZulu-Natal, South Africa |
| Vishal Ramesh Satpute | VNIT Nagpur, India |
| Vishal Saraswat | Robert Bosch Engineering and Business Solutions Pvt. Ltd., India |
| Vivek Dikshit | IIT Kharagpur, India |
| Vivek S. Verma | AKGEC Ghaziabad, India |
| Wael Elmedany | University of Bahrain, Bahrain |

| | |
|---|---|
| Wai Ho Mow | Hong Kong University of Science and Technology, China |
| Warusia Mohamed | Technical University of Malaysia, Malaysia |
| Wei-Chiang Hong | Oriental Institute of Technology, Taiwan |
| Xiao-Zhi Gao | University of Eastern Finland, Finland |
| Yang Zhang | American University, USA |
| Youakim Badr | INSA-Lyon, France |
| Youcef Baghdadi | Sulta Qaboos University, Oman |
| Zhao Yang | Northwest University, China |
| Zoran Bojkovic | University of Belgrade, Serbia |

## Sponsors

- Technical Education Quality Improvement Programme (TEQIP-III)
- Science and Engineering Research Board, Department of Science and Technology, Government of India

# Contents – Part I

# Contents – Part II

# Placing Query Term Proximity in Search Context

Tirthankar Barik and Vikram Singh[✉]

National Institute of Technology, Kurukshetra, Kurukshetra 136119, Haryana,
India
tirthankar.personal@hotmail.com, viks@nitkkr.ac.in

**Abstract.** In the information retrieval system, relevance manifestation is pivotal and regularly based on document-term statistics, i.e. term frequency (tf),
inverse document frequency (idf), etc.. Query Term Proximity (QTP) within
matched documents is mostly under-explored for the relevance estimation in the
information retrieval. In this paper, we systematically review the lineage of the
notion of QTP in IR and proposed a novel framework for relevance estimation.
The proposed framework is referred as Adaptive QTP based User Information
Retrieval (*AQtpUIR*), is intended to promote the document's relevance among
all relevant retrieved ones. Here, the relevance estimation is a weighted combination of document-term (DT) statistics and query-term (QT) statistics. The
notions 'term-term query proximity' is a simple aggregation of contextual
aspects of user search in relevance estimates and query formation. Intuitively,
QTP is exploited to promote the documents for balanced exploitation-
exploration, and eventually navigate a search towards goals. The design analysis asserts the usability of QTP measures to balance several seeking tradeoffs,
e.g. relevance, novelty, result diversity (Coverage and Topicality), and highlight
various inherent challenges and issue of the proposed work.

**Keywords:** Big data analytics · Exploratory search · Relevance manifestation ·
Information retrieval

## 1 Introduction

Information retrieval (IR) is the task of acquiring information system assets from the
collection of those resources that are important to the information needs [1–3]. Full-text
or other content-based indexing used to support the user search [1]. The IR intends to
explore into the searching within document or document searching and also a metadata
search, which describes data as well as text, images or sound databases [2, 4]. An IR
system is a software system that gives access to books, magazines and other records.
The most recognizable IR applications are web search systems [5].

A data object is an entity represented in a contents collection or database by the
information. User queries match the data in the database. In contrast to classic SQL
database queries, the returned results may or may not match the question in the retrieval
of data; thus, outcomes are typically ranked. This ranking of results is a significant
difference in the search for information compared to the pursuit of databases. The most

© Springer Nature Singapore Pte Ltd. 2020
A. Bhattacharjee et al. (Eds.): MIND 2020, CCIS 1240, pp. 1–16, 2020.
https://doi.org/10.1007/978-981-15-6315-7_1

IR schemes calculate the number of the object in the database to match the query and rank it following that value [1, 6]. The user is shown the top-ranking items. You can then iterate the method if the user wants to refine their quest.

One of the essential questions for researching information collection is '*how to define the concept of relevance*' in an operational manner, hence to properly score a relevant document [7, 8]. Generally, a distinct definition leads to another retrieval model. The document is mainly based on different types of word statistics, such as in-document frequencies, reverse document frequencies and document length in most current recovery systems. Still, the closeness of matching query terms to a document has not been exploited. In the proposed work, we wish to place the document where all query terms are close to each other above the document, intuitively. They are distinct from one another, given that we have two documents with the same number of query terms. Thus, closeness to query terms is another possibly helpful heuristic that can be integrated into a recovery model.

The notion of term proximity is widely adapted in the extraction of the documents from the large collection of the documents. The relevance estimation utilized the query term proximity within a document. We intuitively assert that QTP plays a pivotal role in the extraction of diverse and novel user query results. As the proposed QTP measure promote the result objects with proximate query term.

For example, two result objects D1 and D2 are matched for a user query '*Human-Computer Interaction*' [9, 10]. The intuitive estimation places a result object with the closest appearance of query terms within the documents.

$D_1\{$'.. . Human. .. Computer. .. Interaction. . .....'$\}$

$D_2\{$'.............. Human Computer Interaction............'$\}$

The result object $D_2$ is promoted, due to the inherent proximity of user query term.

The term-term proximity of user query is pivotal in the extraction of result objects based on the modeled contextual search intent of the user, during the search. Historically, the query term proximity measures are less-explored and adapted with limited coverage in the information retrieval or related activities, mainly due to the following reason:

(i)   Capturing the user search 'Context' is complex problem.
(ii)  The role of QTP was not validated for relevance estimation, mainly due the lack of clarity on the parameters.

In the paper, we have proposed as the conceptualization of solution three-way coverage of the related work addresses the challenges and related issues in the capacity. The notion of user search context is modelled by modelling four exclusive QTP measures, e.g. *Span, MinCover, MaxDistace* and *MinCover*. Each measure institutively maps the cognitive perception of the user on query terms into the typed query and his intentions over the prospective results. The design challenges and issue are listed in the paper.

## 1.1  Contribution and Outline

The primary contributions of the paper are the novel measures of query term proximity for information retrieval. The proposed notion will explore a new dimension of the relevance estimation in interactive information retrieval (IIR). The proposed measure will contribute to the extraction of diverse and novel results for the user queries. Further, the systematic review of relevant research efforts offers the role of adaption of new aspects, to capture the user contextual aspects into the retrieval process.

The paper is organized as: Sect. 2 presents the literature of the related area, including the brief discussion on the lineage of query term proximity for the retrieval of information in the traditional model and ad-hoc information extraction models. Section 3 described the notions of proposal doe the novel information retrieval adapting QTP in interactive information retrieval. Section 4 analysis of the design challenges involved in the design of the framework and proposed QTP notions. The inherent issues in the implementation *QTP* of for the overall retrieval process, and then concluded.

## 2 Related Work

### 2.1 QTP as Relevance Measure or Heuristic

In traditional information retrieval system, it is highly preferred that document for user queries in which most or all the request query terms appear must be placed higher in the order as compared to others [11, 12]. In the existing literature such as [3, 13–15] support the argument that document statistic, such as term-frequency (TF), inverse document frequency (IDF) and document length, play a pivotal role in the extraction of the relevant document.

In recent research efforts [15–19], it has been widely observed that the proximity of query term within the matched document could be an important factor for this purpose. There are various IR models exists, such as *the Boolean model*, *Vector* Model, etc. [6]. The Boolean model also refereed as exact-match retrieval model. The model matches the user query terms within the document. The matching of both document terms with user query terms concluded as match [20]. The limitation of this model is the lack of a ranking mechanism of the matched document for the user query.

Similarly, the vector space model treats *query-terms* and *document-terms* as vectors in a multidimensional space [6]. This model evaluates the similarity measures via cosine similarity for the retrieval of the relevant documents. The inherent cosine similarity is derived with the generated terms-weights; here, the weight represents the statistical distribution of terms within documents. Vector space does not allow any form of relevance ranking. The model rank the document set based on various term-statistics, but user query terms proximity not exploited.

More recently, in probabilistic model demonstrates '*how likely a document is to be relevant for some user query*' [3]. Let $P(r|d)$ be the probability that the document d is relevant to the query and $P(\bar{r}|d)$ be the probability that d is not relevant to query. The scores of the documents are formalized as, but it is regularly observed that sometimes both $P(r|d)$ and $P(\bar{r}|d)$ are wrongly estimated as user queries contain both lesser query terms and ambiguous in nature. The similarity between *query-terms* and *document-terms* may, therefore, be incorrect or incomplete. The problem of matching emerges from the fact that words used to describe a definition by documents' writers and search engine users can vary. i.e., they are not always semantically related. It has been observed that, for the relevance estimation of information search and the extraction of relevant results (documents or texts) the proximity of user term is rarely adapted. In the tradition benchmarks IR models the estimation is based on document-terms statistics rather query-terms proximity statistics.

The knowledge about term connectivity expresses the proximity of query words in a document [21, 22]. The closer the words appear in the text, the more relevant these terms are. Let $d_a$ and $d_b$ be two documents. The query terms of $q$ appear more proximate in $d_a$ than in $d_b$. Then the probability of relevance measure for $d_a$ is higher than that of $d_b$. Similarly, work discussed in [11, 20], highlights the usability of QTP in retrieval framework. Another work discusses [12], highlights the usability of QTP in retrieval framework.

In particular, other researchers examined proximity based on the BM25 model [23–25] recuperation. Heuristic proximity has been applied to the BM25 recovery function, but their studies are not definitive, and by using proximity, they have not achieved a solid, efficient recovery function. An indirect way of achieving proximity is to use high-order n-grams as text units. It is shown that in [26] bi-gram and tri-gram outperform unigram model. The works discussed in the [11, 20, 21, 27] outlines the importance of retrieval of the relevant document in segments and proximity is often matched. The document segment is processed for matching the term proximity for a user query. This process imposes a proximity constraint on matched terms.

The above-discussed work highlights the potential of QTP for information retrieval. Here, user query consists of query terms and begin by assuming that we can divide a document into certain units. Depending on a particular method of segmentation, the length of every text segment can then be measured by the number of units within the text segment. And the distance between the two terms is equal to the number of units between them. The optimal size of the text segment or sentence size is identified as the. The positional index value of the query terms to be calculated by the number $w$. This value of $w$ is another type of score which is used to rank the documents. This value indicates how bunched together the query terms are in the document. A thus smaller value of $w$ will correspond to a higher score, and the larger value of $w$ will correspond to a smaller score.

## 2.2   QTP for Ad-Hoc Information Retrieval

The information retrieval methods and strategy were reviewed by various studies in the past. One of the earliest studies is conducted by *Keen's*, in which the importance of closeness of query terms is highlighted for the retrieval of information using the '*NEAR*' operator. Though, in existing literature, two key limitations are identified: first of all, the experiments on very limited information sets were performed, so that results could not be well generalized. Secondly, it was created on the foundation of the Boolean model, which is usually considered less efficient than the contemporary complete text recovery systems. A study [28] is one of the follow-up researches that also answer Boolean queries. The [29] and [30] studies tend to be the first to test TREC data sets proximity. Both use '*span*' measure to evaluate proximity.

Similarly, the various studies [22, 31, 32] reveals the role of the proximity of user query terms in the co-related activities of ad-hoc information retrieval, e.g. *Query Completion, Query reformulation, Query suggestion*, Query Expansion, etc. in the past. These activate adapts query terms proximities via various notions to support these activities. In the traditional ad-hoc IR system, to improve the quality of results, the query terms positions are leverages. The QTP is adapted to improve the resulting diversity in post-search tasks. Here, *positional rankings* are commonly used in web search engines and related systems [33–35].

Nevertheless, positioning indexes are well known to require significant quantities of extra space, generally about three times the space of a simple non-positional index. Text data is, however, needed for text snippets to be produced. The notion of time-space variations for the search process is explored via positioning functions and the production of text fragments. Information retrieval models based on proximity usually define a kernel feature on all documents [12]. Nonetheless; situations in different positions can have various levels of impact, particularly technical terminology used by healthcare professionals. Instead of predefining a single kernel like the Gaussian kernel over all documents, the proposed method offers a term with the most appropriate kernel feature at a location.

Data recovery is commonly used in models and algorithms of cyber-physical systems ' wireless networks. The closeness of queries has shown that it is very useful for information collection systems to improve their performance. The proximity to request words cannot individually retrieve documents and should be integrated into original models of recovery. The work discussed in [36] provides the idea of query term embedding, a new way of integrating query term proximity into original models.

This document deals with the question of looking for alternative contract language similar to, but distinct from, a specific clause. Although this is a key activity for the legal transaction, generic search methods provide no effective solution. It shows modern information recovery work to suggest and test new methods for the prototyping of alternative languages [37].

Search engines for full text are important tools for recovery of information. If the document contains query terms close to the other, particularly if the query terms are often used, a document is important in a full-text search. By using additional indexes for each word in a text to store nearby word information at distances between a given the word and the *MaxDistance parameter* [38]

Research is needed to link electronic health records (EHRs) with biomedical literature to enhance clinical decision making. Pseudo-Relevance Feedback (PRF) has proven to be effective in many retraction models and thus suitable for the use of lazy language and clinical jargons on EHR. Prior work defined a collection of conventional PRF-model constraints (axioms) [39]. In the feedback document, however, the meaning of the candidacy term and the relationship between the candidate term and the question term are relevant. Such factors are not taken into account in most processes. Intuitively, words with a higher degree of co-occurrence and a question word tend to be more connected.

In the ad-hoc information retrieval system, both terms statistics plays a pivotal role. The pursuance of the role of statistics, we designed the retrieval framework via keeping two categories of proximity measures: (1) Firstly, *Span*-based and (2) Second *aggregation*-based [40, 41]. In the case of two or more query terms matched with the documents, and then we calculate the proximity by the distance between these matched query terms. Though, modelling the novel notions for query terms proximity is a complex task, due to inherent pre-processing for computation of proximities values and eventually aggregating into single term score to re-rank the matched documents for the user.

## 3  Adapting QTP

The traditional information retrieval system adapted the role of query term proximity for various co-related activities, such as, e.g. *Query Completion, Query reformulation, Query suggestion, Query Expansion*, etc. [35]. The notions of QTP are employed with different notions to support the activities. These activate adapts query terms proximities via various notions to support these activities. In the traditional ad-hoc IR system, to improve the quality of results, the query terms positions are leverages. The *QTP* is adapted to enhance the resulting diversity in post-search tasks. Here, *positional rankings* are commonly used in web search engines and related systems [42].

The role of query term proximity for the interactive information retrieval (IIR) and subsequently for result diversification and novelty is investigated. Our main objective is to design a new set of QTP relevance measures to assist the user in exploratory nature search.

The proposed QTP relevance measures emulate the structural and semantic constraints in the initial type query into the relevance estimation. The proposed estimation will be a two-phase process, in which the initially document-term based relevance prepared using traditional matrices and then *query-term*. In the proposed work, we have designed proximity measures to model the query term proximity, to prepare the relevance estimate and result diversity for a user search. Figure 1 presents a simplified view of proposed QTP measures. The adapted definition of the proposed QTP measure is described below using a working example.

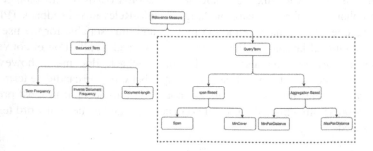

**Fig. 1.** Classification of proposed QTP measures

## 3.1 Proposed QTP Measures

The proposed measures are discussed in the below, for a example document, D. The document is described as,

$$Document\ (D) = \{w_1 w_2 w_1 w_3 w_5 w_4 w_2 w_3 w_4\}$$

The computation of various proposed measure are described below.

**Span:** The span of user query term is defined as the length of the shortest document section covering all query terms within the document, including occurrences that are repeated, and formalized as,

$$Span(w_i,\ w_j) = \{distance(w_i,\ w_j)\,|\,iw_i appears\ at\ least\ once\} \tag{1}$$

For the example document (D) and user query $Q(w_1, w_2)$, the computed span value is 7.

**Mincover:** The length of the shortest document section that includes at least one query term in a document shall be described by min cover.

For the example *document*(D) and user query $Q(w_1, w_2, w_4)$, the computed *Mincover* value is 7.

**MinPairDistance:** The *MinPairDiatnace* of user query terms is evaluated as minimum pair distance of all pairs of matched query terms and formalized as,

$$MinDist = min_{w1,w2} \in Q \wedge D,\ w1 \neq w2\{Dis(w1,w2;D)\} \tag{2}$$

Where D is the document and Q is query set. For the example document D and user query $Q(w_1, w_2, w_3)$ the computed *MinPairDistance* is 1.

**MaxPairDistance:** The *MaxPairDistance* of user query terms are evaluated as the maximum pair distance of all pairs of distinctive matched query terms. The *MaxPairDistance* is formalized as,

$$MaxDist = max_{w1,w2}, \in Q \wedge D,\ w1 \neq w2\{Dis(w1,w2;D)\} \tag{3}$$

Where D is the input document and Q is user query set. For the example document D and user query $Q(w_1, w_2, w_3)$ the computed *MaxPairDistance* is 7.

Next, the information retrieved based on the overall relevance estimation and extraction of the relevant result is described.

## 3.2 Proposed: Two-Phase Relevance Estimation Framework

The proposed relevance estimation framework begins with the pre-processing of the document corpus to extracts the terms of the document. The framework pre-requisites are a large corpus of information documents. Let us assume that the corpus contains $n$ number of documents as $D_1, D_2, ...., D_n$. The pre-processing component generates the equivalent information objects as $O_1, O_2,..., O_n$ for the smooth information matching during the retrieval. These information objects contain the details and referred to as 'document-terms (DT)' of an information object. This logical representation of documents is easier to evaluate the *DT* statistics, e.g. *TF-IDF, document length*, etc.

The relevance estimation directs the evaluation of document-terms statistics for the user query, initially. Thus, *tf-idf* in each document of the given corpus based on user given query, the evaluated DT statistics are kept in temporary storage for later utilization. These statistics imposed for the searching of initially matching document set. Further, The *initially matched objects* ($O_1$, $O_2$, ..., $O_k$) are now goes through the re-arrangement phase. The proposed framework imposed the proximity evaluation of user query terms in these k matched documents. The second phase of matching is intended to offers a user centric list of k documents, as a document with closer appearance of user query terms appears among the higher in the list for user. The conceptual scheme of proposed framework is shown in Fig. 2.

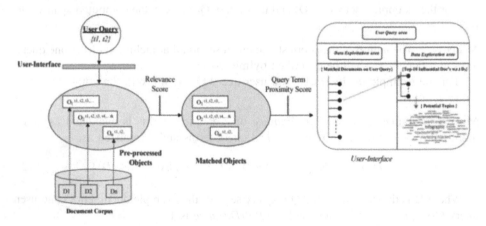

**Fig. 2.** Proposed framework for *relevance estimation*

The evaluation of *QTP* score is an integrated score of sub_scores from various proposed notions. The origin of these proximities notions is derived and based on the definitions adapted, such as given in definition 01–04. The query proximity estimation is the novel contribution of this paper. In framework evaluates the various proximities based on the adapted definitions and eventually, aggregated into a single score for the whole document. The aggregated scores of various proximities into *QT_score* are to re-arrange the entire *m* matched documents. The new list of relevant document is semantically closure to the user-centric, as the re-arrangement is based on terms of proximity within the document.

### 3.3   User Search and QTP Heuristic

The modeling the contextual aspects of user search are pivotal in interactive information retrieval. Though, designing a measure or criteria for modeling the contextual aspect is a multifaceted task, further evaluation strategy to compute the score or statistics is a complex task due to the inherent characteristics. The QTP measure are designed with anticipation that, at the position of search execution the user's perception towards search task, often referred as Cognitive work (CW), evolves and mainly controls by the appropriate keyword selection and reflects in the position of query terms. Thus, proximity among the query terms in an information search is pivotal in the retrieval model (document matching and result ranking).

Our proposal addresses both aspect and its inherent complexity while adapting the query term proximity (QTP) in relevance estimation. The primary objective is to the identification of intrinsic constraint and parameters to represent the contextual aspect of user search and subsequently amalgamate into *QTP* heuristics. The four different QTP notions proposed in the paper are adapted into relevance estimation heuristics and capture the various aspects of the search context.

For informational search, the user submits the data request via a keyword query (Q) containing search terms. The query terms reflects the user information needs in its Traditional presentation, as framework is intended to incorporate the semantic notions, also. The *algorithm 1 'AQtpUIR'*, Adaptive QTP based user information retrieval, as described.

---

**Algorithm**: Adaptive QTP User IR *(AQtpUIR)*

---

**Input**: Document object $O_i$ and User-Query($Q_{t1, \dots tn}$)

**Output**: **Top-K** relevant documents $\{d_1, d_2, \dots, d_k\}$

**Step 1**: *Pre-processing* of all documents $\{d1, d2, \dots, dn\}$
   **For** each document **do**
     derived *docObj($O_i$)* of $d_i$ // equivalent objects created //
**Step 2**: **For** each *docObj* $O_i$ **do**
     *Evaluate* $DT_{score}$; // *tf-idf* values are generated //
**Step 3**: *Extract* *Top-m* matching *docObj*
     *Match(docObj's* terms, $(Q_t)$ terms);
     *If Match* found *then* Store *docObj*
*Extract (docObjs, Top-m)* based on $DT_{score}$;
*Store (matchedDocList($O_{i\dots m}$))*;
**Step 4**: *For* each $O_i$ in *matchedDocList* $(O_{i\dots m})$ **do**
     $x_1$ =Compute ($S_p$ $(O_i, Q_t)$); //evaluate $QTP_{score}$ of objects//
     $x_2$ =Compute ($Min_{cov}$ $(O_i, Q_t)$);
     $x_3$ =Compute ($MinPair_{dst}$ $(O_i, Q_t)$);
     $x_4$ = Compute ($MaxPair_{dst}$ $(O_i, Q_t)$);
**Step 5**: Re-rank *docObjs* based on $QTP_{score}$ and *extract* top-m
Return (*Top-k* documents);

---

The relevance estimation component evaluates the relevance score for the user query and imposes the same for the matching and further for the ranking of the matched document. The various proposed *QTP* notions and then we compute the DT_score.

Based on the score, we rearrange the document. Then, on this rearranged document, we apply some of the proposed methodologies.

We formalized *Span* term proximity for the algorithmic relevance estimations; the strategy is as described in algorithm below. The computation *Span* employs the query term proximity into the relevance estimation and improves the relevance document closer to the user search.

---

***Algorithm 1.1***: Compute Span *Proximity_Score($S_p$)*

---

***Input***:Document object($O_i$)and User-Query($Q_{t1, \ldots tn}$)
***Output***: QTP($q_{t1,t2}$)$_{sp}{}^O{}_i$

---

***For*** each pair of Query-terms($q_{tti,tj}$)
***For*** each object $O_i$
   *Match* the Query-terms ($Q_t$) on Information Object-terms ($O^i{}_t$)
    ***if*** match found ***then***
    *Store*the Pos_Index($O^i{}_t$);    // Positional Index of the key terms//
Retrieve Pos_index(maximum, minimum);
***If*** *these indices cover all query terms at least once* **then**
QTP($q_{t1,t2}$)$_{sp}{}^O{}_i$=*Evaluate*Difference (Pos_index(Max)-Pos_Index(Min);
return (QTP($q_{t1,t2}$)$_{sp}{}^O{}$i);

---

Here the proposed *algorithm 1.1* matches each *user-query* terms with the document terms. In case of a *match*, the positional index of the matched document-term is stored in the initialized data structure. Further, for the evaluation span score, the difference between the minimum and maximum value of the index value is computed. The scope of *span* value is pivotal in the placement of relevant documents among the set of matched list of documents, and further to improve the effects of user relevance. As the Span score steers the positioning of a document in the relevance rank and primarily driven by the closeness of the query terms within the each documents.

Next, *QTP* measure is *Minimum Cover*, as described in *algorithm 1.2*, Here we taken an array *arr[]* whose length is equal to the number of terms in the user query. This array stores the positional index value of each query terms. Positional index is defined as in which position each query term appears in the document. In every iteration we check whether all the elements in the array are non-zero or not.

---

**Algorithm 1.2**: Compute*MinCoverProximityscore*(Min$_{cov}$)

---

**Input**: Document object$O_i$ and  User-Query($Q_{t1, ...tn}$)
**Output**: QTP($Q_{t1,t2}$)$_{Mincov}{}^{O}{}_i$

---

*Initialization*Min$_{cov}$ = len($O_i$)+1
**while** *(length($O_i$))***do**
*for*each query q$_t$
        *Match*Q$_t$ with  the key terms of O$_j$
*Store* its 1$^{st}$occurrences;
*If* none of arr[i] == 0 //arr[i] is used to store the occurrences//
*extract*(min, max) value from arr[i]
*evaluate* difference($x$);
*if*Min$_{cov}$ >$x$**then**
$x$ = Min$_{cov}$;
**return**Min$_{cov}$

---

If non zero, then we takes the minimum and maximum value from this array and calculate the difference between them. Here we take a variable, *Mincov* whose initial value is the length of the document object. If the difference is less than Mincov, then we update the *Mincov* with the difference. Thus in every iteration (in which none of *arr [i] == 0*) we take the difference and check whether it is less than the previous Mincov value. Thus, after alliteration we get the minimum value that indicates the smallest length in which all query terms appear at least once.

Another set of query term proximity is based on the distance-based. When a query has many different terms then we divide them into various pairs of *Query-Term* combinations. The smallest distance for all these pairs is the minimum pair distances (minPair$_{dst}$). Here we take each pair and match them with the document terms.

---

**Algorithm 1.3**: Compute*MinPairDistanceProximityscore(minPairdst)*

---

**Input**: Document Object ($O_i$)and User Query($Q_{t1, ...tn}$)
**Output**: QTP($q_{t1, t2}$)$_{minPairdst}{}^{O}{}_i$

---

**Initialization:** *minPair$_{dst}$*=length( O$_i$)+1
    **For***each pair* of query term(qti ,tj)*inQuery***do**
*Match*(key terms of doc-obj O$_i$);
        Store (Pos_index, $x_i, x_j$,);
obt$_{dst}$= ($x_i$ -$x_j$ );
if*obt$_{dst}$*<*minPair$_{dst}$***then**
*minPair$_{dst}$* = *obt$_{dst}$*;
**end if**
**end for**
Return*minPair$_{dst}$*

---

If match occurred, then we store the positional index of these terms. Then we calculate the difference between these indices. The smallest-difference is the minimum distance between these pairs.

Finally, here also we divide the user query terms into various *Query-Term* combinations. The largest distance for all these pairs is the maximum pair distances (*maxPair$_{dst}$*). Here we take each pair and match them with the document terms. If match occurred, then we store the positional index of these terms. Then we calculate the difference between these indices. The largest-difference is the maximum distance between these pairs.

---

***Algorithm 1.4***: ComputeMaxPairDistance *Proximityscore(maxPair$_{dst}$)*

---

***Input***: Document Object ($O_i$)and  User Query($Q_{t1, ...tn}$)
***Output***: QTP($q_{t1, t2}$)$_{maxPairdst}$$^O_i$
**Initialization:** *maxPair$_{dst}$*=0;
   **For***each pair* of query term(q$t_i$ ,t$j$ )*inQuery***do**
*Match* with thekey terms of doc-obj $O_i$;
      Store (Pos_index,$x_i$ ,$x_j$);
ob$t_{dst}$ = ($x_i$ -$x_j$ );
if*ob$t_{dst}$>maxPair$_{dst}$***then**
*maxPair$_{dst}$ = ob$t_{dst}$*;
   **end if**
**end for**
Return*maxPair$_{dst}$*

---

The primary objective of the proposed framework is to offer user centric document objects during the information search. We assert that, the proposed notions of query term proximity steer the pivotal aspect of relevance estimation and eventually estimate relevance towards context-oriented fashion. In this, the positional dimensions of user query terms within documents is pivotal and also in result ranking.

# 4   Analysis and Challenges

The design of relevance measures for information retrieval is a multifaceted task. The traditional measure considers the matrices related to the document terms and usually based on the quantitative measure, though query proximity measure incorporates the semantics and occurrence of the query terms.

In the paper, we have proposed *Span based* and distance-based measure for QTP estimation. For the estimation of the overall relevance estimation, all measures are aggregated into a singlescore (as *QT_score*).

(a) **Priority of Proximity-types:** The key challenge in modeling of span based measures is that proximity distance value is much higher for relevant documents. But proximity distance value is lesser for the non-relevant documents. This counter intuition shows that significant factor in terms of document relevance can be missed. As user query terms are not uniformly distributed in various documents. Frequency of the query terms varied in every document. But *Span* and *MinCover* favors those documents where frequency is less. The modeling of this dilemma between the document term frequency and proximity distance for information retrieval is a challenging direction. We anticipate that, to direct the biasness, some *normalization factor* is to be introduced.

(b) **Role of each proximity in Overall Relevance:** The rationale of contribution of each proximity notion in overall *QT_score* is complex task, as for each query terms or document set the *QT_score* is volatile and keep changing during the search interactions. We adapted the notion of strength factors for each term proximities and its relevant role into overall relevance during the search.

(c) **Estimation and Modeling of proximities:** The estimation and modeling of distance-based measurer raises challenges to the *state-of-art* approaches. Thus, it is assumed that small distance refers to greater semantic association between document terms and query terms and larger distance to smaller association. Thus, in this paper, we have generated different pairs of query terms and further, evaluated the distance values. The query term pairs are generated, with simple permutation basis. It is widely observed that, some pair of query terms has smaller distance with semantic equivalence. The semantically equivalents query term raises complex challenges to estimation of correct resulting document for the user.

## 5 Conclusion

In this paper, we revisited the notions of query term proximity for the information search. The assessment asserts that intuitive role of the term proximities in the traditional information search strategies and model for the various routine activities of information retrieval. In the evolution of various search systems and need of pursuance to involve user into information interactions, lead to the adaption of novel notions for the relevance of information. To steers the proposed strategy, particularly for the *relevance manifestation,* and enhanced semantic and contextual relevance, as each measure captures different aspects of query terms proximity. The computed QTP scores are adapted to re-rank the initially matched document set, with an objective to introduce the more relevant and diverse result document. The QT based statistics/scores significantly promote the document and incorporate user-preferences context in retrieval framework. The comprehensive assessment affirms the intuitive role of proposed measures in steering the retrieval and data analysis over big database.

The *future scope* of current work may include an *adaptive strategy* for the query terms prediction for prospective user search will emulate a term/word level intents for improved information-search.

## References

1. Baeza-Yates, R., Ribeiro-Neto, B.: Modern Information Retrieval, vol. 463. ACM Press, New York (1999)
2. Croft, B.: The importance of interaction in information retrieval. In: Proceedings of the 42nd International ACM SIGIR Conference on Research and Development in Information Retrieval, pp. 1–2. ACM, July 2019
3. Schütze, H., Manning, C.D., Raghavan, P.: Introduction to information retrieval. In: Proceedings of the International Communication of Association for Computing Machinery Conference, p. 260, June 2008

4. Büttcher, S., Clarke, C.L., Lushman, B.: Term proximity scoring for ad-hoc retrieval on very large text collections. In: Proceedings of the 29th Annual International ACM SIGIR Conference on Research and Development in Information Retrieval, pp. 621–622. ACM, August 2006

5. White, R.W.: Interactions with Search Systems. Cambridge University Press, Cambridge (2016)

6. Croft, W.B., Metzler, D., Strohman, T.: Search Engines: Information Retrieval in Practice, vol. 520. Addison-Wesley, Reading (2010)

7. Rasolofo, Y., Savoy, J.: Term proximity scoring for keyword-based retrieval systems. In: Sebastiani, F. (ed.) ECIR 2003. LNCS, vol. 2633, pp. 207–218. Springer, Heidelberg (2003). https://doi.org/10.1007/3-540-36618-0_15

8. Khennak, I., Drias, H.: A novel hybrid correlation measure for query expansion-based information retrieval. In: Critical Approaches to Information Retrieval Research, pp. 1–19. IGI Global (2020)

9. Idreos, S., Papaemmanouil, O., Chaudhuri, S.: Overview of data exploration techniques. In: ACM SIGMOD International Conference on Management of Data, pp. 277–281 (2015)

10. Patel, J., Singh, V.: Query morphing: a proximity-based approach for data exploration and query reformulation. In: Ghosh, A., Pal, R., Prasath, R. (eds.) MIKE 2017. LNCS (LNAI), vol. 10682, pp. 261–273. Springer, Cham (2017). https://doi.org/10.1007/978-3-319-71928-3_26

11. Liu, X., Croft, W.B.: Passage retrieval based on language models. In: Proceedings of CIKM 2002, pp. 375–382 (2002)

12. Song, Y., Hu, Q.V., He, L.: Let terms choose their own kernels: an intelligent approach to kernel selection for healthcare search. Inf. Sci. **485**, 55–70 (2019)

13. Salton, G., Buckley, C.: Term-weighting approaches in automatic text retrieval. Inf. Process. Manag. **24**(5), 513–523 (1988)

14. Paik, J.H.: A novel TF-IDF weighting scheme for effective ranking. In: Proceedings of the 36th International ACM SIGIR Conference on Research and Development in Information Retrieval (2013)

15. He, B., Huang, J.X., Zhou, X.: Modeling term proximity for probabilistic information retrieval models. Inf. Sci. **181**(14), 3017–3031 (2011)

16. Miao, J., Huang, J.X., Ye, Z.: Proximity-based rocchio's model for pseudo relevance. In: Proceedings of the 35th International ACM SIGIR Conference on Research and Development in Information Retrieval, pp. 535–544. ACM, August 2012

17. Zhao, J., Huang, J.X., Ye, Z.: Modeling term associations for probabilistic information retrieval. ACM Trans. Inf. Syst. (TOIS) **32**(2), 7 (2014)

18. Saracevic, T.: The notion of relevance in information science: everybody knows what relevance is: But, what is it really? Synth. Lect. Inf. Concepts Retrieval Serv. **8**(3), i–109 (2016)

19. Cummins, R., O'Riordan, C.: Learning in a pairwise term-term proximity framework for information retrieval. In: Proceedings of the 32nd International ACM SIGIR Conference on Research and Development in Information Retrieval, pp. 251–258, July 2009

20. Callan, J.P.: Passage-level evidence in document retrieval. In: Croft, W.B., van Rijsbergen, C. (eds.) Proceedings of the Seventeenth Annual International ACM SIGIR Conference on Research and Development in Information Retrieval, Dublin, Ireland, July 1994, pp. 302–310. Spring-Verlag (1994)

21. Kaszkiel, M., Zobel, J.: Effective ranking with arbitrary passages. J. Am. Soc. Inf. Sci. **52**(4), 344–364 (2001)

22. Barry, C.L.: User-defined relevance criteria: an exploratory study. J. Am. Soc. Inf. Sci. **45**(3), 149–159 (1994)

23. Robertson, S., Zaragoza, H.: The probabilistic relevance framework: BM25 and beyond. Found. Trends® Inf. Retrieval **3**(4), 333–389 (2009)
24. Büttcher, S., Clarke, C.L.A.: Efficiency vs. effectiveness in terabyte-scale information retrieval. In: TREC (2005)
25. He, B., Ounis, I.: Term frequency normalisation tuning for BM25 and DFR models. In: Losada, D.E., Fernández-Luna, J.M. (eds.) ECIR 2005. LNCS, vol. 3408, pp. 200–214. Springer, Heidelberg (2005). https://doi.org/10.1007/978-3-540-31865-1_15
26. Song, F., Croft, B.: A general language model for information retrieval. In: Proceedings of the 1999 ACM SIGIR Conference on Research and Development in Information Retrieval, pp. 279–280 (1999)
27. Salton, G., Allan, J., Buckley, C.: Approaches to passage retrieval in full text information systems. In: Proceedings of the 16th Annual International ACM SIGIR Conference on Research and Development in Information Retrieval, pp. 49–58 (1993)
28. Beigbeder, M., Mercier, A.: An information retrieval model using the fuzzy proximity degree of term occurences. In: Proceedings of the 2005 ACM Symposium on Applied Computing. ACM (2005)
29. Clarke, C.L.A., Cormack, G.V., Burkowski, F.J.: Shortest substring ranking (MultiText experiments for TREC-4). In: TREC, vol. 4 (1995)
30. Hawking, D., Thistlewaite, P.: Proximity operators-so near and yet so far. In: Proceedings of the 4th Text Retrieval Conference (1995)
31. Singh, V.: Predicting search intent based on in-search context for exploratory search. Int. J. Adv. Pervasive Ubiquit. Comput. (IJAPUC) **11**(3), 53–75 (2019)
32. Singh, V., Dave, M.: Improving result diversity using query term proximity in exploratory search. In: Madria, S., Fournier-Viger, P., Chaudhary, S., Reddy, P.K. (eds.) BDA 2019. LNCS, vol. 11932, pp. 67–87. Springer, Cham (2019). https://doi.org/10.1007/978-3-030-37188-3_5
33. Arroyuelo, D., et al.: To index or not to index: time-space trade-offs for positional ranking functions in search engines. Inf. Syst. (2019). https://doi.org/10.1016/j.is.2019.101466
34. Zhao, J., Yun, Y.: A proximity language model for information retrieval. In: Proceedings of the 32nd International ACM SIGIR Conference on Research and Development in Information Retrieval, pp. 291–298. ACM, July 2009
35. Song, R., Taylor, M.J., Wen, J.-R., Hon, H.-W., Yu, Y.: Viewing term proximity from a different perspective. In: Macdonald, C., Ounis, I., Plachouras, V., Ruthven, I., White, R.W. (eds.) ECIR 2008. LNCS, vol. 4956, pp. 346–357. Springer, Heidelberg (2008). https://doi.org/10.1007/978-3-540-78646-7_32
36. Qiao, Y., Du, Q., Wan, D.: A study on query terms proximity embedding for information retrieval. Int. J. Distrib. Sens. Netw. **13**(2) (2017). https://doi.org/10.1177/1550147717694891
37. Pitis, S.: Methods for retrieving alternative contract language using a prototype. In: Proceedings of the 16th Edition of the International Conference on Articial Intelligence and Law. ACM (2017)
38. Veretennikov, A.B.: Proximity full-text search by means of additional indexes with multi-component keys: in pursuit of optimal performance. In: Manolopoulos, Y., Stupnikov, S. (eds.) DAMDID/RCDL 2018. CCIS, vol. 1003, pp. 111–130. Springer, Cham (2019). https://doi.org/10.1007/978-3-030-23584-0_7
39. Pan, M., et al.: An adaptive term proximity based rocchio's model for clinical decision support retrieval. BMC Med. Inform. Decis. Mak. **19**(9) (2019). Article number: 251. https://doi.org/10.1186/s12911-019-0986-6

40. Schenkel, R., Broschart, A., Hwang, S., Theobald, M., Weikum, G.: Efficient text proximity search. In: Ziviani, N., Baeza-Yates, R. (eds.) SPIRE 2007. LNCS, vol. 4726, pp. 287–299. Springer, Heidelberg (2007). https://doi.org/10.1007/978-3-540-75530-2_26
41. Svore, K.M., Kanani, P.H., Khan, N.: How good is a span of terms? Exploiting proximity to improve web retrieval. In: Proceedings of the 33rd International ACM SIGIR Conference on Research and Development in Information Retrieval, pp. 154–161. ACM, July 2010
42. Arroyuelo, D., et al.: To index or not to index: time-space trade-offs for positional ranking functions in search engines. Inf. Syst. (2019). https://doi.org/10.1016/j.is.2019.101466

# Identifying Fake Profile in Online Social Network: An Overview and Survey

Shruti Joshi, Himanshi Gupta Nagariya, Neha Dhanotiya, and Sarika Jain[✉]

National Institute of Technology, Kurukshetra, Kurukshetra, India
{shruti_51810006, hnagariya_51810001,
neha_51810004, jasarika}@nitkkr.ac.in

**Abstract.** Online Social Networks (OSNs) presently engage the majority of people, from a child to an adult and even old age people as they spend a good amount of time on these platforms exchanging their information and creating interaction with other people of the world. On one hand, these social networks provide the advantage of direct connectivity between people, information sharing, ways to create a large audience, etc. on the other hand people also misuse them in many ways. Social networking sites are suffering from people who own bulk of fake accounts to take advantage of vulnerabilities for their immoral benefits such as intriguing targeted accounts to click on malicious links or to attempt any other cybercrimes. These actions motivate researchers to develop a system that can detect fake accounts on these OSNs. Several attempts have been made by the researchers to detect the accounts on social networking sites as fake or real, relying on account's features (user-based, graph-based, content-based, time-based) and various classification algorithms. In this paper, we provide an overview of various studies done in this direction and a survey of all the techniques already used and can be used in the future.

**Keywords:** Online Social Network · Feature extraction · Spammer · Fake account detection · Data classification

## 1 Introduction

Nowadays social networking sites have become a wide platform for people to keep in touch with each other, to share information, feelings, photos, posts, status, etc. With the help of OSNs like Twitter, Facebook, Instagram, Pinterest, Google+, LinkedIn, etc. people can easily interact with other people residing in any part of the world. One disadvantage of these sites is that most of the users are unaware of identity theft, loss of privacy, fake profiles, malware, etc. Twitter and Facebook are the most prominent OSNs and are continuously being attacked by spammers to steal personal data, spread rumors, and share false news. These spammers sometimes also use automated programs called social bots that can act like humans and contribute to spread nuisance on the internet. Another major problem while using social networking sites is the fake accounts created with different intentions such as to entrap or mislead people or to spread malicious activities and because of these reasons it has become very important to develop a mechanism to detect spammers.

© Springer Nature Singapore Pte Ltd. 2020
A. Bhattacharjee et al. (Eds.): MIND 2020, CCIS 1240, pp. 17–28, 2020.
https://doi.org/10.1007/978-981-15-6315-7_2

## 1.1   Statistics of Social Media Usage

As of September 2019, there are 2.45 billion Facebook-owned monthly active users worldwide. Following with, Alexa (a web service that ranks websites), the third most visited website is Facebook ensuing Google and YouTube.

As per a survey it was proved that there are more female accounts on Facebook than the total population of females in the world. By this, we can assume how many fake and unwanted accounts are being created. As stated by Statista statistics report in April 2018, the number of active accounts on Twitter has surpassed 336 million, although Facebook is leading with 2196 million users worldwide [6]. As of September 2019, there are 2.45 billion monthly active Facebook users and among them, India has the highest number of users i.e. 270 million users. Approximately there are 1.62 billion active users who log on to Facebook daily. There are 76% of female and 66% of male users and approximately 83 million fake accounts on Facebook. This information was directly provided by Facebook in their reports to Wall Street (SOURCE: Zephoria Digital Marketing) (Fig. 1).

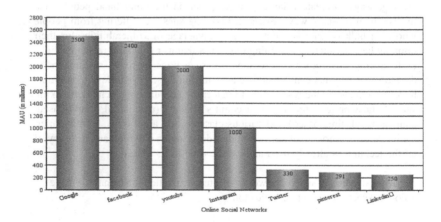

**Fig. 1.**  Monthly active users in the year 2019

## 1.2   Motivation

As we see the number of people using OSNs is increasing, the creation of fake social media accounts is also increasing. The main motivating factor for the identification of these fake accounts is that, these accounts are mostly created to carry out cyber extortion or to commit cybercrimes anonymously or with an untraceable identity as a result of this, the rate of cybercrime has increased noticeably from the last one year. Also, the owner of fake accounts sometimes aims to take advantage of the kindness of people by making false announcements or by spreading fake news through these accounts to usurp money from innocent people. Moreover, people are creating multiple accounts that do not belong to someone and only created to get a hike of votes in online voting systems and so as in online gaming in the greed of getting referral incentives.

Detection of fake accounts on OSNs has attracted many researchers and thus several techniques have been developed using Machine Learning algorithms and by using different features related to an account. However, spammers are also finding ways to withstand such techniques. These defending techniques have complicated detection mechanisms, making it necessary for the continuous development of new spam-detection approaches. The main concern for detection is the accuracy and response time for analyzing features.

## 1.3   Challenges

The previous studies infer that machine learning algorithms are somewhat challenging for the reason that attackers can create some patterns that cannot be trained by machines. Many such challenges can become obstruent in the detection of fake accounts. The below section specified some global and local challenges:

- Single user multiple accounts: Multiple accounts are created and operated by single user for malicious activities or any other illegal activities.
- Making system robust: To build a system which does not get effected by adversarial attacks, or an attacker that learns from failures.
- Difficulties in selection of features: Selecting and finding features which are publicly available and are effective in classifying accounts is another challenge.
- Heterogeneity: Features of different OSNs are unlike in nature so collecting and extracting them is one of the challenge we have seen so far.
- There can be some preventing approach regarding the creation of fake accounts than only just detecting them.
- Integration of feature and graph based techniques are done in only a fewer amount of studies.
- Real time determination of friend request sent by a fake account.

## 1.4   Why Fake Profiles Are Created?

Fake identities in social media are often used in Advanced Persistent Threat cases, to spread malware or a link to it. They are also used in other malicious activities like junk emails/spams or used to artificially increase the number of users in some applications to promote it.

- According to an article a gaming application supported by Facebook provides incentives to the user/player of the application who brings more and more peers to play the game. So, in the greed of incentives, people make fake accounts.
- Huge amount of fake accounts may be created by celebrities or politicians, aiming to show off their large fan base or may be created by the cybercriminals so that their account look more real.
- Applications like in an online survey to get better feedback fake accounts are used e.g. for the increment in the rating of a product/application, fake identities are used by the company or the owner.

## 1.5  Organization

In the rest of the paper, Sect. 2 presents the system overview under the points, data collection, feature selection, feature extraction and classification techniques and also presents the general architecture for identification of fake accounts. Section 3 represents related work done in this direction. Section 4 is findings and discussion in which comparative study of previous researches in done and gaps of existing work are mentioned, Sect. 5 finally concludes the research subject.

## 2  System Overview

OSNs attract various kind of malicious and illegal activities and in the past the community of research has put forward various solutions to the problem [12].

In a general approach for the identification of fake accounts in large scale online social networks following steps are used (Fig. 2):

- Data collection.
- Feature selection.
- Feature extraction.
- Data classification/techniques used.

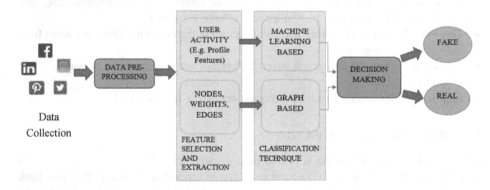

**Fig. 2.** A general architecture for identification of fake account

## 2.1  Data Collection

In this work, we need real-world Facebook, Twitter and other OSN's datasets, which are publicly unavailable. Anonymized datasets of social graph are available including some profile-based feature but the anonymized form cannot be used. Therefore, in some works data was collected from Facebook API, Twitter API, however it is restricted from the data that can be achieved due to privacy issues.

In Boshmaf et al. [2] 100 automated fake accounts were used to send friend requests to 9.6K real users. In Erşahin et al. [3] data is collected manually by three individuals. In BalaAnand et al. [1] data is collected from web scraping framework by python. In Mateen et al. [4] they use the dataset of another researcher. In Khaled et al. [15] used MIB dataset of Cresci et al. [13].

## 2.2   Feature Selection

In this section all the features required for fake account detection are formulated.
Four main categories:

- **User-based:** account age, count of following and followers, count of tweets and, FF ratio.
- **Graph-based:** betweenness centrality, in/out-degree.
- **Content-based:** count of retweets, count of URLs, count of replies, count of digits and characters, and spam words.
- **Time-based:** Tweets sent in a particular time interval, time in days.

In Boshmaf et al. [2] hybrid of user profile and graph property is used. In Mateen et al. [4] Hybrid approach of user-based, graph-based and content-based features is used.

## 2.3   Feature Extraction

After collection of different data attributes, the later step will help in distinguishing the accounts as real or fake by defining and identifying a collection of features extracted from the mentioned data attributes. Four main categories of feature extraction methods are:

- PCA
- Spearman rank-order correlation
- Wrapper feature selection using SVM
- Multiple linear regression

For features, an extraction map reduces technology is used by Boshmaf et al. [2]. Feature extraction by using twitter API Erşahin et al. [3] extract 16 features. As a pre-processing method on social media, they are majorly focusing on the consequences of discretization method because it is the most prominent approach to handle numeric attributes in Naïve Bayes.

In part of feature reduction, all four (mentioned above) data reduction techniques were used by the researcher in Khaled et al. [15].

## 2.4   Classification Techniques

Classification belongs to the category of supervised method and the classification problem is predicting the class of the given dataset that in which category they falls. It is defined in two steps i.e. a classification step and a learning step. In the learning step, a model is trained by a set of labelled data instances and model is constructed, and in the classification step, the model constructed is then used to predict the class labels of the data. The learning step can also be stated as training stage and classification step can be stated as testing stage. In short, in classification technique, we determine target classes by analyzing training dataset (Target classes- fake or real).

The classifiers which are generally used are Linear Classifiers (Logistic regression, Naive Bayes classifier), Support Vector Machine, Quadratic Classifier, Kernel Estimation (k-nearest neighbor), Decision trees (Random forests), Neural Network [19, 20].

Classification methods under data mining are classified into 3 categories:

- Supervised methods.
- Semi-supervised methods.
- Unsupervised methods.

**Supervised Methods:** Supervised methods model both abnormal and normal behaviors. According to this anomaly detection is studied as classification problem having pre-labelled and labelled data as normal or anomalous, this is done using two approaches:

- One, the normal data is pre-labelled and the data is considered as anomalous which is analogous to this model.
- In contrast to the first approach second approach is to define a set of anomalous data objects and if the objects are not present in predefined anomalous data set are considered as normal.

In supervised methods to make the classifier learn is the main aim. A classifier can be formulated in number of ways. For example, it can be Support Vector Machine based, Neural Network based, Bayesian Network based and Random Forest etc.

**Semi-supervised Methods:** As per the name, these methods consists of two sets of data one as labelled and another as unlabelled. So, when few instances or values of the dataset is labelled only then this method is used. Classifier is constructed using this little amount of labelled data and then unlabeled data is labelled using it.

**Unsupervised Methods:** When the data objects are not labelled i.e. the data objects are not attached with any predefined labels such as "normal", "anomalous" then unsupervised methods are used. These methods are usually considered and studied under clustering problem.

### Algorithms Used in Classifying Accounts

In order to classify accounts on the basis of user-based features, content-based features, graph-based features, various machine learning algorithms are used (Fig. 3). Some of the supervised learning classification algorithms are Naive Bayes, Decision Rule-based (Sequential Minimal Optimization, Support Vector Machines (SVM)), Decision Tree classifiers (Random Forest, J48, Random Tree), k-Nearest Neighbor. Out of these popular classification techniques some are mentioned in this paper and they are Naïve Bayes, Support Vector Machine, Neural Network, Random forest [7, 18].

Erşahin et al. [3] used Naïve Bayes learning algorithm on the pre-processed data. BalaAnand et al. [1] used enhanced graph-based semi-supervised learning algorithm. J48, Decorate and Naïve Bayes algorithm were used by Mateen et al. [4]. Khaled et al. [15] work introduced a new technique called SVM-NN (Neural network and Support vector machine) which used hybrid algorithm of SVM and Neural Network for classification. The resultant feature set of SVM is used as the input to train Neural Network model.

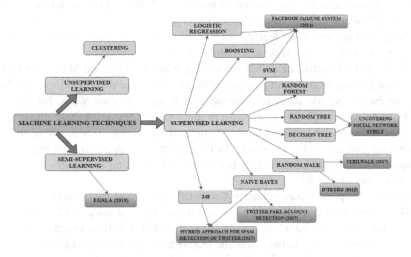

**Fig. 3.** Classification techniques used in existing systems

## 3 Related Work

Inspired by the significance of identification of fake accounts recently researchers have started to examine efficient mechanisms. In most of the previous works, user based and graph based features were majorly used in prediction and classification of accounts. Various studies have been done in this area by using different datasets, feature reduction techniques, classification techniques.

Faurecia Benevenuto et al. [17] detected spammers by using SVM classification algorithm. They collected dataset of twitter and this dataset contains information of 54M users, 1.9B links and approximately 1.8B tweets. Their approach detected 70% of spammers and 96% of non-spammers correctly.

Erşahin et al. [3] collected 16 features using Twitter API, 13 of which were directly collected from API and 3 were created by them using API. As a pre-processing method on the collected data mainly the focus is on the effect of discretization method. By using the discretization technique and using the Naïve Bayes classifier they increase their accuracy from 85 to 90% the shortcoming in that research is they can improve the result by using feature selection. Khaled et al. [15] has reached a classification accuracy of around 98% by using the support vector machine and Neural Network classifier and a hybrid approach of both and compare the accuracy result of the three mentioned classifier.

Yang et al. [14] proposed an approach for the detection of Sybils in Renren. The author used dataset as 50k Sybils and 50k normal user registered on Renren. To train a classification algorithm they use a ground truth clickstream data which can be used to classify the data as Sybil or normal. In classification algorithm they first use SVM and SVM is trained on the basis of clickstream feature i.e. 1. Session level feature, and 2. Feature from click activities. The authors were able to train a classifier with a 99% true-positive rate (TPR) and 0.7% false-positive rate (FPR).

To maximize accuracy BalaAnand et al. [1] used the support vector machine, k-nearest neighbor and random forest classifier and achieved 90.3% accuracy in detecting fake users. And extracted the features from profile attributes user activity values and nodes edge weight as it is graph-based and content based action.

Mateen et al. [4] introduced a hybrid approach for the detection of bots on Twitter. They divide features into 3 main groups and these groups are user-based, content-based and graph-based and use these three mentioned features in their work. Naïve Bayes, J48, Decorate were used as a classification algorithm. They used these classification algorithms on mentioned three features group and found that user-based features are not significant in detecting spammers. In their proposed approach of using a hybrid technique by combining all three features the rate of detecting spammers for Decorate and J48 is increased to 97.6%.

Gupta et al. [5] proposed a mechanism to identify spammers on large scale online social networks and from the several OSNs they chose twitter for their work. A labeled dataset of 1064 Twitter users was used which was acquired from Fabricio Benevenuto et al. [17]. In their work they used, user and tweet specific features. They used a hybrid of Naïve Bayes, Clustering and Decision Trees classification algorithm to achieve higher accuracy.

Sahoo et al. [6] presented a Fake detector framework that can detect fake profiles at the user's homepage using Chrome extension running on the chrome browser. They use a hybrid approach of techniques to detect malicious profiles. They collected twitter dataset from crawler and twitter API. To find out the origin of malicious content they apply a Graph-based traceback mechanism on user based data. As a feature analyzer, they use pertinent and as a detection system, they use chrome extension.

Gurajala et al. [8] in their framework the features used are profile name, URL analysis, account information, creation time and many other features and it uses 6 million no. of accounts. In their proposed model the detection rate is faster and the different features are analyzed even if there is change in the data at runtime.

Boshmaf et al. [2] a ranking based decision making system is used in which low ranks is given to fake accounts and high ranks is given to real account.

Al-Qurishi et al. [11] proposed a method for Sybil-attacks on Twitter. In their work, the data was collected from Twitter API and two dataset, D1 and D2 have been prepared. These datasets contain 25,510 (D1) and 2200 (D2) profiles and out of them for testing process 13,957 and 940 profiles were used respectively. D1 was clean while D2 was not clean i.e. D2 contains noisy profiles. Then they used Deep Neural model for classifying accounts in both datasets and compared the results. They found that the accuracy of D2 was better than D1 i.e. 86% and concluded that noisy and unclean is best for improving the performance of model.

Adikari et al. [10] is slightly different from other papers as they worked on LinkedIn they have collected the limited profile data from the various internet sources and manually worked on some accounts to find if they are fake or real. They have used SVM with Polynomial Kernel on selected features extracted by PCA and achieved 84% accuracy as compared to different approaches using large dataset. As far as we know from our study in most of the work as OSN platform Twitter is chosen because in Twitter information is available publicly by default and this information can be easily accessed with the help of Twitter APIs. The different fake profile detection approaches for different OSNs is summarized in Fig. 4 along with the features used, datasets and techniques which are discussed above in this section expansively [9].

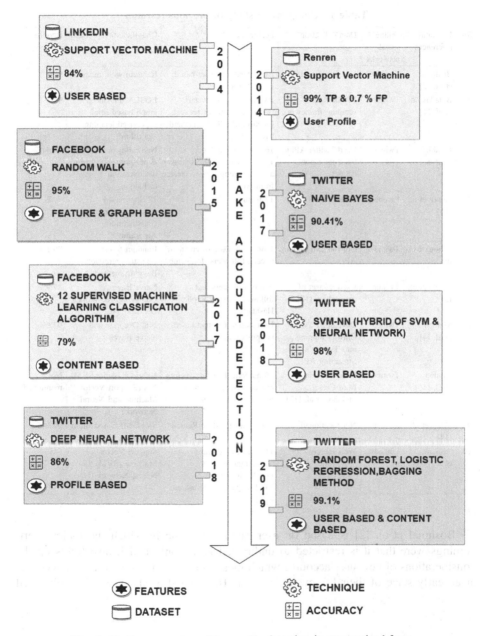

**Fig. 4.** Earlier research on fake profile detection in summarized form

# 4 Findings and Discussions

We have summarized the literature presented in Sect. 3 in tabular format in Table 1 and given a rebuttal of what people have researched in their works and also we have stated the findings and limitations of the reviewed papers.

**Table 1.** Comparative study of previous research

| SN | Literature references | Online social networks | Data collection | Features used | Classification approach | Reported accuracy |
|---|---|---|---|---|---|---|
| 1. | Boshmaf et al. [2] | Facebook | Not mentioned | Basic Features, user-based, graph based | Random walk method | 95% |
| 2. | BalaAnand et al. [1] | Twitter | Python web-scraping framework | Average time between tweets, Fraction of retweets, Fraction of URLs, Standard tweet length | EGSLA (enhanced graph based semi-supervised learning algorithm) | 90.3% |
| 3. | Erşahin et al. [3] | Twitter | Used Twitter API to build their own dataset | 16 features gathered. 13 of which are directly taken and remaining 3 were created from API | Naïve Bayes and data is pre-processed using discretization technique | 90.41% |
| 4. | Gupta et al. [16] | Facebook | Facebook API | 17 features | 12 Supervised Machine Learning Classification Algorithm | 79% |
| 5. | Sahoo et al. [6] | Twitter | Crawler and twitter API | Profile ID, Date of creation, tweets, followers, following, etc. | Random forest, Logistic regression, Bagging method | 99.1% |
| 6. | Gupta et al. [5] | Twitter | Used dataset of researchers [17] | No. of followers and followees, URLs Replies Hashtags | Naïve Bayes, Clustering Techniques, Decision Tree | 87.9% |
| 7. | Mateen et al. [4] | Twitter | Developed Twitter Crawler tapping into Twitter's Streaming API | User based, Content based, Graph based | J48, Decorate and Naïve Bayes | 97.6% |
| 8. | Khaled et al. [15] | Twitter | Used MIB dataset from Cresci, Stefano, et al. [13] | 16 numerical feature vectors reduced using four data reduction techniques | Hybrid classifier SVM-NN (Support Vector Machine and Neural Network) | Not mentioned |
| 9. | Yang et al. [14] | Renren | Not mentioned | Users registered on Renren 50 k normal and 50 k Sybils | SVM, MLE maximum likelihood estimation | 99% T.P 0.7% F.P |
| 10. | Adikari et al. [10] | LinkedIn | Web sources | 11 features including No_Languages, Profile_Summary, No_Edu_Qualifications, etc. | Support Vector Machine (SVM) and Neural Network (NN) | 84% |

Boshmaf et al. [2] is based on user ranking scheme in which the major short-comings were that it is restricted to undirected graph only and it also holds up the considerations of new user accounts which means that it is not able to detect accounts at an early stage of their life-cycle. Whereas BalaAnand et al. [1] used graph-based algorithm and the accuracy somewhere limited because of not using hybrid classifiers, using hybrid classifiers the accuracy can be increased. Erşahin et al. [3] are lacking feature selection in their approach they only tested the accuracy before and after discretization of data and targeting to find the content of tweet as their future work. Gurajala et al. [8] have the limitation of identifying a proportionately small percentage of fake accounts. The approach mentioned in Aditi Gupta et al. [16] has achieved relatively low accuracy i.e. 79% as compared to many more existing systems.

The LinkedIn fake profile detection by Adikari et al. [10] stated their limitation as verification of the sources according to which the data has been collected and in case of cloning attack it is difficult to tell that which profile is real and which one is fake.

## 5 Conclusion

This paper presents a thorough study of important techniques used to identify fake account in Online Social Networks (OSNs). In this paper major approaches and a wide variety of approaches applicable for determination of fake accounts in OSNs are analyzed. An effort has been done to cover maximum essential techniques out of all the existing techniques used in this direction. Some of the previous approaches, including the dataset statistics are tabulated and compared. Comparison of different techniques like content-based, graph-based, user-based, time-based, etc. is done and also recently proposed designs, their importance and limitations are also analyzed. Many researches have already been carried out to a certain extent to solve the problem of detecting fake accounts but more convincing actions are still required to be taken. There is a need to provide a system or approach which can understand user's information in more fast, reliable and efficient manner.

## References

1. BalaAnand, M., Karthikeyan, N., Karthik, S., Varatharajan, R., Manogaran, G., Siva-parthipan, C.B.: An enhanced graph-based semi-supervised learning algorithm to detect fake users on Twitter. J. Supercomput. **75**(9), 6085–6105 (2019). https://doi.org/10.1007/s11227-019-02948-w
2. Boshmaf, Y., et al.: Integro: leveraging victim prediction for robust fake account detection in OSNs. In: NDSS, vol. 15, pp. 8–11, February 2015
3. Erşahin, B., Aktaş, Ö., Kılınç, D., Akyol, C.: Twitter fake account detection. In: 2017 International Conference on Computer Science and Engineering (UBMK), pp. 388–392. IEEE, October 2017
4. Mateen, M., Iqbal, M.A., Aleem, M., Islam, M.A.: A hybrid approach for spam detection for Twitter. In: 2017 14th International Bhurban Conference on Applied Sciences and Technology (IBCAST), pp. 466–471. IEEE, January 2017
5. Gupta, A., Kaushal, R.: Improving spam detection in online social networks. In: 2015 International Conference on Cognitive Computing and Information Processing (CCIP), pp. 1–6. IEEE, March 2015
6. Sahoo, S.R., Gupta, B.B.: Hybrid approach for detection of malicious profiles in Twitter. Comput. Electr. Eng. **76**, 65–81 (2019)

7. Jia, J., Wang, B., Gong, N.Z.: Random walk based fake account detection in online social networks. In: 2017 47th Annual IEEE/IFIP International Conference on Dependable Systems and Networks (DSN), pp. 273–284. IEEE, June 2017

8. Gurajala, S., White, J.S., Hudson, B., Matthews, J.N.: Fake Twitter accounts: profile characteristics obtained using an activity-based pattern detection approach. In: Proceedings of the 2015 International Conference on Social Media & Society, p. 9. ACM, July 2015

9. Xiao, C., Freeman, D.M., Hwa, T.: Detecting clusters of fake accounts in online social networks. In: Proceedings of the 8th ACM Workshop on Artificial Intelligence and Security, pp. 91–101. ACM, October 2015

10. Adikari, S., Dutta, K.: Identifying fake profiles in linkedin. In: PACIS, p. 278, June 2014

11. Al-Qurishi, M., Alrubaian, M., Rahman, S.M.M., Alamri, A., Hassan, M.M.: A prediction system of Sybil attack in social network using deep-regression model. Future Gener. Comput. Syst. **87**, 743–753 (2018)

12. Masood, F., et al.: Spammer detection and fake user identification on social networks. IEEE Access **7**, 68140–68152 (2019)

13. Cresci, S., Di Pietro, R., Petrocchi, M., Spognardi, A., Tesconi, M.: Fame for sale: efficient detection of fake Twitter followers. Decis. Support Syst. **80**, 56–71 (2015)

14. Yang, Z., Wilson, C., Wang, X., Gao, T., Zhao, B.Y., Dai, Y.: Uncovering social network sybils in the wild. ACM Trans. Knowl. Disc. Data (TKDD) **8**(1), 1–29 (2014)

15. Khaled, S., El-Tazi, N., Mokhtar, H.M.: Detecting fake accounts on social media. In: 2018 IEEE International Conference on Big Data (Big Data), pp. 3672–3681. IEEE, December 2018

16. Gupta, A., Kaushal, R.: Towards detecting fake user accounts in Facebook. In: 2017 ISEA Asia Security and Privacy (ISEASP), pp. 1–6. IEEE (2017)

17. Benevenuto, F., Magno, G., Rodrigues, T., Almeida, V.: Detecting spammers on Twitter. In: Collaboration, Electronic Messaging, Anti-Abuse and Spam Conference (CEAS), vol. 6, no. 2010, p. 12, July 2010

18. Stein, T., Chen, E., Mangla, K.: Facebook immune system. In: Proceedings of the 4th Workshop on Social Network Systems, pp. 1–8, April 2011

19. Kolankar, P., Patel, R., Dangi, N., Sharma, S., Jain, S.: Exploiting the most similar cases using decision tree to render recommendation. In: International Conference on Recent Developments in Science, Engineering and Technology, pp. 290–304. Springer, Singapore, November 2019

20. Jain, Y., NamrataTiwari, S., Jain, S.: A comparative analysis of various credit card fraud detection techniques. Int. J. Recent. Technol. Eng. (2277–3878), **7**(5S2), 402–407 (2019)

# An Efficient Graph Based Trust-Aware Recommendation System

Gaurav Mishra$^{(\boxtimes)}$, Sumit Kumar, Rahul Gupta, and Sraban Kumar Mohanty

Computer Science and Engineering, PDPM Indian Institute of Information
Technology, Design and Manufacturing, Jabalpur, Jabalpur, India
{gaurav.m,sumitkumar,rahulgupta,sraban}@iiitdmj.ac.in

**Abstract.** With the increase in amount of information, it becomes
important to build recommendation systems which can map and provide the relevant information based on the preferences, tastes and trust
of users. The data clustering is applied in recommendation system to
reduce the computational overhead. It has been shown empirically that
with the increase in number of clusters, the rating coverage decreases
monotonically. To reduce the impact of clustering, the rating prediction
is computed in terms of the user similarity, trust and Jaccard similarity
with each term having some coefficient to give them weights. The optimal
weights are decided for each clusters which are finally used to make the
recommendation. Calculation of optimal parameters is one of the expensive steps and they are fixed for each users of the clusters. In this paper,
we dynamically compute the optimal parameters for each pair of users
instead of using static optimal parameters for each clusters. The optimal parameters in the proposed approach are individually calculated for
two users according to the ratio of Pearson, trust and Jaccard similarity
between them. It helps us to reduce the complexity of the system as well
as it results into increasing the accuracy of overall recommendations.
Experiment results on real datasets illustrate that the our improved 2D-
Graph method defeats the competing approaches based on accuracy and
rating coverage.

**Keywords:** Recommendation system · Graph clustering · Trust ·
Rating coverage

## 1 Introduction

Recommender systems have been evolving rapidly with the advancement in technology, research and infrastructure. Recommender systems are applied in various
areas such as E-commerce, movies, music, search-query, social-media and many
more. Collaborative and content-based recommender systems are widely adopted
[3]. Collaborative filtering approaches utilize the past behaviour of users and the
similarity between users for performing recommendations. Collaborative filtering approaches often suffer from problems like rating coverage, data sparsity and

© Springer Nature Singapore Pte Ltd. 2020
A. Bhattacharjee et al. (Eds.): MIND 2020, CCIS 1240, pp. 29–42, 2020.
https://doi.org/10.1007/978-981-15-6315-7_3

cold start problems [14]. Data Sparsity occurs when there are less number of ratings present in a recommender system [15], that is caused when user rates only few number of ratings in a recommender system. The cold-start problem occurs on the recommendation of new users. To achieve accurate recommendations, a large amount of data on a user is required which increases the computational overhead on the system.

To reduce this issue, various clustering techniques have been used in recommender system to solve the problems in collaborative filtering-based recommender system. Similar batch of users or items are grouped together in clustering methods. The essential theme is that similar user may have the matching likes and dislikes. Correctness of rating predictions can be improved by clustering approaches. Finding the actual clusters is an issue in clustering techniques. Bad clustering not only decreases the accuracy but it also minimizes the coverage of the system. There should be sufficient quantity of users in a cluster for more correctness and coverage in recommender system [14]. Dakhel et al. [2] presented an approach using K-means clustering algorithm for recommendation system [2,8]. Usually K-means algorithm uses the Euclidean distance as de-similarity measure in order to make the clusters. Initially it takes random points as center of the clusters and gradually moves toward getting the best centers for the clusters. In order to get the best centers, every point has to be compared with all the centers, involving more computations [11]. Later in 2013, an efficient K-means algorithm was proposed [12] which reduces the time complexity, maintaining the quality of clusters. Patil et al. [8] shown that Hierarchical clustering algorithm Chameleon performs better than Dakhel et al. [2] approach, because K-means based approaches suffers from various drawbacks one of them being the domain knowledge to estimate the number of clusters. But the clusters are naturally formed in chameleon based approach [8].

In real life scenarios two users might be having same mind set on some set of items but they may have opposite likes on other set of items, which was proposed by Xu et al. [17]. So they enhances the idea of [5] by not making the prediction for the user choice using the entire set of ratings, instead they used subgroups for making predictions.

Today everyone is connected to other people through social networks, which shows the friendship between two people and we know that people are more influenced by the people whom they trust more. In a way social network provides trust information of an individual which can be used to determine his/her choice. External social information is used for improving the precision of the recommendation in Trust aware recommender system as shown in [9,10,13]. This extra information about the user also helps to overcome the problem of sparsity which was proposed in the seminal paper of Massa Avesani [13] for the improvement of the recommender system. Other studies have been carried out to use clustering based approaches in trust enabled recommender systems. Prime aim is to leverage the benefit of clustering approach for trust enabled recommender systems. DuBois et al. [4] adopted the trust as the prime metric for enhancing the correctness of the recommender systems. Various techniques of graph mining were also adopted to upgrade the quality of the systems [1,14].

A diverse network was developed by combining an exact trust graph and graph of user ratings to overcome the problem of sparsity by Zhang et al. [18]. Co-clustering algorithm was also adopted by them to get more consistent and error free subgroup of items regarding user choices or preference.

The work presented here continues the lines of research of Sheugh et al. [16]. Specifically, we have taken forward the approach by Sheugh et al. [16] who proposed to make a 2D graph using Pearson correlation coefficient and trust propagation as weights of the graph. The constructed 2D graph is passed to the customized K-medoids algorithm for generating the clusters then optimal parameters are decided for each cluster which is finally used to make the recommendation. The optimization stage has high time complexity for calculating the optimal parameters for getting minimum mean absolute error. This high complexity limits the approach for the application of large size datasets. To reduce these limitations, we propose a method to dynamically decide the optimal parameters for each pair of users instead of using static optimal parameters for each clusters [16]. Using this approach also helps us to reduce the complexity of the system as well as it results into increasing the accuracy of overall recommendations. Experimental results on real datasets depict that the improved 2D-Graph method defeats other competing approaches based on accuracy and rating coverage.

The rest of the paper is presented as follows. The proposed technique is demonstrated in the Sect. 2. The experiment analysis are reported and demonstrated in Sect. 3. Section 4 demonstrate the conclusion and future work.

## 2 Proposed Work

The proposed algorithm consists of two phases namely offline and online phases. The overall flow of the recommender system is shown in Fig. 1. In offline phase, the major portion of the required computations are carried out which partitions the group of all users into some non-overlapping clusters [16], so that the system should respond quickly to the inquiries of online users. The offline phase composed of two major stages which are taken from the idea of [16]. In the first stage, 2D graph is constructed by incorporating the trust data with Pearson similarity measure. In the second phase, a set of feasible partitioning is generated by feeding the graph into 2D graph clustering technique [16]. In online phase, the rating prediction is carried out for a target item corresponding to a user. We first map the target user to the cluster it belongs. We compute Pearson similarity, Trust measure, and Jaccard similarity between the outside user and the users in the cluster who have given rating for the target item. The overall similarity is computed between the two users which is fusion of Pearson similarity, Trust measure and Jaccard similarity measure. This makes the basis for the rating prediction [16]. The details of the proposed technique is described in the subsequent subsections.

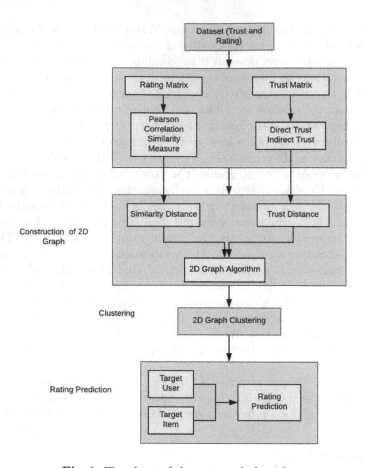

**Fig. 1.** Flowchart of the proposed algorithm.

## 2.1  Construction of the 2D Graph

In this section, the directed graph is constructed from the dataset using Pearson Correlation Coefficient (PCC) similarity measure and trust information.

**Similarity Between the Users.** The generally used similarity measure in collaborative filtering recommendation system are Cosine similarity, Pearson Correlation Coefficient (PCC) and Jaccard similarity measures. These similarity measures are adopted for predicting the ratings. The preffered similarity measure is PCC.

**Trust Information Between the Users.** Trust information tells whether a user trusts other users or not by using which we can recommend efficiently. Trust between users is computed by taking direct and indirect trusts. Indirect trust between users is computed by considering up to six degree of propagation.

**The Nodes and Edges of the 2D Graph.** To construct a 2D graph, the trust detail is combined with PCC similarity information [16]. The nodes and edges of 2D graph show the construction of the directed 2D graph where users are connected through doubly weighted edges as shown in Fig. 2. Graph is generated by taking users as the node of the graph and their Pearson similarity and trust information are considered for edge weights in the graph. For example, the weights between user B and C is (0.8, 0) which means Pearson similarity of 0.8 but there is no trust between user B and C.

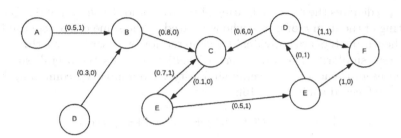

**Fig. 2.** Illustration of graph construction phase. The pair (X, Y) represents the Pearson and trust similarity.

### 2.2 Clustering Phase

In this phase, the clustering approach is accomplished by filtering approach. To generate a set of feasible partitioning without much reduction in rating coverage, a minimum acceptable rating coverage is used to put a constraint on coverage. To accomplish 2D graph clustering, the customized K-medoids algorithm is used to cluster the computed 2D-Graph into some non-overlapping groups of users. The aim is to group like-minded users into the same cluster [16]. In K-medoids clustering algorithm, we can select a center of a cluster as one of the existing users present in every iteration. Mathematically, the objective function of the K medoids clustering algorithm.

$$F = min \sum_{C_E \in C} \sum_{u,v \in C_E} dist(u,v) \tag{1}$$

where user $u$ and $v$ are present in cluster $C_E$ and and $C$ refers the set of clusters and $dist(u,v)$ is the similarity between users $u$ and $v$ in the 2D graph. The distance in 2D Graph clustering algorithm is applied as follows [16]:

$$dist^2(u,v) = dist_S^2(u,v) + dist_T^2(u,v) \tag{2}$$

where $dist_S(u,v) = 1 - W_S^{2DGraph}(u,v)$ denotes the similarity distance and $dist_T(u,v) = 1 - W_T^{2DGraph}(u,v)$ depicts the trust distance.

## 2.3  Rating Prediction

In online phase, whether an item should be recommended to an user or not is decided by predicting the rating of an item for the user. For rating prediction, the weighted average method is used for incorporating the rating information of other users in the cluster to that item. The rating for the target item is computed as [16]:

$$r_{u,k} = \frac{\sum_{v \in C_u} W(u,v).r_{v,k}}{\sum_{v \in C_u} |W(u,v)|} \tag{3}$$

where $r_{u,k}$ denotes the predicted rating of the item $k$ for the user $u$ and $r_{v,k}$ refers the rating of the item $k$ of user $v$ who is located in the same cluster containing $u$ [16]. The parameters are individually calculated for two users to give the weights to different similarity measures. Here $W(u,v)$ represents the overall similarity between users $u$ and $v$. The overall similarity is computed by combining PCC, Trust and Jaccard similarities [16]:

$$W(u,v) = \alpha.PCC(u,v) + \beta.T(u,v) + \gamma.J(u,v) \tag{4}$$

such that

$$\alpha + \beta + \gamma = 1$$

where $\alpha$, $\beta$ and $\gamma$ refers the weight given to Pearson, Trust and Jaccard similarity respectively [16]. Here $PCC(u,v)$ denotes the Pearson, $T(u,v)$ refers the Trust and $J(u,v)$ refers the Jaccard similarity measures which show the social similarity between users $u$ and $v$ and estimated as [16]:

$$J(u,v) = \frac{|T_u \bigcap T_v|}{|T_u \bigcup T_v|} \tag{5}$$

where, $T_u$ and $T_v$ refer the set of trusted neighbors of users $u$ and $v$ respectively.

The optimization stage described in [16] has high time complexity for calculating optimal parameters for getting minimum mean absolute error, as optimal parameters are chosen by checking for all values of $\alpha$, $\beta$ and $\gamma$ between 0 and 1. Figure 3 illustrates the prediction approach used in [16]. In the previous approach optimal parameters are fixed for all users which is shown in Fig. 3.

Based on these issues, the proposed method dynamically decides the optimal parameters for each user. The optimal parameters $\alpha$, $\beta$ and $\gamma$ in the proposed approach are individually calculated for two users $u$ and $v$ according to the ratio of Pearson, trust and Jaccard similarity. The parameters are calculated so as to give more weights in the overall similarity to that similarity measure which has higher value. If the value of $PCC(u,v)$ is less than or equal to zero, we take $W(u,v)$ equal to zero because it means that user $u$ and $v$ are dissimilar. There is no point to consider the contribution of users in clusters that are dissimilar with target user, as considering them, the quality of rating prediction is degraded. This method effectively calculates overall similarity measure $W(u,v)$ according

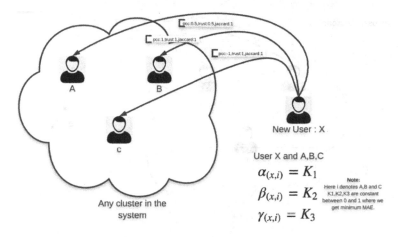

**Fig. 3.** Illustration of prediction phase in [16].

to the weights of similarity measure. The parameters $\alpha$, $\beta$ and $\gamma$ are calculated as follows:

$$\alpha = \frac{PCC(u,v)}{PCC(u,v) + T(u,v) + J(u,v)} \tag{6}$$

$$\beta = \frac{T(u,v)}{PCC(u,v) + T(u,v) + J(u,v)} \tag{7}$$

$$\gamma = \frac{J(u,v)}{PCC(u,v) + T(u,v) + J(u,v)} \tag{8}$$

For calculating $\alpha$, $\beta$, and $\gamma$, the above formula is used to ensure that all three similarity measures used, get their coefficient values in proportion to their values. Figure 4 shows an illustration using three users where optimal parameters are dynamically calculated for users $A$, $B$ and $C$ respectively. The parameters of each users are computed based on their PCC, trust and Jaccard similarity. It gives the illustration on how proposed approach is efficient than the approach described in [16].

Recommendation algorithm should not have high complexity involved because that will increase the system response time. In the proposed algorithm the searching phase for $\alpha$, $\beta$, and $\gamma$ is removed that reduces the time taken by the model significantly. Instead, here we use dynamic values of $\alpha$, $\beta$, and $\gamma$ to decide proportion of the similarities for each user, which not only helps to produce better results but also improves the overall complexity of the system.

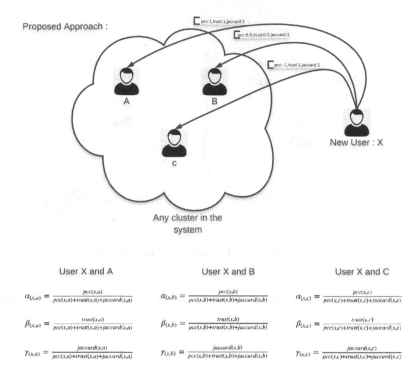

**Fig. 4.** Illustration of prediction phase of the proposed technique.

## 3    Results and Discussions

We perform experiment on two real datasets for evaluating the performance of the proposed technique. Each dataset is randomly splitted into a test and training set. The training set is used to find out the optimal partition and testing set is employed in the prediction phase to compute the efficiency of the system. Our proposed approach is evaluated with the 2D-graph clustering algorithm [16], MV clustering algorithm [7] and merge [6] based on F1 measure, mean absolute error and rating coverage to assess the quality of the recommendation system.

### 3.1    Datasets

Epinions and FilmTrust datasets are used for implementation which are taken from [6,13]. It contains the data about users and the movies to which they have rated in between 1 to 5 and 0.5 to 4.0 respectively. It also contains the trust information between two users, if they trust each other then its value is 1. Table 1 depicts the detailed description of the datasets. Figure 5a and 5c show the rating and trust information of users respectively. Figure 5b shows the average rating, maximum rating and minimum rating given by a randomly selected ten users from the dataset. The dataset information of Epinion dataset is illustrates in Fig. 6.

**Table 1.** The detailed information of the datasets.

| Datasets | Number of users | Number of items | Number of ratings | Scale | Range | Number of trust statements |
|---|---|---|---|---|---|---|
| FilmTrust | 1508 | 2071 | 35.5K | 0.5 | [0.5 4] | 1853 |
| Epinions | 5000 | 10000 | 77.1K | 1 | [1 5] | 205K |

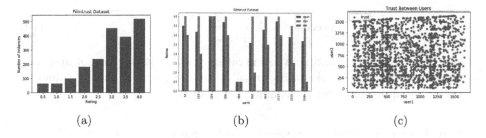

(a)          (b)          (c)

**Fig. 5.** Description of the Film trust datasets: (a) The number of times a particular rating is given over 2000 random samples. (b) The mean, max and min ratings given by randomly selected ten users are shown. (c) The trust information between users are shown.

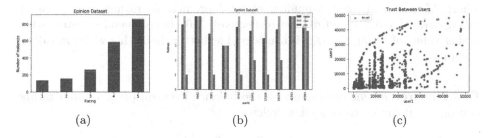

(a)          (b)          (c)

**Fig. 6.** Description of Epinions datasets: (a) The number of times a particular rating is given over 2000 random samples. (b) The mean, max and min ratings given by randomly selected ten users are shown. (c) The trust information between users are shown.

## 3.2 Evaluation Measure

In this section, evaluation measures are described to compute the efficiency of the recommendation system.

**Accuracy.** Mean absolute error (MAE) is used to evaluate the accuracy of the system. It indicates the average amount of error made while making prediction for individual input. It is calculated as follows:

$$MAE = \sum_{i=1}^{N} \frac{\mid r_i - r_p \mid}{N} \tag{9}$$

where $r_i$ and $r_p$ are actual and predicted rating respectively. Lower values of mean absolute error (MAE) indicates comparatively better recommender system.

**Precision.** Calculation of precision is done as follows:

$$precision = 1 - \frac{MAE}{r_{max} - r_{min}} \tag{10}$$

where $r_{max}$ denotes the maximum movie rating possible in the dataset and $r_{min}$ denotes the minimum movie rating possible in the dataset. Higher values of precision are appreciated for a recommender system.

**Rating Coverage.** Rating coverage is another parameter to evaluate the performance of the recommendation system which is defined as:

$$RC = \frac{M}{\Omega} \tag{11}$$

where $M$ and $\Omega$ shows the number of total predictable ratings and count of ratings available in the test dataset respectively [16]. Recommender system with higher values of rating coverage is considered as better than other with low rating coverage.

**F1 Measure.** $F1$ measure indicates the balance between precision and rating coverage and can be calculated as follows:

$$F_1 = \frac{2 \times precision \times RC}{precision + RC} \tag{12}$$

Higher values of $F1$ measure is desired from a better recommender system.

### 3.3  Result Analysis

The experimental results of different techniques on Epinions and FilmTrust datasets based on $MAE$, $RC$ and $F1$ measures are shown in Table 2 and 3 respectively. Results depict that our approach attains the better quality than the competing methods on both the datasets.

**Table 2.** Illustration of MAE, RC and F results on FilmTrust dataset.

| Measure/method | Merge [6] | MV [7] | 2D-graph [16] | Improved 2D-graph |
|---|---|---|---|---|
| MAE | 0.7080 | 0.7100 | 0.6586 | 0.5810 |
| RC | 0.9506 | 0.9000 | 0.8608 | 0.9500 |
| F1 | 0.8822 | 0.8595 | 0.8479 | 0.8881 |

**Table 3.** Illustration of MAE, RC and F results on Epinions dataset.

| Measure/method | Merge [6] | MV [7] | 2D-graph [16] | Improved 2D-graph |
|---|---|---|---|---|
| MAE | 0.8200 | 0.9600 | 0.8098 | 0.7959 |
| RC | 0.8000 | 0.0900 | 0.8648 | 0.9300 |
| F1 | 0.7975 | 0.1609 | 0.8298 | 0.8607 |

Figure 7 illustrates the $F1$ measure on FilmTrust and Epinions datasets. $F1$ measure value on Epinions dataset shows significant improvement over competing approaches since the trust information in the FilmTrust dataset is less than the Epinions dataset. Figure 8 shows the MAE value on FilmTrust and Epinions dataset. The MAE value of our approach is close to the 2D-Graph methods. Figure 9 demonstrates the rating coverage of the proposed technique with competing approaches. The proposed approach attains the better rating coverage as compared to the competing methods. The proposed method takes nearly same rating coverage value on the FilmTrust datasets. The experiment results illustrate that our approach depicts the significant improvement over the competing methods.

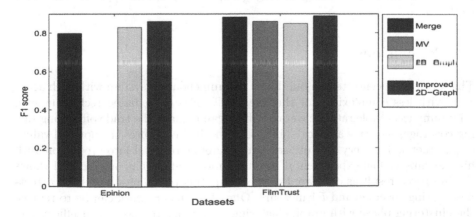

**Fig. 7.** Illustration of F1-measure on different algorithms on FilmTrust and Epinion datasets.

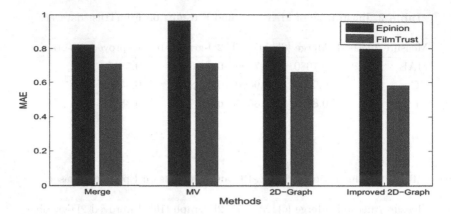

**Fig. 8.** Illustration of the min absolute error (MAE) of the proposed algorithm with other competing approaches.

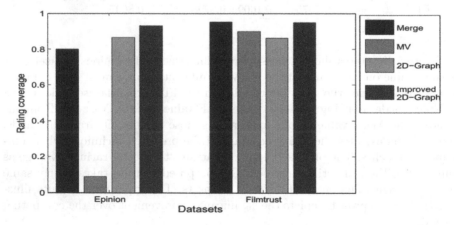

**Fig. 9.** Illustration of the rating coverage (RC) of the proposed approach with other methods.

## 4   Conclusions

This work is concentrated on building a recommendation system with high accuracy with less complexity. For that we used a clustering based technique with minimum acceptable rating coverage which can manage the trade off among rating coverage, accuracy and scalability. Our method computes the optimal values of parameters for every pair of users and therefore resulted into prediction with high accuracy. The experimental results demonstrated that out method shows the improved result as compared to the competing techniques based on correctness, rating coverage and $F1$ measure. One of the future work can be to replace the clustering phase with graph clustering algorithms to study their efficacy.

# References

1. Bellogin, A., Parapar, J.: Using graph partitioning techniques for neighbour selection in user-based collaborative filtering. In: Proceedings of the Sixth ACM Conference on Recommender Systems, pp. 213–216. ACM (2012)
2. Dakhel, G.M., Mahdavi, M.: A new collaborative filtering algorithm using K-means clustering and neighbors' voting. In: 2011 11th International Conference on Hybrid Intelligent Systems (HIS), pp. 179–184. IEEE (2011)
3. Di Noia, T., Rosati, J., Tomeo, P., Di Sciascio, E.: Adaptive multi-attribute diversity for recommender systems. Inf. Sci. **382**, 234–253 (2017)
4. DuBois, T., Golbeck, J., Kleint, J., Srinivasan, A.: Improving recommendation accuracy by clustering social networks with trust. Recomm. Syst. Soc. Web **532**, 1–8 (2009)
5. George, T., Merugu, S.: A scalable collaborative filtering framework based on co-clustering. In: Fifth IEEE International Conference on Data Mining (ICDM 2005), pp. 4–pp. IEEE (2005)
6. Guo, G., Zhang, J., Thalmann, D.: Merging trust in collaborative filtering to alleviate data sparsity and cold start. Knowl. Based Syst. **57**, 57 68 (2014)
7. Guo, G., Zhang, J., Yorke-Smith, N.: Leveraging multiviews of trust and similarity to enhance clustering-based recommender systems. Knowl.-Based Syst. **74**, 14–27 (2015)
8. Gupta, U., Patil, N.: Recommender system based on hierarchical clustering algorithm chameleon. In: 2015 IEEE International Advance Computing Conference (IACC), pp. 1006–1010. IEEE (2015)
9. Jamali, M., Ester, M.: TrustWalker: a random walk model for combining trust-based and item-based recommendation. In: Proceedings of the 15th ACM SIGKDD International Conference on Knowledge Discovery and Data Mining, pp. 397–406. ACM (2009)
10. Jiang, M., Cui, P., Wang, F., Zhu, W., Yang, S.: Scalable recommendation with social contextual information. IEEE Trans. Knowl. Data Eng. **26**(11), 2789–2802 (2014)
11. Jothi, R., Mohanty, S.K., Ojha, A.: DK-means: a deterministic K-means clustering algorithm for gene expression analysis. Pattern Anal. Appl. **22**(2), 649–667 (2019). https://doi.org/10.1007/s10044-017-0673-0
12. Liao, Q., Yang, F., Zhao, J.: An improved parallel K-means clustering algorithm with MapReduce. In: 2013 15th IEEE International Conference on Communication Technology, pp. 764–768. IEEE (2013)
13. Massa, P., Avesani, P.: Trust-aware recommender systems. In: Proceedings of the 2007 ACM Conference on Recommender Systems, pp. 17–24. ACM (2007)
14. Moradi, P., Ahmadian, S., Akhlaghian, F.: An effective trust-based recommendation method using a novel graph clustering algorithm. Phys. A **436**, 462–481 (2015)
15. Nilashi, M., Jannach, D., bin Ibrahim, O., Ithnin, N.: Clustering-and regression-based multi-criteria collaborative filtering with incremental updates. Inf. Sci. **293**, 235–250 (2015)

16. Sheugh, L., Alizadeh, S.H.: A novel 2D-Graph clustering method based on trust and similarity measures to enhance accuracy and coverage in recommender systems. Inf. Sci. **432**, 210–230 (2018)
17. Xu, B., Bu, J., Chen, C., Cai, D.: An exploration of improving collaborative recommender systems via user-item subgroups. In: Proceedings of the 21st International Conference on World Wide Web, pp. 21–30. ACM (2012)
18. Zhang, W., Wu, B., Liu, Y.: Cluster-level trust prediction based on multi-modal social networks. Neurocomputing **210**, 206–216 (2016)

# Permission Based Access Control
# for Healthcare Systems

Shaswata Saha$^{(\boxtimes)}$ ⓘ and Sarmistha Neogy

Jadavpur University, 188, Raja S.C. Mallick Road,
Kolkata 700 032, West Bengal, India
shaswata97@gmail.com

**Abstract.** The objective of this work is to present a secure and privacy-protected environment to manage Personal Health Record (PHR) data stored in distant cloud. The work aims at providing a cloud-based data storage solution that ensures maximum visibility but not at the cost of data privacy. It presents a technique by which users can read and update data stored in cloud storage depending on whether they are allowed to access that data. For this, data encryption has been used on the data to be stored in the cloud. This has been combined with a permission-based access control mechanism. Experiments show that the access-control mechanism works successfully and that data is accessible to only those who are permitted to access it. The work also passes state-of-the-art security attacks.

**Keywords:** Access control · Cloud storage · Personal health record · Hash function · Encryption

## 1 Introduction

Arguably the most important word in today's era of digital boom is data. Everyday an enormous amount of data is generated by various institutions, like companies, governments, educational institutions, hospitals etc. With the increase in data, the need for it's storage and maintenance is also important. This has lead to the increased demand of cloud [1] because of their large scalability. Clients store their data at a distant cloud server that is managed by unknown people.

The increased use of cloud has also brought with it the need for data security. This is because there is a potential lack of control and transparency when a third party Cloud Service Provider (CSP) holds the data. Trusted computing and applied cryptographic techniques [2] may offer new tools to solve these problems. However, more research needs to be done to make cloud computing more secure.

Encryption is a useful tool for protecting the confidentiality of sensitive data. This is because even if an intruder gets access to the database, the data remains protected even after the database has been successfully attacked or stolen. Encryption can provide protection for the sensitive data stored in the database, reduce the legal liability of the data owners, and reduce the cost to society of fraud and identity theft, only with the assumption that the encryption is done successfully and the inverse of these measures is known only to members of client institutions.

© Springer Nature Singapore Pte Ltd. 2020
A. Bhattacharjee et al. (Eds.): MIND 2020, CCIS 1240, pp. 43–56, 2020.
https://doi.org/10.1007/978-981-15-6315-7_4

However, in some of these places, like hospitals, because of the sensitive nature of the data involved, the need to securely and seamlessly share data among multiple parties including healthcare providers, payers, government agencies, and patients becomes a necessity. In short, not all data is accessible to every member. For example, in a healthcare system, the nurse may not get all the details of a patient that the doctor gets. Also a doctor must not get details of any patient whom (s)he is not monitoring. Thus, access to a seemingly ignorable piece of cloud data must also be controlled which leads to fine-grained access control.

This work discusses a fine-grained access control scheme for personal health record (PHR) in healthcare systems. It deals with privacy of patients' data from Cloud Service Providers (CSP) and the distribution of elementary data to users in the system based on their access permissions. It also addresses security issues to be dealt with from a "curious" CSP, collusion among users, and collusion between a user and the CSP.

## 2  Related Works

In this section, we will review some of the works on secure data storage and retrieval and user access revocation problem.

Yang et al. [3] proposed an attribute-based encryption and proxy re-encryption based fine-grained data sharing. Samanthula et al. [4] proposed a secure data sharing solution similar to the technique proposed by Yang et al., with the exception that in place of attribute based encryption, homomorphic encryption is used. However, in both these methods, for each pair of user (that is, patient and data consumer), there is an encryption key pair. Thus a large amount of storage space is needed only for the keys.

Basu et al. [5] proposed a Fusion platform for a patient-centric data management system in healthcare application. One key is generated for each patient. Hence, a considerable amount of storage space is required for the key itself. Also, an efficient key retrieval strategy is needed. In 2017, Sengupta [6] developed an attribute-based user authorization model for e-healthcare systems. The model uses attribute trees and Lagrange's polynomial to grant or deny access to a user. However, the model does not consider access of data by a data miner. Thus, data mining activities in this model becomes difficult.

In 2019, Mandal [7] proposed a blockchain-based data storage and access scheme for storing patient data in cloud. The mutable data is stored in a non-relational database, whereas, the data that must be accessible but immune to modification is stored in the blocks of a blockchain due to their immutable nature. The work also proposed a hierarchical blockchain scheme that drastically reduces the search time of the immutable data. However, this work deals with search operations only.

Gasarch et al. [8] and Mitra et al. [9] proposed solutions that do not need the entire data to be encrypted. However there exists curious CSPs, who may want to look into the data provided to them and infer meaning from them, if possible. Thus, in the current work, a fine grained access control method is presented that encrypts entire dataset using a single key and retrieves or modifies data based on access permissions.

## 2.1   Secure Hash Algorithm

The Secure Hash Algorithms, or SHA, are a family of cryptographic hash functions designed to keep data secured. The first SHA algorithm, known as SHA-0 is a 160 bit hash function published by the National Institute of Standards and Technology (NIST) in 1993 [10]. It is based on the Message Digest 5 (MD5) hash algorithm and is mainly used for digital signature schemes. In 2001, NIST published three new hash functions, namely, SHA-256, 384 and 512; whose hash value sizes are 256 bits, 384 bits and 512 bits respectively. In this work, the SHA-256 hash algorithm has been used for generating digital signatures. This is because, even after 18 years since its inception, it is still the state-of-the-art technology for such purposes.

## 2.2   RSA Cryptography

Rivest–Shamir–Adleman (RSA) is a public key cryptosystem widely used for data transmission, publicly described in 1977. In public-key cryptosystems, the encryption key, which is based on two large prime numbers, is public whereas the decryption key is kept private (secret). The prime numbers must be kept secret so that the ciphertext is not decrypted [11]. RSA cryptosystem is used in this work because of its widespread usage even today.

# 3   Proposed Method

## 3.1   Contributions

This paper proposes a permission based scheme to achieve fine-grained access control over cloud data. It uses encryption and digital-signature based permission technique to address the above issues. This work provides the following features:

**Efficient user revocation:** In this technique, revocation of user or user privileges on a certain piece of data does not require re-encryption of the entire dataset or distribution of new keys to existing users. The cloud simply removes user privilege(s) from the permission list.

**Efficient joining of a new or previously revoked user:** Just like revocation, new user admission also does not need data re-encryption or key distribution. Privileges of the new user are added to the permission list. Also, previously revoked users are treated as new users so that if they are enrolled with new set of permissions then they would not be able to access the data that they could previously access.

**Prevention of collusion between a revoked user and an authorized user:** When a user is revoked, all keys associated with him/her are deleted from the permission list. Thus, even if the revoked user stores the keys, these would be invalid from the moment the user is revoked. Thus collusion between a revoked user and a valid user would be unsuccessful.

**Prevention of collusion between the user and the CSP:** The dataset is encrypted by an asymmetric encryption scheme. The keys of this scheme are accessible only to the Database Administrator (Data Admin). Thus even if CSP provides the required data to the user, it can be decrypted with the help of the Data Admin only. Needless to say that without decryption the data would be useless to the user.

**Prevention of collusion between the user and the Data Admin:** Even the Data Admin cannot edit any data in the cloud if he/she is not permitted to do so. Thus, if a user wants to get access to some data with the help of the Data Admin, the Data Admin has to try all combinations of permission from the permissions list to bypass the permission validator.

### 3.2 Architecture

In this section, the architecture of our permission based healthcare data access control scheme is discussed. Data is healthcare systems is private and extremely sensitive. A single piece of data, like blood pressure or bilirubin count, may not be sensitive. However, the correlation of the same with some other piece of data like patient name or address may become extremely sensitive. For example, a data scientist A may want the number of patients suffering from diabetes. The Healthcare system must be designed in a way such that the data scientist gets only the count and not other details about the patients suffering from diabetes. However, a doctor B must know the past medical records if his patient is suffering from diabetes. Also, the same Doctor B may be eligible to access data records of a Patient X but may not be able to see or update data related to another Patient Y. To sum up, although both A and B are registered users of the hospital, the permission each of them enjoys over each piece of data is different. It is the duty of the designers of the healthcare system to ensure that only the users with sufficient permission get access to the data.

Thus the proposed method centers around the concept of permission. Although permission based attempts have been proposed in the past, they can largely be categorised into Role Based Access Control (RBAC) or Attribute Based Access Control (ABAC). However, both RBAC and ABAC make the generalisation that every user having the same role or same attribute permission will be allowed to operate on the same type of data, which may not always be the case. Also, whether every user can work on the data of every patient is not discussed.

This has inspired us to attempt this method. If a user wants to read or update a piece of data in the Health Database, (s)he must have a 'Read' or 'Update' permission for that data respectively. However, the CSP must not be aware of the access permissions, the working model or the data within the Database. The schematic diagram of the solution is shown in Fig. 1.

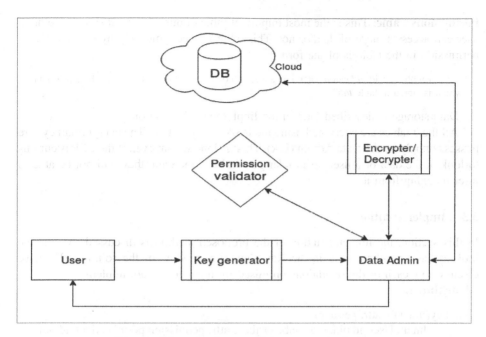

**Fig. 1.** Schematic diagram of the proposed solution

Based on the nature of operations on the Database, people may be categorised into 3 groups:

**User:** Users are the clients who make queries to read or update data from the database. Users can be doctors, nurses, patients or any employee or client of the hospital.

**Cloud Service Provider (CSP):** A CSP or a Cloud Service Provider provides cloud service to the hospital, i.e., the CSP stores the Healthcare Database and provides or edits the data as per instructions from the client.

**Data Admin(DA):** The Data Admin or DA is the bridge between the Users and the CSP. The Admin receives requests from the users, checks whether the user is eligible to work on the data, encrypts values and names of tables and attributes, and sends appropriate queries to the CSP. The CSP sends data to the DA depending on the query. The Admin, on receiving the data decrypts it and sends it to the user.

The proposed method has 3 types of tables namely – Health data, Users and Permissions. The structure of the 3 tables are discussed below:

**Health Data Tables:** These tables store the details of the patients. The primary key of each such table is patient_id. There may be other attributes too, like patient name, address, blood pressure, platelet count, etc. So it is quite evident that there may be multiple tables to store the data of patients.

**Users Table:** This table stores the details of the users. There is only one such table. It has a primary key named user_id. The table may also contain other details like user name, designation etc.

**Permissions Table:** This is the most important table of our scheme. It stores whether a user can access a piece of data or not. This table is accessible only by the DA. Every permission in the table is of the form:

"A user with user_id *uid* can read('*r*') or write('*w*') or both('*b*') patient *pid's* attribute *attr* data which is stored in table *tab*"

Data storage is described later in the Implementation section.

All the 3 tables are encrypted using the RSA cryptosystem. The encryption keys are possessed only by the Data Admin (DA). This is done so that even if the CSP is curious to look at the data or a user or intruder gets hold of the data, they will not be able to infer meaning from it.

### 3.3   Implementation

In this section, the implementation of the proposed method is discussed. At first we look at the algorithms used in the Key Generator module of the solution. Then we discuss how each of the operations promised by the solution are implemented.
**Algorithm 1.**

gen_key(uid, tab, attr, perm, pid)
       Input: User_id uid, table tab, attribute attr, permission perm, patient_id pid
       Output: $h_{fin}$, Digital signature to be stored or searched in the Permissions
table
       1. $h_1$ <- SHA-256(uid)
       2. $h_2$ <- SHA-256(tab)
       3. $h_3$ <- SHA-256(attr)
       4. $h_4$ <- SHA-256(perm)
       5. $h_5$ <- SHA-256(pid)
       6. $h_{fin}$ <- $h_1 + h_2 + h_3 + h_4 + h_5$


**Algorithm 2.**

gen_key_user(uid, tab, attr, perm)
       Input: User_id uid, table tab, attribute attr, permission perm,
       Output: $h_{fin}$, Digital signature required to search in the Permissions table
when data is to be searched for multiple patients
       1. $h_1$ <- SHA-256(uid)
       2. $h_2$ <- SHA-256(tab)
       3. $h_3$ <- SHA-256(attr)
       4. $h_4$ <- SHA-256(perm)
       5. $h_{fin}$ <- $h_1 + h_2 + h_3 + h_4$


**Uniqueness of the signature:** Permissions are stored in the database in the form of digital signatures, each of size 256*5 = 1280 bits for a regular user or 256*4 = 1024 bits for a surveyor. To make sure that a user cannot forge a permission signature, we have to ensure the uniqueness of the signatures.

Different users must not be able to generate the same signature. However, a user may try to access data accessible to another user by entering their *user_id* during data query and mimic their activities. To avoid this, the proposed method does not allow users to enter their uids by themselves. The users have to go through a login module where they sign in using their uid and password to access the database. Once a user logs into the system using their unique *user_id*, this *user_id* will be used to generate permission signatures throughout the session. Thus, the only way a user can generate a signature belonging to another user is by logging into the system using the credentials of that user.

The function must not give the same output for different inputs. In other words, the function defined above must be a one-to-one function. We will try to prove this by contradiction.

Let

$$h_{fin}(x_1) = h_{fin}(x_2) \text{ such that } x_1 \neq x_2$$

where $x_1$ and $x_2$ are the 5-tuples which store the (uid, tab, attr, perm, pid) in that order. Now, since the strings given by the function $h_{fin}$ are equal, it means that each segment of corresponding 256 bits are also equal, i.e., $h_1$ through $h_5$ in both strings are equal. Now, since the hash outputs of the values of uid in $x_1$ and $x_2$, ($h_1$ of both $x_1$ and $x_2$), are equal and considering that SHA-256 is almost collision resistant, therefore the uid in both $x_1$ and $x_2$ must also be same. The same can also be proven for the values of tab, attr, perm and pid (in $x_1$ and $x_2$) from the hash strings $h_2$, $h_3$, $h_4$ and $h_5$ (of both $x_1$ and $x_2$) respectively. Now since the corresponding values in the 5-tuples $x_1$ and $x_2$ are equal, therefore, $x_1 = x_2$. So we have a contradiction. Thus the proposition $h_{fin}(x_1) = h_{fin}(x_2)$ such that $x_1 \neq x_2$ does not hold. The proposition $h_{fin}(x_1) = h_{fin}(x_2)$ is true only if $x_1 = x_2$.

Now we look at how the operations are implemented. At first, a database is created and the structure of the tables are specified by the DA. Relational tables are used here. Once created, the database is sent to the CSP for storing them in the cloud. Once it is done, the DA communicates with the users, who may raise request for the following:

**User Registration:** When a new user is enrolled into the system, (s)he has to go through the registration procedure. A unique user_id is generated and sent to the user. User information is collected by the DA, encrypted using his/her public key and sent to the CSP for entering a new row in the Users table.

**Patient Registration:** Large number of patients are admitted every day in every hospital. When a new patient is admitted, a patient_id is generated and given to the patient. Information about the patient is taken and encrypted by the DA. The DA then requests the CSP to create new rows in the appropriate Health Data tables and fill them with the encrypted values. The patient is then allotted a doctor and nurse/s according to the policy of the hospital. Once the DA receives the list of permissions of the users who can read or update the patient data, keys for each permission in the list is generated using the gen_key() algorithm. The DA then requests the CSP to store these keys accordingly in the Permissions table.

**Adding new permission to the Permissions table:** When the DA has to provide a new permission to a user, the DA sends uid, tab, attr, perm and pid values to the gen_key() algorithm, encrypts the output using DA's public key and stores the ciphertext in the Permissions table.

**Reading and updating data:** If a user with user_id 'U' wants to read 'r' or update 'w' data of a patient with patient_id 'P' about an attribute 'A', then the table 'T' storing that attribute, is first found. The strings U, P, T, A and characters 'r'/'w'/'b' are passed to the gen_key() algorithm. The resulting key *Perm* is then sent to the DA. *Perm* is then encrypted by the public key of the DA to create the string *EPerm*. The DA then sends a query to the CSP to search *EPerm* in the Permissions table. If the value is found and the user had sent a *read* request, the corresponding attribute value is queried from the CSP by the DA. Upon receiving the value from the CSP, the DA decrypts it using its private key and sends it to the user. If it is an *update* request, the updated attribute value is encrypted by the DA and sent to the CSP for updation. The CSP sends a 'success' message to the DA after the table is updated successfully.

Patients can only access data from the Health Data table if patient_id matches the patient_id of the data queried. If matches, *read* or *update* is done as mentioned above.

Similarly, users can also read data from the Users table if their user_id match the user_id of the data searched by them. If the two are same, *read* or *update* is done by the DA and the CSP as already mentioned.

Data from the Permissions table can only be searched or updated by the DA.

**Permission revocation:** If the hospital decides to revoke a certain permission with respect to some attribute of data, user_id, patient_id, the table and attribute where the data is stored, and the type of access (read/write), are given to the Key Generator module. The module passes these values to the gen_key() algorithm and sends the result *Perm* to the DA. The DA creates the *EPerm* using the public key. Then the DA asks the CSP to delete this *EPerm* from the Permissions table, if present.

**User or patient revocation:** When the DA gets request for user or patient revocation, the DA finds the user_id or patient_id and generates key $k$ using SHA-256 algorithm. Then it sends a *DELETE* request to the CSP. The DA requests the CSP to delete all keys $k'$ in the Permissions table where $k$ is a substring of $k'$. Thus, the DA ensures that even if the user or patient later joins with the same user_id or patient_id respectively, they will not be able to view or modify the data they were allowed access to in the past.

In all these requests it is assumed that a user may request data for a particular user. However, in real world, there may exist users like surveyors who would like to execute aggregation operations on the PHR data. This is where the gen_key_user() comes into play. The following aggregation operations are supported by the proposed method.

**Keyword Search:** The proposed method is capable of performing keyword searches. If a user wants to search a keyword of an attribute, the DA checks if (s)he is eligible to view the data using the gen_key_user() algorithm. The DA sends the user_id, the table and attribute of the data required and the '$r$' permission for read operation, to the gen_key_user() algorithm. If permission matches, the DA encrypts the keyword and sends it to the CSP to search the data. Since the encryption used here is deterministic encryption, the keyword must be present only in the form of the ciphertext generated by the DA, if the keyword is at all present in the table.

**Count:** The Count method is based on the keyword search method. Count is an aggregate method and does not reveal the original data. Thus the user searching for the count of a keyword will never be able to identify even a single patient_id. Just like the *Keyword Search* operation, the values user_id, table, attribute and the character 'r' (read) is sent to the gen_key_user() algorithm of the Key Generator module. The algorithm sends the hashed string *Perm* to the DA. The DA then encrypts it to create *EPerm* and requests the CSP to check if any of the strings in the Permissions table starts with this string., i.e., if there exists at least one patient for whom the user is eligible to view that attribute. If yes, then the user is also eligible to get the count of that attribute. If the user is eligible, the DA encrypts the keywords and requests the CSP to find the count of the encrypted keyword.

**Joins:** This method is able to perform join operations between tables. If a user wants to read data of some attributes A from the join of t tables based on some conditions X, then the following steps are undertaken:

1. The set of attributes present in X, i.e., $A_X$ is found.
2. $S = A \cup A_X$
3. Repeat for each attribute s in S, only those patient rows, whose data can be seen by the user if the user is a general user, i.e., a non-surveyor. This is done by sending (user_id, table, attribute s, read/write permission, patient_id) to gen_key() for validation. For a surveyor, all the patient rows are selected but they are reduced to only those attributes of S which the surveyor is eligible to view. For each attribute s in S the 4-tuple (user_id, table, attribute s, read permission) is sent to gen_key_user() function for checking eligibility.
4. Thus each of the t tables is reduced to only those rows and attributes which can be seen by the user.
5. The join operation is performed on these tables.

# 4 Experiments and Results

This section shows a simulation of the application developed for the proposed method. The codes are written in Java. The server used here is an Apache Server and the data are stored in a MySQL database.

At first, the DA logs into the admin mode of the system using user name and password. After successful login of the DA, new users are registered into the system. The user_id of each user is automatically generated to ensure uniqueness. Other details like name, role, etc. are taken as input from the user. Table 1 shows the Users table after all the operations are completed.

**Table 1.** Users table after registration

| User_id | Name | Role |
|---------|--------|--------|
| u001 | Admin1 | Admin |
| u002 | Doctor1 | Doctor |
| u003 | Nurse1 | Nurse |
| u004 | Doctor2 | Doctor |

After the successful registration of the 3 users, patients are registered by the DA during the time of their admission. Information such as name, age, etc. are entered by the patients themselves. The patient_id of each patient is auto-generated in the same manner as the user-id in the previous operations. The Health_Data table is shown in Table 2.

**Table 2.** Health_Data table after patient admission

| Patient_id | Name | BP_high | BP_low | Age | Glucose |
|------------|----------|---------|--------|-----|---------|
| p001 | Patient1 | 130 | 90 | 35 | 148 |
| p002 | Patient2 | 105 | 75 | 42 | 89 |
| p003 | Patient3 | 160 | 100 | 52 | 196 |

Now, the DA provides permission to some users to access/modify some of the data in the Health_Data table. For inserting every new permission, the DA enters the user_id, the patient_id, table_name, the column_name and the read/update/both access.

The final Permissions table after inserting some new permissions is shown in Table 3. Although the original Permissions table contains data in hashed form, the table given below contains it's simplified equivalent.

**Table 3.** Permissions table after all the operations

| User_id | Patient_id | Attribute | Access |
|---------|------------|-----------|------------|
| u002 | p001 | Name | Read |
| u002 | p001 | BP_high | Read/Write |
| u003 | p001 | BP_high | Read/Write |
| u003 | p001 | BP_low | Read/Write |

Now, the users test the integrity of the access control scheme. Doctor1 logs into the client mode of the system using his user_id and password. The doctor tries to view and update the name of patient with id p001 in the following manner:

1. Doctor1 asks the algorithm to "Show" data.
2. Then the doctor enters the table name and column name where the required data exists
3. Finally, Doctor1 enters the patient_id (here, p001).
4. The doctor then asks to "Update" the name of the patient to "Patient4" by entering the same credentials.

According to the Permissions table, i.e., Table 3, Doctor1 is allowed to read the name of the patient but cannot modify it. Thus, after Doctor1 completes Step 3, the user gets the name "PATIENT1". However, after step 4, Doctor1 sees a message "*Record cannot be updated*". Thus, the Health_Data table remains the same as shown in Table 2.

Now, Doctor1 tries to read the name of another patient p002, who is not under his/her supervision, by repeating steps 1–3 as shown above. However, the screen shows the message "*you are not authorized to get this data or wrong query*". Similarly, (s)he then tries to read and update the BP_high attribute of p001 in Table 2 to 125. The updated Health_Data table is shown in Table 4. The updated value of BP_high is marked in bold. From Table 3 it can be seen that the doctor is allowed to do both the operations. Thus, the system conducts those operations successfully.

**Table 4.** Health_Data table operations performed by Doctor1

| Patient_id | Name | BP_high | BP_low | Age | Glucose |
|---|---|---|---|---|---|
| p001 | Patient1 | **125** | 90 | 35 | 148 |
| p002 | Patient2 | 105 | 75 | 42 | 89 |
| p003 | Patient3 | 160 | 100 | 52 | 196 |

After this operation, Nurse1 logs into the system using his/her user_id and password. The nurse tries to read the name of patient p001. But, according to Table 3, she does not have this permission. So, the system restricts him/her from getting the name. Then (s)he tries to read the BP_high attribute of the patient. This time (s)he succeeds because the Permission table grants this access to Nurse1. Nurse1 gets the value 125 on her screen as shown in the updated Health_Data table, i.e., Table 4.

It must also be noted that permissions can be updated at any point of time by the DA. For example, at the present state of the Permissions table if Nurse1 tries to get the glucose value of patient p001 (s)he cannot access the data because the nurse is not eligible to do so. However, let us suppose that the DA gets instruction from the administration that Nurse1 be given this permission and the DA does so. Now, if Nurse1 tries to get the data (glucose value) again, (s)he will get the data this time.

Thus, the experiments and results are evident of the fact that the access control system is foolproof. All the experiments have produced the desired results. The users can read and update data stored in the server. But they are restricted by the permissions granted to them by the administration via the Data Admin (DA).

# 5   Security Analysis

This section analyses the security aspect of the proposed method and compares it to some state-of-the-art access control methods.

## 5.1   Collision Attack

Collision attack prevention is one of the security tests that hash-based cryptographic systems must pass to prove their security. It tries to find two different inputs for which the hash function may produce the same output value. This is because if a malicious user or unregistered hacker can mimic the hash output of another innocent user, then the former will be able to access and modify data accessible to the latter. Not only does it lead to data breach and data inconsistency but it also makes the innocent user liable for any such error. In Sect. 3.3, we have proved that the hash function that has been proposed for the creation and maintenance of the Permissions table is a one-to-one function, i.e., if two inputs manage to give the same output they must be identical to each other. Thus, the proposed method passes the collision attack.

## 5.2   Reverse Attack

Reverse attack [12] is done by a valid user with malicious intentions with their own secret parameters and trying to guess the secret parameters of another user to get data that the malicious user is not permitted to view or update. As seen in the first Case of the Sect. 4, a user cannot enter credentials of another user in the Permissions module. This is because the user_id is automatically taken as input from the current session. Thus, for a malicious user A to get the data permitted for another user B, A must log-in using the user_id and password of B.

## 5.3   External Attack

External attack [12] is the phenomenon by which an invalid user tries to access cloud data. If the user can access data stored in the cloud, then the privacy of data, as sensitive as patient information, will be compromised. Thus, the proposed technique must be immune to external attacks. Since the user does not have a valid user_id and password, (s)he will not be able to login to the module. Even if the user manages to bypass the login module, the user cannot bypass the Permissions module. This is because the Permissions table does not contain any valid permission with the credentials of the invalid user. Sometimes, malicious users, like curious CSPs, may get hold of the entire cloud data. However, this data would still be meaningless to the user because the entire data is encrypted and the decryption key is stored with the DA.

## 5.4   Other Attack

Legitimate use may also lead to breach of privacy. This will be hard to detect. However, this can be dealt with by adopting proper measures to control access to data, even to a legitimate user. Authorization is to be carefully looked into. In the work [13] the authors proposed a flexible security model especially for data centric applications in cloud computing based scenario. This security model ensures data confidentiality, data integrity and fine grained access control to the application data.

## 6 Conclusion

This work uses state-of-the-art security techniques like SHA-256 hashing and RSA cryptography to provide a fine-grained access control scheme in healthcare applications. Different types of data are kept in separate tables in encrypted manner. Thus any intruder or curious CSP cannot infer the data. Permissions are stored in the form of digital signature due to their one-wayness thus ensuring security. User registration and revocation are elementary operations and does not require new keys to be distributed or used for encryption. The method also allows a user to use the count and join operations apart from the search operation. However, the proposed work is still not ready for operations like range comparisons, mean, sum and other mathematical operations due to the encrypted nature of the data. The possibility of these operations would be explored in the future.

## References

1. Armbrust, M., et al.: A view of cloud computing. Commun. ACM **53**(4), 50–58 (2010)
2. Yang, Z., Zhong, S., Wright, R.N.: Privacy-preserving queries on encrypted data. In: Gollmann, D., Meier, J., Sabelfeld, A. (eds.) ESORICS. LNCS, vol. 4189, pp. 479–495. Springer, Heidelberg (2006). https://doi.org/10.1007/11863908_29
3. Yang Y., Zhang, Y.: A generic scheme for secure data sharing in cloud. In: Proceedings of the 40th International Conference on Parallel Processing Workshops, pp. 145–153, Washington DC (2011)
4. Samanthula, B.K., Howser, G., Elmehdwi, Y., Madria, S.: An efficient and secure data sharing framework using homomorphic encryption in the cloud. In: Proceedings of the 1st International Workshop on Cloud Intelligence, Cloud-I 2012, Istanbul (2012)
5. Basu, S., et al.: Fusion: managing healthcare records at cloud scale. IEEE Comput. **45**(11), 42–49 (2012)
6. Sengupta, J.: Design of attribute based user authorization model for e-healthcare. Masters in Distributed and Mobile Computing Thesis, Jadavpur University, Kolkata, India (2017)
7. Mandal, S.: Design of secure storage and access for cloud based data. Masters in Distributed and Mobile Computing Thesis, Jadavpur University, Kolkata, India (2019)
8. Gasarch, W.: A survey on private information retrieval. Bull. EATCS **82**, 72–107 (2004)
9. Mitra, G., Barua, S., Chattopadhyay, S., Sen, S., Neogy, S.: Accessing data in healthcare application. In: Thampi, S., Madria, S., Wang, G., Rawat, D., Alcaraz Calero, J. (eds.) Security in Computing and Communications. SSCC 2018. CCIS, vol. 969. Springer, Singapore (2019). https://doi.org/10.1007/978-981-13-5826-5_23
10. Kasgar, A.K., Agrawal, J., Sahu, S.: New modified 256-bit MD5 algorithm with SHA compression function. Int. J. Comput. Appl. **42**(12), 47–51 (2012)
11. Rivest, R., Shamir, A., Adleman, L.: A method for obtaining digital signatures and public-key cryptosystems. Commun. ACM **21**(2), 120–126 (1978)

12. Liu, C-H., et al.: Secure PHR Access Control Scheme for Healthcare Application Clouds. In: Proceedings of the 2013 42nd International Conference on Parallel Processing, pp. 1067–1076, Lyon (2013)
13. Saha, S., Das, R., Datta, S., Neogy, S.: A cloud security framework for a data centric WSN application. In: ACM Digital Library Proceedings of the 17th International Conference on Distributed Computing and Networking, Article No. 39 (2016)

# 5W1H-Based Semantic Segmentation of Tweets for Event Detection Using BERT

Kunal Chakma[1]([✉])[iD], Steve Durairaj Swamy[1][iD], Amitava Das[2][iD],
and Swapan Debbarma[1]

[1] National Institute of Technology Agartala, Agartala 799046, Tripura, India
kchakma.cse@nita.ac.in
[2] Wipro AI Lab, Bangalore, India
https://www.kunalchakma.com

**Abstract.** Detection of events from Twitter has been one of the significant areas in the Text Mining domain due to the volume of content generated by online users. Twitter is considered as one of the top sources for disseminating information to the users. Due to the short length of texts on Twitter, the content generated is often noisy, which makes the detection of events very difficult. Though research on Twitter event detection has been in existence, most of them focused on implementing statistical measures rather than exploiting the semantics. The work presented in this paper presents an approach for the semantic segmentation of Twitter texts (tweets) by adopting the concept of 5W1H (Who, What, When, Where, Why and How). 5W1H represent the semantic constituents (*subject, object* and *modifiers*) of a sentence and the actions of *verbs* on them. The relationship between a *verb* and the semantic constituents of a sentence forms the basis for representation of an event. The basic approach of the proposed system is to segment the tweets based on the 5W1H contextual word embeddings generated with the help of recent state-of-the-art technology and then clustering the tweets for the representation of possible events. We compared our approach with a simple baseline system that does not segment the tweets. We evaluated the performance of both the approaches by measuring the cosine similarity of the tweets under a cluster. Our 5W1H segmentation approach produced a similarity score above **82%** for the most similar tweets in a cluster against the baseline system that scored below **70%**.

**Keywords:** 5W1H · Semantic Role Labeling · Twitter event detection · BERT

## 1 Introduction

In the present decade, there has been a tremendous growth of user-generated content on the Internet due to the upsurge in social media services. Twitter is one such social networking service or a microblogging service that has gained tremendous success recently. Twitter as a microblogging service allows its users

© Springer Nature Singapore Pte Ltd. 2020
A. Bhattacharjee et al. (Eds.): MIND 2020, CCIS 1240, pp. 57–72, 2020.
https://doi.org/10.1007/978-981-15-6315-7_5

to share and communicate with friends and family about real-world events and also as a medium to express the user's opinion or sentiments on topics of interest [1]. According to the Topic Detection and Tracking (TDT) project [2], an *event* is "an unusual thing that occurs in a certain moment". Becker et al. [3] define an event as the discussion and publication of a substantial volume of a time-ordered stream of Twitter messages of some real-world occurrences. Dou et al. [4] define an event as "a phenomenon that causes a variation in the amount of text data that addresses the relevant topic at a given time". We borrowed Hasan et al.'s [5] concept of an event that describes an event in social media as the discussion on an event-associated subject instigated by users' interest either shortly after the occurrence or in anticipation of it.

Detection of events from social media, particularly from Twitter, has drawn significant attention in the text mining domain. According to Internet Live Stats[1], the number of tweets published on an average is 6000 per second, 350,000 per minute, 500 million per day and around 200 billion per year. The volume of information published on Twitter is humongous and useful for performing tasks such as political campaigning, launching of a product, conducting surveys, publishing of breaking news even before conventional electronic and print media. All such activities are possible representatives of an event. Initially, Twitter was launched in 2007, with a message unit length of only 140 characters which was later extended to 280 characters by the end of 2017. This powerful feature of Twitter makes it unique as the maximum amount of information is incorporated with a minimum length of text. The compact unit enables information updates in real-time, which helps the users to interact intensively and get timely updates for the detection of events. For example, the report in [6] states that it is faster to detect earthquake events on Twitter than on conventional media. However, event detection from the Twitter stream is difficult and challenging. There are several reasons such as a) short and noisy content, b) informal nature of tweets, c) diverse and fast-changing topics, d) mixing of multiple languages, and e) huge data volume.

Previous studies on Twitter event detection as discussed in the later sections, mostly focus on statistical measures such as word frequency occurrences, n-grams; and tweet metrics like the number of followers, user mentions, hashtags etc. Such measures sometimes are an overestimation of the real scenario and are often misleading. Therefore, it is vital to exploit the semantic attributes of tweets in addition to the statistical measures for developing better solutions for the stated problem. Exploiting the semantic attributes of tweets for overcoming the limitations of statistical approaches for event detection on Twitter is the primary reason for the motivation of the presented work.

This paper reports on a system for Twitter event detection by segmenting the tweets based on the extraction of the 5W1H (*Who did what to whom, when, where, why and how*) constituents. 5W1H represent the actions of a *verb* on the semantic constituents of a sentence such as *subject*, *object* and *modifiers*. The *subject* in a given sentence is the nouns or named entities (names of Persons,

---

[1] https://www.internetlivestats.com/.

Locations or Organizations) whereas, the *object* could be nouns or pronouns that depends on the *object* type. In the basic form, *object* is the recipient of the action (*verb*) performed by the *subject*. Therefore, the relationship between a *verb* and the other semantic components forms the basis for the information contained in a given text. For this reason, the 5W1H concept is used in journalism for covering a news story [7]. A news article is deemed complete in journalism when all 5W1H constituents are present. Therefore, the extraction of 5W1H can play an essential role in the event detection task.

The major contribution of our work is:

- Creation of a Twitter corpus on 3 general topics: Demonetization, Me too movement in India and US Presidential elections of 2016
- Segmentation of tweets based on the 5W1H concept
- Identification of events by clustering the tweets after extracting the 5W1H constituents

The rest of the paper is organized as follows. Section 2 describes the working of the proposed implementation. Section 3 presents our experiments. Section 4 presents the results and analysis. Section 5 presents related works. The paper finally concludes in Sect. 6.

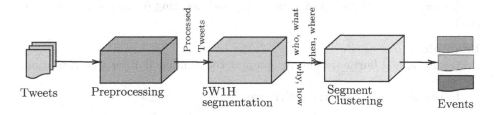

**Fig. 1.** 5W1H based event detection framework

## 2  System Overview

In this section, we present our event detection framework as shown in Fig. 1. Our framework consists of four components: *preprocessing of tweets, segmentation of tweets, detection of event segments* and *clustering event segments*. After collecting the tweets, we preprocess them by lowercasing the texts, removing non-ASCII characters, trailing URLs, and retweets. After curating the tweets, we segmented them by extracting the 5W1H components by a deep neural network implementation [8]. The extracted segments belonging to the same event are then clustered together based on their semantic similarity in the next phase. We describe each phase of our framework in the rest of this section.

## 2.1  Tweet Segmentation

In this section, we discuss on segmentation of a tweet based on the extraction of the 5W1H constituents. In the English language, the basic semantic components of a sentence are the *subject, verb* and an optional *object* (for example: "He eats fruits"). The *verb* describes the actions of the *subject* on the *object*. These semantic constituents are called semantic roles and the task of identifying them is called Semantic Role Labeling (SRL) [10]. Several lexical resources such as PropBank [11], FrameNet [12] and Verbnet [13] have been developed for SRL task. In our framework, we have only used the verb senses defined in PropBank [11] and adopted the concept of 5W1H as the semantic constituents. The 5W1H represents the semantic constituents of a sentence which are comparatively simpler to understand and identify. The concept of 5W1H is widely used in journalism for covering a news story. The 5W1H is known as the answer to questions of a reporter and thus serves as the basis for information gathering. A news story is considered as complete information when all the 5W1H components are present and answers to the question of *Who did what, when, where, why and how*. Based on these premises, we model our tweets, as stated below.

Let us represent the sequence of words in a tweet as $w = \{w_1 w_2 \ldots w_n\}$ with $X$ being the attribute to which $w$ is mapped such that $X$ is the tuple $\langle WHO, WHAT, WHEN, WHERE, WHY, HOW \rangle$ in 5W1H.

Let us consider the event of someone (Kunal) meeting (event) someone (Anupam).

**Example 1**
Yesterday, Kunal hurriedly met Anupam at the seminar hall for a presentation.

In the above example, the 5W1H are:

- **Who:** Kunal
- **What:** met Anupam
- **When:** Yesterday
- **Where:** at the seminar hall
- **Why:** for presentation
- **How:** hurriedly

We, therefore, model a tweet similar to [14] by segmenting them into the 5W1H structure:

$$\psi_{5W1H}(w) = \bigcup_{X \, \epsilon \, 5W1H} \psi_X(w) \tag{1}$$

where, the set of words in the text $w$ are represented with $\psi_X(w)$ which are then classified to the attribute $X$ such that $X \, \epsilon \, 5W1H$. Given a tweet $t \, \epsilon \, \tau$, $t$ is segmented by splitting $t$ into segments, $t = \langle s_1 s_2 \ldots s_m \rangle$ where each $s_i$ is one of the 5W1H defined in Eq. 1.

SRL is a classification task that requires the predicate and corresponding semantic role identification first then the classification of the semantic roles. The segmentation step of our framework requires the identification and classification of verbs and the corresponding semantic roles in the form of the 5W1H. We, therefore, used our [8] attention [9] based deep neural network system for 5W1H component identification and classification task.

## 2.2 Event Segment Detection

A predicate, according to the Oxford dictionary[2], is part of a sentence containing a verb that makes a statement about the verb's subject. In most of the cases, we consider the predicates of sentences or clauses as the trigger for an event. For example, in the following tweet: *"Clinton is losing states by a few thousand votes"*, *Clinton* is the subject, and *is losing states by a few thousand votes* is the predicate. Here, the presence of terms like *losing* and *votes* are the indicators of an event. We, therefore, consider entity mentions or temporal/spatial arguments as event arguments. Similar to SRL arguments for predicates, entity mentions or temporal/spatial arguments serve as specific roles in events.

We define the seven most relevant and abstract semantic components of an event as: *action*, $agent_{sub}$, $agent_{obj}$, *location*, *time*, *causal* and *manner*. We map the 5W1H arguments to the event arguments by adopting the following procedure: 1) we set verbs to represent actions ($action = verb$), 2) we set SRL subject as $agent_{sub} = who$, 3) we set SRL object (direct or indirect object) as $agent_{obj} = what$, 4) we represent event location by setting the SRL spatial argument which is $location = where$, 5) we set SRL temporal argument as event time which is $time = when$ 6) we set SRL causal argument representing the cause of the event as $causal = why$ and 7) Manner modifier specifies how an action is performed. Therefore, we set it as $manner = how$. Based on the structured information described above, we convert each component and the tweet to its vector representation, discussed further in this section. The vectors of each component are then concatenated along with the embeddings of the tweets in the order: *tweet*, $action = verb$, $agent_{sub} = who$, $agent_{obj} = what$, $location = where$, $time = when$, $causal = why$ and $manner = how$ as shown in Fig. 2. All the components of 5W1H may not be present in all the tweets. We therefore, set the corresponding vector to be "NIL" (i.e. NaN) if there are missing event arguments.

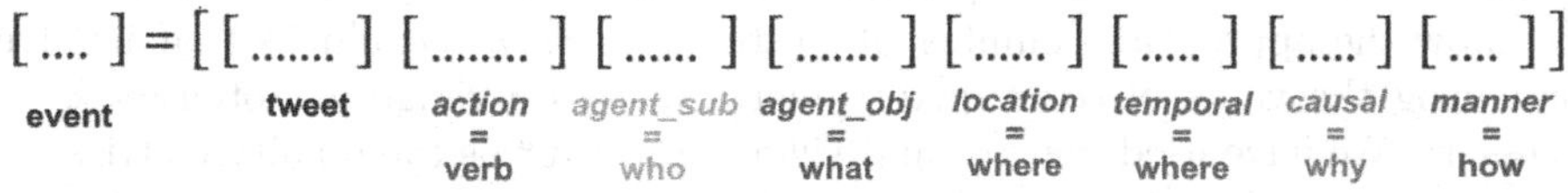

$$[ \dots ] = [ [ \dots ] [ \dots ] [ \dots ] [ \dots ] [ \dots ] [ \dots ] [ \dots ] [ \dots ] ]$$

| event | tweet | action = verb | agent_sub = who | agent_obj = what | location = where | temporal = where | causal = why | manner = how |

**Fig. 2.** Event vector representation

---

[2] https://bit.ly/37GtJWl.

**Segment Vector Representations.** Sentence level embeddings based on Word2Vec [15] or GloVe [16] do not perform well as the context of the words are not stored by these techniques. For SRL, the primary tasks are to identify the predicate and the corresponding role arguments. A predicate may have different meanings depending on the context. For example, the verb *act* has different meanings in *"I was angry when I saw his violent act against animals."* and *"First National Bank of Chicago will act as trustee"*[3]. In the first case, *act* refers to an action, whereas, in the second case, *act* refers to role-playing, and accordingly, the roles are defined. Therefore, the context of the predicate (verb) is important. We, therefore, model this as a sequence labelling task. The year 2018 had seen a breakthrough in the Natural Language Processing (NLP) domain when BERT (Bidirectional Encoder Representations from Transformers) [17] was introduced. Due to the tremendous success of BERT on several NLP tasks, we exploited BERT's capabilities to generate our embeddings. BERT uses special tokens [CLS] and [SEP] to mark a sentence for embedding. The architecture of our model is shown in Fig. 3. Each tweet and the corresponding 5W1H components are input to BERT to generate embeddings for the full tweet and the corresponding 5W1H. *emb_whole_tweet* and *emb_5W* represent the embeddings for the tweet and its 5W1H respectively. These embeddings are then concatenated to form the embedding *emb_T*. The next layer of our model is a pooling layer where we applied different pooling strategies (described in Sect. 3.3). The final layer generates the contextualized vectors $v$. To encode the tweets with the 5W1H components, we designed the input as "[CLS] tweet [SEP]" for a tweet, "[CLS] verb [SEP]" for the verb, and similar structure for the 5W1H components, allowing the representation of the predicate and the corresponding 5W1H to interact with the entire sentence via appropriate attention mechanisms. We feed the sequences into the BERT encoder to obtain the contextual representation using the pre-trained BERT uncased base model.

## 2.3   Event Clustering

Based on the contextual representations identified in the previous step, we group them into clusters where each cluster corresponds to a possible event. We used k-means [18] clustering for grouping the events. The k-means algorithm requires the number of clusters $k$ to be specified before the clustering is done. Since we do not know the appropriate number of clusters, a *priori*, techniques that involve comparing the value of some quality metric across a range of potential $k$s is necessary. We have used *inertia*[4] and *silhouette score*[5] as the quality metrics for choosing the number of clusters $k$. *Inertia* is a measure of how internally coherent clusters are and *silhouette score* is a method of interpretation and validation of consistency within clusters of data. The K-means algorithm is designed to select

---

[3] http://verbs.colorado.edu/propbank/framesets-english-aliases/act.html.

[4] https://scikit-learn.org/stable/modules/clustering.html#clustering-performance-evaluation.

[5] https://en.wikipedia.org/wiki/Silhouette_(clustering).

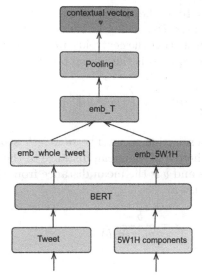

**Fig. 3.** Model architecture on BERT

the centroids that minimize *inertia* and maximize the *silhouette score*. We have chosen the value of $k$ based on decreasing *inertia* and increasing *silhouette score*. The selection of the best $k$ is further described in the following sections.

## 3   Experimental Setup

### 3.1   Dataset

We collected tweets on three different topics: *demonetization*[6], *US Elections 2016*[7] and *Me Too Movement*[8]. We pre-processed the tweets by removing Non-English tweets, *retweets* and lower-casing the tweets. We finalized a total of 16,374 tweets: 3484 on 'demonetization', 6558 on 'Me too' and 6332 on 'US Elections 2016' after pre-processing.

### 3.2   Baseline Clustering

Our baseline is a simple TF-IDF [19] vectorization of the tweets. The vectorization normalizes the token counts according to the fraction of tweets in which the token appears. As mentioned in Sect. 2.3, we start with different values of clusters $k = [2, 5, 10, 20, 30, 50]$. Based on the quality metrics such as *inertia* and

---

[6] https://en.wikipedia.org/wiki/2016_Indian_banknote_demonetisation.

[7] https://en.wikipedia.org/wiki/2016_United_States_presidential_election.

[8] https://en.wikipedia.org/wiki/Me_Too_movement_(India).

*silhouette score*, we chose $k = 10$ as the most possible number of clusters. This is because for $k = 10$, a fall in *inertia* increases the *silhouette score* as seen in Fig. 4(a). A lower *inertia* suggests that the centroids are chosen in such a manner that the within-cluster sum-of-squares is the minimum which is defined as:

$$\sum_{i=0}^{n} min_{u_j \; \epsilon \; C} \left( \|x_i - y_j\|^2 \right) \tag{2}$$

where, $u_j$ is the mean and $x_i$ a selection point. The *silhouette score* $s$ is measured by two parameters $a$ and $b$ where $a$ is the mean distance of the sample from all other points of the same class and $b$ is the mean distance from the sample to all other points in the nearest cluster.

$$s = \frac{b - a}{max(a, b)} \tag{3}$$

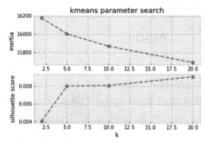
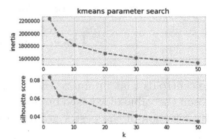

Inertia vs. Silhouette score for Baseline System    Inertia vs. Silhouette score for 5W1H System

**Fig. 4.** Selection of best value of $k$ for clustering

## 3.3    5W1H Based Clustering

As discussed in Sect. 2.2, we input our tweets into BERT with 'bert-base-uncased' pre-trained model, which has 12 layers of transformers [20] with 768 hidden layers. We have used a client-server implementation of BERT known as *bert-as-service* [21]. We set *max_seq_len* to NONE to use the longest sequence dynamically with specific *pooling_strategy* such as *REDUCE_MEAN*, *REDUCE_MAX*, and *REDUCE_MEAN_MAX*. *bert-as-service* allows us to take the average of the hidden state of the encoding layer on the time axis by setting the *pooling_strategy* to *REDUCE_MEAN*. With *REDUCE_MAX*, we can take the maximum of the hidden state of the encoding layer on the time axis. Using $REDUCE\_MEAN\_MAX$, we can separately perform $REDUCE\_MEAN$ and $REDUCE\_MAX$ and then concatenate them together on the last axis, resulting in sentence encodes of 1536 dimensions. We experimented with different *pooling_layer* that determines the encoding layer to which pooling is applied. For example, in a 12-layer BERT model, the layer closest to the output is represented by $-1$, and the layer closest to the embedding layer is represented by $-12$. All the different combinations of *pooling_strategy* and *pooling_layer* produced almost similar results. However, $REDUCE\_MEAN\_MAX$ and *pooling_layer* $-2$ (the second-to-last encoding layer), produced the best clustering results, which are reported in the next section.

## 4    Results and Analysis

There are two kinds of validity indices to measure the quality of clustering results: external indices [22] and internal indices [23]. An external index is a consensus calculation between two partitions, in which the first partition is the labeled clusters and the second partition is the clusters generated by the clustering algorithm. In other words, under external indices, the results of a clustering algorithm are tested based on a defined cluster structure of a data set. Internal indices are used to calculate a clustering structure's correctness without any external knowledge. Under internal indices, the results are evaluated using the inherent quantity and characteristics in the data set. *inertia* and *silhouette score* already discussed in Sect. 2.3 are the internal validity index measures that are used to determine the optimal number of clusters. Since manual annotation of the tweets for labelling the clusters is not feasible, external indices such as *precision* and *recall* cannot be measured. However, for measuring the quality of the clusters, we measured the semantic similarity of the tweets using a new state-of-the-art [24] system. The semantic similarity of the tweets under a particular cluster by the baseline and our 5W1H based system is shown in Fig. 9 and Fig. 10. The central most region of the similarity matrix of Fig. 10 shows that the similarity score is above **82%** and in fact, the quality of the cluster thus produced is significant. On the other hand, the central region of the similarity matrix for the baseline system (Fig. 9) shows that the similarity score is below **70%**. These observations show that the quality of the clusters produced by our 5W1H approach is better and significant than that of the baseline system.

The dimensionality of the feature space is too high for direct visualisation techniques. Therefore, we visualise our clusters with a dimensionality reduction technique called t-SNE [25]. A t-SNE plot of the clustering results with the number of clusters $k = 10$ for the baseline and 5W1H approach are reported in Fig. 5. From Fig. 5, it is observed that our 5W1H approach does better clustering than the baseline approach. In Fig. 6, it is observed that the baseline approach generated clusters with cluster label 8 and 9. Cluster number 9 represents the *"Me too*

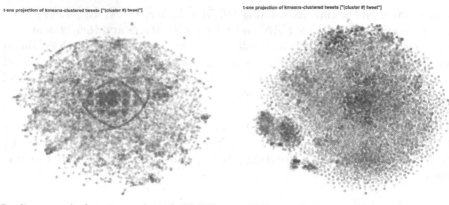

Baseline system's clustering results with TF-IDF vectorization

5W1H system's clustering results with contextualized vectors

**Fig. 5.** Overall clustering for $k = 10$

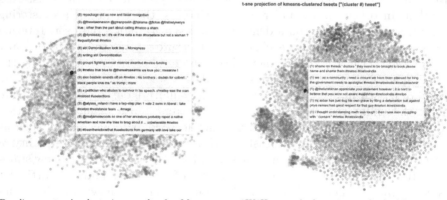

Baseline system's clustering results for Me too movement

5W1H system's clustering results for Me too movement

**Fig. 6.** Cluster representation of Me too movement

*movement"* whereas cluster number 8 contains tweets from both *"demonetization"* and *"US Elections"* topics. On the other hand, our 5W1H approach generated cluster number 1 with a clear representation of the *"Me too movement"*. Similarly, a comparison of the clusters for *"US Elections"* and *"demonetization"* are shown in Figs. 7 and 8 respectively.

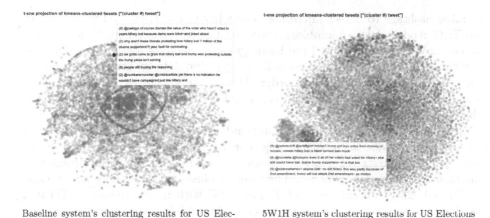

Baseline system's clustering results for US Elections

5W1H system's clustering results for US Elections

**Fig. 7.** Cluster representation of US Elections

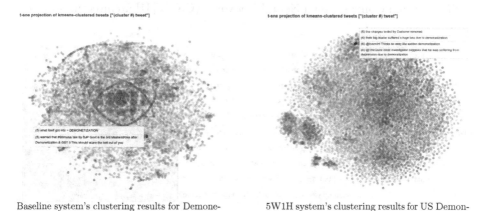

Baseline system's clustering results for Demonetization

5W1H system's clustering results for US Demonetization

**Fig. 8.** Cluster representation of Demonetization

## 5 Related Works

Detection of events from Twitter is not a new topic of research. However, due to the extensive studies done earlier with the then available tools and state-of-the-art techniques, research in this domain still has significance at the present time. In this section, we discuss some of the related works in Twitter event detection that motivated us for doing this research work. Atefeh and Khreich [26] presented a survey paper which mostly focused on the literature from before the year 2012. In a later survey paper by Hasan et al. [5] presented a survey of several event detection techniques from Twitter in the past few years. They presented several open issues in the Twitter event detection domain, and we tried to address some of them in our research work. 5WTAG [14] is a system for automatic generation of topic hashtags to detect microblog topics from Sina Weibo[9]. The authors of 5WTAG modelled the microblogs based on the five Ws(When, Where, Who, What, hoW). They generated the hashtags by segmenting a microblog with the 5W components such that the words forming a candidate hashtag come from the same 5W clause and in the same order. They evaluated the extracted candidate hashtags by computing the semantical completeness and correctness for ranking the candidate hashtags.

Twevent [27] proposed a segmentation-based event detection system from tweets. Tweets were segmented using a segment score of "stickiness" in their approach, and bursty segments were selected based on segment prior probability distribution, and user diversity. They finally clustered the tweets into events. SEDTWik [28] is an extension of Twevent [27] with more features. SEDTWik used hashtags, retweet count, user popularity, and follower count as the key features. They achieved better results by giving more weightage to hashtags. Dabiri and Heaslip [29] presented a deep learning-based system for traffic event detection from the Twitter stream. They used both Recurrent Neural Networks (RNN) [30] and Convolutional Neural Networks (CNN) [31] architectures on top

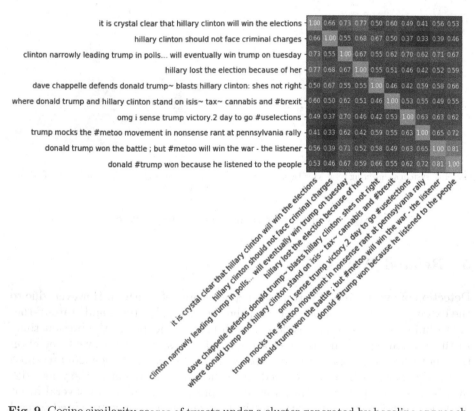

**Fig. 9.** Cosine similarity scores of tweets under a cluster generated by baseline approach

---

[9] https://en.wikipedia.org/wiki/Sina_Weibo.

**Fig. 10.** Cosine similarity scores of tweets under a cluster generated by our 5W1H approach

of word embeddings. TwitterNews+ [32], is a system for event detection from the Twitter stream in real-time which integrates inverted indexes and incremental clusters to detect major as well as minor events considered to be newsworthy. They utilized several parameters such as $M$ (number of most recent tweets), $tS_i$ (expiry time for an event cluster), $tsr$ (cosine similarity threshold) and fine-tuned them to achieve the best performance.

Unlike Twevent [27] and SEDTWik [20] where a segment of a tweet is an n-gram with no semantic structure, our 5W1H segmentation approach provides a highly semantically rich structure which helps in better clustering of the events. Though we modelled the tweets similar to 5WTAG [14], the two approaches are different in terms of their use. The primary emphasis of 5WTAG is to construct a candidate hashtag from the 5 W segments whereas, our 5W1H based segmentation is oriented towards establishing the relationship between the predicates and the corresponding arguments and using this relationship for clustering the tweets.

# 6   Conclusion

The explosive growth in user-generated content on social media such as Twitter has attracted considerable interest in the academia and the industry. Twitter is considered as one of the top sources for providing information on ground backing news, discussions on trending topics, or topic of interests to the users. The discussions on Twitter could be the references to the occurrence of potential events which could be significant to the users. However, detecting events from Twitter is a difficult task due to the nature of tweets. Tweets are short in length, often noisy, and users often do not follow grammatical structure while posting on Twitter. In this paper, we presented a Twitter event detection system by segmenting the tweets with the 5W1H components, which are essential semantic constituents of information. We performed experiments with our 5W1H based segmentation of the tweets and compared them with a simple TF-IDF vectorization approach. We used the recent state-of-the-art technology for generating contextualized embeddings from the 5W1H components, which we later used for generating the clusters. The dataset used in our work are very generic, and the approach adopted could be extended to detect specific events related to disasters, sports and terror activities. In future, we intend to include experiments with other clustering techniques and compare the clustering quality. We also intend to test our approach on accessible event detection datasets and compare our approach with other similar event detection systems.

# References

1. Kwak, H., Lee, C., Park, H., Moon, S.: What is Twitter, a social network or a news media? In: WWW, pp. 591–600. ACM, Raleigh (2010)
2. James, A.: Topic Detection and Tracking: Event-Based Information Organization, 1st edn. Springer, Boston (2002). https://doi.org/10.1007/978-1-4615-0933-2
3. Becker, H., Naaman, M., Gravano, L.: Beyond trending topics: real-world event identification on Twitter. In: Proceedings of the Fifth International Conference on Weblogs and Social Media, Barcelona, Catalonia, Spain, 17–21 July 2011 (2011)
4. Dou, W., Wang, K., Ribarsky, W., et al.: Event detection in social media data. In: Proceedings of the IEEE VisWeek Workshop on Interactive Visual Text Analytics - Task Driven Analytics of Social Media Content, pp. 971–980 (2012)
5. Hasan, M., Orgun, M.A., Schwitter, R.: A survey on real-time event detection from the Twitter data stream. Inf. Sci. 44(4), 443–463 (2017)
6. Sakaki, T., Okazaki, M., Matsuo, Y.: Earthquake shakes Twitter users: real-time event detection by social sensors. In: WWW, pp. 851–860 (2010)
7. Wilson, T., Medine, P.: The Art of Rhetoric (1560): G - Reference Information and Interdisciplinary Subjects Series. Pennsylvania State University Press (1999)
8. Chakma, K., Das, A., Debbarma, S.: Deep semantic role labeling for tweets using 5W1H: Who, What, When, Where, Why and How. Computación y Sistemas 23(3), 751–763 (2019). https://doi.org/10.13053/CyS-23-3-3253
9. Bahdanau, D., Cho, K., Bengio, Y.: Neural machine translation by jointly learning to align and translate. In: Proceedings of the ICLR Conference, San Diego, USA, pp. 1–15 (2015)

10. Gildea, D., Jurafsky, D.: Automatic labeling of semantic roles. Assoc. Comput. Linguist. **28**(3), 245–288 (2002)
11. Palmer, M., Gildea, D., Kingsbury, P.: The proposition bank: a corpus annotated with semantic roles. Comput. Linguist. J. **31**(1), 71–105 (2005)
12. Baker, C.F., Fillmore, C.J., Lowe, J.B.: The Berkeley framenet project. In: 1998 Proceedings of the 36th Annual Meeting of the Association for Computational Linguistics and 17th International Conference on Computational Linguistics, vol. 1, pp. 86–90 (1998)
13. Schuler, K.K., Palmer, M.S.: VerbNet: abroad-coverage, comprehensive verb lexicon. Ph.D. thesis. University of Pennsylvania, Philadelphia, PA, USA (2005)
14. Zhao, Z., Sun, J., Mao, Z., Feng, S., Bao, Y.: Determining the topic hashtags for Chinese microblogs based on 5W model. In: Wang, Y., Yu, G., Zhang, Y., Han, Z., Wang, G. (eds.) BigCom 2016. LNCS, vol. 9784, pp. 55–67. Springer, Cham (2016). https://doi.org/10.1007/978-3-319-42553-5_5
15. Mikolov, T., Sutskever, I., Chen, K., Corrado, G., Dean, J.: Distributed representations of words and phrases and their compositionality. In: Advances in Neural Information Processing Systems, vol. 26 (2013)
16. Pennington, J., Socher, R., Manning, C.D.: GloVe: global vectors for word representation. In: Empirical Methods in Natural Language Processing, pp. 1532–1543 (2014)
17. Devlin, J., Chang, M., Lee, K., Toutanova, K.: BERT: pre-training of deep bidirectional transformers for language understanding. arXiv preprint arXiv:1810.04805 (2018)
18. Jin, X., Han, J.: K-means clustering. In: Sammut, C., Webb, G.I. (eds.) Encyclopedia of Machine Learning. Springer, Boston (2011). https://doi.org/10.1007/978-0-387-30164-8_425
19. Jin, X., Han, J.: TF-IDF. In: Sammut, C., Webb, G.I. (eds.) Encyclopedia of Machine Learning. Springer, Boston (2011). https://doi.org/10.1007/978-0-387-30164-8_832
20. Vaswani, A., et al.: Attention is all you need. CoRR, (abs/1706.03762) (2017)
21. Xiao, H.: BERT-as-service (2018). https://github.com/hanxiao/bert-as-service
22. Dudoit, S., Fridlyand, J.: A prediction-based resampling method for estimating the number of clusters in a dataset. Genome Biol. **3**(7), 1–21 (2002). https://doi.org/10.1186/gb-2002-3-7-research0036
23. Thalamuthu, A., Mukhopadhyay, I., Zheng, X., Tseng, G.C.: Evaluation and comparison of gene clustering methods in microarray analysis. Bioinformatics **22**(19), 2405–2412 (2006)
24. Reimers, N., Gurevych, I.: Sentence-BERT: sentence embeddings using siamese BERT-networks. In: Proceedings of Empirical Methods in Natural Language Processing. Association for Computational Linguistics (2019). http://arxiv.org/abs/1908.10084
25. Maaten, L., Hinton, G.: Visualizing data using t-SNE (2008)
26. Atefeh, F., Khreich, W.: A survey of techniques for event detection in Twitter. Comput. Intell. **31**, 132–164 (2015)
27. Li, C., Sun, A., Datta, A.: Twevent: segment-based event detection from tweets. In: Proceedings of the 21st ACM International Conference on Information and Knowledge Management, CIKM 2012, New York, NY, USA, pp. 155–164 (2012)
28. Morabia, K., Murthy, B., Lalita, N., Malapati, A., Samant, S.: SEDTWik: segmentation-based event detection from tweets using Wikipedia. In: Proceedings of the 2019 Conference of the North American Chapter of the Association for Computational Linguistics: Student Research Workshop, pp. 77–85 (2019)

29. Dabiri, S., Heaslip, K.: Developing a Twitter-based traffic event detection model using deep learning architectures. Expert Syst. Appl. **118**, 425–439 (2019)
30. Sherstinsky, A.: Fundamentals of recurrent neural network (RNN) and long short-term memory (LSTM) network. CoRR, (abs/1808.03314) (2018)
31. Yamashita, R., Nishio, M., Do, R.K.G., Togashi, K.: Convolutional neural networks: an overview and application in radiology. Insights Imaging **9**(4), 611–629 (2018). https://doi.org/10.1007/s13244-018-0639-9
32. Hasan, M., Orgun, M.A., Schwitter, R.: Real-time event detection from the Twitter data stream using the TwitterNews+ Framework. Inf. Process. Manag. **56**(3), 1146–1165 (2019)

# Sarcasm Detection in Tweets as Contrast Sentiment in Words Using Machine Learning and Deep Learning Approaches

Chandra Prakash Singh Sengar$^{(\boxtimes)}$ and S. Jaya Nirmala$^{(\boxtimes)}$

National Institute of Technology Tiruchirappalli, Tiruchirappalli, India
chandraprakashsinghsengar30@gmail.com, sjaya@nitt.edu

**Abstract.** Sarcasm is a remark that clearly means the opposite of what is said, made to criticize something in a humorous way. The main goal of the proposed work is to identify sarcasm in plain text. Sarcasm detection in a text is a difficult task due to lack of context of the tweet, lack of user's character and personality and lack of expression and body language. We present a novel method in feature engineering based on the contrast in phrases of the sarcastic sentence. It can recognize the positive phrases followed by negative situation phrase (example- I can't wait for the algebra exam tomorrow!) and the inverse of it in sarcastic tweets. It has been done by getting the sentiment of various parts of the tweet by dividing the tweet. Features to know the context of words used in a sentence were extracted by many different methods. We used a neural network model using the ReLU activation function for the detection of sarcasm in tweets, which improves the f1-score as compared to machine learning approaches. It is found that the neural network model outperforms the machine learning model in terms of accuracy and f1-score.

**Keywords:** Sarcasm detection · Neural network · Contrast sentiment phrases · Twitter data

## 1 Introduction

Sarcasm is basically an ironic utterance that is a form of speech, where what the speaker says is not the same as what he means. The message in sarcasm is implicit Sarcasm is often used to express critical attitude, insult, and sense of humor. Sarcasm is verbal communication that depends on pitch and tone of voice which helps in defining sarcasm, but to identify in the written text it is even more difficult. Sarcastic texts can generally be seen in user-generated text such as on Facebook, Twitter, and Amazon product reviews. Most of the Natural Language processing work has a lot of challenging problems and one of the major issues which affect the efficiency of the NLP models is sarcasm. More precisely in areas such as sentiment analysis and text summarization, sarcasm might result in a completely wrong analysis of data (example-This phone has an awesome battery back-up of 2 h). These challenges of sarcasm and their benefits have led to an interest in sarcasm detection. Sarcastic texts can be hard to understand not only for the machine but also for a human sometimes because of the common topic and historical information need to share between two people to make the

© Springer Nature Singapore Pte Ltd. 2020
A. Bhattacharjee et al. (Eds.): MIND 2020, CCIS 1240, pp. 73–84, 2020.
https://doi.org/10.1007/978-981-15-6315-7_6

sarcastic statement successfully. A variety of words are used together in the sarcastic statement makes it hard to successfully extract features. It has been seen in sarcastic tweets that it has embedded incongruity in the form of words and phrases themselves, as mentioned in the example below.

- I thoroughly **enjoyed** taking exam. #sarcasm
- I **love** being ignored. #sarcasm
- I never forget faces, but in your case, I'll be **glad** to make an exception. #sarcastic
- @user my flight is delayed……. **Amazing**. #sarcasm
- **Love** you when you don't text me back. #sarcasm

Sarcastic tweets follow a pattern where a positive phrase is followed by a negative situation, where positive polarity words are Bold and negative situation words are Underline.

We are using data from Twitter [1]. The reason to use tweets is that on Twitter where people write sarcastic comments, they also write #sarcasm or #sarcastic. Hence, categorizing or labeling data is easy for training the model. It has some drawbacks such as noise and subjectivity of sarcasm. This work has discussed the feature engineering to extract most of the features from contrast sentiment in sarcastic tweets. We also take into account the N-grams feature up to N = 2 and topic modeling for recognizing the pattern. Design machine learning and neural network with ReLU logit function models to detect sarcasm using extracted features and check which model learns better on these features. The neural network recall is less. The contrast features have provided more insights into training models and, gets the primary goal is to analyze whether the text is sarcastic or not.

# 2  Related Work

Research interest grew rapidly toward sarcasm detection in text with the popularity growth of social networking sites and e-service such as e-commerce, e-tourism, and e-business [13]. The companies are very keen on utilizing sentiment and sarcasm detection for marketing strategies to analyze customer emotion towards their brands [7, 13]. Mathieu Cliche [15] had collected a lot of sarcastic tweets text by the help of #sarcasm or #sarcastic hashtag from Twitter [4] and regular tweets text by ensuring that tweets do not have #sarcasm or #sarcastic hashtag in it using Twitter API [5]. The same dataset is used in this work for training purpose. The values of the positivity and negativity score assigned by the SentiWordNet dictionary [6]. Miruna Pislar and Mathieu Cliche [8, 9] have used files, by the help of that emojis are translated to their descriptions, emoticons are translated to their descriptions, slang is corrected, and abbreviations are expanded in the dataset for better analysis in the text. Ellen Riloff et al. [3] shows the contrast between positive sentiment phrases in a negative situation in the sarcastic statement, which is the common pattern that occurs in the user-generated sarcastic text on social networking sites. Parash dharwar et al. [12] has given an overview of feature selection for the text data to identification sarcasm and, Abhijit Mishra et al. [21] shows the harnessing of cognitive features for sarcasm detection, which is useful in feature engineering. Our work used updated traditional feature engineering processes and as well as more effective features to train the model.

Logistic regression is the appropriate regression analysis to conduct when the dependent variable is dichotomous (binary) [10]. Poria et al. [14] explain the Convolutional neural network is effective at modeling the hierarchy of features, which is essential to learn the context of words. ReLU is faster to compute than the sigmoid function, and its derivative is faster to compute [11]. This makes a significant difference in training and inference times for neural networks.

## 3 Proposed Work

The block diagram of the proposed sarcasm detection system shown in Fig. 1.

### 3.1 Gathering the Dataset

The gathering of a dataset requires great care on authenticity and reliability. Twitter can fulfill all characteristics for the best place to gather text data to analyze and as many distinct samples as we want. Twitter allows limited characters that lead to discussions or expressed neatly without wasting words, which helps in the analysis of the text. [2] had gathered tweets for over two months using Twitter API and tweepy library [16] based on hashtag present in the Tweets. If '#sarcasm' or '#sarcastic' present in the tweet, then it is considered as sarcastic tweet text otherwise non-sarcastic or regular tweet text. Dataset consists of about 1,51,900 sarcastic tweets text [4] and 3,30,692 non-sarcastic tweets text [5]. The whole dataset is in the English language only.

### 3.2 Pre-processing

The raw data that was gathered from Twitter has some demerits, it is noisy and unlabeled. '#sarcasm' or '#sarcastic' hashtag in Tweets was meant to be sarcastic, but it is possible that others might not be able to guess because sarcasm is subjective (example- what a great vacation I have been having so far!). The noise was removed through various steps and data consistency is maintained throughout the data cleaning process.

- Remove all the tweets which have URL (http), remove whitespace and, remove user tag (@user) in it.
- The non-ASCII characters were removed present in it.
- The hashtag had been split and, then remove all hashtag sign (#). Also, remove friend tag and all indication of sarcasm or sarcastic from remaining tweets.
- After the above three stages, individual tweets should be three words long [17], otherwise, it must be discarded because tweets cannot be sarcastic with two words.
- Duplicate tweets have been removed if present in the corpus.
- Emoticons (example- ":-(" : "bad"), expand contraction (example- "doesn't": "does not") and slang (example- "yay!": "good") have been replaced by word, which describe emotion behind it using dictionary[8] and, easy to recognized by the

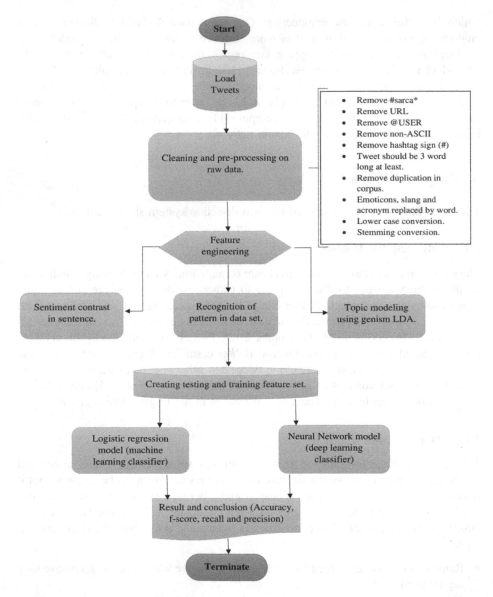

**Fig. 1.** Sarcasm detection architecture.

sentiment analysis. This had been improved the number of dimensions of the feature.

- Lower case conversion and, stemming have also been done on whole texts because lower case makes similarity in the text, which is good for analysis and, stemming converts a variety of words to their standard illustration to get the sentiment of a word defiantly in the dictionary [6] (Table 1).

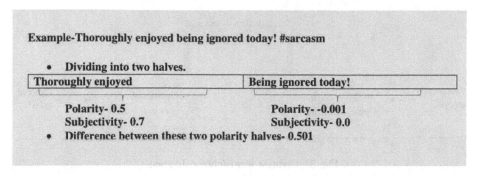

**Fig. 2.** Polarity and subjectivity diagram of two halves and their difference.

**Table 1.** Number of tweets in dataset after pre-processing on sarcastic and regular dataset.

| Dataset | Number of tweets |
|---|---|
| Sarcastic dataset | 25,273 |
| Regular dataset | 1,17825 |

### 3.3   Feature Extraction of the Tweet

Feature engineering is the core step of natural language processing work. The dataset is in annotated text form which cannot be provided as an input to machine learning or deep learning model directly for classification. Hence, to train models we need to give more focus view of tweets. Which unique characteristic makes a tweet or sentence sarcastic or not? That question must be answered so, these basic features from tweets to be extracted for model training.

Now, multiple different feature set were extracted, which are task-specific for classification model as follows.

**Contrast Sentiment Features.** Sarcasm or irony is when a negative situation is described with positive words or saying the opposite of what is meant (example-thoroughly enjoyed being ignored today!). The sarcastic statement can be identified when there is a contract in the statement with their situation as shown in Fig. 3. The goal here is to create a classifier model for tweets or statements that can recognize the contrast of positive sentiments with a negative situation and vice versa. Base research work [3] shows frequently two divided halves of sarcastic tweets have contrast polarity and subjectivity as mentioned in Fig. 2. Different kinds of sarcastic statements show contrast on multiple levels of division. Hence, to extract the best feature from the dataset we have modified feature extraction engineering to get more insight into the dataset. Now, we have following feature being extracted.

- Full tweet polarity and subjectivity.
- Half tweet (1/2 and 2/2) polarity and subjectivity.
- Third parts of tweet (1/3, 2/3 and 3/3) polarity and subjectivity.
- Fourth parts of tweet (1/4, 2/4, 3/4 and 4/4) polarity and subjectivity.

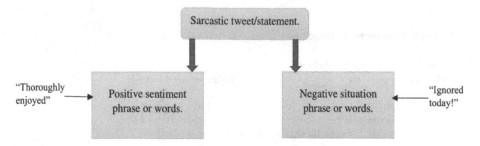

**Fig. 3.** Contrast words/phrase diagram.

- Difference between the polarity of two halves.
- Difference between minimum and maximum polarity of third.
- Difference between minimum and maximum polarity of fourth.

Textblob library [18] and dictionary using SentiWordNet [6] was used to find polarity and subjectivity. This method provides the highest number of features to train the model.

**Recognizing Patterns.** It has been seen often that some words come together in one tweet or statement (example- Saturday, party, night, friends, etc.). The question is that, is it possible to discover a group of words that mostly comes together in sarcastic or non-sarcastic tweets? Topic modeling is an unsupervised learning technique that is capable of scanning a corpus, detecting phrase pattern and words within them, and clustering similar word groups that best characterize a corpus. These groups are called topics. We are able to find the topics associated with sarcastic or non-sarcastic tweets using Latent Dirichlet Allocation (LDA). LDA views a document or corpus as a bag of words. It works on reverse engineering of an assumption that the way a document was generated by picking a set of topics and then for each topic picking a set of words. We have used the gensim library [19] that took tweets and topic modular and returned a topic vector feature using LDA. The topic vector is the decomposition of each tweet as a sum of topics. It is one of the best features extracted and makes learning easier and more accurate.

**N-grams Feature Extraction.** Using N-grams on the hypothesis that would be helpful in identifying sarcastic tweets as they are not separated from the context around it and are more identifiable at word level. When performing machine learning tasks related to NLP on sequence-based datasets N-grams not only helps to learn words but also learn words in that context, which provides a better understanding of the meaning of the words. More precisely, unigram and bigram are the simple, effective and scalable approach for feature extraction. Bi-gram are used to capture words used in a negative or positive context (example- the staff were not friendly, terrible really). In the last example the word 'friendly' is positive but by looking the word nearby, we could understand the word is used in a negative context. Bi-gram are really helpful in sarcasm detection and it captures the border context of the words as mentioned in Fig. 4.

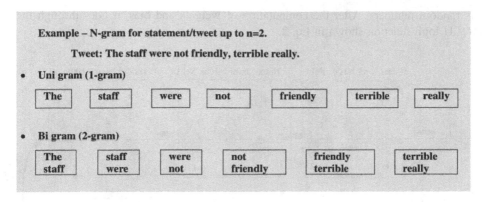

Fig. 4. N-gram diagram.

## 3.4 Building the Model

**Logistic Regression.** It is the statistical model used to assign the probability of certain events or classes between 0 and 1. Sarcasm detection comes under binary classification, where two outcomes are possible in each sample of tweets. Hence, the dichotomous variable has been involved with the prediction of the outcomes. The regression algorithm deals with the plotting of feature set coordinate with their values and then try to get the most accurate function possible that can predict the output values of input features. Mathematically, the logistic regression model has two variables dependent and independent, whereas the dependent variable with two values is represented by indirect variables shown in Eq. 1.

$$P(x) = \frac{e^{\left(\beta_0 + \beta_1 x_1 \ldots \ldots \beta_{nx_n}\right)}}{e^{\left(\beta_0 + \beta_1 x_1 \ldots \ldots \beta_{nx_n}\right)} + 1} = \frac{1}{e^{-\left(\beta_0 + \beta_1 x_1 \ldots \ldots \beta_{nx_n}\right)} + 1} \in [0, 1] \tag{1}$$

**Neural Network.** The neural network was developed with the help of open-source AI libraries and data flow graphs. TensorFlow was used, for creating large scale neural networks with many layers. It allows building data flow graph and mathematical computation at every node of the graph according to the requirement of the model. TensorFlow takes both data flow graph and input together and process it in the background and generate output in a python file, which boost the performance and avoid compatibility issue in python.

Our model is designed with an input layer of 23 neurons, three hidden layers of 100 neurons each and an output layer of two neurons, one for each sarcastic and non-sarcastic classification as mentioned in Fig. 5. Here, the output neurons work as binary classifiers. The output was recorded as an encoded array for easy extraction and comparison. The corresponding indexes to the classes are 0 and 1 in the output array. The first layer takes the feature set as input. Initially, weights and biases are initialized as random numbers. After the computation of weights and bias, it goes through the ReLU logit function shown in Eq. 2.

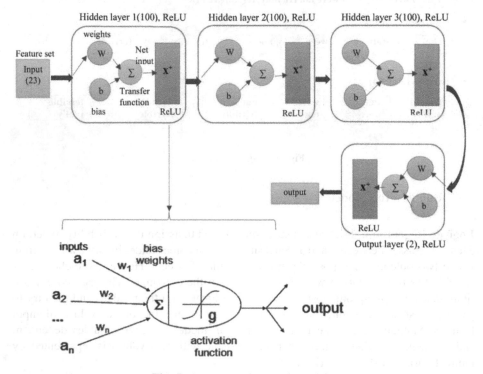

**Fig. 5.** Deep neural network model.

$$f(x) = x^+ = \max(x, 0) \tag{2}$$

Similarly, the output of the first hidden layer goes to the second hidden layer as the input and computation of weight, bias and ReLU logit function take place. Similar computation happens on the third hidden layer, whose output goes through the output layer as input.

Then that final value considered as the output of the neural network. TensorFlow was used to established backpropagation to facilitate learning and data flow in the neural network.

### 3.5    Training and Testing

All the pre-processing and testing required for the machine learning approach on this research has been on a system that has a configuration of Intel (R) Core (TM) i5-4200 CPU @ 1.60–2.30 GHz and 4 GB RAM. The deep learning approach or neural network has been build using Tensorflow 1.0 on Google Colab.

**Logistic Regression Model.** The dataset was divided into a training set and testing set using scikit-learn library [20]. The training set and testing set are divided in the ratio of 75:25%. The model was trained using the same training set. A 10-fold cross-validation technique was used on the testing set to analyze the results.

**Neural Network Model.** The same extracted feature was provided to train the model. The training set and testing set are divided in the ratio of 3:1. Adam optimizer and batch processing have been used for training the neural network to minimize the mean cost throughout the epochs. The goal here is to minimize the cost of the trained model. The training set used to train the neural network and 80 epochs of training were done. In each epoch, a batch size of 50 was used and the loss has collected. Batch processing is the number of times an entire dataset is processed in epochs. This process helps the neural network to learn accurately. It is evident from Fig. 6 that loss is reducing continuously after every epoch, which means the neural network is learning in every epoch.

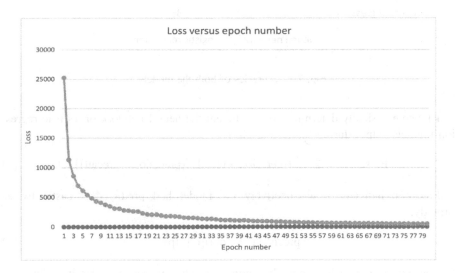

**Fig. 6.** Loss versus Epoch.

# 4 Result and Analysis

The raw data collected from Twitter was pre-processed and features were extracted from each tweet. Deep learning and machine learning models give the ability to computers to learn from the feature set and make a prediction on the tweet, whether it is sarcastic or not. To get a better sense of all three feature extraction approaches, contrast sentiment feature gives deeper insights into data and played a major role to train the classification model. The neural network had learned positive sentiment and negative situation phrases effectively. The neural network model works much better than the machine learning model for sarcasm detection on this kind of feature sets as shown in Fig. 7.

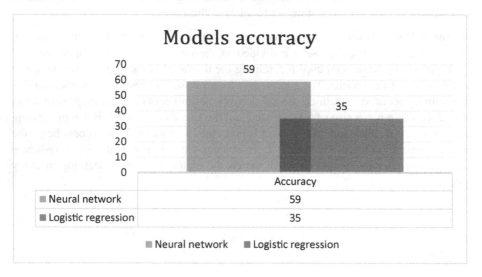

**Fig. 7.** Accuracies of both the models.

F1-Score basically determines how efficient the neural network or logistic regression predicts output during the testing phase.

$$F1\,score = 2 * ((precision * recall)/(precision + recall)) \qquad (3)$$

Precision indicates how effectively the model had predicted sarcastic tweets correctly.

$$precision = tp/(tp + fp) \qquad (4)$$

The recall is the indicator that how sarcastic tweets did classifier label as sarcastically.

$$recall = tp/(tp + fn) \qquad (5)$$

where, tp = ture positive, fp = false positive and, fn = false negative.

Accuracy is a measure of the degree of the nearness of predicted sarcastic or regular tweets to its actual nature (Table 2).

$$Accuracy = correctly\,predicted\,tweets/total\,testing\,tweets \qquad (6)$$

F1-score and accuracy of the neural network are 0.698 and 0.58449 respectively. The recall and precision of the model are 0.23 and 0.63 respectively.

**Table 2.** Confusion matrix of the neural network.

|                   | Predicted sarcastic | Predicted regular |
|-------------------|---------------------|-------------------|
| Actual sarcastic  | 1424                | 4846              |
| Actual regular    | 839                 | 6573              |

Paper uses different feature engineering methods such as contrast sentiment, patter reorganization, and N-gram to know the context of the word in tweets to get a variety of features from the text for the training, which can give a large dissimilar feature set for sarcasm detection. Polarity and subjectivity of contrast phrases of a tweet by dividing the tweet into various parts turn out to be the best feature. Machine learning and deep learning approaches are able to identify sarcasm in tweets, but the neural network model outperforms the logistic regression model with the same feature set due to the presence of non-linear data in the corpus.

## 5    Conclusion and Future Scope

Using a single type feature extraction to train a sarcasm detection model is not enough. Our works identify one kind of sarcasm, which is most common in tweets that is positive phrases to explain the negative situation. According to that, we proposed the method for feature extraction and, these features can be used to recognize sarcastic tweets more accurately.

The f1-score and accuracy can be increased by making sarcastic data balance to regular data, which currently is unbalanced that is 25273 sarcastic sentences and 117825 regular sentences. Sarcasm identification precision can be more accurate if we will be able to find more features from a dataset. In future work more features like part-of-speech tag, sarcasm occurs due to number (example- We drove so slowly.......only 160 km/h.), and "liked-prefixed" sarcasm (example- Like those guys believe a word they say.) added to the model.

## References

1. Twitter. https://twitter.com/
2. http://www.thesarcasmdetector.com/about/
3. Riloff, E., Qadir, A., Surve, P., Silva, L., Gilbert, N., Huang, R..: Sarcasm as contrast between a positive sentiment and negative situation. In: Proceedings of EMNLP, pp. 704–714 (2013)
4. Sarcastic tweets database. https://github.com/MathieuCliche/Sarcasm_detector/blob/master/app/twitDB_sarcasm.csv
5. Regular tweets database. https://github.com/MathieuCliche/Sarcasm_detector/blob/master/app/twitDB_regular.csv
6. Words dictionary. https://github.com/MathieuCliche/Sarcasm_detector/blob/master/app/SentiWordNet_3.0.0_20130122.txt
7. Marketing brand value. https://sproutsocial.com/insights/twitter-data/

8. Files are used to replace tweet slang, emoticons, and emoji by words: https://github.com/ MirunaPislar/Sarcasm-Detection/tree/master/res/emoji
9. Function that replace slag to words. https://github.com/MathieuCliche/Sarcasm_detector/ blob/master/app/exp_replace.py
10. Logistic Regression. https://en.wikipedia.org/wiki/Logistic_regression
11. Rectified liner unit. https://en.wikipedia.org/wiki/Rectifier_(neural_networks)
12. Dharwal, P., Choudhury, T., Mittal, R., Kumar, P.: Automatic sarcasm detection using feature selection. In: 2017 3rd International Conference on Applied and Theoretical Computing and Communication Technology (iCATccT), pp. 29–34, Tumkur (2017)
13. Popescu, A.-M., Etzioni, O.: Extracting product features and opinions from reviews. In: Proceedings of the Conference on Human Language Technology and Empirical Methods in Natural Language Processing (HLT 2005). Association for Computational Linguistics, pp. 339–346, USA (2005). https://doi.org/10.3115/1220575.1220618
14. Poria, S., Cambria, E., Hazarika, D., Vij, P.: A deeper look into sarcastic tweets using deep convolutional neural networks. In: Proceedings of COLING (2016)
15. Mathieu Cliche repository. https://github.com/MathieuCliche/Sarcasm_detector
16. Documentation for the Tweepy module. http://docs.tweepy.org/en/v3.5.0/api.html
17. Tungthamthiti, P., Shirai, K., Mohd, M.: Recognition of sarcasm in tweets based on concept level sentiment analysis and supervised learning approaches. In: Proceedings of the 28th Pacific Asia Conference on Language, Information and Computation, PACLIC 2014, pp. 404–413. Faculty of Pharmaceutical Sciences, Chulalongkorn University (2014)
18. Textblob library. https://textblob.readthedocs.io/en/dev/
19. Gensim library documentation. https://pypi.org/project/gensim/
20. Scikit-learn library. https://scikit-learn.org/stable/
21. Mishra, A., Kanojia, D., Nagar, S., Dey, K., Bhattacharyya, P.: Harnessing cognitive features for sarcasm detection. arXiv preprint arXiv:1701.05574 (2017)

# Personal Health Train on FHIR: A Privacy Preserving Federated Approach for Analyzing FAIR Data in Healthcare

Ananya Choudhury$^{(\boxtimes)}$ (iD), Johan van Soest(iD), Stuti Nayak(iD),
and Andre Dekker(iD)

Department of Radiation Oncology (MAASTRO), GROW School for Oncology
and Developmental Biology, Maastricht University Medical Centre+,
Maastricht, The Netherlands
ananya.choudhury@maastro.nl

**Abstract.** Big data and machine learning applications focus on retrieving data on a central location for analysis. However, healthcare data can be sensitive in nature and as such difficult to share and make use for secondary purposes. Healthcare vendors are restricted to share data without proper consent from the patient. There is a rising awareness among individual patients as well regarding sharing their personal information due to ethical, legal and societal problems. The current data-sharing platforms in healthcare do not sufficiently handle these issues. The rationale of the Personal Health Train (PHT) approach shifts the focus from sharing data to sharing processing/analysis applications and their respective results. A prerequisite of the PHT-infrastructure is that the data is FAIR (findable, accessible, interoperable, reusable). The aim of the paper is to describe a methodology of finding the number of patients diagnosed with hypertension and calculate cohort statistics in a privacy-preserving federated manner. The whole process completes without individual patient data leaving the source. For this, we rely on the Fast Healthcare Interoperability Resources (FHIR) standard.

**Keywords:** Personal health train · FHIR · FAIR

## 1 Introduction

We live in an era of information explosion and artificial intelligence. Modern society is creating and making use of data like never before. With new devices and application, the amount of data generated is increasing both in terms of number of individuals an number elements per individual. However, as more and more data are created, people and government are increasingly becoming aware of whether or not it is ethically and legally right to use the data in an unrestricted manner. Of all the information about a person, his medical records are inherently privacy sensitive and confidential. As, such in the healthcare sector, it is important to protect patient privacy. The data protection law in the U.S.A., the HIPAA Act, limits sharing of sensitive data. In the E.U., the General Data Protection Regulation sets a well-formulated directive for securing confidentiality and privacy of citizens so that the data is not available publicly without

A. Bhattacharjee et al. (Eds.): MIND 2020, CCIS 1240, pp. 85–95, 2020.
https://doi.org/10.1007/978-981-15-6315-7_7

explicit, well informed specific consent, and cannot be used to identify a subject without additional information stored separately. PIPEDA in Canada, the Data Protection Act (P.D.A.) in the U.K., the Russian Federal Law on Personal Data, the I.T. Act in India and the China Data Protection Regulations (CDPR), all reflect the increasing global awareness regarding the importance of data privacy and confidentiality [1–4].

Current healthcare data sharing platforms are focused on performing queries on remote data sources and obtaining the results of these data queries. This means that interpretation of this data happens at the receiving end, rather than at the sending end. During this interpretation, issues can occur due to missing provenance or understanding the healthcare process on the sending side. The rationale of the infrastructure (PHT) - is that instead of requesting and receiving data, we are interested in asking a specific question and receiving a corresponding answer. PHT infrastructure is designed to deliver questions and algorithms which can be executed at data source institutes [5]. In this paper, we present a methodology for privacy-preserving analysis of healthcare data using HL7 FHIR standard.

The entire execution is fully controlled by the data source institutes, which means that interpretation and processing will happen at the data source institute as well, rather than at the receiving institute. Hence, we are sharing only the needed knowledge and information about a patient, instead of asking for data. PHT by design is made flexible for existing analysis tools, systems, or configuration in the hospital infrastructures. To perform this interpretation at the source, we need computational resources at the data source institute. More specifically, we need a location within the source institute where applications are received and can be executed in a safe (or sandboxed) environment. This allows the source institute to monitor who is requesting data, for what purpose, and what information is being sent back. This concept of having secure and safe compute resources at the source is not new. Large technology companies are already building towards this view of keeping data sources local, and only centralizing aggregated result statistics. These solutions are marketed using umbrella terms such as the "Intelligent Edge" [6], or and are already implementing similar concepts [7].

From a security perspective, this method reduces the data duplication need. By asking questions (instead of performing data queries), results can be stored, although the original data source is not duplicated. In recurring situations, this means the question needs and can be asked again. Recurrence of any question is an inefficient approach, however, makes the data provenance trail easier. When patients withdraw access to certain kinds of information/data, access management can be effectuated directly and enforced in future questions. In the current situation, all duplications of data need to be accounted for (resulting in a large provenance trail), and the information needs to be removed from these duplications. Second, this approach introduces advantages in terms of audit trails. Next to the regular information stored in audit trails (who requested what data, for which purpose, and stand at what time?), it clarifies the processing for a specific question. For example, an easy request asking for a patient's body-mass index (BMI) will send an application to the data source, this application retrieves the height and weight of the patient, calculates the BMI. and only sends this BMI value back to the system asking the question. This means that for audit trailing, we do know which processes and applications processed the data, as well as the exact method of processing. Figure 1 shows the difference between the traditional approach and the PHT approach of knowledge sharing.

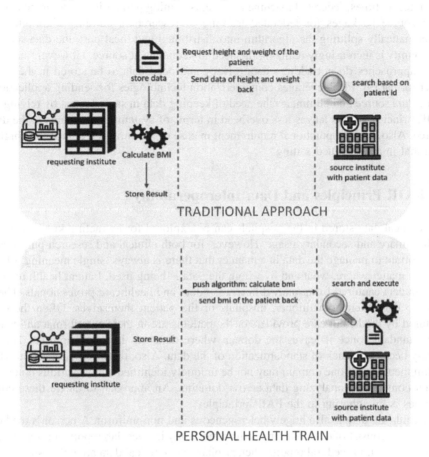

**Fig. 1.** Traditional approach vs Personal Health Train

Although such an infrastructure would work in an ideal-world situation where there is semantic interoperability, we have to cater for a realistic situation. Hence, such an infrastructure where data stays at the source needs proper definitions of where we can find data (Findable), how we can access this data (Accessible), how we can interpret (Interoperable) the data available, and how we can (Re)use the data. This means that this infrastructure heavily relies on the FAIR (Findable, Accessible, Interoperable, Reusable) principles [8]. This does not mean that every data source is publicly available; however, it should be clear how to use this data. As we are sending applications to the source, it also means that these applications need to be able to interpret FAIR data descriptions. These applications need to act on these descriptions to be able to read the (different) data structures present within the source location. Hence, these trains should be programmed to switch data structures (Interoperability) dynamically and to be able to access multiple internal data sources (Accessibility). In our approach, this means algorithms and applications need to be able to interpret FAIR data standards, instead of humans.

In recent times, federated machine learning is gaining popularity. Vendors releasing open source packages for federated learning to researchers building algorithms by mathematically splitting the algorithm into distributed and local part, the data science community is increasingly realizing the need to keep data at source. However, many of these approaches do not address data privacy and need data to be stored in the same exact format [9]. PHT leverages containerization technologies for sending applications to the data source and eliminates the need of keeping data in same format by relying on FAIR principles. This leaves less overhead in terms of system requirements at the data source. Also, the computational requirement in case of a centralized approach is higher than that in a distributed setting.

## 2    FAIR Principles and Data Interoperability

The clinical data stored in the hospitals can be explored for extracting knowledge for both primary and secondary usage. However, for both clinical and research purposes it is important to manage the data in a manner that there is always 'single meaning' of the data no matter where, what and by whom the data is being used. Patient health records contain data captured from many different vendors and healthcare professionals. These may be the general practitioner, hospitals or the patient themselves. Often the data captured by the health care providers or the patients are in their own format and is not understandable once it leaves the domain where data was initially captured. This is largely because of lack of standardization of the data. Also, the data that is identifiable within the realm of one domain may not be uniquely identified across various domains, which complicates analyzing data across domains. An approach to tackle these complexities is by adhering to the FAIR principles.

Healthcare data is also hugely heterogeneous and non-uniform. A person's medical record may consist of data that ranges from radiology images, lab reports, prescriptions, medication list, procedural reports, dietary plans etc. Clinical data are either structured: such as coded data and laboratory results, or unstructured: such as clinical notes and free text comments. Imaging data for those stored in DICOM format contain the structured metadata, whereas the image itself is unstructured [10]. The completeness of scientific and clinical knowledge that can be extracted needs both unstructured and structured data to be harnessed.

Whereas structured data is easier to process, data correctness and completeness becomes a major concern. Unstructured data, on the other hand, contains a detailed description of the clinical condition that is easily understandable by humans but difficult to process by the computer due to lack of standard description and terminology usage. The data landscape in healthcare and the usage of these data for knowledge extraction for better care is hindered by lack of data interoperability and data quality at the source.

Interoperability as defined in the IEEE standard glossary "…is the ability of two or more systems or components to exchange information and use the information that has been exchanged". Interoperability can be sub divided further as syntactic or structural interoperability and semantic interoperability [11]. Standardization of the data at the source is one way of ensuring interoperability; however, we argue that standardization alone is insufficient for several reasons.

First, the healthcare data exchange standards viz. HL7 Version 2.X and 3.X, OpenEHR and ISO 13606, HL7 CDA, XDS, ODM etc. and more recently the restful HL7 FHIR provide a format for specifying the information so that structure of the information remains same. However, with so many options of standardizing the data, different vendors choose different standards, again raising questions of syntactic interoperability. Thus, structuring data at the source might be a suggested option but not the ultimate solution. Secondly, use of a vocabulary based semantically interoperable system based on terminology and coding standards such as SNOMED CT and WHO Family of classification (ICD, ICF, ICH, ICHI, ICD-O) has already been in practice. However, even though different parties can agree on using the same terminology for their concept representation, understanding the clinical meaning out of it has still been an issue widely unaddressed or minimally addressed. For example, if a patient is admitted in the hospital with fracture in his tibia, this can be coded in an appropriate terminology for example using SNOMED CT. However, the coding terminology is not sufficient to know the following: how the fracture occurred, whether it caused any external injuries and whether the patient suffered from any injury induced diseases and symptoms. As such, keeping semantic consistency of data is more important than structuring the data.

HL7 Version 2.X and 3.X both structures the information and has a rich information model backing it. However, associating the data with terminology services like SNOMED CT, HL7 could only enable semantic interoperability to a certain extant while still failing to communicate the meaning of the clinical context. OpenEHR structures the data in a hierarchical manner based on one or more of the 300 complex archetypes. This emphasizes more on the data persistence rather than the clinical semantic interoperability. It is also common practice to exchange clinical information and documents using XDS. XDS uses a XML-based information representation and a central document registry. Queries to the database is based on health record metadata such as patient id etc.

In the light of all the discussion, HL7 FHIR seems to be a promising solution for achieving interoperability in the simplest possible way. FHIR has a rich information model and structures data in XML and JSON formats. FHIR also provides a RESTful way for querying and exchanging the data. The data elements are encoded in healthcare coding terminologies such as SNOMED CT, ICD and LOINC. All FHIR resources hence can be queried in a uniform way without having to look into the actual data. The FHIR community publishes data structuring guidelines in the form of resources. These resources can be customized for individual requirement or adapted as it is. FHIR extends the capabilities of HL7 version 2.x and version 3.x messaging protocols with a rich information model. Until the advent of HL7 FHIR, ODM was presumed to be the best data exchange standard for clinical research. ODM gained more popularity in clinical research for achieving semantic interoperability [12]. ODM is a cross platform data exchange standard for sharing between heterogeneous systems and allows integration of multiple data sources. CDISC ODM is a close match for FHIR though; ODM lacks a rich information model. This limits ODM to use its own coding system unlike FHIR where external semantics source is easily incorporated.

One of the primary challenges in achieving semantic interoperability with FHIR will be to make the existing data, modelled in FHIR resources. Many ideas has been proposed in mapping OpenEHR, CDISC ODM, XDS etc. into FHIR [13–15].

## 3 Methods and Materials

The sensitive nature of patient health records bring challenges surrounding secondary usage of such data. Protecting patient privacy on one hand and making data available for research is a tradeoff faced traditionally in healthcare research. In the previous section we have described how it is possible to share insights from the data, without data having to leave from its origin, hence protecting patient privacy at its core [16, 17].

In this section, we describe the detailed methodology for using distributed health records for secondary usage. We use PHT as the infrastructure for federated data querying and statistical analysis of HL7 FHIR data. One of the pre-requirements for PHT is that the data at the source should be FAIR. We make use of data from two public data repositories and set it up in two data stations [18, 19]. We used the open source implementation of PHT infrastructure [20].

***FAIR Data Stations:*** FAIR data stations are hosted within the organizational and IT system boundary of the hospital. Each data station contains FAIR data and are connected securely to the central server.

***Central Server:*** All communication between the researcher and the data stations occur through the central server. The server acts as a message broker between the data stations and the researcher. The central server also stores the result received from the data stations.

***Train:*** Trains are the containers carrying the algorithms and data query from the researcher to the data station. The researcher designs a train. The most common way to build trains are to wrap the algorithm and scripts in a Docker container.

***Private Train Repository:*** The repository contains algorithms wrapped in containers. The researcher initiates a task by requesting the central server. For this implementation, the train repository is hosted in Docker hub [21].

***Track:*** The track is the metaphor used to describe all communication happening between the researcher, central server and the data stations. The individual components communicate in a RESTful way with each other. Figure 2 shows the schematic diagram of the infrastructure.

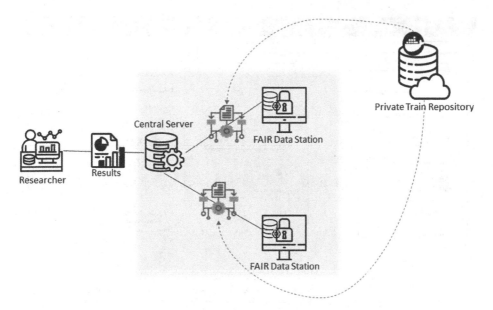

**Fig. 2.** Schematic diagram of personal health train infrastructure

The prerequisite of PHT is to host data in a FAIR repository. The FHIR resources and coding terminology makes data interoperable syntactically and semantically. All FHIR repositories can be accessed using the <base_url> of the repository. The central resource of FHIR is the patient resource. All other items such as patient observations, diagnostic reports, treatment plans etc. are organized as interlinked XML or JSON files and can be accessed by a unique <uri> assigned to it.

Example: All patients who were born after January 1, 1990

https://example.fhirserver.com:8000/Patient?birthDate=ge01-01-1990

The experiment consists two data stations set up with FHIR resources obtained from two public FHIR data repositories [18, 19]. The two data stations are connected to the PHT infrastructure. We build a train containing the FHIR query and an algorithm to calculate summary statistics. The researcher sends the train to all the data stations to calculate patient cohort statistics. At the data stations, the infrastructure component pulls the specified Docker image from Private Docker registry.

The algorithm for the distributed task consists of a master algorithm running in the researcher's machine. The master algorithm co-ordinates the task among the data stations and the researcher through the central server. The master algorithm also aggregates the results obtained from the individual data stations. The node algorithm wrapped in a Docker container runs at the data station. The node algorithm consists of a data query that loads the data locally and temporarily inside the Docker container. The execution of the node algorithm at the data station is controlled by the infrastructure component running at the data station. The node algorithm computes statistics locally inside the Docker container and sends only the results to the central server. When all the node algorithms complete execution and sends the result back to the server, the master algorithm is notified. The master algorithm retrieves the individual results from the central server and aggregates them to calculate the final output. Figure 3 shows the distribution of algorithms as Master and Node algorithm.

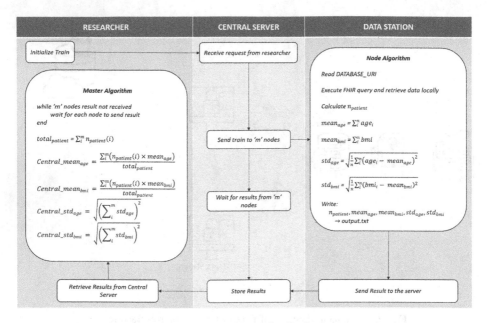

**Fig. 3.** Algorithm distribution

The master algorithm can also handle complex task such as coordinating and aggregating an iterative distributed machine learning process. Figure 4 shows how the node algorithm executes inside the data station. The node algorithm interacts with the FAIR data repository through an environment variable *DATABASE_URI* set by the infrastructure. The DATABASE_URI, at each data station contains the value of the actual url of the data repository. This keeps the algorithm and the researcher agnostic of the location of actual database. The node algorithm receives input from the master algorithm in the form *JSON* string and writes the result in *output.txt*, which is sent to the central server as *JSON* string.

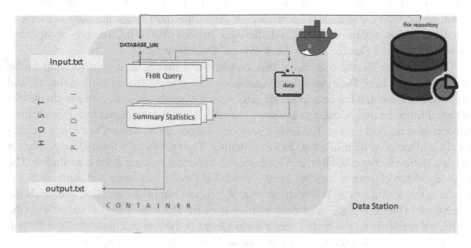

**Fig. 4.** Node algorithm running inside Docker container.

# 4 Results

The aim of the experiment was to calculate summary statistics of patient cohorts from distributed FHIR sources without making the data leave the source. The research question was to retrieve *"All matching patients born before 01-01-1990, who are diagnosed with **hypertension** and fetch **age** and **body mass index**."* For the patients diagnosed with hypertension, we send a second query which checks *"Is the hypertension patient also diagnosed with **diabetes**"*. The FHIR queries for fetching data are shown below:

*<base_url>*Condition?_include=Condition:patient.birth-Date=le1990-01-1&code=http://snomed.info/sct|38341003

*<base_url>*Observation?subject=*<patient_id>*&category=http://hl7.org/fhir/observation-category|vital-signs&code=http://loinc.org|39156-5

*<base_url>*Condition?subject=*<patient_id>*&code=http://snomed.info/sct|44054006

The first query retrieves all patients who are diagnosed with hypertension specified by SNOMED CT code *38341003* and who are born before *01-01-1990*. The second query fetches the BMI report for each patient. BMI in LOINC is coded as *39156-5*. Finally, the third query retrieves if the patient has also been diagnosed with type 2 diabetes mellitus, identified by SNOMED CT code *44054006*.

Table 1 shows the summary statistics obtained from the distributed cohorts and the aggregated summary statistics. We calculates mean age and BMI. A total of 398 patient information was retrieved from both the sources and mean and standard deviation (std) of age and BMI calculated. Figure 5 shows the age and BMI plot from the two data sources.

**Table 1.** Summary Statistics

| Dataset | Patient Cohort Count | Diabetes | Age | | BMI | |
|---------|----------------------|----------|------|------|------|------|
| | | | Mean | Std | Mean | Std |
| FHIR Endpoint 1 | 199 | 26 | 49.72 | 21.14 | 32.46 | 7.94 |
| FHIR Endpoint 2 | 99 | 18 | 50.2 | 19.63 | 31.74 | 8.2 |
| Total | 398 | 44 | 50.05 | 28.85 | 31.98 | 8.2 |

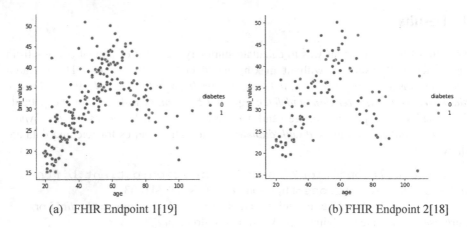

(a)   FHIR Endpoint 1[19]                    (b) FHIR Endpoint 2[18]

**Fig. 5.**   Age and BMI plot of hypertension patients.

## 5   Discussion and Conclusion

In this paper, we showed that PHT, existing healthcare standards and containerization technology can be leveraged for achieving data agnostic, privacy preserving distributed data analytics. Compared to other data sharing platforms or infrastructures, PHT has a significant advantage of scalability and flexibility. Since technologies around the globe are being developed in a very fast speed, it is impossible to ask all hospitals, clinics or other health providers to update their data format, methods of storing data, coding systems in the same speed. With PHT, it is possible to make use of these differently formatted data as long as we have enough metadata description associated with the data. The concept of sending applications and questions instead of requesting data creates many new opportunities both for primary and secondary use of clinical data. It acts as a bridge between the researcher requiring data and healthcare providers containing the data while serving everyone's interests. However, PHT and other existing similar infrastructures do not fix the problems of data preparation and data cleaning, data structure and semantic interoperability.

The paper is part of an ongoing project where we aim to train a machine learning model for predicting diabetes for patients diagnosed with hypertension in a privacy preserving federated manner. The different data sets are geographically and organizationally distributed and are governed by privacy and confidentiality laws. For training a machine learning model it is important for us to know the data distribution at the source. This is essential step before designing a complete machine learning algorithm, as the data distribution at the source impacts the choice of algorithms, hyper-parameter selection and model optimization. Hence, the work presented in this paper is a preliminary but important step. This will be further investigated by including machine learning algorithms in the proposed solution approach for predicting diabetes among patients.

# References

1. General Data Protection Regulation (GDPR): Final text neatly arranged. https://gdpr-info.eu/. Accessed 09 July 2019
2. China Data Protection Regulations (CDPR)—China Law Blog. https://www.chinalawblog.com/2018/05/china-data-protection-regulations-cdpr.html. Accessed 26 Mar 2019
3. Data protection - GOV.UK. https://www.gov.uk/data-protection. Accessed 09 July 2019
4. The Personal Information Protection and Electronic Documents Act (PIPEDA) - Office of the Privacy Commissioner of Canada. https://www.priv.gc.ca/cn/privacy-topics/privacy-laws-in-canada/the-personal-information-protection-and-electronic-documents-act-pipeda/. Accessed 09 July 2019
5. Beyan, O., et al.: Distributed analytics on sensitive medical data: the personal health train. Data Intell. 96–107 (2019). https://doi.org/10.1162/dint_a_00032
6. Intelligent Edge – Future of Cloud Computing—Microsoft Azure, https://azure.microsoft.com/en-us/overview/future-of-cloud/. Accessed 15 Feb 2020
7. Konečný, J., McMahan, H.B., Ramage, D., Richtárik, P.: Federated optimization: distributed machine learning for on-device intelligence. arXiv:1610.02527 [cs] (2016)
8. Hagstrom, S.: The FAIR Data Principles. https://www.force11.org/group/fairgroup/fairprinciples. Accessed 12 Mar 2019
9. Using TFF for Federated Learning Research | TensorFlow Federated. https://www.tensorflow.org/federated/tff_for_research. Accessed 15 Feb 2020
10. DICOM Standard, https://www.dicomstandard.org/. Accessed 15 Feb 2020
11. Oemig, F., Snelick, R.: Healthcare Interoperability Standards Compliance Handbook: Conformance and Testing of Healthcare Data Exchange Standards. Springer, Cham (2016). https://doi.org/10.1007/978-3-319-44839-8
12. Tapuria, A., Bruland, P., Delaney, B., Kalra, D., Curcin, V.: Comparison and transformation between CDISC ODM and EN13606 EHR standards in connecting EHR data with clinical trial research data. Digit Health 4 (2018). https://doi.org/10.1177/2055207618777676
13. Leroux, H., Metke-Jimenez, A., Lawley, M.J.: ODM on FHIR: towards achieving semantic interoperability of clinical study data. 10
14. Boussadi, A., Zapletal, E.: A Fast Healthcare Interoperability Resources (FHIR) layer implemented over i2b2. BMC Med. Inf. Decis. Making. 17, 120 (2017). https://doi.org/10.1186/s12911-017-0513-6
15. Mandel, J.C., Kreda, D.A., Mandl, K.D., Kohane, I.S., Ramoni, R.B.: SMART on FHIR: a standards-based, interoperable apps platform for electronic health records. J. Am. Med. Inf. Assoc. 23, 899–908 (2016). https://doi.org/10.1093/jamia/ocv189
16. Deist, T.M., et al.: Infrastructure and distributed learning methodology for privacy-preserving multi-centric rapid learning health care: euroCAT. Clin. Transl. Radiat. Oncol. 4, 24–31 (2017). https://doi.org/10.1016/j.ctro.2016.12.004
17. Jochems, A., et al.: Distributed learning: developing a predictive model based on data from multiple hospitals without data leaving the hospital – a real life proof of concept. Radiother. Oncol. 121, 459–467 (2016). https://doi.org/10.1016/j.radonc.2016.10.002
18. HAPI FHIR. http://hapi.fhir.org/. Accessed 16 Feb 2020
19. HL7 FHIR API—Synthea, https://synthea.mitre.org/fhir-api. Accessed 16 Feb 2020
20. IKNL/VANTAGE6. Integraal Kankercentrum, Nederland (2020)
21. Docker Hub. https://hub.Docker.com/. Accessed 16 Feb 2020

# Analyzing the Linguistic Structure of Questions to Make Unanswered Questions Answered

Shashank Bhatt and Tapas Kumar Mishra[(✉)]

National Institute of Technology, Rourkela, Rourkela, India
{218cs3439,mishrat}@nitrkl.ac.in
https://mishra-tapas.github.io/

**Abstract.** There are many questions present on Question and Answer websites like quora.com, stackoverflow.com, mindthebook.com, yahoo.com, etc. which are open. There are many factors for which a question remains open; namely, subjectivity, vagueness, openendedness, ambiguity, etc. To find the reason why the question is open, there is a need to design an automatic framework that is designed to deal with the issues of question's answerability. There are two types of questions: *open* questions which are unanswered and *answered* questions. We study the linguistic structure of question text on which we have to perform certain linguistic activities. There are 2 types of activities: first is "User-level" and second is "Question-level". These two type of activities can give many discriminating factors to define the answerability of a question and also distinguishes the answered question from the unanswered one. The motivation of the current paper is to analyze the linguistic structure of the questions so that minimal changes to an unanswered question makes it answered.

**Keywords:** Social networks · Text processing · Quora questions

## 1 Introduction

There are many website now a days present in the world which are Question and answers website, or simply Q&A's website in short. One may wonder the need of such websites. The main reason such websites exist is - there are many question in mind of the users which are either open or user not being a specialist in the domain is un aware of. In fact, the same question may come to mind of different users as well. So, the users post their questions to such Q&A websites. Such questions come in the dashboard of other members who have subscribed to the same category and many of them may choose to answer the question. Quora[1] is one of the most followed Q&A websites with many anonymous user as well authorized users. From the countries like the U.S (United

---

[1] www.quora.com

A. Bhattacharjee et al. (Eds.): MIND 2020, CCIS 1240, pp. 96–110, 2020.
https://doi.org/10.1007/978-981-15-6315-7_8

States) number of visitors is 23.9%, from India number of visitors is 38.2% and from Canada number of visitors is 3.4%, this all data is provided by Alexa[2] updated after November 2019. There are many policies, bots, content editing schemes and review team which help to maintain Quora with a larger number of question posted daily as well as its answer by different type of users. User may be anonymous as a guest or user may be an verified and authorised account. Quora allows the users to interact with the website in different ways, such as: 1. posting a question; 2. following a question (if the user is interested in various answers to the particular question); 3. following other users (if the user is interested in answers by a particular user); 4. answering unanswered questions or giving alternate explanations to other answered questions; 5. commenting on answers and upvoting as well as downvoting, etc. There are many website base on Q&A like Quora: MindtheBook, Amazon's Askville, Yahoo! Answers, Stack Overflow, SuperUser.com, Answers.com etc. However, due to rich content and social structure as a main part of the Quora, Quora is the most popular among the Q&A websites, The key of any Q&A website is the standard of the questions along with their answers. In the paper, our concern is with the question's answerability on Quora, that is, whether a question posted is answered or not.

Quora has an organized list of questions according to the particular topics (like Mathematics and Physics, English words, India News, Indian Right, BQ Business, Joking Insanely, News18 Movies, Technology Untangled, Relationship Help, Life and Understanding, Python Learners, Your Story Daily Updates, Travel Nomads & Guides, Mind & Muscle, Indian History, Islam and Muslims, Express Sports, etc.). The unanswered question referred as *open questions*. We have to focus on the open questions to find out the reason behind they remaining answered or to make the questions more precise. For example, consider the following question which was posted in Quora on June 23, 2011, and was answered on April 22, 2013: "What are the most promising advances in the treatment of traumatic brain injuries?"[3]. There are many possible reasons for this question remaining open for so long: the question may be hard to answer or question may not be clear to the other user or there may be lack of specialists in the field. Therefore, it is key to recognize the open questions and take required measures: steps should be taken so that the good questions get ample attention and are visible to the domain specialists where as bad questions need to be removed.

## 2    Objective

We detect some of the characteristics based on different feature of question text (include open and answered both). We analyze text in such a way that one can discriminate between an open question before answered to after answered. To achieve this, we find methods through which we can detect the difference in some values with its respective question. In our experiment, analysis is done on

---

[2] www.alexa.com.

[3] https://www.quora.com/What-are-the-most-promising-advances-in-the-treatment-of-traumatic-brain-injuries.

linguistic activities of question text: how these activities can affect the question's answerability on Quora. The single most important task here is to identify language patterns based on which a human expert can discriminate between a question remaining open or getting answered. Based on these linguistic activities, we can efficiently differentiate between the open and the answered questions. Our objective is to use this characterization to design an efficient model that can discriminate an open question from a question that will be answered in near future. Moreover, linguistic characterization also improves the accuracy of the prediction framework (Table 1).

**Table 1.** Example of dataset

| Question | Link | After answered |
|---|---|---|
| Can you unscramble the word "cta"? | https://tch504930.tch.www.quora.com/Can-you-unscramble-the-word-cta | Can you unscramble the word "cta"? |
| What is the Hindi translation of Bawarchi" in English? | https://tch504930.tch.www.quora.com/What-is-the-Hindi-translation-of-Bawarchi-in-English | What is the Hindi translation of "Bawarchi" in English? |
| Is India leading on the right path in terms of jobs? | https://www.quora.com/Is-India-leading-on-the-right-path-in-terms-of-jobs | Is India leading on the right path in terms of jobs? |
| What is the Hindi translation of "Baharon Phool Barsao" in English? | https://www.quora.com/unanswered/What-is-the-Hindi-translation-of-Baharon-Phool-Barsao-in-English | No |
| What is the Hindi meaning of near? | https://www.quora.com/unanswered/What-is-the-meaning-of-Negative-Energy-Absorption-NEA-in-Hindi | What is the meaning of Negative Energy Absorption (NEA) in Hindi? |
| Is the number 25 odd or even? | https://www.quora.com/Is-the-number-25-odd-or-even | Is the number 25 odd or even? |

## 3   Related Works

The authors in [5] study the same problem of designing a model for making unanswered questions answerable through user-level and question level analysis. However, their model uses large number of features. As we will discuss in the subsequent sections, many of these features are redundant and the accuracy of models improve once those features are eliminated. The authors in [1] propose a model in which they provide the prediction for the number of answers the asker

**Table 2.** Examples of open questions with respect to linguistic activities

| Question | Question_Link | Topics | Linguistic activities |
|---|---|---|---|
| How can I make a robot? | https://www.quora.com/q/technologyandscience/How-to-make-a-robot | Physics, Technology, Science | Low ROUGE_LCS |
| Which is better between RRBJE and diploma trainee in NTPC? And difference between them?? | https://www.quora.com/q/engineeringfaternity/Which-is-better-between-RRBJE-and-diploma-trainee-in-NTPC-And-difference-between-them | Indian Engineering Services, Indian Space Research Organisation (ISRO), GATE Preparation | High POS tag diversity, lengthy |
| There is realy only one satellite of earth. Is there is more? | https://www.quora.com/q/engineeringfaternity/'There-is-realy-only-one-satellite-of-earth Is-there-is-more | Indian Engineering Services, Indian Space Research Organisation (ISRO), GATE Preparation | High PosTagDiversity, lengthy |

will get before posting a question: this prediction is totally based on the question text and topic assigned to that question. Moreover, the model provides the warning to the asker so that at the time of posting a question, the frustration level of asker reduces and question asking capablities is enhanced. Their model works on yahoo.com. The authors in [7] search different aspects of unusual features present in Q&A website like Quora. They create an anonymity grid: this grid is created to differentiate between the perception of the anonymity of the user posting question and which helps the community to answer to a valid user. The authors' model looks for the first response time and observes that it is the lowest for topics that are on personal and sensitive issues. The authors compute various parameters like anonymity ratio, question types, structural analysis, word usage, POS analysis, sentimental analysis and psycho-linguistic analysis on question text. A question can have many different answer. The aim of the asker is to pick the best answer according to its question. To achieve this, the authors in [10] design a model for ranking of answers. They were working on two modules, a Disconnected Learning Segment and a Online Inquiry Part. In the Disconnected Learning Segment, they create a data driven preceptions on positive, negative, impartial preparing tests and they mutually fuse these three different tests after this shut shape arrangement for this model is determined. In the Online Inquiry Part, first they collect the group of answers connected to a question and then they find a possiblity for the given question by means of discovering its comparative questions.

There are many topic tag to a question which is kind of similar, quora moderator analyse the topics and merge them manually. The authors in [8] proposed a model in which they used two step approach that detect and combine two or more similar topic uniquely which is tag to a question. The authors in [6] analyze a large dataset that contains many questions of different topics; they proposed a regression model to predict popularity of topics and genereate some important feature. The authors in [11] proposed a model that detects a domain expert on Quora specific to a topic. The authors in [14] find out meaningful relationships between information of the user and the quality of their answers. In [3], the authors present a opinion extraction model based on user's profile. The authors in [9] proposed a model that can recognize different type of "insincere" questions and take appropriate actions.

### 3.1 Dataset

Quora's robot.txt file was blocked for web based crawler by Quora itself. Therefore, we prepared a dataset by manually fetching a question as shown on the Table 2. We explored topics like Mathematics and Physics, English words, India News, Indian Engineering Services, Indian Space Research Organisation (ISRO), GATE Preparation Indian Right, BQ Business, Joking Insanely, News18 Movies, Technology Untangled, Relationship Help, Life and Understanding, Python Learners, Your Story Daily Updates, Travel Nomads & Guides, Mind & Muscle, Indian History, Islam and Muslims, Express Sports, etc. The dataset is manually fetched from Quora during June 2019 to November 2019.

## 4    Description of Methodology

In this section, we identify various user level linguistic activities on question text posted by the user. We observe that there are meaningful differences in the linguistic structure of "open question" and "answered questions". Most of the features that we define are simple, instinctive and can be easily retrieved automatically from the data. Hence the framework is practical, economical, and highly scalable. We divide linguistic activities into two types: 1) User-level linguistic activities related to the style of user-posted a Question; 2) Question-level linguistic activities which are mostly handling the moderator team itself.

### 4.1    Linguistic Activities (User-Level)

There are a various aspect of the Question text while posting a question like editing, adding, deleting, posting, commenting and many more on another hand we also have activities which perform on the text of the question only, In our experiment, we are more focused on the activities which are more related to our text, so that we can compare "open Question" to "answered one".

1) Linguistic pattern of the user while Posting a Question: Quality text of the question is very important and that is why we have to examine them. The key features in the linguistic structure are POS tags, word-character usage and use of out-of-vocabulary words.

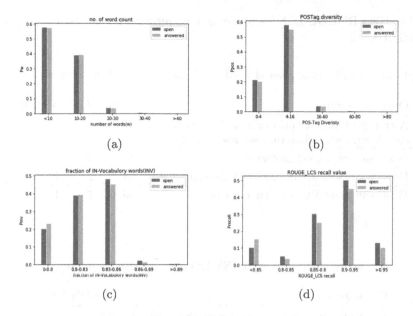

**Fig. 1.** Comparison of distribution of a) no. of words in the question b) fraction of In-Vocabulary words c) POS tag diversity d) ROUGE-LCS recall for open questions vs answered question.

In Fig. 1(a), there are more number of word used by the asker of open question as compare to answered one. In Fig. 1(b), We just find out the functional word (correct word/ or the word which is present on the English dictionary/ chat words frequently used in social media). We compare the words with GNU[4] Aspell dictionary to check their presence or absence. Further, we are using GitH[5] project: latest updated dictionary is present in which all of latest word of English up to $23^{rd}$ november 2019 is contained approximately 466k English words. In Fig. 1(c), POS-TAG indicates that text is related to the grammatical aspect, which means grammatical category that gives an expression about how an event, action, or state, denoted by a verb, increases over time. For POS-TAG generation, we use POS tagger SCMU Tagger [2,10] for identifying and generate a confidence value of particular tag use in the text.

$$\text{POS-TAG diversity} = -\sum\nolimits_{j \in POS^{set}} p_i \times log(p_i)$$

$p_j$ is the probability of the $j^{th}$ POS in the set of POS tags. In Fig. 1(d), we calculate the ROUGE-LCS[6] recall value. It is defined as "by how far can edit a question can make a difference to the its original version". for finding text summarization of a particular domain, we need to find a recall value of ROUGE

---

[4] http://aspell.net/.

[5] https://github.com/dwyl/english-words.

[6] https://github.com/google-research/google-research/tree/master/rouge.

LCS [4]. High ROUGE LCS value means the question has a small change to it original version.

**Table 3.** Examples of number of words with question length in term of character

| Open_Question | NOC | NOW | NF/FW |
|---|---|---|---|
| Astrology: I am a Capricorn Sun Cap moon and cap rising... what does that say about me? | 86 | 16 | 1 |
| How can I be a good geologist? | 30 | 7 | 1 |
| How do I read and find my YouTube comments? | 43 | 9 | 1 |
| What can make Physics easy to learn? | 36 | 7 | 1 |

**Table 4.** Examples of the fraction of INV-OOV words with its respective questions

| Open_Question | frac_INV_OOV |
|---|---|
| What are some special cares for someone with a nose that gets stuffy during the night? | 0.875 |
| What Game of Thrones villain would be the most likely to give you mercy? | 0.714285714 |
| How do we prepare for UPSC? | 0.666666667 |
| What are some examples of products that can be make from crude oil? | 0.846153846 |

2) Psycholinguistic analysis: Analysis can be done observing the user pattern of writing a question, we can find the emotion of the user while posting a question, Here is one application for the text analysis known as LIWC [12] (refer Table 12). LIWC gives an emotion (like social, anger, positive, negative, sadness, happiness, and many more) significance value and also LIWC captures the asker's aspects related to Psychology. LIWC takes a document as input and gives output scores as input is given.

3) Other Editing Activities: Several user-related activities like commenting, editing, deletion of irrelevant answers, the addition of answers, tagging a new/remove/edit topic, many more. But in this paper, we are notfocused on those activities we are not performing any activities on these activities.

## 5    Result Analysis and Discussion

### 5.1    Prediction Feature

All those activities perform by the User comes Under User-level linguistic activities while Question-level linguistic activities is related to the question like the

**Table 5.** POS tagset from Gimpel et al. (2011) [2]

| N | Common noun |
|---|---|
| O | Pronoun (personal/WH; not possessive) |
| ^ | Proper noun |
| S | Nominal + possessive |
| Z | Proper noun + possessive |
| V | Verb including copula, auxiliaries |
| L | Nominal + verbal (e.g. i'm), verbal + nominal (let's) |
| M | Proper noun + verbal |
| A | Adjective |
| R | Adverb |
| ! | Interjection |
| D | Determiner |
| P | Pre- or postposition, or subordinating conjunction |
| & | Amp; coordinating conjunction |
| T | Verb particle |
| X | Existentialthere, predeterminers |
| Y | X + verbal |
| # | Hashtag (indicates topic/category for tweet) |
| @ | At-mention (indicates a user as a recipient of a tweet)marker |
| ~ | Discourse marker, indication of continuation across multiple tweets |
| U | URL or email address |
| E | Emoticon |
| $ | Numeral |
| , | Punctuation |
| G | Other abbreviations, foreign words, possessive endings, symbols, garbage |

number of time editing, addition, commenting, deletion perform by the moderators of the team. The User-level linguistic activities fundamentally related to the pattern of question which a user can post. We are going to extract some of the features related to User-level linguistic activities. For the prediction, we use the following features.

1) Question text has features like the length of the text, number of characters present in the question text. As first feature of our model, we consider the fraction of non-frequent word to the functional word. The functional word means the total number of words present in the string. Refer to Table 3 for a sample of the feature.
2) Suppose while Posting a question, an user can have correct or incorrect word in its question text. We need to find out a correct word from the question text

**Table 6.** Examples of POS Diversity with its repective questions

| open_Question | POS diversity |
|---|---|
| Astrology: I am a Capricorn Sun Cap moon and cap rising... what does that say about me? | 0.329220556 |
| How can I be a good geologist? | 0.130599187 |
| How do I read and find my YouTube comments? | 0.163930056 |

by checking each word of the question text from the GNU Aspell dictionary as well as "Word.text" (dictionary corpus) from github[7]. Further, a fraction of INV word to functional word is the next feature of our model, refer to Table 4 for this feature sample.

$$Frac\text{-}INV\text{-}OOV = number\text{-}of\text{-}INV/number\text{-}of\text{-}fW$$

**Table 7.** POS tags

| token | POS-TAG | confidence(x) | token | POS-TAG | confidence(x) |
|---|---|---|---|---|---|
| Astrology | N | 0.7978 | How | R | 0.9851 |
| : | , | 0.9715 | can | V | 0.9975 |
| I | O | 0.9958 | I | O | 0.9987 |
| am | V | 0.9993 | be | V | 0.9999 |
| a | D | 0.9964 | a | D | 0.9779 |
| Capricorn | ^ | 0.9519 | good | A | 0.9972 |
| Sun | ^ | 0.997 | geologist | N | 0.9966 |
| Cap | ^ | 0.9701 | ? | , | 0.9977 |
| moon | N | 0.9616 | | | |
| and | & | 0.9984 | How | R | 0.9785 |
| cap | N | 0.9227 | do | V | 0.9954 |
| rising | V | 0.9902 | I | O | 0.9991 |
| ... | , | 0.9571 | read | V | 0.9983 |
| what | O | 0.9951 | and | & | 0.9958 |
| does | V | 0.9982 | find | V | 0.999 |
| that | O | 0.8913 | my | D | 0.9785 |
| say | V | 0.9971 | YouTube | ^ | 0.9264 |
| about | P | 0.9713 | comments | N | 0.96 |
| me | O | 0.999 | ? | , | 0.9979 |
| ? | , | 0.9978 | | | |

3) We find out POS tag of each word of the question text (for both open and answered) which is present in our corpus. Then, we generate the probability of each question which is further known as POS-TAG diversity of the questions.

---

[7] https://github.com/dwyl/english-words.

**Table 8.** Example of LDA topical diversity

| open_question | lda_score(K = 10) | lda_score(K = 20) | lda_score(k = 30) |
|---|---|---|---|
| Astrology: I am a Capricorn Sun Cap moon and cap rising... what does that say about me? | 0.100000001 | 0.0650515 | 0.049237377 |
| How can I be a good geologist? | 0.06505152 | 0.040051509 | 0.02963586 |
| How do I read and find my YouTube comments? | 0.100000001 | 0.0650515 | 0.049237377 |
| What can make Physics easy to learn? | 0.06505152 | 0.040051507 | 0.029635863 |
| What was your first sexual experience like? | 0.065051523 | 0.040051513 | 0.02963586 |

**Table 9.** Example of ROUGE-LCS recall score

| open_Question | answered_one | ROUGE_LCS_R_1 | lda_score(k = 30) |
|---|---|---|---|
| Astrology: I am a Capricorn Sun Cap moon and cap rising... what does that say about me? | I'm a triple Capricorn (Sun, Moon and ascendant in Capricorn) What does this say about me? | 0.4375 | 0.049237377 |
| How can I be a good geologist? | What should I do to be a great geologist? | 0.444444444 | 0.02963586 |
| How do I read and find my YouTube comments? | How can I see all my Youtube comments? | 0.5 | 0.049237377 |
| What can make Physics easy to learn? | How can you make physics easy to learn? | 0.625 | 0.029635863 |
| What was your first sexual experience like? | What was your first sexual experience? | 0.833333333 | 0.02963586 |

POS-TAG diversity is a feature to the model, refer to Table 5, 6, 7 for the example of POS's with its confidence value and POS-tag diversity values. In Table 5, there are 25 POS tag which has its respective meaning.

Confidence value of particular POS-TAG = number-of-times-particular-tag-present-in-the-question/number-of-times-particular-tag-present-in-our-corpus

In Table 6, example of POS Diversity is calculated with its respective question present on the database. In Table 7, each question is divided into token then attached with respective POS-tag and generate its respective confidence value.

$$\text{POS-TAG diversity} = -\sum\nolimits_{j \in POS^{set}} p_i \times log(p_i)$$

$p_j$ is the probability or the confidence of the $j^{th}$ POS in the set of POS tags.

4) For topic distribution, we use LDA (latent Dirichlet allocation). LDA is a very famous generative probabilistic model which generates a probability distribution of the topic present in the document. For a question $Q_i$, LDA considers all the words in the question present in the document. While performing LDA for out experiment, we consider topic (K) = 10, 20 and 30 and find out $p(topic_k|D_i)$ for a document $D_i$ containing all the words of the $i_{th}$ question. Each of these $p(topic_k|D_i)$ for $k = 1, \ldots, K$ act as a feature of the model (Tables 8 and 9).

Steps to perform LDA[8] :

– collection of data (text) in form of a data set
– data pre-processing: 1. tokenization 2. remove words which have length less than 3 character 3. remove all stop words 4. Lemmatization of each word which means (third person are changed to first person as well as future and past tense converted into present). 5. stemming of word which means word converted to root form
– create a dictionary with frequency of each token from Pre-processed data
– remove token who have less than 15 documents or more that 0.5 documents(fraction of total corpus size, not absolute number)
– keep only the first 100000 most frequent tokens and save dictionary in form of corpus.
– create TF-IDF model.
– Train out LDA model using genism.models.lda.multicore and save it. For each topic, we will explore the words occurring in that topic and its relative weight.
– Running LDA using TF-IDF
– Performance evaluation by classifying sample document using LDA bag of word model

---

[8] https://towardsdatascience.com/topic-modeling-and-latent-dirichlet-allocation-in-python-9bf156893c24.

- Performance evaluation by classifying sample document using LDA TF-IDF model.
- Testing model on unseen document

5) Discussion about topical diversity of LDA so here we find out the LDA topical diversity named as "Topic Div" of a question $(q_i)$ from the document topic distributions obtained above as follows and use this value of each question as a feature.

$$\text{Topic-Div}(q_i) = -\sum\nolimits_{k=1}^{K} p(topic_k|D_i) \times logp(topic_k|D_i)$$

6) ROUGE-LCS recall of the question text at the end of the observation period of the prediction with reference to the original question text posted by the asker.

### 5.2   Prediction Model

As we perform our experiment on the different database by just extracting user-level linguistic activities on Question text, we labeled unanswered question as an "Open Questions" in our database and we labeled answered Question text as an "Answered Question".

The classifier which we are choosing for our experiment is SVM. SVM's are very good when we have no idea on the data, works well with even unstructured and semi structured data like text, images and trees. The kernel trick is real strength of SVM. With an appropriate kernel function, we can solve any complex problem, unlike in neural networks. When compared to ANN models, SVMs give better results. In additional we are performing SVM with known validation named as "tenfold cross-validation" and achieve 84.01% accuracy with a high average precision (Table 10).

**Table 10.** Performance of various methods (K = 10, 20, 30). First 5 lines for t = 1 month

| K | Accuracy | Precision | Recall | F Score | ROC |
|---|---|---|---|---|---|
| 10 | 75.99% | 0.8966 | 0.6995 | 0.7443 | 0.7598 |
| 20 | 84.01% | 0.9071 | 0.7688 | 0.8263 | 0.8403 |
| 30 | 83.66% | 0.7953 | 0.76 | 0.8235 | 0.8368 |

## 6   Conclusion and Future Work

If an user posts a question and does not get any answer, the most likely reason is a wrongful way of framing the question. This may create a bad impression of the website on the user's mind leading to the user leaving the platform. Our main work is to detect such questions and recommendation of correction to the user may result in answers from the community. The benefit of user-level linguistic style for feature extraction is that it can be directly extended to other Q&A websites.

In this paper, we use user-linguistic activities to find out the features effecting answerability of the question and we can improve the way of delivery of questions by the user. For the experiment, we use the data available on Kaggle.com[9]. First, we observe that the pattern to write the question or language related to the question is one of the important factors that is considered by human judges: this factor helps to decide whether a question is answerable or not. By these user-level linguistic activities, discrimination of open question to answered question is done efficiently. Our proposed prediction framework achieves an accuracy of 84.01% (see Table 12) with high precision and recall for observation outperforming the baseline methods convincingly. We observed that through user-level linguistic activities, we can extract quality of features easily and efficiently as compared to others. Some of the reasons for better accuracy of our model as compared to earlier models are: 1. we are using the different data set, because as we concert about it that we cannot able to use a crawler (crawler is blocked by Quora itself) and also we are using a different data set as a comparison to analyzing the linguistic structure of question texts to characterize answerability in Quora [5]; 2. in this paper, we are working on user-level linguistic activities and not working on question level linguistic activities because these include many factors which have to be maintained by Quora team members.

## 7    List of Abbreviation

Refer to Table 12 for the list of abbreviation (Table 11)

**Table 11.** Sample of feature extracted with two zero represent the class of open question and one represent the class of answered question

| character_length | num_of_word | POS_DIV | ROUGE_LCS_R | frac_INV_OOV | lda_score (K = 10) | lda_score (K = 20) | lda_score (k = 30) | Y_question |
|---|---|---|---|---|---|---|---|---|
| 86 | 16 | 0.329220556 | 1 | 0.5625 | 0.100000001 | 0.0650515 | 0.049237377 | 0 |
| 30 | 7 | 0.130599187 | 1 | 0.571428571 | 0.06505152 | 0.040051509 | 0.02963586 | 0 |
| 43 | 9 | 0.163930056 | 1 | 0.555555556 | 0.100000001 | 0.0650515 | 0.049237377 | 0 |
| 36 | 7 | 0.130599187 | 1 | 0.571428571 | 0.06505152 | 0.040051507 | 0.029635863 | 0 |
| 90 | 16 | 0.212735971 | 0.4375 | 0.5625 | 0.100000001 | 0.0650515 | 0.049237377 | 1 |
| 41 | 9 | 0 | 0.444444444 | 0.666666667 | 0.06505152 | 0.040051505 | 0.02963586 | 1 |
| 38 | 8 | 0 | 0.5 | 0.5 | 0.100000001 | 0.0650515 | 0.049237377 | 1 |
| 39 | 8 | 0.030087911 | 0.625 | 0.75 | 0.065051536 | 0.040051513 | 0.029635863 | 1 |

---

[9] https://www.kaggle.com/quora/question-pairs-dataset.

**Table 12.** List of abbreviation

| | |
|---|---|
| Q&A | Questions and answers |
| QUORA | www.quora.com |
| ALEXA | www.alexa.com |
| i.e., | That is |
| POS | Part of speech |
| ROUGE LCS | ROUGE load current substation recall value |
| LIWC | Linguistic Inquiry & word count |
| SVM | Support vector machine |
| LR | Logistic Regression |
| RF | Random forest |
| POS-TAG | Tag/symbol which is used for part of speech |
| CQA | Characteristics based on Question/answer |
| OOV | Out of vocabulary word or word which is not present in the dictionary |
| INV | In Vocabulary word or word which is present in dictionary |
| NOC | Number of characters in string |
| NOW | Number of Words in string |
| NF/FW | Division of Functional word to total number of word |
| fract_INV_OOV | Fraction of IN- vocabulary word to total number of word present in the string |
| Confidence (x) | Accuracy or Probability of the POS-TAG in a question |

# References

1. Dror, G., Maarek, Y., Szpektor, I.: Will my question be answered? Predicting "Question Answerability" in community question-answering sites. In: Blockeel, H., Kersting, K., Nijssen, S., Železný, F. (eds.) ECML PKDD 2013. LNCS (LNAI), vol. 8190, pp. 499–514. Springer, Heidelberg (2013). https://doi.org/10.1007/978-3-642-40994-3_32
2. Gimpel, K., et al.: Part-of-speech tagging for Twitter: annotation, features, and experiments, vol. 2, pp. 42–47, January 2011
3. Kumar, A., Praveen, S., Goel, N., Sanwal, K.: Opinion extraction from quora using user-biased sentiment analysis. In: Bhateja, V., Nguyen, B.L., Nguyen, N.G., Satapathy, S.C., Le, D.-N. (eds.) Information Systems Design and Intelligent Applications. AISC, vol. 672, pp. 219–228. Springer, Singapore (2018). https://doi.org/10.1007/978-981-10-7512-4_22
4. Lin, C.-Y., ROUGE: a package for automatic evaluation of summaries. In: Text Summarization Branches Out, pp. 74–81. Association for Computational Linguistics, Barcelona, July 2004

5. Maity, S.K., Kharb, A., Mukherjee, A.: Analyzing the linguistic structure of question texts to characterize answerability in quora. IEEE Trans. Comput. Soci. Syst. **5**, 816–828 (2018)
6. Maity, S.K., Sahni, J.S.S., Mukherjee, A.: Analysis and prediction of question topic popularity in community q&a sites: a case study of quora. In: Ninth International AAAI Conference on Web and Social Media (2015)
7. Mathew, B., Dutt, R., Maity, S.K., Goyal, P., Mukherjee, A.: Deep dive into anonymity: large scale analysis of quora questions. In: Weber, I., Darwish, K.M., Wagner, C., Zagheni, E., Nelson, L., Aref, S., Flöck, F. (eds.) SocInfo 2019. LNCS, vol. 11864, pp. 35–49. Springer, Cham (2019). https://doi.org/10.1007/978-3-030-34971-4_3
8. Mathew, B., Maity, S.K., Goyal, P., Mukherjee, A.: Competing topic naming conventions in quora: predicting appropriate topic merges and winning topics from millions of topic pairs. In: Proceedings of the 7th ACM IKDD CoDS and 25th COMAD, pp. 125–133 (2020)
9. Mungekar, A., Parab, N., Nima, P., Pereira, S.: Quora insincere question classification. National College of Ireland (2019)
10. Owoputi, O., O'Connor, B., Dyer, C., Gimpel, K., Schneider, N., Smith, N.A.: Improved part-of-speech tagging for online conversational text with word clusters. In: Proceedings of NAACL-HLT, 2013, pp. 380–390, January 2013
11. Patil, S., Lee, K.: Detecting experts on quora: by their activity, quality of answers, linguistic characteristics and temporal behaviors. Soc. Netw. Anal. Min. **6**(1), 5 (2016)
12. Pennebaker, J., Chung, C., Ireland, M., Gonzales, A., Booth, R.: The development and psychometric properties of liwc2007, January 2007
13. Soni, S., Navale, V.: Analyzing structure of question texts to characterize answerability in quora using SEO: a survey
14. Zhou, Z.-M., Lan, M., Niu, Z.-Y., Lu, Y.: Exploiting user profile information for answer ranking in CQA. In: Proceedings of the 21st International Conference on World Wide Web, pp. 767–774 (2012)

# Applicability of Structured and Unstructured Communication Techniques in Emergency Environment

Vipin Kumar Pandey[ID], Diwakar Deep Tirkey, Mubassir Rahman, and Suddhasil De[✉][ID]

Computer Science and Engineering Department, NIT Patna,
Patna 800005, Bihar, India
{vipin.pandey,suddhasil.de}@acm.org, diwakardeep3@gmail.com,
9919mubashir@gmail.com

**Abstract.** Peer-to-Peer (P2P) from of networking is among the best communication strategy for any emergency scenario. An important characteristic of such network deployed for handling emergency communication is the dynamicity and heterogeneity of the nodes. Due to this behaviour, the number of nodes joining and leaving the topology would be rapid resulting in expensive network maintenance. The communication requirement for such networks suits a dynamic approach for handling as per the changing network topology for a reliable and efficient solution. For applicability of different P2P communication types such as structured, unstructured, cluster and hierarchical P2P are analysed. Different emergency scenario is created in OMNeT++ simulator and analysed on parameters like Packet drop ratio, Throughput and End-to-End delay resulting to the outcome that no single P2P communication strategy is perfect.

**Keywords:** Peer-to-Peer · Structured P2P · Unstructured P2P · Emergency · Applicability

## 1 Introduction

Peer-to-Peer (P2P) networking [17] allows multi-node communication in the network, in which there are no central control and coordination. Each participant (which is a computing device) in that network is referred as "peer"; data present in the P2P network is distributed among all its peers. Each peer assumes the role of both 'server' and 'client' at the same time; their simultaneous roles also bestow on them all necessary responsibilities and capabilities. Moreover, each

This work is carried out with the support by the Science and Engineering Research Board, a statutory body of the Department of Science and Technology (DST), Government of India, under grants number ECR/2016/002040.

© Springer Nature Singapore Pte Ltd. 2020
A. Bhattacharjee et al. (Eds.): MIND 2020, CCIS 1240, pp. 111–124, 2020.
https://doi.org/10.1007/978-981-15-6315-7_9

peer is allowed to join and to leave the network at any time. A typical P2P network is created as an overlay on top of the traditional TCP/IP network stack, and is based on TCP/IP protocol suite for data delivery.

There are two primary communication models in networking—(i) client/server model and (ii) peer-to-peer model. The major difference between the two model is the former support centralized behaviour where the server act as a single point of contact while in former each peer can be a client or server supporting the decentralized behaviour of the overall network. In emergency scenario [1] where the churn rate of peers are high [14] client server model can be very detrimental. Also for rapid deployment arranging a single machine to carry out the whole server responsibility will be a difficult task in comparison to distributing the server responsibility among various peers in the region.

The above discussed P2P model is implemented over the traditional link, i.e. overlay network. Overlay network is abstracted as a network with virtual or logical links as its connectivity; each link indicates a path in underlying network, where the path may traverse through its multiple physical links. P2P overlay network is broadly classified as two types—(i) structured and (ii) unstructured. In structured overlay, peers are organized according to some specific topology. This orderly arrangement ensures that search for a file/resource in the network is carried out efficiently by any node, even when occurrence of that resource is much rare. This is because, structured network has an organized topology which contain the information of its successor and predecessor node due to which searching process become easier. Examples of this network include Chord [18], DHT [13], CAN [9] etc.

In unstructured overlay, peers of the network are randomly connected to a subset of peers. This configuration is beneficial for its simplicity, but doesn't satisfy the scalability particularly well. The scalability problem arises from the fact that entire network need to be searched to find the required content. The flooding approach for searching reduces the response time of the whole network. Examples of this category of network include Gnutella [16], BitTorrent etc. Gnutella is a scalable and decentralized P2P network. Clustering [12] is one of the important methods for extending the lifetime of P2P overlay in wireless network. It involves grouping of the peer nodes into clusters and selecting the cluster heads (CHs) from all the clusters. Hierarchical clustering [11] groups data over different variety of scale forming a cluster tree. This technique arranges the overlay into a hierarchy of groups according to some specified weight function for improving network lifetime.

On the basis of above, the identified two primary challenges regarding p2p network type selection in emergency are: (1) Trying to find out universal solution for any kind of topography where the emergency network is to be deployed. (2) Selecting parameters to decide upon the applicability of Structured P2P or Unstructured P2P in the emergency. This paper has tried to address both the challenges by carrying out validation through simulation in different topography by applying Structured P2P like Chord/DHT, Unstructured P2P like Gnutella or Cluster based approach for emergency network deployment. The contribution of this paper for addressing above mentioned challenges are: (1) Firstly, for different topography of the emergency affected region structured, unstructured or cluster based approach is simulated. (2) Comparison is been carried out to analyse the performance to have a universal solution or some hybrid solution which gives best results in all possible combination.

The remaining paper is organized as follows. Starting with Sect. 2 provides the necessary background and the related works. Section 3 discusses about the challenges need to overcome for experimentation. Section 4 details experiment result and finally Sect. 5 concludes the best suitable applicability for different emergency network topography with future scope.

## 2    Background and Related Works

In this section, necessary background and the related works are discussed.

### 2.1    Communication Model

In traditional networking there are two major type of communication models, i.e. client/server model and peer-to-peer model.

**Client Server Model.** In Client Server model, relationship is such that a server has to respond with the resource a client has requested. Traditionally client request the service and the Server response the request of the client. The client server communication model is centralized form of communication model where clients are totally dependent on the server. As the load increases at the server the performance of the model starts deteriorating at a greater pace. So, this model has a bottleneck of centralization.

**Peer-to-peer (P2P) Model.** A P2P network is a multi-node communication approach with no emphasis on coordination or central control. Every node (whether in form of mobile device or a computer) in a P2P network is a peer with both client and server capabilities and the data available on the network is distributed among them. This capabilities/responsibilities of acting as a client and a server of peer makes this model distributed in nature.

### 2.2    P2P Network Type

There are different types of P2P networks available based on the underlying structure i.e. structured, unstructured, cluster and hierarchical type as detailed below.

**Structured P2P Networks.** In every decentralized and dynamic environment where structured p2p overlay networks [7] is applied, joining and leaving of peers have been a major issue since the origination. Each DHT [13] application tries to employ a specific mechanism to deal with such phenomenon. But when large set of churning of peers in a short time interval takes place, the system will surely enter in a crashing tendency. There are very few studies available which are examining the impact of churn problem. In [15], study is done on the resilience and scalability, so that system can be made fault-resilience for a worst case joining and leaving of peers. They focused on maintaining a balanced network even though in the presence of high churn rate. In Structured P2P Networks the underlying topology is fixed and scope for extending it to fit for any underlying topography is not explored much.

**Unstructured P2P Networks.** Gnutella [16] is a prominent unstructured p2p network [8] of very early stage; however, there have been concerns about its scalability since its origin. A lot of interesting solution have appeared since then. Many researchers have claimed of improving the performance of unstructured system [6], acknowledging solution's predominance and simplicity in today's world. Many such recent solutions for unstructured system have suggested utilising an alternative for the flooding operations, for example random walk technique or restrictive flooding approach. At the same time there have been proposals for improving flooding itself; as in the earlier approach, flooding is carried out in several successive rounds where time-to-live (TTL) field is getting increased, until enough responses are received. The above modified approach can effectively improve the response time of the overall system vis-a-vis reducing the searching time for the popular files.

**Hierarchical Cluster Network.** There were various issues in flooding an unstructured network, so to cater the flooding problem, the clustering technique [10] was used. In this approach the links are created on top of unstructured P2P overlay network for organizing peers according to their interests or common properties. Mainly clustering can help in limiting the flooding iteration cycle which reduces the number of peers to which query is sent. This enforces that query are sent only to those peers which are more likely to have relevant data objects. That results in overall improvement of scalability of the deployed network.

### 2.3   Related Works

The P2P form of communication paradigm is stabilized area of research where lot of work based on simulation of P2P Structured [4] and P2P Unstructured [2] communication method in Static environment is carried out in different works [3,19]. As the network start expanding and the underlying nodes forming the setup becomes dynamic in nature, the structured and unstructured form of P2P communication moved towards other forms such as cluster and hierarchical P2P network. In [11], cluster based P2P network is been deployed in a dynamic environment where classification of node is been carried out as a super node, emergency node and general node to specify the role in the cluster as per requirement. In another work [5], a hierarchical cluster model is been deployed in a dynamic environment to setup an emergency network for carrying out the communication, a tree data structure is been maintained to restrict the packets for those branches which are not in the destination set.

As discussed earlier, in dynamic environment where each and every node is mobile and dynamic with random topology. The related works are available applying any of the P2P communication type; however, as far as my knowledge there are very few specific work is available where comparison among existing work is done between different type of P2P communication network and its performance. The earlier work lacks comparison related to different network topography based on structured, unstructured, cluster and hierarchical network and trying to find out which type of network is best suited in which certain dynamic environment. This kind of work required comparison to be carried out based on following parameters—(i) Packet Loss, (ii) Delay, (iii) Control message and (iv) Power consumption.

# 3   Proposed Applicability Mechanism

This section presents the proposed applicability mechanism for selection of structured or unstructured P2P network for any underlying topology.

Applicability is an important characteristic to decide the best suited P2P network for any unknown scenario. In a real time scenario, where the topography can be of varied nature with different time-lines, selecting the most appropriate P2P network type with priori knowledge or no-priori knowledge is the major objective. The established fact about the limitations of the different type of P2P network is been validated through simulation to arrive at a universal or hybrid solution. This solution should be such that it gives optimum performance irrespective of the varied topography of the region where it is applied. The different structured, unstructured and cluster based network is tried to come up with a universal solution. Also the parameters that have a major effect on applicability of the type of network to be chosen for a defined topology is also analysed to improve the network performance. There were various challenges which have an impact in obtaining the proposed universal solution applicability to any topography. The details of the parameters having an impact on simulated experimentation are discussed below:

*Mobility.* Dynamic nature of ad-hoc network results in exhibiting frequent and unpredictable topology modifications. The mobile peers establish routes among themselves dynamically as they move. Figure 1 shows initial position of the nodes. Figure 2 shows the changed network topology or the next position of the nodes after time (here, few seconds).

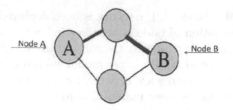

**Fig. 1.** Initial network topology

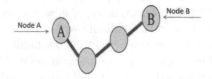

**Fig. 2.** Network topology after some time

*Limited Resources.* When the resources available in the region where the emergency network need to be deployed is limited in nature then issues arises in creating and sustaining the dynamic communication among the nodes. The basic operations of nodes which are carried out is following—(1) Neighbor discovery, (2) Update route and (3) Sending and receiving of the packets etc.

*Scalability.* As the network start growing the number of message that needs to be traversed through whole network also increases. The earlier unstructured P2P network didn't fare well on scalability parameters. Overall, the network has to be flexible so as to allow more number of peers anywhere and any time, without affecting the performance of network.

*Churn.* It deals with the sudden burst in arrival and departure of peers (it can be thought as events where any user can switch-off his/her PC at any time or leave the network due to mobile nature of the node). Churn becomes a challenging and essential aspect in building a scalable P2P system. The different mobility models available in the simulated environment gives different behaviour for the different P2P network deployed.

*Latency.* Since in the highly dynamic environment churn rates are high due to which the nodes take few time in updating its routing table which results in packet transmission delays. Also sometimes due to packet loss there is delay in the packet transmission to the required destination which results in overall delay for the whole network as a unit. In dynamic environment where network-partitioning is also a scenario the latency can be huge collapsing the whole network.

*Search Issues.* Flooding based search is used in unstructured overlay. Which is extremely wasteful in terms of bandwidth. A large linear part of the network is covered irrespective of hit found. In this enormous number of redundant messages are sent. This is carried out by all users in parallel which leads to local load growth linearly with size.

# 4    Experiment and Results

The analysis of the structured, unstructured and cluster network in dynamic environment carried out in a simulated environment using OMNeT++ is discussed below:

## 4.1    Structured P2P Network

As discussed in the Sect. 2 this type of network is carried out with a fixed underlying structure which are best for static routes; however for dynamic routes where routing table change dynamically performance changes. In the following discussed simulation example this scenario is simulated. The routing table are changed by applying Advanced On-Demand Vector (AODV) routing protocol. In the network, a series of AODV-routers are placed. These are mobile hosts that have AODV and IP forwarding enabled. Six of the hosts are laid out in a chain, and are stationary. Their communication ranges are specified so that each host can only reach the adjacent hosts. Destination host moves up and down along the chain, and is only in the communication ranges of one or two nearby hosts.

NetworkConfigurator is set-up not to add static routes, The AODV protocol is used to configure the routing tables. Source-Host is configured to ping destination-Host. Since each host is capable of reaching the adjacent hosts only, the ping packets are relayed to destination-Host through the chain. As the network topology changes because of node mobility, the AODV protocol dynamically configures the routing tables. To reduce clutter, we set the destination Filter parameter of the visualizer to destinationHost. When destination-Host starts to move downwards as shown in Fig. 3a, packets get routed along the chain to the host that is currently adjacent to destination-Host. Finally, this host relays the packets to destination-Host. As the node moves as shown in Fig. 3b, routing tables are kept up to date by AODV to relay the packets along the chain to destination-Host. On the way back, the lower hosts are not involved with the relay of packet, and the routing tables entries remain unused for some time, after which they are timed out and removed. When destination-Host gets to the top of the scene as shown in Fig. 3c, the process starts over again. The visualizer continually reacts to changes in the routing tables, and updates the visualization accordingly.

## 4.2    Unstructured P2P Network

For simulating an unstructured P2P network, the experimentation is setup. Initially mobile nodes join the network as shown in Fig. 4a. Next they determine which other nodes are alive on the network. For this purpose, "ping" packet

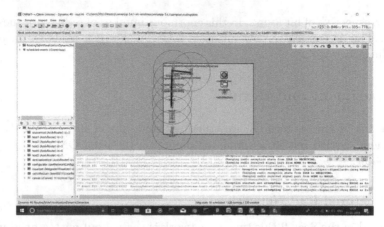

(a) Initial mobile destination host moving in downward direction

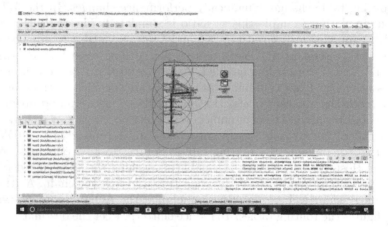

(b) Node moving downward while connecting with their neighbour nodes

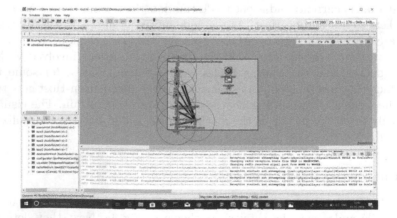

**Fig. 3.** Structured P2P Network in dynamic environment

is advertised to declare each peer's presence in the network. Other peers, on receipt, reply back with the respective "pong" packet for confirmation as shown in Fig. 4b. Also the ping packet is forwarded to other connected peers. A pong packet consists of—(1) IP address, (2) port number and (3) route through which pong packet come back.

An important aspect in unstructured P2P Network is searching, in such network a node ask other peer if they have the file you desire. Peers check to see if they have matches, it will respond and send the packet to the connected peers as shown in Fig. 4c. Continues for TTL (how many hops a packet can go before it dies, typically). Once a peer respond with a Query Hit (contains contact information). File transfer use direct connection using AODV protocol.

### 4.3   Cluster P2P Network

One of the important protocol which is used to simulate cluster based approach is LEACH. In this protocol among the entities present, some are randomly chosen as Cluster Heads (CHs). Their role is to balance the overall energy requirement of the whole network as well as reducing the size of data received from peers in the same cluster before forwarding it to the centralized data unit for further processing. This is done to improve the overall time required for transmitting the data through the network that has been setup.

In cluster based P2P network some of the important parameters have been setup before carrying out simulations. A network has been deployed for 100 randomly-deployed nodes in 500 square meters area. Then distance d is calculated for all the node with their neighbouring nodes and compared with the threshold th value of distance. This is carried out to segregate nodes and place them in an optimally selected cluster to which the node distance is minimal with respect to the respective cluster head. Using this process it is been assured that all the nodes are segregated and put in the same cluster based upon the minimal distant value as shown in Fig. 5a.

An optimal route is sought among the large coverage set of nodes for fastest transfer of information. If destination node and source node is under the same coverage set, then only transmission can take place, otherwise there will be a background search for an alternate path. At the starting of route searching, source will seek all the possible paths to reach the destination with having additional information of the direction of traversal to strike out those path which are strictly opposite to the destination node.

The Fig. 5b displays the graph of the number of live nodes per unit time. It shows that with the lapse of the time the energy of the nodes gradually get dissipated due to which it starts dying, which means they are not able to transmit or receive the packets and becomes dead to the network i.e. churn rate rises. Initially the nodes are live so we can see the number of live nodes maximum but as shown in the Fig. 5c dead nodes start increasing as the time increases due to the dissipation of the energy of the nodes. The Fig. 5d shows the graph of the average Residual Energy of the all the nodes as time passes by, which indicates that as time passes energy gets dissipated gradually of all the nodes. The Fig. 5e

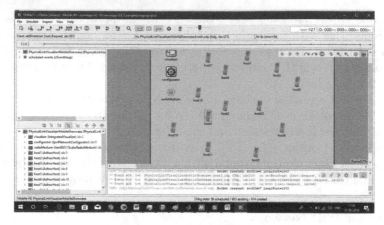

(a) Mobile nodes in random topology

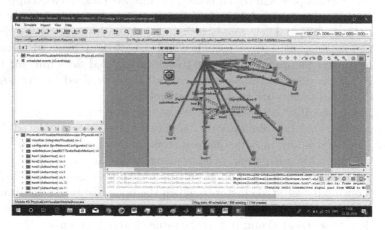

(b) Ping Pong process of all the nodes

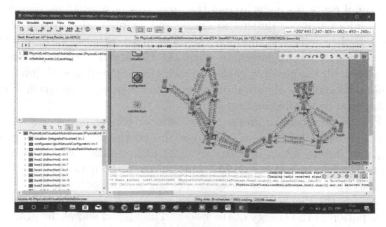

(c) Random graph network topology

**Fig. 4.** Unstructured P2P Network

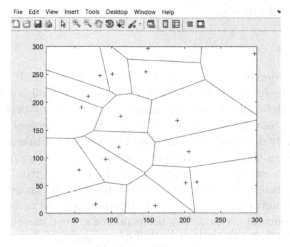

(a) Cluster Network

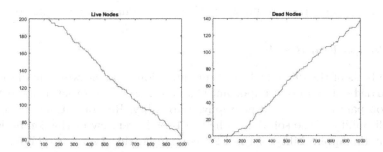

(b) Live nodes v/s No. of rounds (c) Dead nodes v/s No. of rounds

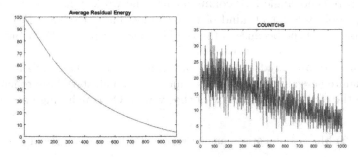

(d) Energy v/s No. of rounds    (e) Cluster heads per unit time

**Fig. 5.** Cluster based P2P Network

shows that as the number of nodes dies due to the dissipation of the energy the total number of the nodes also get decreases, due to which the number of the cluster heads also decreases.

### 4.4 Simulation

To achieve the objective of best suitable applicability of P2P communication model in an emergency scenario OMNeT++ simulation tool is selected. It supports built in code available for P2P model types and any other user defined code for carrying out the comparison. To create an emergency scenario, 100 nodes are randomly deployed in the region of 500m * 500m taken for simulation. The mobility model chosen for simulation is `RandomWaypoint` model due to its similarity with an emergency scenario where there is no fixed path of movement of nodes forming the network. Thee different P2P model types for e.g. Structured, Unstructured, Clustered and Hierarchical type is simulated for the underlying environment created. The performance is been measured on different parameters like Packet drop ratio (PDR), Throughput and End-to-End delay for different P2P communication type. For implementing Cluster and Hierarchical form, some built in implementation is available for e.g. LEACH protocol is used for obtaining comparison result with other P2P form of implementation.

### 4.5 Comparison Result

On the basis of the different P2P communication type, network simulation has been carried out to obtain important characteristics. The table enclosed here is drawn on parameters like Topography, Scalability, Response-time and Universal applicability of the solution to have a broad overview of the comparison to arrive at the applicability of the P2P communication type for different topology in an emergency scenario. It can be observed from Table 1 that all the different P2P Network type performs differently when the underlying scenario changes. There is no single P2P communication network type structure which is universally applicable for all kind of topography. The structured P2P network has fixed topology type because of the rigid data structure like Distributed Hash Table (DHT) which limits it dynamicity. Next comes the unstructured P2P network which suits any kind of topography but it didn't scale well in terms of network maintenance and searching. So due to which clustered approach is tried to improve the overall response time of the system. On concluding lines it can be

**Table 1.** Comparison among various P2P network method.

| P2P network type | Topography | Scalability | Response-time | Universal solution |
|---|---|---|---|---|
| Structured | Fixed | Rigid | Fast | No |
| Unstructured | Variable | Poor | Worst | Yes |
| Cluster-Hierarchical | Variable | Good | Fast | Hybrid |

said that as the topography and nodes become dynamic, no single form can be universal solution and a hybrid approach is applied to optimize the performance.

## 5 Conclusion and Future Work

On the basis of the experimentation performed in OMNeT++ simulation environment the applicability of P2P network in different topography was analysed. It was observed that for different dynamic condition in any topography where emergency network is deployed, there is no any P2P network best suited for all the environment. For e.g. if the topography is more of uniform side then structured network is best suited. Similarly, if we have lesser number of mobile nodes and we have to cover a large area then in this scenario unstructured network performs better and if the area where emergency network needs to be deployed is huge and peers are less then the hierarchical network is the best suited type.

On carrying out the simulation it was observed that there are areas where improvement in P2P network topography type would result in reliable and efficient network. There is no any single topography best suited for all kind of dynamic environment. But as a future scope of work there can be best heuristic approach to find a way that the network itself can choose automatically the best possible topography to handle any dynamic environment.

## References

1. Abraham, I., Awerbuch, B., Azar, Y., Bartal, Y., Malkhi, D., Pavlov, E.: A generic scheme for building overlay networks in adversarial scenarios. In: Proceedings International Parallel and Distributed Processing Symposium, pp. 9-pp. IEEE (2003)
2. Ali, S., Sewak, A., Pandey, M., Tyagi, N.: Simulation of P2P overlays over manets: impediments and proposed solution. In: 2017 9th International Conference on Communication Systems and Networks (COMSNETS), pp. 338–345. IEEE (2017)
3. Barjini, H., Othman, M., Ibrahim, H., Udzir, N.I.: Shortcoming, problems and analytical comparison for flooding-based search techniques in unstructured P2P networks. Peer-to-Peer Netw. Appl. **5**(1), 1–13 (2012). https://doi.org/10.1007/s12083-011-0101-y
4. Baumgart, I., Heep, B.: Fast but economical: a simulative comparison of structured peer-to-peer systems. In: Proceedings of the 8th Euro-NF Conference on Next Generation Internet NGI 2012, pp. 87–94. IEEE (2012)
5. Cao, S., Wei, Y., Chen, X.: A robust cluster-based dynamic-super-node scheme for hybrid peer-to-peer network. J. China Univ. Posts Telecommun. **14**, 21–26 (2007)
6. Chawathe, Y., Ratnasamy, S., Breslau, L., Lanham, N., Shenker, S.: Making gnutella-like P2P systems scalable. In: Proceedings of the 2003 Conference on Applications, Technologies, Architectures, and Protocols for Computer Communications, pp. 407–418 (2003)
7. Chowdhury, F., Kolberg, M.: Performance evaluation of structured peer-to-peer overlays for use on mobile networks. In: 2013 Sixth International Conference on Developments in eSystems Engineering, pp. 57–62. IEEE (2013)
8. Cohen, E., Shenker, S.: Replication strategies in unstructured peer-to-peer networks. ACM SIGCOMM Comput. Commun. Rev. **32**(4), 177–190 (2002)

9. Falchi, F., Gennaro, C., Zezula, P.: A content–addressable network for similarity search in metric spaces. In: Moro, G., Bergamaschi, S., Joseph, S., Morin, J.-H., Ouksel, A.M. (eds.) DBISP2P 2005-2006. LNCS, vol. 4125, pp. 98–110. Springer, Heidelberg (2007). https://doi.org/10.1007/978-3-540-71661-7_9

10. Hsiao, R., Wang, S.D.: Jelly: a dynamic hierarchical P2P overlay network with load balance and locality. In: 24th International Conference on Distributed Computing Systems Workshops, Proceedings, pp. 534–540. IEEE (2004)

11. Hu, C.L., Kuo, T.H.: A hierarchical overlay with cluster-based reputation tree for dynamic peer-to-peer systems. J. Netw. Comput. Appl. **35**(6), 1990–2002 (2012)

12. Krishna, P., Vaidya, N.H., Chatterjee, M., Pradhan, D.K.: A cluster-based approach for routing in dynamic networks. ACM SIGCOMM Comput. Commun. Rev. **27**(2), 49–64 (1997)

13. Li, J., Stribling, J., Gil, T.M., Morris, R., Kaashoek, M.F.: Comparing the performance of distributed hash tables under churn. In: Voelker, G.M., Shenker, S. (eds.) IPTPS 2004. LNCS, vol. 3279, pp. 87–99. Springer, Heidelberg (2005). https://doi.org/10.1007/978-3-540-30183-7_9

14. Liu, Z., Yuan, R., Li, Z., Li, H., Chen, G.: Survive under high churn in structured P2P systems: evaluation and strategy. In: Alexandrov, V.N., van Albada, G.D., Sloot, P.M.A., Dongarra, J. (eds.) ICCS 2006. LNCS, vol. 3994, pp. 404–411. Springer, Heidelberg (2006). https://doi.org/10.1007/11758549_58

15. Loguinov, D., Kumar, A., Rai, V., Ganesh, S.: Graph-theoretic analysis of structured peer-to-peer systems: routing distances and fault resilience. In: Proceedings of the 2003 Conference on Applications, Technologies, Architectures, and Protocols for Computer Communications, pp. 395–406 (2003)

16. Ripeanu, M., Foster, I.: Mapping the gnutella network: macroscopic properties of large-scale peer-to-peer systems. In: Druschel, P., Kaashoek, F., Rowstron, A. (eds.) IPTPS 2002. LNCS, vol. 2429, pp. 85–93. Springer, Heidelberg (2002). https://doi.org/10.1007/3-540-45748-8_8

17. Schollmeier, R.: A definition of peer-to-peer networking for the classification of peer-to-peer architectures and applications. In: Proceedings First International Conference on Peer-to-Peer Computing, pp. 101–102. IEEE (2001)

18. Stoica, I., Morris, R., Karger, D., Kaashoek, M.F., Balakrishnan, H.: Chord: a scalable peer-to-peer lookup service for internet applications. ACM SIGCOMM Comput. Commun. Rev. **31**(4), 149–160 (2001)

19. Vishnumurthy, V., Francis, P.: A comparison of structured and unstructured P2P approaches to heterogeneous random peer selection. In: USENIX Annual Technical Conference, pp. 309–322 (2007)

# Effect of Filtering in Big Data Analytics for Load Forecasting in Smart Grid

Sneha Rai[ID] and Mala De[⊠][ID]

Department of Electrical Engineering, NIT Patna, Patna, India
sneharai0212@gmail.com, mala.de.in@ieee.org

**Abstract.** With the introduction of smart metering infrastructure in the power system, the availability of real-time data for every node in a smart grid has become possible. This has led to the availability of big data in power system. The analysis of this huge set of data requires a different method of treatment. Machine learning-based tools are being used in this environment for load forecasting. But this huge data set requires appropriate pre-processing for bad data removal, missing data identification, normalization of largely varying datasets, etc. to enable the load forecaster to perform better. The present paper focuses on the analysis of different filters or pre-processors in the performance of multiple load forecasting methods in the case of smart grid. The paper uses a practical smart grid data to implement the same.

**Keywords:** Data filtering/Pre-processing · Smart grid · Load forecasting · Regression · Big data

## 1 Introduction

Due to the emergence of a smart grid for redistribution of electrical power, a large number of smart meters are installed at various nodes for collecting real-time power consumption data. This large volume of real-time data opens up new avenues for different power system analyses like load forecasting, system planning, resource allocation, maintenance scheduling, etc. [1]. Load forecasting is very much essential for optimum planning and operation of various electric utilities [2]. It can be classified into four categories depending upon the period; very short-term forecasting - which are usually for forecasting loads over periods of few minutes to an hour, short-term load forecasting which forecasts for few hours to a week ahead, medium-term forecasting which forecasts from few weeks to a month ahead, and long-term forecasting which is over few months to an year ahead [3]. The forecasts for different time horizons are used for different operations. Long term forecasting is important for capacity planning and mid-term and short term forecasting is crucial for secure day to day operation of any power system. This task of forecasting becomes harder due to the temporal nature of

This work is supported by the Science & Engineering Research Board, a statutory body of Department of Science and Technology (DST), Government of India, under grants number ECR/2017/001027.

the load consumption data caused by the unpredictability of the end-user. Hence, an efficient load forecaster is one of the most important requirements for successful operation of a power system.

With the increasing advancement in communication technology, the use of smart meter has increased to a large extent in the smart distribution network. The smart meters collect and communicate the load data in real-time at every node of the smart grid. This leads to collection of huge data at every instant of time. The traditional power system analysis methods used for load forecasting, mostly can't handle these huge sets of data available in real-time. Hence this has led to a different era of power system analysis in the presence of big data. Another point worth mentioning is – the variation in load for any individual node, over a day, is much higher than that of the variation for all the nodes in the network as the load is a dynamic quantity. Hence, load prediction for an individual node becomes harder due to its continuously varying nature. The availability of real-time data for individual nodes has opened up new avenues in power system forecasting and subsequently, its operation.

The classical methods of load forecasting required to be updated in the presence of this big data. Due to the dynamically changing nature of this data and presence of bad data, the choice of a proper filtering method becomes vital and affects the performance of a load forecaster in a big way. The raw data collected from smart meters contain various outliers such as noise, error due to communication link failure, and missing or abnormal data. These unwanted data should be filtered out to obtain good and accurate forecasting performance. But, while filtering bad data, care must be taken not to filter the actual data out. Hence, data pre-processing is an integral step in load forecasting as the quality of the data affects the ability of the prediction model to undergo proper training with the training information (data set) [4]. Data pre-processing includes data cleaning i.e. filling the missing values due to meter or link failure, smoothing the noisy data, removing outliers and inconsistencies from the entire dataset, and normalization of the raw data without altering the original characteristics of the actual load.

## 2  Related Work

In the past, there have been several works based on the load forecasting with the help of various load forecasting methodologies. These methods can be broadly classified into two types: Classical methods and Modern methods. Classical methods include regression analysis like MLR [5] and time series methods like ARIMA [6], exponential smoothening methods [7], and Kalman filtering [8]. The modern method of forecasting in presence of big data mainly includes neural network (NN) based prediction models like feed-forward neural network (FFNN) [9, 10], general regression neural network (GRNN), recurrent neural network (RNN) [11], convolution neural network (CNN) [12], and regression-based on support vector machines (SVM) [13, 14], deep learning-based CNN [15]. The performance of a regression model is very much dependent upon the quality of data used for training the regressors. In [4] and [16] some works are presented which have used the pre-processing filters like moving average (MA), moving median (MAD), Gaussian and GRRN based filter as well.

The present work focuses on a case study for a practical smart grid based at NIT Patna campus which is a perfect combination of different types of loads including residential, academic and small scale industry (the laboratories in the various departments consists of large machines which can be considered equivalent to a small scale industry). As a preliminary work, this paper attempts to identify a suitable pre-processing method that may be applied to the data being obtained from the smart meters and results in a better load prediction performance. In this paper, different load forecasting methods are used to forecast the future load of a particular node of the smart grid with and without pre-processing of the available real-time data. The moving average filter (MAF) and Gaussian filter (GF) are two established and widely used filtering techniques used in the case of load forecasting in the presence of big data. Hence, the effect of these two data pre-processing methods on the performance of various linear and non-linear regression techniques has been explored and compared in this paper. For the testing purpose, the real-time load data of a particular node in the smart grid is considered.

The remainder of this paper is organized as follows. The description of the test system along with sample data is presented in Sect. 3. Section 4 describes the methodology that includes various regression methods and pre-processing techniques used for the load prediction model for the specified dataset. The validation of the effectiveness of the applied pre-processing methods for the different load prediction methods is presented in Sect. 5. Finally, the conclusion is drawn in Sect. 6.

## 3 System Data and Input Parameters

To show the effectiveness of different filtering techniques on the performance of the load forecasting methods, practical system data is used. The load data required to show the applicability is the real-time load consumption data which is obtained from the smart meters located at various points inside the NIT Patna campus. The load data is collected in real-time by these smart meters at the different nodes at a pre-specified time interval (viz. 1 min interval, 5 min interval, etc.). This load data is then logged and communicated to the controller computer via wireless communication. At a given node different parameters of load data e.g. active-reactive power, line, and phase voltages, currents, power factor, frequency, etc. can be obtained at desired time interval.

The dataset used in this work consist of daily average load for six months ranging from 15th July 2019 to 15th January 2020. As a case study, the load prediction performance has been evaluated for a particular node namely Girls Hostel (GH) node in this network. In this paper, we are trying to predict the daily average load of this particular node for a month using the known daily average load data of previous months. Hence, for this particular load prediction, the sample load data required should be daily average load. A sample set of this load data for the node under consideration i.e., GH node for two time periods of 28 days are shown in Fig. 1. This average daily load is also directly available from the logged historical data for this network. The figure presents the load for 56 days ranging from 15-12-2019 to 13-01-2020 and 15-07-2019 to 13-08-2019. This is only a representational dataset; the data used for analysis here are of six month's duration. The load consumption shown in the second column is the amount of load that is consumed at a particular node in the last 24 h in kW.

| National Institute of Technology - Patna | | National Institute of Technology - Patna | |
| Patna | | Patna | |
| Log Date / Time | GIRLS HOSTEL | Log Date / Time | GIRLS HOSTEL |
|---|---|---|---|
| 15-12-2019 00:00 | 398.72 | 15-07-2019 00:00 | 318.08 |
| 16-12-2019 00:00 | 124.08 | 16-07-2019 00:00 | 733.36 |
| 17-12-2019 00:00 | 105.28 | 17-07-2019 00:00 | 885.76 |
| 18-12-2019 00:00 | 115.36 | 18-07-2019 00:00 | 860.40 |
| 19-12-2019 00:00 | 98.80 | 19-07-2019 00:00 | 657.60 |
| 20-12-2019 00:00 | 101.28 | 20-07-2019 00:00 | 289.20 |
| 21-12-2019 00:00 | 88.56 | 21-07-2019 00:00 | 294.88 |
| 22-12-2019 00:00 | 91.68 | 22-07-2019 00:00 | 808.56 |
| 23-12-2019 00:00 | 110.00 | 23-07-2019 00:00 | 743.28 |
| 24-12-2019 00:00 | 93.84 | 24-07-2019 00:00 | 647.52 |
| 25-12-2019 00:00 | 97.60 | 25-07-2019 00:00 | 610.96 |
| 26-12-2019 00:00 | 95.52 | 26-07-2019 00:00 | 625.04 |
| 27-12-2019 00:00 | 91.04 | 27-07-2019 00:00 | 178.48 |
| 28-12-2019 00:00 | 112.56 | 28-07-2019 00:00 | 144.32 |
| 29-12-2019 00:00 | 102.72 | 29-07-2019 00:00 | 631.20 |
| 30-12-2019 00:00 | 115.84 | 30-07-2019 00:00 | 543.04 |
| 31-12-2019 00:00 | 110.64 | 31-07-2019 00:00 | 551.52 |
| 01-01-2020 00:00 | 104.88 | 01-08-2019 00:00 | 424.72 |
| 02-01-2020 00:00 | 110.00 | 02-08-2019 00:00 | 429.20 |
| 03-01-2020 00:00 | 111.28 | 03-08-2019 00:00 | 137.76 |
| 04-01-2020 00:00 | 112.56 | 04-08-2019 00:00 | 156.00 |
| 05-01-2020 00:00 | 104.88 | 05-08-2019 00:00 | 675.44 |
| 06-01-2020 00:00 | 356.32 | 06-08-2019 00:00 | 989.04 |
| 07-01-2020 00:00 | 313.28 | 07-08-2019 00:00 | 855.68 |
| 08-01-2020 00:00 | 140.80 | 08-08-2019 00:00 | 681.36 |
| 09-01-2020 00:00 | 122.24 | 09-08-2019 00:00 | 714.24 |
| 10-01-2020 00:00 | 230.80 | 10-08-2019 00:00 | 181.44 |
| 11-01-2020 00:00 | 131.68 | 11-08-2019 00:00 | 198.80 |
| 12-01-2020 00:00 | 102.40 | 12-08-2019 00:00 | 238.16 |
| 13-01-2020 00:00 | 118.40 | 13-08-2019 00:00 | 658.56 |
| Total Consumption | 4113.04 | Total Consumption | 15863.6 |

**Fig. 1.** Sample dataset of Girls Hostel (GH) node

This load consumption data will be used as input for determining the parameters of load forecaster and once trained; it will be able to forecast the daily average load of the node for any future date.

It has been seen that the electrical consumption at a residential building is predominantly decided by weather factors like temperature and humidity of any area. The GH node is the node that supplies power to the residential girls' hostel building. Hence, along with the historical load consumption, the other input factors used for load forecasting are the weather parameters known as the THI index. Moreover, day and season have a considerable effect on the load consumption pattern and are taken as input features for the forecasting model. Day factor is also considered to be an important feature as we can see from Fig. 1 that the amount of load in the given node varies with the variation of day and day of a month also influence the load trend due to seasonal variation. Hence, day and month must be considered as a training parameter to design a proper load forecaster.

The sample six month dataset used for analysis is divided into two parts: training and testing dataset. 75% of the load data from 15th July 2019 to 1st December 2019 with a sampling period of 24 h is used for training the model. Remaining 25% of the load data is used for testing and validation of the obtained load forecasting models.

## 4 The Methodology

Different regression methods are used to build the load forecaster for forecasting daily average load for a month using the last 5 months of data for training. The raw data collected from smart meters are first pre-processed using the two above mentioned filters for pre-processing and then the processed data is used to build the prediction models. It has been seen in literature that for different types of system datasets, different regression methods become effective and produce accurate results. Hence, multiple regression methods are used to forecast the load under consideration and then a comparison is drawn to decide on the most suitable one. The different regression methods are described below.

### 4.1 Regression Methods

MLR is a linear regression method that describes the relationship between the dependent variable i.e. load with two or more independent variables like temperature, humidity, day, time, etc. It has one disadvantage that the method suits linear forecasting but the pattern of the load is mainly non-linear. The double exponential smoothening method is a univariate technique that is most suitable for the data having a trend. It assigns decreasing exponential weights as the observation gets older. The recent observations are given more weight than the older ones. The method is mainly based on two components: level component and trend component. The moving average is a technique that calculates the overall trend in a dataset. The simple moving average method is a traditional time series prediction technique that uses the average of past observations to predict the future one period forecast. This implies equal weights for all the past data points. FFNN is a non-linear regression technique that can learn from the experience as a human brain to build a multivariate model. It is the basic form of NN having one input, one output and one hidden layer with *n* number of neurons. SVR is slightly different from other regression techniques as it uses the basic idea of a classification algorithm to predict a real variable rather than a class. It takes into account the non-linearity present in the data to build the prediction model.

## 4.2    Data Pre-processing

Multiple pre-processing techniques can be used to process the data before it is used to train a forecaster. These pre-processors are

- Moving average filter (MAF): It is a simple low pass filter that takes $m$ input samples at a time and calculates the average of those samples to produce a single output data. The smoothness of the output increases with the increasing length of the filter as the sharp modulations in the data are made increasingly blunt without altering the original characteristics of the data.
- Gaussian filter (GF): It is a type of filter whose impulse response is a Gaussian function. One added advantage of the Gaussian filter is that its Fourier transform is centered on zero frequency and hence, the relative removal of outliers is more effective in the case of Gaussian filter as compared to moving average filter [17]. It is used to reduce the noise from the time series data as it is isotropic.

In the present paper, the pre-processing also includes the normalization of the actual load data followed by the filtration process. Normalization is required here as the variation in the load data over different seasons are wide due to change in weather condition and this trend of wide variation gets lost during the model training. To reduce the difference in the data, it is normalized on a scale of [0, 1]. The normalization is done using (1).

$$x_{new} = \frac{x - x_{min}}{x_{max} - x_{min}} \tag{1}$$

Where; $x$ is the actual load at a given instant, $x_{min}$ and $x_{max}$ is the minimum and maximum values of load in the entire dataset used for analyses and $x_{new}$ is the normalized load at that particular instant.

After normalization, the normalized data is filtered using MAF and GF for removing the outliers present in the data.

## 4.3    Prediction Accuracy

The forecast accuracy is determined by using mean absolute percentage error (MAPE) which is a common metric used in the field of load forecasting. It is calculated as:

$$MAPE = \frac{1}{N} \left| \sum_{i=1}^{N} \frac{(y_i - \tilde{y}_i)}{y_i} \right| \times 100 \tag{2}$$

Where; $y_i$ is the actual load and $\tilde{y}_i$ is the forecasted load, $N$ is the number of samples used for testing.

Lower MAPE value represents improved prediction, i.e., the predicted load is nearer to the actual load. For all the above mention regression technique based forecasters, the MAPE values are calculated for the predicted daily average load and the one with minimum MAPE value is the most accurate load predictor for this particular node.

## 5   Results - Effect of Filtering or Pre-processing

The different pre-processing methods are applied to the actual load dataset for the GH node and the obtained filtered and normalized data is used as training and testing dataset for building the load prediction model by the different regression techniques.

Figure 2 shows the actual load curve of the GH node without pre-processing. This curve indicates the daily variation of load for a few months (training data, 75% of the dataset) at the GH node. This data is then pre-processed using multiple techniques namely GF and MAF. The load curves after applying the GF technique is presented in Fig. 3. On the other hand, the processed load waveform with the MAF technique is shown in Fig. 4. For these curves, it can be analyzed that by using GF, the actual characteristics of the raw data is more preserved as compared to MAF for the given node and time frame. The MAF smoothens the load data more as compared to GF which seems not necessary for smaller number of training samples used in this case. However, the performance of the prediction may vary by changing the sampling period and duration of the training and testing dataset

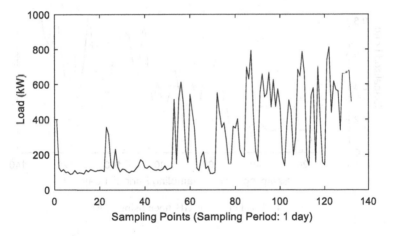

**Fig. 2.**  Actual load of GH node

The different load forecasters are – MLR, Holt's Method, MA, FFNN, and SVR. Once the forecasters are trained using this filtered and unfiltered dataset, these are tested for the test dataset and their performance is evaluated. The comparison of the performance is based on the MAPE value defined in (2).

The prediction results obtained using the mentioned pre-processing methods are shown in Table 1. These results have been obtained after the iterative evaluation of the methods implemented. From the results, it is seen that for the given test dataset, the MAPE obtained after the GF method of data pre-processing is lower and in a comparable range for all the linear and non-linear regression techniques compared to MAF.

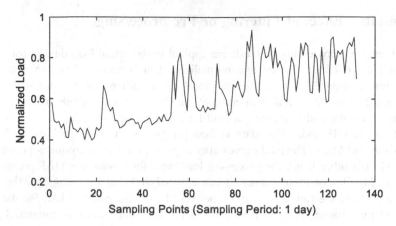

**Fig. 3.** Load curve of GH node using GF

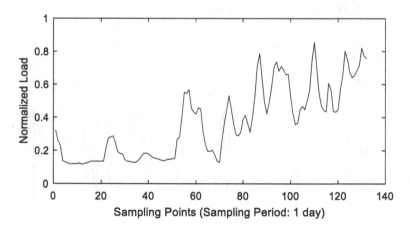

**Fig. 4.** Load curve of GH node using MAF

**Table 1.** Performance evaluation of pre-processing with various regression method

| Regression methods | Performance parameter | Signal pre-processing methods | | Raw waveform |
|---|---|---|---|---|
| | | MAF | GF | |
| MLR | MAPE | 21.18 | 3.64 | 31.64 |
| Holt's | MAPE | 10.28 | 8.64 | 5.97 |
| MA | MAPE | 4.45 | 9.9 | 30.45 |
| FFNN | MAPE | 24.43 | 3.83 | 30.29 |
| SVR | MAPE | 23.46 | 3.15 | 29.84 |

The above table shows the value of MAPE for all the regressors. It can be seen that the MAPE for all the regressors other than Holt's method is very high and unacceptable when unfiltered data is used. Only Holt's method could predict the load with accuracy. When pre-processing is introduced, the prediction accuracy improved for most of the forecasters. But the improvement in accuracy is much more in the case of GF compared to MAF.

A comparison plot of actual and predicted load for test data by various regression techniques using GF for data pre-processing is also shown in Fig. 5. It can be seen that FFNN, SVR, and MLR gives better prediction accuracy as compared to MA and Holt's method. The Holt's double exponential smoothening method mainly predicts the trend in the load data which includes determining the speed and direction of movement of the actual load, therefore the plot of Holt's method for testing dataset is a straight line with an increasing slope which denotes the trend component of the predicted load. Holt's method performs better without filtering. But for all other regression-based load forecasters/predictors, data filtering or pre-processing improves the prediction accuracy and for this particular load dataset, GF proved to be best.

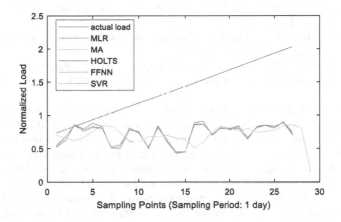

**Fig. 5.** Comparison plot of actual load and forecasted load using GF

## 6 Conclusion

This paper shows the effect of different filtering techniques in the case of load forecasting in the presence of big data for a smart grid environment. A practical data set from a real-life smart grid proves the validity of the result. The comparison of different filtering methods in case of load forecasting based on multiple regression techniques is presented in this paper. The comparison of MAF and GF for the used test dataset shows that for all types of predictors, GF performs much better than the MAF in this study. The performance is compared based on the MAPE value of these predictors. The processed data obtained by GF performs better in this case as the nature of load contains a lot of variation and by using GF the actual load characteristics are much more preserved as compared to MAF. However, the performance of the predictors may vary with the sampling period and duration of the dataset. This work can be extended for all other nodes in the network for short-term, mid-term and long-term load forecasting.

# References

1. Wen, L., Zhou, K., Yang, S., Li, L.: Compression of smart meter big data: a survey. Renew. Sustain. Energy Rev. **91**, 59–69 (2018)
2. Majidi, M., Zare, K.: Integration of smart energy hubs in distribution networks under uncertainties and demand response concept. In: IEEE Transactions on Power Systems (2018)
3. Hayes, B., Gruber, J., Prodanovic, M.: Short-term load forecasting at the local level using smart meter data. In: IEEE Eindhoven PowerTech, Eindhoven, pp. 1–6 (2015)
4. Nose-Filho, K., Lotufo, A.D.P., Minussi, C.R.: Preprocessing data for short-term load forecasting with a general regression neural network and a moving average filter. Presented at the IEEE Trondheim Power Tech, Trondheim, Norway, 19–23 (2011)
5. Zhang, P., Wu, X., Wang, X.: Short-term load forecasting based on big data technologies. CSEE J. Power Energy Syst. **1**(3), 59–67 (2015)
6. Moshkbar-Bakhshayesh, K., Ghofrani, M.B.: Development of a robust identifier for NPPs transients combining ARIMA model and EBP algorithm. IEEE Trans. Nuclear Sci. **61**(4), 2383–2391 (2014)
7. Ji, P.R., Xiong, D., Wang, P., Chen, J.: A study on exponential smoothing model for load forecasting. In: Proceedings of 2012 Power and Energy Engineering Conference (APPEEC), Shanghai, China, 1–4 (2012)
8. Hagan, M.T., Behr, S.M.: The time series approach to short term load forecasting. IEEE Trans. Power Syst. **2**(3), 785–791 (1987)
9. Blissing, D., Klein, M.T., Chinnathambi, R.A., Selvaraj, D.F., Ranganathan, P.: A hybrid regression model for day-ahead energy price forecasting. IEEE Access **7**, 36833–36842 (2019)
10. Singh, P., Dwivedi, P.: Integration of new evolutionary approach with artificial neural network for solving short term load forecast problem. Appl. Energy **217**, 537–549 (2018)
11. Buitrago, J., Asfour, S.: Short-term forecasting of electric loads using nonlinear autoregressive artificial neural networks with exogenous vector inputs. Energies **10**, 40 (2017)
12. Tian, C., Ma, J., Zhang, C., Zhan, P.: A deep neural network for short-term load forecast based on LSTM and convolution neural network. Energies **11**, 3493 (2018)
13. Zhang, X., Wang, J., Zhang, K.: Short-term electric load forecasting based on singular spectrum analysis and support vector machine optimized by Cuckoo search algorithm. Electr. Power Syst. Res. **146**, 270–285 (2017)
14. Selakov, A., Cvijetinovic, D., Milovic, L.: Hybrid PSO-SVM method for short-term load forecasting during periods with significant temperature variations in the city of Burbank. Appl. Soft Comput. **16**(3), 80–88 (2013)
15. Wen, L., Zhou, K., Yang, S.: Load demand forecasting of residential buildings using a deep learning model. Electr. Power Syst. Res. **179** (2020)
16. Nose-Filho, K., Lotufo, A.D.P., Minussi, C.R.: Short-term multinodal load forecasting using a modified general regression neural network. IEEE Trans. Power Deliv. **26**(4), 2862–2869 (2011)
17. Hussein, E.M.A.: Preprocessing of Measurements, pp. 97–123. Elsevier (2011)

# Distance Invariant RGB-D Object Recognition Using DSMS System

Rahul Patekar$^{(\boxtimes)}$ and Abhijeet Nandedkar

Department of Electronics and Telecommunication, SGGSIE&T,
Nanded, Maharashtra, India
rahugpatekar@gmail.com

**Abstract.** In computer vision, object recognition has gained a lot of attention due to its numerous practical usage. For real-world applications, it is necessary to consider conditions like object images are captured from multiple viewpoints, change in illumination and different distance locations of objects from the camera for better recognition. In this work, a new CVPR34K RGB-D dataset is proposed consisting of RGB-D images which are acquired from different distance location from the camera. A distance invariant RGB-D object recognition system is introduced using Depth Estimation, Scale data with Unit Depth and Multimodal Convolutional neural network with SVM (DSMS). The proposed DSMS system is divided into three parts. First, the Depth Estimation is introduced to detect distance location of acquired RGB-D object image. The second stage consists of several preprocessing operation to normalize input RGB-D data with respect to a reference distance. The final stage is to learn features from normalized RGB and depth images and performed RGB-D object recognition. The experimental results show that the DSMS method achieves comparable performance to state-of-the-art methods on the RGB-D object dataset. Effectiveness of our method is clearly observed for the cases when distance location RGB-D object image is changed in proposed CVPR34K Dataset.

**Keywords:** Object recognition · Distance invariant · Multimodal convolutional neural network · Depth estimation · Scale data

## 1  Introduction

In recent years, depth cameras have become more popular and the RGB-D object recognition application has got more attention. With the help of depth cameras, the number of visual information increases which contains RGB and depth modality. The RGB-D dataset [12] is a publically available large dataset of 300 household objects. The objects were placed on a turntable and the camera is mounted at three different height with fixed distance and RGB-D image acquired from different angles. The RGB images contain extra geometric information about the object texture, shape, appearance, and color information. The

© Springer Nature Singapore Pte Ltd. 2020
A. Bhattacharjee et al. (Eds.): MIND 2020, CCIS 1240, pp. 135–148, 2020.
https://doi.org/10.1007/978-981-15-6315-7_11

RGB data can be easily interfered by occlusion, low contrast, illumination, and poor color quality, etc. However, the depth data is used to enhance the object recognition accuracy due to the robustness of depth measurement to color and light variation. Depth data provide plenty of information about the shape and spatial geometry of the object in scenes. The RGB-D object recognition deal with the machine to recognize the object class using RGB and depth information.

The object recognition performance of the system is influenced by images that are under-lighted or over-lighted. Since image quality may be very simply affected by changing climate, or camera that has been used to acquire the image. These circumstances lead to the image that could endure from loss of essential information. The purpose of image enhancement is to improve the quality of an image, bring out information that's hidden in an image for object recognition applications. Ying et al. [19] presented work on the exposure fusion framework as an image enhancement algorithm. The image enhancement algorithm provide an accurate contrast enhancement which leads to realistic results for the input images. Pierre et al. [14] proposed the variational contrast enhancement algorithm for RGB images. This work introduced the variational models both for the enhancement of gray-scale images and color images with their advantages and disadvantages.

There are two approaches in the literature for object recognition depending on the feature extraction procedures, namely hand-crafted features and machine-learned features. The hand-crafted feature extraction methods such as SIFT [13], SURF [2], color histogram [1], etc. capture a subset of cues which are used for the recognition task. Khan et al. [10] presented an approach to construct new features using a feature combination of various feature extraction techniques such as principal component analysis (PCA), wavelet moments, local binary pattern (LBP) and color correlograms for RGB-D images. Their work used $K$-nearest neighbor ($K$-NN) as a classifier for better object recognition results. Bo et al. [4] demonstrated depth kernel descriptors for object recognition. This paper introduced best features representation from a set of kernel features on depth images that model size, 3D shape, and depth edges in a single framework. Bo et al. [3] presented hierarchical kernel descriptors that apply kernel descriptors recursively to form image-level features. These features provide a consistent way and conceptually simple way to generate image-level features from pixel attributes.

However, the problem with hand-crafted feature extraction methods is that these do not extend to different modalities and different datasets. Machine-learned feature extraction methods are based on automatic feature extraction. The convolutional neural network (CNN) [11] is the most famous feature extraction technique due to its capability of obtaining generic features. Jin et al. [9] described a method to jointly use the handcrafted features and machine-learned features for RGB-D object recognition. In this work, the authors used locality-constrained linear coding based spatial pyramid matching for hand-crafted features and convolution neural networks for machine-learned features. These extracted features were classified by using SVM [5,8]. Socher et al. [16] proposed a model based on the combination of a recursive neural network and a CNN for learning features and classification of RGB-D images. The CNN was pre-trained in an unsupervised way to learn low-level features. The learned features were used as inputs to multiple RNN to learn a higher level features. Wang et al. [18] presented a multimodal CNN-based learning structure for RGB-D object recognition. This framework exploited the complementary information between RGB-D modalities and similarity within modalities. The multimodal framework could be used for the different multimodal recognition applications. Zia et al. [21] proposed the use of three-dimensional CNN to completely exploit the 3D spatial information from disparity data and also pre-trained two-dimensional CNN used to learn features from color images. The authors presented a hybrid 2D/3D CNN that can be initialized with pre-trained 2D CNN and can be trained on the small RGB-D dataset.

Rahman et al. [15] introduced a novel multimodal deep CNN architecture for RGB-D object recognition which composed of three streams with two different types of deep CNN. A combined architecture of the joint network of colorjet, surface normal and RGB streams was used for object recognition. Eitel et al. [6] worked on recent progress on CNN and introduced RGB-D architecture for object recognition. This paper focuses on two crucial ingredients for handling depth data with CNN's and a multi-stage training methodology. The first, an effective encoding of depth information for CNN that enables learning without the need for large depth datasets. The second, a data augmentation scheme for robust learning with depth images by corrupting them with realistic noise patterns.

Sun et al. [17] presented a method that extends the original PCANet for RGB-D data. The RGB and depth data were preprocessed to meet the requirement of the network input layer. The features from RGB-D data were extracted by the two stages RGB-D PCANet which consists of binary hashing, cascaded PCA and block-wise histograms with SVM as a classifier. The support vector machine is a well-known method in pattern classification and regression model.

In this work, the new CVPR34K RGB-D dataset is proposed to verify the performance of the Depth Estimation, Scale data with Unit Depth and Multimodal Convolutional neural network with SVM (DSMS) system for RGB-D objects recognition in which objects are placed at different distance locations from the camera. It overcomes the limitation of the existing RGB-D dataset [12], consisting of images with a fixed distance of objects from the camera. This work also introduces a distance invariant RGB-D object recognition system. The three stage algorithm is proposed to recognize RGB-D objects which are placed at different distance location from the camera.

The remaining paper is organized as follows: Sect. 2 gives a brief idea about dataset creation, Sect. 3 describes the proposed approach to recognize RGB-D object images, in Sect. 4 experimental results are discussed and Sect. 5 concludes the work.

## 2    CVPR34K RGB-D Object Dataset Creation

The existing RGB-D object dataset [12] contain images of household objects in which the objects were placed on the turntable at a fixed distance from the camera and video frames were captured for one complete rotation of the turntable with three viewpoints. In the RGB-D dataset, objects do not have depth and illumination variations, i.e. object distance from the camera does not vary and image acquired with the uniform light source. Depth information plays a vital role to recognize objects from different distant locations. Hence, it is necessary to include distance variations to acquire RGB-D object images.

In this work, the Panasonic HDC-SDT750, a 3D camera is used for the creation of CVPR34K RGB-D object dataset. The camera has a 3D conversion lens, capable of recording 3D images. The 3D conversion lens comprises of fixed 14 mm inter-ocular distance and a fixed focal length of 58 mm. It has two lenses which simultaneously records 2 images using side-by-side format having a frame size of $(1080 \times 1920)$ pixels in one video file whereas the size of the left and right image is equal to $(980 \times 828)$. These two left and right images are referred to as stereoscopic images and used to find depth image.

The CVPR34K RGB-D dataset is generated for an object having three depth information in RGB-D images. For this purpose, objects are placed at three different distance locations from the 3D camera on a turntable. The objects are placed at a distance of 83 inches, 106 in., and 120 in. away from the camera, which is referred to as minimum distance (D1), medium distance (D2) and maximum distance (D3) locations, respectively. In general, if the distance between object and camera increases then there is a certain amount of light variation observed in acquired images. Therefore, CVPR34K RGB-D dataset has three different depth and illumination information in acquired images. The video is recorded for a complete one rotation of the turntable with each object. The CVPR34K RGB-D object dataset includes 45 object classes and a total of 180 distinct objects in the whole dataset. The dataset consists of object classes such as apple, banana, coffee cup, food packet, etc. are as shown in Fig. 1.

For each distance, D1, D2 and D3 the RGB-D object images are cropped by using the output of the depth estimation stage. For example, apple image size is $(175 \times 320)$ for D1, $(115 \times 250)$ for D2 and $(95 \times 190)$ for D3 locations from the camera. Figure 1 represents multiple objects which are captured from three different distance location. Three different distance locations having control over creating different illumination images (i.e. L1, L2, and L3) under the same light source for D1, D2 and D3 distance location from the camera. There are in total 34,624 images, in which 10,275 images acquired from a minimum distance with L1 illumination; 11,814 images are captured from a medium distance with L2 illumination and 12,535 images are procured from a maximum distance location from the camera under L3 illumination, for roughly 70 images per object. The proposed CVPR34K dataset will be made public on the web [22].

**Fig. 1.** Objects from the CVPR34K RGB-D Object Dataset *(Note: Each object is shown here belongs to three different distant locations)*

# 3    Proposed Approach for Distance Invariant RGB-D Object Recognition

A distance invariant RGB-D object recognition involves identifying common RGB-D objects placed at different locations from the camera. In this work, the distance invariant RGB-D object recognition system is introduced with three different depth variation. The distance invariant RGB-D object recognition system is proposed using Depth Estimation, Scale data with Unit Depth and Multimodal Convolutional neural network with SVM (DSMS). The DSMS approach is divided into three stages such as: Sect. 3.1 Depth Estimation, Sect. 3.2 RGB-D normalization and Sect. 3.3 Feature Extraction and Classification (Fig. 2).

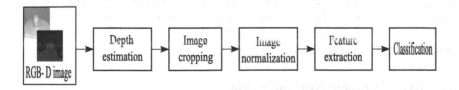

**Fig. 2.** DSMS system for distance invariant RGB-D object recognition

## 3.1    Depth Estimation

The proposed CVPR34K dataset consists of RGB-D object images acquired from three different distance location from the camera. In the process of making a fully automatic distance invariant RGB-D object recognition system, it is essential to determine the depth location of the input RGB-D image. All RGB-D images are acquired from the 3D camera have the same size (980 × 828) as in the dataset creation section. But, size, appearance, and shape of the object in RGB-D images are varied based on distance location from the camera.

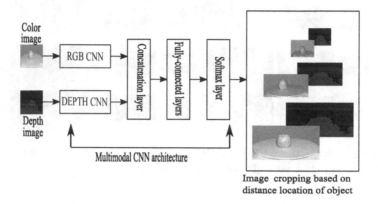

**Fig. 3.** Depth estimation for RGB-D images

It is noted that the object are placed at different distance location, but their position is at the center of the image. The position of an object play an important role when image cropping is to performed based on distance location from the camera using the depth estimation stage. The depth estimation stage provides initial information about the object location from the camera. This initial information is required to select the crop region of the object in the RGB-D image. In this case, it is important to estimate three distance locations object in RGB-D images. The RGB-D object images acquired with each distance location from the camera have unique features like shape, appearance, width, height, and area cover by an object in an image. The depth image has a unique depth range for these three depth locations from the camera. Therefore, the features in RGB-D images are extracted by multimodal CNN to perform depth estimation, as shown in Fig. 3.

## 3.2 RGB-D Image Normalization

The proposed scale data with unit depth stage is essential to provide a uniform distance RGB-D object images, as shown in Fig. 4.

This process transforms the RGB-D image taken from a given distance image to a reference distance RGB-D image. In proposed method, unit depth term is represented for reference distance location of an object. The reference distance location of object is used to convert multiple depths RGB-D object image to single (uniform) depth RGB-D object image with different data scaling operations. In this work, the D1 distance of the proposed CVPR34K dataset (83 in.)

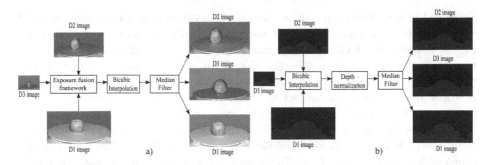

**Fig. 4.** Conversion of different distance images to uniform distance RGB-D images. a) Scale RGB image with unit depth, b) Scale depth image with unit depth

is considered as a reference distance location of an object. The data scaling color channels (RGB image) with unit depth consists of exposure fusion framework [19], bicubic interpolation [7] and median filtering; whereas data scaling for depth channel (disparity image) with unit depth includes bicubic interpolation, depth normalization, and median filtering. It is observed that RGB images captured from different distance locations have variation in illumination. To create a uniform distance RGB image, the algorithm must have an accurate contrast for each distance image. The exposure fusion framework [19] is an image enhancement algorithm which provides an accurate contrast enhancement images that are under-lighted or over-lighted.

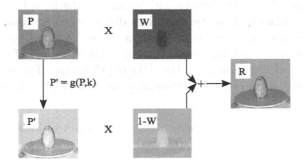

**Fig. 5.** Exposure fusion framework for RGB image enhancement algorithm

Figure 5 shows an exposure fusion framework for the RGB image enhancement to obtain an image well exposure. In this algorithm, an input image is fused with different exposure and mathematically it is represented as:

$$R = Q \circ P + (1 - Q) \circ g(P, k) \tag{1}$$

where $P$ is the input image, $Q$ is the weight map of the image, $g$ is the Brightness Transform Function and $k$ has given exposure ratio and $R$ is the final enhanced image. Although a depth image can withstand against color and light variation so it is not necessary to have contrast enhancement for depth image. Figure 4 shows that RGB-D object image acquired from different distance location from the camera have different size of an object in images which belong to the same class. The motivation behind the bicubic operation is to provide a uniform appearance of the object in the RGB-D image. The bicubic interpolation is used to resample the images to increase or decrease the image resolution. It resamples the resolution of D3 distance images and D2 distance images of the CVPR34K dataset to have the same resolution as that of the reference distance object images (i.e. D1). To increase or decrease image resolution with the smoother interpolated surface, bicubic interpolation is helpful. The bicubic interpolation uses a cubic convolution algorithm which determines the gray level value from the weighted average of the sixteen closest pixels to the specified input coordinates and allocates that value to the output coordinates, the first 4 one-dimension. The bicubic convolution interpolation kernel is:

$$W_{B.I} = \begin{cases} (a+2)\,|x|^3 - (a+3)\,|x|^2 + 1 & \text{for } |x| \leq 1 \\ a\,|x|^3 - 5a\,|x|^2 + 8a\,|x| - 4a & \text{for } 1 < |x| < 2 \\ 0 & \text{otherwise} \end{cases} \tag{2}$$

where $a$ is generally taken as $-0.5$ to $-0.75$

The median filtering operation is a statistical non-linear filter that is used to remove the noise and preserve the dominant edges of the RGB-D object images. The median filter helps in forming uniform distance RGB-D images. However, the depth image may have a different depth range depending on distance location from the camera. The depth image with minimum distance location from the camera has a maximum disparity, a medium distance has medium disparity and a maximum distance has a minimum disparity range. To provide a uniform depth range to all distance depth images, a depth normalization by a factor $N$ is done with respect to reference distance (i.e. D1) depth image. The parameter $N$ is computed for test image by using minimum distance depth image as reference distance:

$$N = \frac{Maximum\ depth\ value\ in\ reference\ image}{Maximum\ depth\ value\ in\ test\ image} \tag{3}$$

### 3.3 Feature Extraction and Classification

The normalized RGB-D images are fed as input to a multimodal convolutional neural network (MCNN). The MCNN architecture is used to learn the low level, mid-level and high-level features from the RGB-D images. The purpose of the support vector machine (SVM) algorithm is to find out a hyperplane in an N-dimensional space that distinctly classifies the feature points extracted from the fully-connected layer (FC5) of MCNN. Feature extraction and classification steps are discussed in the next section.

**Multi-modal CNN Architecture.** The three different CNN structures as shown in Fig. 6 are used to learn color, depth, and both color and depth features for object image recognition. MCNN consists of RGB and depth modalities with additional fully-connected layers. The concatenation layer used to join RGB and DEPTH CNN. The multimodal CNN architecture consists of four convolution layers, two max-pooling layers and two fully-connected layers in both modalities. The output of the two modalities is concatenated and is followed by four fully-connected layers. In each modality, input images are rescaled to $(80 \times 80)$. The first convolution layer has 96 kernels of size $(7 \times 7)$ with stride 2. For second to fourth convolution layers, 112, 128 and 128 kernels are used respectively. This layers have kernel of size $(3 \times 3)$ and stride of 1 is maintained.

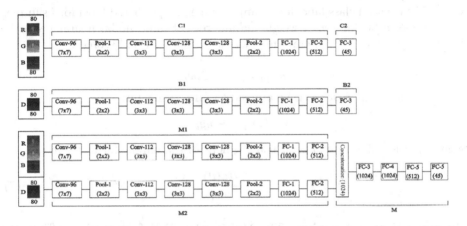

**Fig. 6.** Different type of CNN structures. (a) RGB CNN, (b) DEPTH CNN,(c) RGB-D CNN. *(Note: C1, C2, B1, B2, M, M1 and M2 are parameters of the network)*

There are two max-pooling layers followed by the first and fourth convolution layer. The two fully-connected layers used after convolution layers have the sizes of 1024 and 512, respectively. The last fully-connected layers of two modalities are concatenated to form a vector of size 1024. The concatenation layer combines the feature vector of both color and depth modalities.

This is followed by four fully-connected layers with 1024, 1024, 512 and 45 nodes, respectively. The nodes 45 in the last fully-connected layer indicate a number of classes to be learned. In the case of the depth estimation stage, 45 output nodes are replaced with three representing depth location for the CVPR34K dataset. The Rectified Linear Unit (ReLu) non-linearity function [11] is applied to the output of all convolution and fully-connected layers except for the last fully-connected layer which has softmax loss function. In the proposed method, Adadelta [20] is used as an optimizer to update the weights of the network. The similar architecture is used in depth estimation stage except for a number of nodes in the last fully-connected layer with reference to distance variation available in the dataset.

The RGB CNN and DEPTH CNN architectures are trained on color and depth images independently by scratch training. Pre-trained weights of RGB CNN and DEPTH CNN are used to initialize parameters of multimodal CNN before concatenation. The weights of the last four fully-connected layers are randomly initialized. While training multimodal CNN, the parameter of RGB CNN and DEPTH CNN are kept fixed and only the parameter of the last four fully-connected layers are updated. The algorithm calculate a separate loss for each class label per observation and sum the result. The cross-entropy loss function is to calculate the loss of multimodal CNN:

$$L(\theta) = -\sum_i Y_i \, log(\hat{Y}_i) \tag{4}$$

where $Y_i$ be actual class label for $i$ sample and $\hat{Y}_i$ be predicted label for $i$ sample.

Assume $w$ be the set of weight parameters of multimodal neural network. Let the parameter at $t^{th}$ iteration as $w_t$ the updating rule becomes:

$$w_{t+1} = w_t + \triangle w_t \tag{5}$$

The general approach can be applied to any parameter:

$$\triangle w_t = -\eta g_t \tag{6}$$

where $\eta$ = learning rate. The $g_t$ is a gradient of the parameter at $t^{th}$ iteration:

$$g_t = \frac{\partial L(\theta)}{\partial w_t} \tag{7}$$

**Support Vector Machine.** The Multimodal CNN framework is effectively learned to combine features from both RGB-D modalities. These extracted features have different characteristics of color and depth modality and shared information between both modalities. The SVM is used to find optimal hyperplane which has a large margin to perform distance invariant RGB-D object recognition. For real-world data, the extracted features are non-linear and have inseparable planes. To classify this features, SVM uses kernel function for transforming the input feature space to a higher-dimensional space. The proposed algorithm uses SVM along with radial basis function for distance invariant RGB-D object recognition. The hyper-parameters for SVM are selected as Penalty parameter of the error term at 1.0 and Tolerance for stopping criterion is at 0.001.

## 4    Experimental Results

The aim of the experiment is to evaluate the effectiveness of the DSMS system for RGB-D object recognition. RGB-D dataset [12] and the proposed CVPR34K dataset are used to evaluate the performance of the proposed system. Experiments are performed on a high-performance system with Intel Xenon E5-2695 v4 processor with 64 GB RAM and TITAN Xp GPU of 12GB RAM. The details of the datasets and experimental results are discussed in the following section:

## 4.1 Datasets and Experimental Parameter

**RGB-D Dataset.** The RGB-D object dataset [12] consists of a fixed distance RGB-D object image with 51 object classes. The RGB-D dataset consists of RGB-D images recorded by Kinect style 3D camera with 34,000 RGB-D object images for training and 6,900 images for testing.

**CVPR34K Dataset.** The CVPR34K RGB-D object dataset includes variation in distance of objects from the camera. It includes RGB-D object images of 45 object classes. The dataset has a total of 34,624 RGB-D images recorded by Panasonic HDC-SDT750 3D camera with three different distance locations from the camera. 10,275 images captured from minimum distance, 11,814 images captured from medium distance and 12,535 images are captured from maximum distance location with roughly 70 images per object. The CVPR34K dataset created for mixed distance and inter-distance invariant RGB-D object recognition. In the mixed distance, minimum, medium and maximum distance RGB-D object images are combined whereas, the randomly selected 23,198 images are kept for training and 11,426 images are used for testing. However, in inter-distance, minimum and maximum distance images (22,810 images) are used for training and medium distance images (11,814 images) are used for testing.

The primary step in proposed algorithm is to detect distance location of RGB-D object images by using multimodal CNN as mentioned in Depth Estimation Section. The input image is cropped based on a distance location from the camera. For distance invariant RGB-D object recognition, it is essential to convert different distance RGB-D object data into uniform distance RGB-D object data.

In proposed algorithm input image is cropped based on a distance location from the camera. The distance location of RGB-D object image is detected by using multimodal CNN as mentioned in Depth Estimation Section. For distance invariant RGB-D object recognition, it is essential to convert different distance RGB-D object data into uniform distance RGB-D object data. The Sect. 3 describes RGB-D image normalization to make a uniform distance RGB-D object data with the help of reference distance location. The exposure fusion framework is used as an accurate enhancement algorithm for under-lighted or over-lighted input RGB image. The RGB-D normalization stage consists of bicubic interpolation for rescaling the resolution of input RGB-D object image (D3 and D2) with reference RGB-D object image (D1). The median filter with a kernel size of $(5 \times 5)$ is applied to variation in distance RGB-D images for minimizing noise. The depth normalization by $N$ is applied to depth images using D1 as 44 and D3 as 19 maximum disparity value. Similarly, using D1 as 44 and D2 as 27 maximum disparity value, the algorithm produced $N$ as 2.333 for maximum distance images, and $N$ as 1.629 for medium distance images as expressed in Eqs. 3. The Adadelta optimizer is used to train the multimodal CNN. The batch size is kept to 128 and training is carried out for 300 iterations. To select parameters of the network, minimum loss iteration is considered and it is generally obtained within 30 iterations.

## 4.2    Result on RGB-D Dataset and CVPR34K RGB-D Dataset

The proposed DSMS system is applied to solve fixed distance, inter-distance and mixed distance RGB-D object recognition using the RGB-D object dataset and CVPR34K RGB-D dataset. Table 1 shows the comparison of object recognition accuracy of baseline methods and proposed DSMS on the fixed distance RGB-D dataset.

**Table 1.** Comparison between the baseline and DSMS method on RGB-D object dataset

| Method | RGB | Depth | RGB-D |
| --- | --- | --- | --- |
| HKDES [3] | $76 \pm 2.2$ | $75 \pm 2.6$ | $84 \pm 2.2$ |
| Kernel DES [4] | $74 \pm 1.9$ | $78 \pm 2.7$ | $86 \pm 2.1$ |
| RGB-D CNN with 4 channel [11] | $78 \pm 2.1$ | $81 \pm 1.4$ | $82 \pm 1.9$ |
| Multimodal CNN [18] | $80 \pm 1.6$ | $82 \pm 2.9$ | $86 \pm 3.1$ |
| Fus-CNN (jet) [6] | $84 \pm 2.7$ | $83 \pm 2.7$ | $91 \pm 1.4$ |
| Proposed DSMS method | $87 \pm 2.4$ | $86 \pm 1.8$ | $92 \pm 2.6$ |

Table 2 shows the performance of the DSMS method for mixed distance RGB-D object recognition on the CVPR34K dataset. Mixed distance has D1, D2, and D3 distance images, it provides different depth information during training and more generic features are extracted leads to improvement in accuracy.

**Table 2.** Comparison between the baseline and DSMS method for Mixed distance RGB-D object recognition on CVPR34K dataset

| Method | RGB | Depth | RGB-D |
| --- | --- | --- | --- |
| RGB-D CNN with 4 channel [11] | $88 \pm 1.7$ | $86 \pm 2.4$ | $90 \pm 0.9$ |
| Multimodal CNN [18] | $90 \pm 2.2$ | $88 \pm 2.3$ | $91 \pm 1.8$ |
| Fus-CNN (jet) [6] | $92 \pm 1.3$ | $91 \pm 2.1$ | $93 \pm 1.4$ |
| Proposed DSMS method | $95 \pm 2.8$ | $93 \pm 2.9$ | $96 \pm 2.6$ |

Table 3 shows the performance of the DSMS system for inter-distance RGB-D object recognition on the CVPR34K dataset. The inter-distance consists of minimum and maximum distance images as training and medium distance images as testing. Minimum and maximum distance images have a significant difference in depth range compared to medium distance. Hence, test accuracy depends on the learning of minimum and maximum distance objects which results in better performance compared to other existing methods.

**Table 3.** Comparison between the baseline and DSMS method for Inter distance RGB-D object recognition on CVPR34K dataset

| Method | RGB | Depth | RGB-D |
| --- | --- | --- | --- |
| RGB-D CNN with 4 channel [11] | 68 ± 1.4 | 33 ± 3.5 | 71 ± 2.2 |
| Multimodal CNN [18] | 70 ± 1.6 | 34 ± 2.6 | 72 ± 2.6 |
| Fus-CNN (jet) [6] | 71 ± 2.5 | 38 ± 2.8 | 73 ± 0.9 |
| Proposed DSMS method | 77 ± 1.2 | 42 ± 1.8 | 79 ± 2.1 |

## 5 Conclusion

In this work, the problem of object recognition in RGB-D images is handled. The CVPR34K RGB-D dataset is introduced to include distance variations in the RGB-D dataset. In the proposed dataset, three different distance locations are considered while capturing RGB-D object images. Depth Estimation, Scale data with Unit Depth and Multimodal Convolutional neural network with SVM (DSMS) system is presented to achieve distance invariant RGB-D object recognition. The depth estimation and feature extraction stages are performed by MCNN which includes two modules, namely RGB CNN and DEPTH CNN. The depth estimation stage can extend the model to predict many depth locations of RGB-D object images. The second stage includes RGB-D data normalization with reference to minimum distance RGB-D object image. The features are extracted by MCNN using normalized RGB-D data and the final output is predicted by SVM. The experimental results show that DSMS has improved performance compared to state-of-the-art methods on the RGB-D dataset. Also, it is observed that when the object distance is varied from the camera in the CVPR34K RGB-D object dataset, the performance of DSMS is quite satisfactory. In future work, multiple distance locations with multiple backgrounds will be considered while acquiring RGB-D object images for more robust and accurate distance and background invariant RGB-D object recognition.

## References

1. Abdel-Hakim, A., Farag, A.: CSIFT: a SIFT descriptor with color invariant characteristics. Comput. Vis. Pattern Recogn. **2**, 1978–1983 (2006)
2. Bay, H., Tuytelaars, T., Van Gool, L.: SURF: speeded up robust features. In: Leonardis, A., Bischof, H., Pinz, A. (eds.) ECCV 2006. LNCS, vol. 3951, pp. 404–417. Springer, Heidelberg (2006). https://doi.org/10.1007/11744023_32
3. Bo, L., Lai, K., Ren, X., Fox, D.: Object recognition with hierarchical kernel descriptors. In: CVPR (2011)
4. Bo, L., Ren, X., Fox, D.: Depth Kernel descriptors for object recognition. In: IEEE/RSJ International Conference on Intelligent Robots and Systems, pp. 821–826 (2011)
5. Chang, C., Lin, C.: LIBSVM a library for support vector machines. ACM Trans. Intell. Syst. Technol. (TIST) **2**, 1–39 (2011)

6. Eitel, A., Springenberg, J., Spinello, L., Riedmiller, M., Burgard, W.: Multimodal deep learning for robust RGB-D object recognition. In: IEEE/RSJ International Conference on Intelligent Robots and Systems (IROS), pp. 681–687 (2015)
7. Fadnavis, S.: Image interpolation techniques in digital image processing: an overview. Int. Eng. Res. Appl. **4**, 70–73 (2014). 2248-962270
8. Hsu, C., Chang, C., Lin, C.: A practical guide to support vector classification. BJU Int. **101**(1), 1396–400 (2010)
9. Jin, L., Gao, S., Li, Z., Tang, J.: Hand-crafted features or machine learnt features? Together they improve RGB-D object recognition. In: IEEE International Symposium on Multimedia, pp. 311–319 (2014)
10. Khan, W., Phaisangittisagul, E., Ali, L., Gansawat, D., Kumazawa, I.: Combining features for RGB-D object recognition. In: Electrical Engineering Congress (iEECON) International, pp. 1–5 (2017)
11. Krizhevsky, A., Sulskever, I., Hinton, G.E.: ImageNet classification with deep convolutional neural networks. In: Advances in Neural Information and Processing Systems (NIPS), vol. 60, no. 6, pp. 84–90 (2012)
12. Lai, K., Bo, L., Ren, X., Fox, D.: A large-scale hierarchical multi-view RGB-D object dataset. In: IEEE International Conference on Robotics and Automation, pp. 1817–1824 (2011)
13. Lowe, D.: Distinctive image features from scale-invariant keypoints. Int. J. Comput. Vis. **60**, 91–110 (2004). https://doi.org/10.1023/B:VISI.0000029664.99615.94
14. Pierre, F., Aujol, J.F., Bugeau, A., Steidl, G., Ta, V.T.: Variational contrast enhancement of RGB images (2015)
15. Rahman, M., Tan, Y., Xue, J., Lu, K.: RGB-D object recognition with multimodal deep convolutional neural networks. In: IEEE International Conference on Multimedia and Expo (ICME), pp. 991–996 (2017)
16. Socher, R., Huval, B., Bhat, B., Manning, C., Ng, A.: Convolutional-recursive deep learning for 3D object classification. In: International Conference on Neural Information Processing Systems, vol. 1, pp. 656–664 (2012)
17. Sun, S., Zhao, X., Xu, J., Tan, M.: RGB-D object recognition based on RGBD-PCANet learning. In: IEEE International Conference on Mechatronics and Automation (ICMA), pp. 1075–1080 (2017)
18. Wang, A., Lu, J., Cai, J., Cham, T., Wang, G.: Large-margin multimodal deep learning for RGB-D object recognition. IEEE Trans. Multimed. **17**(11), 1887–1898 (2015)
19. Ying, Z., Li, G., Ren, Y., Wang, R., Wang, W.: A new image contrast enhancement algorithm using exposure fusion framework. In: Felsberg, M., Heyden, A., Krüger, N. (eds.) CAIP 2017. LNCS, vol. 10425, pp. 36–46. Springer, Cham (2017). https://doi.org/10.1007/978-3-319-64698-5_4
20. Zeiler, M.: ADADELTA: An Adaptive Learning Rate Method. arXiv:1212.5701v1 [cs.LG] (2012)
21. Zia, S., Yüksel, B., Yüret, D., Yemez, Y.: RGB-D object recognition using deep convolutional neural networks. In: IEEE International Conference on Computer Vision Workshops (ICCVW), pp. 887–894 (2018)
22. Patekar, R., Nandedkar, A.: CVPR34K RGB-D Object dataset. https://drive.google.com/file/d/1vOiBPkwoLecj0hHQMP8s1kJHQsZXQEuT/view?usp=sharing

# Single Look SAR Image Segmentation Using Local Entropy, Median Low-Pass Filter and Fuzzy Inference System

R. Lalchhanhima[1,2(✉)], Debdatta Kandar[2], and R. Chawngsangpuii[1]

[1] Mizoram University, Mizoram, India
chhana.mizo@gmail.com
[2] North Eastern Hill University, Shillong, India

**Abstract.** Synthetic Aperture Radar (SAR) image segmentation based on intensity information alone poses severe inaccuracy due to the presence of speckle noise. The multiplicative speckle noise produces salt and pepper noise effect in the end product of the image and thereby making it difficult to segment the images efficiently. Moreover, due to the same reason, by applying the classical methods which are based on thresholding and clustering, satisfactory results are often not achieved. Since the SAR images as they are in their original state cause a severe obstacle in segmentation, here it is proposed to first extract the roughness information feature in terms of local entropy and median filtered image; and then feed to the fuzzy inference system. The fuzzy inference system then takes inputs from two different features and decide the segmentation criteria. The end result from the Fuzzy classifier is then thresholded using Otsu's method to get the final segmented image. The proposed method simplifies the segmentation by generalizing the possible spatial features to be extracted and incorporated in the segmentation process while resulting to efficient and effective results.

**Keywords:** Image segmentation · Local entropy · Fuzzy inference system · Speckle noise · SAR image · Medium low-pass filter

## 1 Introduction

Digital Image Processing (DIP) is one of the hot topic of discussion in the computing field. It is being applied in different areas such as photography, remote sensing and various computer vision applications [1–4]. Though it is desired to have a perfect image for processing, images are usually contaminated with imperfection or noise that comes from different sources. Optical instruments suffer from chromatic aberrations and atmospheric conditions play a degradable role in image quality. Conditions like difference of reflectivity from one surface to another, lighting conditions, Sensor sensitivity, sensor density, aperture, shutter speed; they all affect the image quality [5–7]. So, when image is captured, no matter where it is the application area, it usually requires preprocessing. The

© Springer Nature Singapore Pte Ltd. 2020
A. Bhattacharjee et al. (Eds.): MIND 2020, CCIS 1240, pp. 149–159, 2020.
https://doi.org/10.1007/978-981-15-6315-7_12

preprocessing task is to make the image more presentable to the actual usage of the image. In case of photography, the task is to make the image more presentable to the human eye. In the X-ray, CT scan images, the task is to highlight the interest areas in the image and so on.

Synthetic Aperture Radar (SAR) imaging is used for land surface imaging and are based on active radar, i.e., self-illuminating and hence they are not affected by weather conditions but are severely affected by speckle noise that degrades the image quality [8]. So, speckle noise processing is one of the primary task in SAR images [9]. Since the existing thresholding methods works well only when the pixel intensity of the object is substantially different from the background pixels, thresholding based segmentation techniques can not be directly applied for SAR image segmentation.

There are different types of image segmentation methods and can be broadly classified into - thresholding, region based, edge based, clustering and active contours [10]. The simple thresholding based segmentation technique works by determining the threshold value and the result is a two class or binary segmentation. Region based segmentation starts with seed pixels and conditionally expands to the neighboring pixel until some given criteria is met. Edge based segmentation technique works by determining gradient and thereby finding the edges of regions that is used for segmentation into different regions. The model based segmentation tries to determine incorporate knowledge from the training data and then formulate mathematical formula by approximating the known data.

Though there are a number of existing image segmentation methods available, the recent and most effective ones mainly rely on the statistical pro distribution of image intensity and In this work, attempt is made to extract roughness feature of the SAR image and the extracted feature forms one of the feature for classification purpose. Another feature is obtained by filtering out the noises by applying low-pass median filter. The specific use of median filter instead of mean filter is that it exhibit more robust property towards noisy data [11–13]. These two derived features are then fed to a fuzzy inference system wherein classification is done based on the derived feature and then give result. The result obtained from the fuzzy inference system is then subject to Otsu's thresholding method [14] to give the final result.

The rest of the paper is organized as follows: the following section discusses about the related works done in regard to image segmentation. The third section deals with potential features that could be extracted from a SAR image and fuzzy based classification using different feature sets. The results and findings are discussed in the subsequent section.

## 2    Related Works

Image segmentation has been proposed for several types of SAR images. Most recent publications are based mainly on level-set methods [15–17], active contour methods [18–21], while there are other models such as based on key pixels

[22], clustering methods [23–26], fuzzy based classifiers [27–29] etc. Most of the proposed models work mainly on the statistical distribution of SAR image pixels and they usually require supervised modelling for segmentation. The main drawbacks of the aforementioned segmentation methods are the requirement of several number of SAR image data for training. There are also proposed segmentation methods that are based on the spatial properties of SAR image data in which derived features are extracted such as entropy, average brightness and roughness information [9, 30–33].

## 2.1 Feature Extraction

Feature extraction is the process of selection of dimensionally reduced but attain necessary properties for desired segmentation criteria. As was mentioned earlier, the actual pixel values, when used for segmentation criteria results to undesired segmentation because they do not attain the potential and probable quality for segmentation [34, 35]. Therefore it is hereby proposed to extract features which are Roughness Feature and the other one is feature extracted from average intensity information. This roughness feature could be roughness information, variance, entropy and other statistical methods that can generate texture and roughness criteria. In this work, local entropy is determined and is used as a feature to find two different regions in the SAR image. Out of the recent publications, Rodrigues et al. uses roughness information of SAR data modelled by $G_I^0$ and $G_A^0$ for segmentation [9] and Nobre et al. also use Renyi's Entropy for segmentation purpose [30]. These features are actually the superpixels and are determined from the neighbouring pixels and contain feature value that corresponds to the related area. Therefore it is very much apprehended that these features could be the key basis on which segmentation be done.

Apart from the features based on the roughness, there are a number of smoothing techniques available. The simplest are mean filters, median filters and mode filters. There are also Gaussian [36], Butterworth [37,38] low pass filters as well. Since the image we are going to consider is a SAR image that is contaminated by speckle noise and applying these low-pass filters reduce the effect of speckle noise to a large extent. The filters work mainly like the following:

$$O(r,c) = \sum_{i=-k}^{k} I(r+i, c+j) \times M(i,j) \qquad (1)$$

Where

$O(r,c)$ = Output in the $r^{th}$ row and $c^{th}$ column
$I$ = Input image in the form of 2-D matrix
$M$ = Filtering mask matrix having size $2 * k$

The masks may be chosen with a window of $3 \times 3$, $5 \times 5$ or higher dimension as we wish. Smaller window removes small sharp edges and spots whereas larger window removes larger edges or spots. And in using smaller windows, the pixel under consideration is affected by less number of pixels around them and when using larger window, farther pixels play roles in the pixel under consideration. We also have an option of using Butterworth filter, Gaussian filter or Mean filter.

## 2.2  Fuzzy Classification

Fuzzy Logic is one of the most useful logic nowadays. We have been witnessing the real-time usage of Fuzzy Logic in our everyday life and also the performance of devices that are running on Fuzzy Logic [43]. It's nature of tolerance towards imprecision and the real-world friendly nature of its operation further added to its expansion. Therefore, taking into account the nature of SAR image segmentation, Fuzzy Logic could play a very important role [29].

Instead of using boolean values in logical calculation, fuzzy logic uses fuzzy values, i.e., some range of numbers. This allows classification of cold and hot, which is somewhat odd in the case of boolean logic [44]. So, in fuzzy logic, it is possible to describe the belongingness of some variable to a class using membership functions. For instance, water may be hot or cold, but it may not be precise to say $50\,°C$ is the boundary between hot and cold. So, we may say that the coldness at $0\,°C$ is at maximum and coldness at $100\,°C$ is minimum. In between there could be linear interpolation. Likewise, the hotness of water at $0\,°C$ is zero, whereas the hotness of water at $100\,°C$ is maximum, or definitely hot.

Fuzzy classification is based on the Fuzzy Logic in the sense that the classification will not be based on boolean values, i.e., 0's and 1's alone, but on the fuzzy nature of the subjects. Here, we propose using one of soft-computing method - Fuzzy Logic. The Fuzzy Inference System (FIS) is designed in such a way to take in multiple parameters, process and produce the result in terms of belongingness to different classes. The main aim is to classify them into different classes or clusters based on the roughness feature value and the average brightness value, which is synonymous to segmentation based on two different intensity levels. The difference being usage of roughness parameter and average intensity in place of intensity level. But since the roughness feature alone is not giving out good result, it is also included the intensity level information as a support. However, using the raw intensity level in the image is again resulting to unsatisfactory result, the image is first subjected to smoothening and then use each of the output pixel values as intensity feature.

Otsu's thresholding method works by finding the optimal threshold value so that the two different classes (inter-class) have the largest variance while the pixels belonging to the same class, the variance is minimised [14]. So, it is an optimal threshold value.

## 3  Methodology

The proposed methodology is a combination of feature extraction and Fuzzy classification. In the feature extraction part, we extract the roughness feature and average brightness features. The roughness feature extracted is in the form of simple local entropy of the image. The local entropy highlighted the randomness in the pixel location and the brightness feature takes the average intensity around the pixel. Those two features are fed into Fuzzy Inference System for classification. The output of the FIS is then de-fuzzified in order to get the final segmented image.

### 3.1  Roughness Feature Extraction Using Local Entropy

Entropy is the measures of impurity, disorder or uncertainty in a bunch of dataset [31]. In a situation where an image is to be segmented but contaminated by noise severely, segmentation may not be easy. So, we proposed to determine the different regions in an image may be done on the basis of randomness. In a SAR image, there could be different types of reflection properties in which different types of region provide different pattern of reflections [32,39–41]. For instance, water bodies reflect less amount of energy than forest regions and there would normally be less unpredictability in the case of water than in forest regions. Using this difference, we could determine the randomness of a region and use this information to segment the regions.

The local entropy can be determined using the following formula [42]:

$$Entropy = -\sum p(X) \log_2 p(X) \tag{2}$$

Where

$p(x)$ is the probability of an event $x$ happening
$x$ is the random variable.

Whereas it is also possible to use other statistical model to calculate texture and randomness, this particular feature provides more differentiation of the model under consideration, i.e., to segment forest cover area and water body.

Since the end product of SAR image is basically a bitmap grayscale image contaminated by speckle noise that appears in the form of salt and pepper effect. So, the correlation between the actual pixel value and the actual targeted segment is very low. Therefore, it is required to have another feature that is not only the pixel intensity value, but possess the possibility that it differentiates on that basis. So, it is proposed here to obtain the roughness feature for each of the pixels in the image.

### 3.2  Low-Pass Smoothing Filter

The median low-pass filters exhibit more robustness towards noisy data. Therefore, we chose median filter over other filters as SAR image is severely contaminated by speckle noise. This median filtered image is obtained through the use of window size $3 \times 3$ as the image is small enough and the pixel graininess is just found to be sufficient. The median filter picked the middle value amongst the 9 neighbouring pixel values. So, this median filter is immune to outlier data points which are present in noisy data.

### 3.3   Fuzzy Inference System

In order to make classification based on the previously extracted features, FIS is designed with 2 inputs and 1 output. Inputs are named entropy and intensity. Each of the inputs are having 2 membership functions each are named as low and high. The range is normalised in the range [0–255] as per the grayscale image standard. The trimf type membership functions are defined with parameters [0 0 255] and [0 255 255] for low and high respectively. The output is designed with 4 nos of trimf type membership functions having parameters [0 0 130], [30 95 220], [15 140 270] and [128 255 357] respectively.

The input variables take input from each of the entropy and median filtered image and linked with the output by means of 4 fuzzy rules. The output of the fuzzy system is again fuzzy values and are then thresholded using Otsu's method.

## 4   Experimental Results

For testing the performance of segmentation, a single look SAR HH polarimetric image is used [45] which is in Fig. 1. The image is HH polarimetry and is having the size 400 × 400. The ground truth in Fig. 3 (a) is derived from the google earth image of the same location provided in [45]. The result of segmentation using k-means clustering [46] and Otsu's thresholding [14] methods are given in Fig. 2 (a) and (b) respectively.

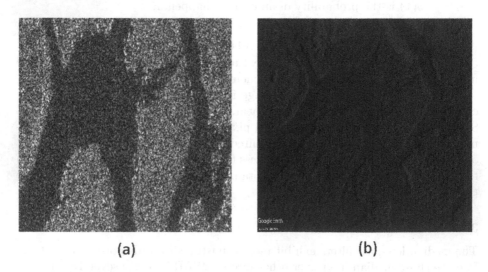

(a)                                        (b)

**Fig. 1.** (a) Source image, (b) Corresponding google image

The methods used for comparison of performance are a median regularized level set for hierarchical segmentation of SAR images proposed by Braga et al.

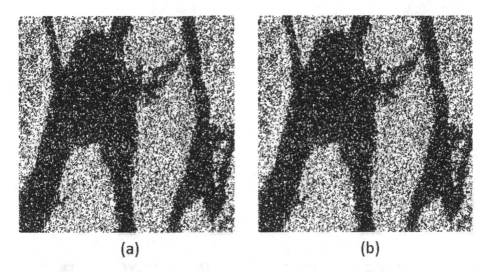

**Fig. 2.** Result of SAR image segmentation using classical methods (a) Using k-means clustering, (b) Using Otsu thresholding

[10], SAR Image Segmentation Using the Roughness Information proposed by Rodrigues et al. [9] and SAR image segmentation with Renyi's entropy proposed by Nobre et al. [30].

The output of the proposed algorithm is given in Fig. 4 in which Fig. 4 (a) is the roughness feature output and 4 (b) is the median filtered image output. The final output is given in 4 (c).

The performance of each of the algorithms are given in the Table 1.

**Table 1.** Performance evaluation

| Method | TP+TN | FP+FN | Accuracy percent |
|---|---|---|---|
| k-means | 102452 | 57548 | 64.03 |
| Otsu | 120505 | 39495 | 75.32 |
| Braga et al. [10] | 154501 | 5499 | 96.56 |
| Rodrigues et al. [9] | 143476 | 16524 | 89.67 |
| Nobre et al. [30] | 149413 | 10587 | 93.38 |
| Proposed method | 158801 | 1199 | 99.25 |

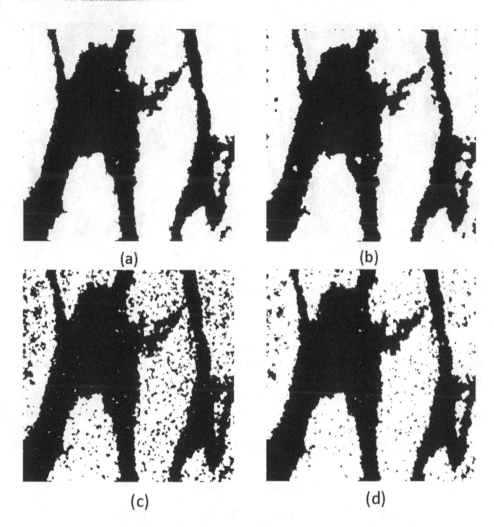

**Fig. 3.** (a) Ground truth image derived from Fig. 1 (b)–(d) Output of algorithms provided by [9,10,30]

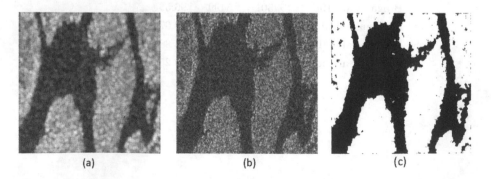

**Fig. 4.** (a) Normalised output of local entropy, (b) Median filtered image, (c) Final output

# 5  Conclusion

After running the experiments and from the results in Table 1, the proposed simple algorithm performs at par or even better than the existing algorithms proposed recently. With simple to understand concepts and the use of Fuzzy Logic, the algorithm can be tuned and can be used for incorporation of different other algorithms to give neutral output.

The experiments indicate that the concept of roughness information in the SAR image can be used for supervised classification and segmentation of SAR images subject to extraction of information and training using different SAR data. So, this feature can be useful even when intensity information could not suffice for segmentation purpose.

# References

1  Taneja, A., Ranjan, P., Ujjlayan, A.: A performance study of image segmentation techniques. In: 2015 4th International Conference on Reliability, Infocom Technologies and Optimization (ICRITO) (Trends and Future Directions), pp. 1–6. IEEE (2015)

2. Pal, N.R., Pal, S.K.: A review on image segmentation techniques. Pattern Recogn. **26**(9), 1277–1294 (1993)

3. Dey, V., Zhang, Y., Zhong, M.: A review on image segmentation techniques with remote sensing perspective (2010). na

4. Jiao M.-L.: A review on latest interferometric synthetic aperture radar researches. In: 2009 WRI World Congress on Software Engineering (2009)

5. Strangman, G., Franceschini, M.A., Boas, D.A.: Factors affecting the accuracy of near-infrared spectroscopy concentration calculations for focal changes in oxygenation parameters. Neuroimage **18**(4), 865–879 (2003)

6. Morgan, S.P., Khong, M.P., Somekh, M.G.: Effects of polarization state and scatterer concentration on optical imaging through scattering media. Appl. Opt. **36**(7), 1560–1565 (1997)

7. Hoh, S.T., et al.: Factors affecting image acquisition during scanning laser polarimetry. Ophthalmic Surg. Lasers Imaging Retina **29**(7), 545–551 (1998)

8. Aggarwal, S.: Satellite Remote Sensing and GIS Applications in Agricultural Meteorology. World Meteorological Organisation, Switzerland (2004)

9. Rodrigues, F.A.A., Neto, J.F.S.R., Marques, R.C.P., de Medeiros, F.N.S., Nobre, J.S.: SAR image segmentation using the roughness information. IEEE Geosci. Remote Sens. Lett. **13**(2), 132–136 (2016)

10. Braga, A.M., Marques, R.C.P., Rodrigues, F.A.A., Medeiros, F.N.S.: A median regularized level set for hierarchical segmentation of SAR images. IEEE Geosci. Remote Sens. Lett. **14**(7), 1171–1175 (2017)

11. Sun, T., Neuvo, Y.: Detail-preserving median based filters in image processing. Pattern Recogn. Lett. **15**(4), 341–347 (1994)

12. Wang, Z., Zhang, D.: Progressive switching median filter for the removal of impulse noise from highly corrupted images. IEEE Trans. Circuits Syst. II: Analog Digit. Sig. Process. **46**(1), 78–80 (1999)

13. Toh, K.K.V., Isa, N.A.M.: Noise adaptive fuzzy switching median filter for salt-and-pepper noise reduction. IEEE Sig. Process. Lett. **17**(3), 281–284 (2009)

14. Otsu, N.: A threshold selection method from gray-level histograms. IEEE Trans. Syst. Man Cybern. **9**(1), 62–66 (1979)
15. Yongfei, W., He, C., Liu, Y., Moting, S.: A backscattering-suppression-based variational level-set method for segmentation of sar oil slick images. IEEE J. Sel. Top. Appl. Earth Obs. Remote Sens. **10**(12), 5485–5494 (2017)
16. Li, C., Huang, R., Ding, Z., Gatenby, J.C., Metaxas, D.N., Gore, J.C.: A level set method for image segmentation in the presence of intensity inhomogeneities with application to MRI. IEEE Trans. Image Process. **20**(7), 2007–2016 (2011)
17. Lin, S., Wen, X., Xu, H., Yuan, L., Meng, Q.: A precise and stable segmentation algorithm of SAR images based on random weighting method and modified level set. IEEE Access **7**, 8039–8047 (2018)
18. Song, H., Huang, B., Zhang, K.: A globally statistical active contour model for segmentation of oil slick in SAR imagery. IEEE J. Sel. Top. Appl. Earth Obs. Remote Sens. **6**(6), 2402–2409 (2013)
19. Han, B., Yiquan, W., Basu, A.: Adaptive active contour model based on weighted RBPF for SAR image segmentation. IEEE Access **7**, 54522–54532 (2019)
20. Meng, Q., Wen, X., Yuan, L., Xu, H.: Factorization-based active contour for waterland SAR image segmentation via the fusion of features. IEEE Access **7**, 40347–40358 (2019)
21. Garrido, L., Guerrieri, M., Igual, L.: Image segmentation with cage active contours. IEEE Trans. Image Process. **24**(12), 5557–5566 (2015)
22. Shang, R., Yuan, Y., Jiao, L., Hou, B., Esfahani, A.M.G., Stolkin, R.: A fast algorithm for SAR image segmentation based on key pixels. IEEE J. Sel. Top. Appl. Earth Obs. Remote Sens. **10**(12), 5657–5673 (2017)
23. Xiang, D., Tang, T., Hu, C., Li, Y., Yi, S.: A Kernel clustering algorithm with fuzzy factor: application to SAR image segmentation. IEEE Geosci. Remote Sens. Lett. **11**(7), 1290–1294 (2014)
24. Shang, R., et al.: A spatial fuzzy clustering algorithm with Kernel metric based on immune clone for SAR image segmentation. IEEE J. Sel. Top. Appl. Earth Obs. Remote Sens. **9**(4), 1640–1652 (2016)
25. Zhang, W., Liu, F., Jiao, L., Hou, B., Wang, S., Shang, R.: SAR image despeckling using edge detection and feature clustering in bandelet domain. IEEE Geosci. Remote Sens. Lett. **7**(1), 131–135 (2010)
26. Seljuq, U.: Synthetic aperture radar (SAR) image segmentation by fuzzy c-means clustering technique with thresholding for iceberg images. Comput. Ecol. Softw. **4**(2), 129 (2014)
27. Wan, L., Zhang, T., Xiang, Y., You, H.: A robust fuzzy c-means algorithm based on Bayesian nonlocal spatial information for SAR image segmentation. IEEE J. Sel. Top. Appl. Earth Obs. Remote Sens. **11**(3), 896–906 (2018)
28. Guo, Y., Jiao, L., Wang, S., Wang, S., Liu, F., Hua, W.: Fuzzy superpixels for polarimetric SAR images classification. IEEE Trans. Fuzzy Syst. **26**(5), 2846–2860 (2018)
29. Javed, U., Riaz, M.M., Ghafoor, A., Cheema, T.A.: SAR image segmentation based on active contours with fuzzy logic. IEEE Trans. Aerosp. Electron. Syst. **52**(1), 181–188 (2016)
30. Nobre, R.H., Rodrigues, F.A.A., Marques, R.C.P., Nobre, J.S., Neto, J.F.S.R., Medeiros, F.N.: SAR image segmentation with Renyi's entropy. IEEE Sig. Process. Lett. **23**(11), 1551–1555 (2016)
31. Wu, Y., Zhou, Y., Saveriades, G., Agaian, S., Noonan, J.P., Natarajan, P.: Local Shannon entropy measure with statistical tests for image randomness. Inf. Sci. **222**, 323–342 (2013)

32. Kekre, H.B., Gharge, S., Sarode, T.K.: SAR image segmentation using vector quantization technique on entropy images. arXiv preprint arXiv:1004.1789 (2010)

33. Wang, W., Xiang, D., Ban, Y., Zhang, J., Wan, J.: Superpixel segmentation of polarimetric SAR images based on integrated distance measure and entropy rate method. IEEE J. Sel. Top. Appl. Earth Obs. Remote Sens. **10**(9), 4045–4058 (2017)

34. Lang, F., Yang, J., Li, D., Zhao, L., Shi, L.: Polarimetric SAR image segmentation using statistical region merging. IEEE Geosci. Remote Sens. Lett. **11**(2), 509–513 (2014)

35. Haker, S., Sapiro, G., Tannenbaum, A.: Knowledge-based segmentation of SAR data with learned priors. IEEE Trans. Image Process. **9**(2), 299–301 (2000)

36. Deng, G., Cahill, L.W.: An adaptive Gaussian filter for noise reduction and edge detection. In: 1993 IEEE Conference Record Nuclear Science Symposium and Medical Imaging Conference, pp. 1615–1619. IEEE (1993)

37. Butterworth, C.: Filter approximation theory. Engineer **7**, 536–541 (1930)

38. Roberts, J., Roberts, T.D.: Use of the Butterworth low-pass filter for oceanographic data. J. Geophys. Res.: Oceans **83**(C11), 5510–5514 (1978)

39. Zhao, W., Wang, F., Zhang, Q., Li, M., Lian, X., Wu, Y.: Unsupervised SAR image segmentation based on conditional triplet Markov fields. IEEE Geosci. Remote Sens. Lett. **11**(7), 1185–1189 (2014)

40. Zhang, P., Li, M., Yan, W., Liu, G., Chen, H., Jia, L.: Unsupervised sar image segmentation using a hierarchical tmf model. IEEE Geosci. Remote Sens. Lett. **10**(5), 971–975 (2013)

41. Hu, L., Xing, X.: SAR segmentation and recognition based SCM. In: 2013 IEEE International Conference on Green Computing and Communications and IEEE Internet of Things and IEEE Cyber, Physical and Social Computing, pp. 1533–1537. IEEE (2013)

42. Kannappan, P.: On Shannon's entropy, directed divergence and inaccuracy. Probab. Theory Relat. Fields **22**(2), 95–100 (1972)

43. Lee, C.-C.: Fuzzy logic in control systems: fuzzy logic controller. II. IEEE Trans. Syst. Man Cybern. **20**(2), 419–435 (1990)

44. Yager, R.R., Zadeh, L.A.: An Introduction to Fuzzy Logic Applications in intelligent Systems, vol. 165. Springer, New York (2012)

45. Nobre, R. H., et al.: GRSS SAR/PolSAR Database (2017)

46. MacQueen, J., et al.: Some methods for classification and analysis of multivariate observations. In: Proceedings of the Fifth Berkeley Symposium on Mathematical Statistics and Probability, Oakland, CA, USA, vol. 1, pp. 281–297 (1967)

# An Edge Detection and Sliding Window Based Approach to Improve Object Localization in YOLOv3

Shaji Thorn Blue and M. Brindha$^{(\boxtimes)}$

Department of Computer Science and Engineering, National Institute of Technology, Tiruchirappalli, Tiruchirappalli, Tamil Nadu, India
shajithornblue@gmail.com, brindham@nitt.edu

**Abstract.** Object detection is considered as a challenging field in computer vision. Once an object has been detected, the next challenge is object localization where a rectangular boundary box is drawn around the location of detected object. The proposed framework addresses the problem of object localization by improving its precision. You only look once or YOLOv3 is one of the well-known object detection algorithm with its state-of-the-art object detection and real time capabilities. Because of this reason, the proposed scheme uses YOLOv3 as the base algorithm. In this work, COCO dataset is used to detect an object, and to improve the precision of boundary box this work make use of edge detection, thresholding and morphological operation. Also, redundant edge removal algorithm is proposed to remove redundant edges and boundary box construction algorithm draws rectangular boundary box around detected object. When compared with YOLOv3, the proposed model produces significantly better results when boundary boxes around detected object is concern.

**Keywords:** YOLOv3 · Object detection · Object localization · Boundary box

## 1 Introduction

Humans are considered as one of the most advance intelligence that exists on planet earth. The main contributor to this intelligence is the human brain. From the start, many studies have taken place to understand how the human brain work and there have been many attempts to mimic the same. With the discovery of computers, it has become evident how powerful the human brain is. When it comes to very basic tasks like distinguishing between cat and dog, our brain does it in a fraction of seconds while it has taken multiple decades of development in the field of computer science to achieve the same. Even with so much advancement, when accuracy and object localization are concerned, computers still fall behind the capabilities of the human brain.

The field of computer vision focuses on giving the ability to machines so that they can see and extract meaningful information out of it. Nowadays, object detection and localization have emerged as a popular field in computer vision. Object detection deals with finding the objects that are present in an image. Due to the introduction of the deep neural network, machines are now able to detect an object with very high accuracy. The

© Springer Nature Singapore Pte Ltd. 2020
A. Bhattacharjee et al. (Eds.): MIND 2020, CCIS 1240, pp. 160–174, 2020.
https://doi.org/10.1007/978-981-15-6315-7_13

history of the neural network can be found even in 1940s [1], where inspiration has been taken from the human brain to solve the learning problems. With the introduction of algorithms like back-propagation, the neural network becomes popular in 1980s and 1990s. Due to insufficient training data and computational resources, the neural network becomes unpopular in the early 2000s.

In recent years, due to the advancement that has been done in the area of computer vision, a sudden boom has been observed in the usage of object detection in industrial applications. These advancements have been made possible due to the increase in the popularity of deep learning in 2006. The factors that are responsible for this popularity are large-scale training datasets with proper annotation and development of GPU systems with high-performance parallel computing. Till now many advanced algorithms have been proposed that tackle the problem of object detection.

Object localization is the second challenge that needs to be solved after object detection. Object localization deals with precisely locating the detected object. With recent object detection tasks like self-driving cars, Unarmed Ariel Vehicles or UAVs that are being used in military operations, locating a ship using satellite data, etc., precision plays an important role. For example, every millimeter of the precision matter when challenges like pedestrian detection [2] or mapping the path for a self-driving car is concerned. Many hardware sensors have been used in self-driving cars and UAVs to achieve the same. Software solutions can help in solving these problems and help industries to make more cost-efficient technologies. This work focuses on the problems of object localization in the YOLOv3 [21] algorithm.

## 2  Background and Related Work

Object detection has always been considered as a challenging task in the field of computer science. Traditionally, the object detection method relies on some hand-picked features of an object with very little scope of trainable architecture. To detect an object, scanning the entire image using a multi-scale sliding window seems to be a natural choice. However, this method was computationally expensive with too many redundant windows. Then some feature extraction techniques have been introduced where some visual features have been extracted. Some of the features extraction techniques are SIFT [3], Haar-like [4], HOG [5]. Also, due to different scenarios like different lighting condition, different backgrounds, diversity in appearances, the task of manually picking up features become difficult.

With recent improvements in the deep neural network and accessibility of large-scale datasets with a proper annotation such as ImageNet [6], this task has been shifted to trainable architecture. Here, two types of framework have been introduced. The first one follows the traditional object detection approach i.e. at first, a regional proposal has been generated and then each region is classified into a different category. However, in the second approach, object detection has been seen as a regression or classification problem. The work that has uses region proposal-based method are R-CNN [7], Fast R-CNN [8], Faster R-CNN [9], R-FCN [10], FPN [11] and Mask R-CNN [12]. The work that uses regression-based models are Multibox [13], G-CNN [14], AttentionNet [15], YOLO [16], YOLOv2 [17], SSD [18], DSSD [19], DSOD [20], YOLOv3 [21].

R-CNN [7] was introduced by Ross Girshick in 2014. R-CNN [7] uses selective search [22] and generates about 2k region for each image. Then each region is cropped into a fixed resolution which has been passed through the CNN module to extract features. SVM [23] is used to score these region proposals and non-max suppression is used to produce final bounding boxes at desire object location. R-CNN [7] worked well when it comes to object detection techniques but training turned out to be expensive in terms of space and time. Also, this algorithm suffers from inaccurate localization of the object. Girshick then introduces Fast R-CNN [8] where efficiency and accuracy both are improved. With the development of Region Proposal Network or RPN, Faster R-CNN [9] has been introduced. Faster R-CNN [9] was able to achieve a frame rate of 5 FPS on GPU. However, even though Faster R-CNN [7] is performing quite well, none of the above-mentioned algorithms can be used for real-time applications.

In 2016, YOLO [16] is introduced, which is proposed by Redmon. YOLO [16] divides the image into $S \times S$ grid and each grid predicts the object that is in the center of the grid. Apart from that, these grids also help in finding bounding boxes with their corresponding confidence score. YOLO [16] was able to achieve a speed up to 45 FPS in real-time and a Fast YOLO i.e. a simplified version of YOLO [16] is able to achieve a speed up to 155 FPS. Later in 2016, YOLOv2 [17] was introduced which bring several changes like anchor boxes, multi-scale training and dimension clustering. A further improvement has been done in YOLO [14] series with the introduction of YOLOv3 [21], where Features Pyramid Network (FPN) has been added to detect small objects in an image with several added features. With the introduction of the YOLO [16] series, the potential of object detection in the real-time applications has been unlocked with state-of-the-art object detection capabilities.

In 2019, first work [24] has been done to improve the boundary box of YOLOv3 [21]. It adds a new layer of edge detection to find the edges of the object and draw boundary boxes according to their edges while maintaining the real-time capabilities of YOLOv3 [21]. However, this work fails to detect sharp object that are present in the image and when there are too much noise and redundant details. The proposed work focuses on solving these problems using redundant edge removal algorithm with added optimization that will be suitable in all conditions.

The motivation behind this work comes from the recent advancement in computer vision and real-time usage of object detection. In some of the recent works [25–30], YOLOv3 [21] has been extensively used to solve the problem. Be it in the field of medical science where cell counting has been considered as a most challenging task or detecting vehicles using aerial infrared images which can be useful for military operations. In all of these cases, precision plays an important role and the proposed framework pays attention to improve the accuracy of rectangular boundary boxes around the detected objects.

The rest of the work is structured as follows: Proposed framework is discussed in Sect. 3. Section 4 shows intermediate steps and discusses the result that has been obtained in different scenarios. Finally, Sect. 5 concludes this work.

## 3  Proposed Work

To improve the accuracy of the boundary box, a new structure has been introduced. The proposed work has been divided into two stages. In the first stage, the proposed methodology starts with an image and passes it through YOLOv3 [21] algorithm. YOLOv3 [21] algorithm detects the class of objects present in an image and draws a boundary box according to the position of objects. Then, to improve the accuracy of the boundary box constructed by YOLOv3 [21] algorithm, the resulting image is pre-processed first and then passed through the proposed framework that consist of image pre-processing, redundant edge removal algorithm and boundary box construction algorithm. The final image contains objects with an accurate boundary box much closer to the ground truth when compared with YOLOv3 [21] algorithm. A high-level diagram of this work is shown in Fig. 1.

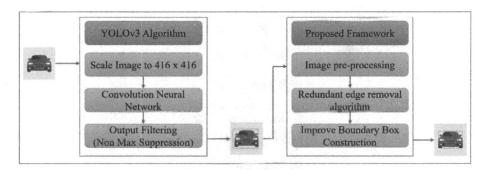

**Fig. 1.** Block diagram of proposed framework

### 3.1  YOLOv3 Algorithm

YOLOv3 [21] is the third iteration of the YOLO family for object detection. It provides with few improvements over YOLOv2 like DarkNet-53 with shortcut connections, better object detection with feature map unsampling and concatenation. It contains 53 convolution layers therefore it has been named DarkNet-53, In the convolution layer, each layer contains a normalization layer and Leaky ReLU activation function. Here pooling is not used and a stride factor of 32,16 and 8 have been used in the convolution layer to downsample the feature map and to make a prediction at a different scale. This approach helps in preventing loss of low-level features.

YOLOv3 [21] is a regression-based object detection technique. YOLOv3 [21] algorithm starts by changing the size of an image to 416 × 416, and then the network divides the image into grids of size $S \times S$. Next, this image is passed through convolution neural network, which results a tensor containing numbers i.e. $[pc, bx, by, bh, bw, c]$. Here, $(pc)$ denotes prediction confidence that illustrates whether a particular box contains an object of a particular class or not, $(bx, by)$ denotes $(x, y)$ coordinates of the object, $(bh, bw)$ denotes height and width of the object and $(c)$ denotes class confidence of the object. In YOLOv3 [21], each cell predicts 3 bounding boxes. To reduce the number of boundary boxes that have been detected first, boxes are filtered based on object prediction confidence score. Boxes with a score below 0.5 are ignored and then Non-max suppression is applied to remove remaining false-positive boxes. The proposed work uses pretrained weight of the COCO dataset to identify the class of detected objects.

## 3.2    Image Pre-processing

YOLOv3 [21] algorithm produces an output image that contains a boundary box around the detected object along with the class of the object. In the next stage, the proposed work takes the output image produced by YOLOv3 [21] algorithm and goes through a series of operations that will be discussed in the upcoming section. An overview of image pre-processing has been shown in Fig. 2.

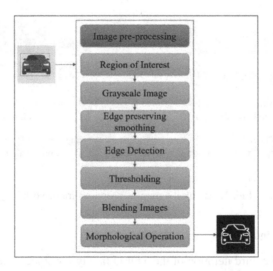

**Fig. 2.**  Steps involve in image pre-processing

**Region of Interest (ROI).** The boundary box drawn by YOLOv3 [21] is in a close approximation of the object, but it is not completely accurate. So, this work expands the rectangle drawn by YOLOv3 [21] by 2% on each side and separates the region to work with. Following this approach, this study only focuses on the region where the object has already been detected. This approach saves unnecessary computation which otherwise had to be done on the whole image. The proposed work calls this as the region of interest or ROI.

**Grayscale and Edge-Preserving Smoothing.** Once the region of interest is separated, next this work converts the RGB image to a grayscale image. Since one of the goals of the proposed methodology is to extract edges of the detected object, this work chooses to apply edge-preserving smoothing. Edge-preserving filters preserve the edges by limiting itself to smoothing at edges while smoothing away noise or textures from the image. The proposed work uses a median filter. In the median filter, median of all pixels in a kernel area is calculated and the center element is replaced with it. The proposed work uses a kernel size of 21 × 21 and found that it produces the best result. This operation processes the edges while removing the noise.

**Edge Detection.** Edge detection is one of the key operations of the proposed work. Therefore, the proposed methodology uses one of the most popular edge detection algorithms i.e. Canny Edge Detection. Canny Edge detection algorithm requires two threshold value, i.e. *minValue* and *maxValue*. Any edge with intensity gradient greater than the *maxValue* will be considered as edges, let's call it as "sure-edge", and the values that are lower than *minValue* will be considered as non-edges. Values in-between *minValue* and *maxValue*, if connected with "sure-edge" pixel, they will also be considered as part of edges else they will be considered as non-edges. The proposed work creates two edge detected images with different *minValue* and *maxValue*. In first image, the *minValue* and *maxValue* are as follows: *minValue* = 10, *maxValue* = 200.

Since it is going to cover the widest range of edges, the proposed work calls it "canny-wide". For the second image, the *minValue* and *maxValue* are calculated as follows.

$$minValue = max(0, (1-\beta) * m) \tag{1}$$

$$maxValue = min(255, (1+\beta) * m) \tag{2}$$

Here, $\beta$ is taken as 0.33 and $m$ is the median of the single channel pixel intensities. Since *minValue* and *maxValue* are calculated according to the median value, the proposed work calls it "canny-auto".

**Thresholding.** After edge detection, the proposed work applies thresholding to both "canny-wide" and "canny-auto" image. This work uses an adaptive threshold where the threshold value of each pixel depends upon neighboring pixel intensities. To find threshold value $t(x, y)$, first, a region of size $b \times b$ has been chosen. Next, a weighted average of $b \times b$ region has been calculated using gaussian weighted average. At last, a constant value c has been subtracted from the resulting value, to get the threshold value of a region.

$$t(x, y) = gausavg(x, y) - c \tag{3}$$

Here, $b$ is taken as 21 and constant $c$ is taken as 7. Since threshold value has been calculated for both "canny-wide" and "canny-auto", the proposed work calls the resulting image as "threshold-wide" and "threshold-auto" respectively.

**Blending Images.** In the next step, the proposed work blends both the images i.e. "threshold-wide" and "threshold-auto". The proposed work blends the images according to their weights.

$$blendimg = \alpha.img1 + \beta.img2 \tag{4}$$

Here, $\alpha$ is 0.7 and $\beta$ is 0.3. The *img1* and *img2* are "threshold-wide" and "threshold-auto" respectively.

**Morphological Operation.** At the last stage of image pre-processing, this work applies a morphological operator. In morphology operation, each pixel is adjusted based on the neighboring pixel. There are four basic morphological operators namely erosion, dilation, opening and closing. Due to the way canny edge detection works, there were many small gaps that have been present between two consecutive edges. Therefore, the proposed work uses dilation as a morphological operator. Dilation helps us to fill up those gaps and the make boundary more visible by adding pixels to the boundary of the object. The proposed work applies dilation to blended image and calls the resulting image as "preprocess-image".

### 3.3   Redundant Edge Removal Algorithm

While working with an edge detection algorithm, one of the major problems that have been faced is redundant details. The redundant details are the edges that are not associated with the detected object. For example, in a scenario where one person is standing near a tree or stairs, the redundant details are the edges associated with trees or stairs. This is the major problem that is present when one tries to improve the rectangular boundary box around a detected object. A block diagram of this step is shown in Fig. 3. In the block diagram, sw_width is referred to the sliding window width and percent_diff is referred to the percentage difference between "preprocessed image" and threshold-auto" image.

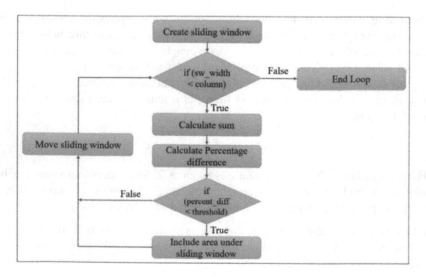

**Fig. 3.**  Block diagram of removing redundant edges

```
Algorithm 1: Redundant edge removal algorithm
Input: "processed-image" and "threshold-auto" images
Output: "final-image" where redundant edges are removed.
threshold = 80
height = processed_image.height()
width = processed_image.width()
width_const = 0.05 * width
sw_width = width_const
sw_height = height
final_image.shape() = processed_image.shape()
x, y = 0
while (sw_width < width)
   sum_processed = sum (processed_image[x:sw_width, y:sw_height])
   sum_auto = sum (threshold auto[x:sw_width, y:sw_height])
   percent_diff = ((abs (sum_processed – sum_auto))/ sum_processed) * 100
   if (percent_diff < threshold)
    final_image [x: sw_width, y: sw_height] = processed_image [x: sw_width,
y: sw_height]
    x = sw_width
   sw_width = sw_width + width_const
return final_image
```

To solve this problem, the idea that is being proposed is to create two edge detected images. In the first image, this work focuses on covering the most highlighted edges, while in the second image, this work focuses on covering the widest range of edges. This is achieved by changing the threshold values of canny edge detection algorithm. After this, the proposed work finds the region where both images have common edges while discarding the remaining part of the image. An overview of this step is shown in Fig. 3.

This step starts by creating a sliding window. The sliding window width is calculated as 5% of the width of the image and sliding window height is same as that of image. In this work, "preprocess-image" and "threshold-auto" image have been taken for comparison. A new image is being created in which the sliding window data of "threshold-auto" image is copied when a certain threshold is exceeded. To calculate the threshold, all pixel intensity value of the sliding window region is summed up i.e.

$$sum_{pi} = \sum_{x}^{m} \sum_{y}^{k} pixel\_intensities \tag{5}$$

$$sum_{ta} = \sum_{x}^{m} \sum_{y}^{k} pixel\_intensities \tag{6}$$

Here $m$ represents the width of the sliding window and $k$ represents the height of the sliding window. After sum has been calculated for both images, the next step is to obtain a common part that is present in both images. To find this common part percentage difference between the sum of images is calculated.

$$percentage\ difference = \left(\frac{sum_{pi} - sum_{ta}}{sum_{ta}}\right) * 100 \qquad (7)$$

A comparison has been made between the percentage difference and threshold value. If the percentage difference is less than the threshold value, then sliding window data is copied into the newly created image. After that, the sliding window is moved to next area. The proposed work repeats the same step until sliding window covers the whole width of the image and returns the newly created image. In the proposed work, the threshold value for this comparison has been taken as 80. This work calls this image "final-image".

### 3.4　Error Calculation and Improved Boundary Box Construction

At last, this work draws the boundary box. To draw boundary box, a similar concept of sliding windows has been used which is responsible for calculating error in edges of the boundary box. This work creates four sliding windows i.e. left, right, top and bottom. To calculate the dimension of a sliding window, the height of left and right sliding window is same as that of "final-image" and the width of left and right sliding window is calculated as 5% width of "final-image". Similarly, the height of top and bottom sliding window is calculated as 5% height of "final image" and the width is same as that of "final-image". Left sliding window move from left to right, right sliding window move from right to left, top sliding window move from top to bottom and bottom sliding window move from bottom to top. At each position, the sliding window lookup for edges and calculate a threshold value. To calculate the threshold value of each sliding window, mean is calculated i.e. finding the sum of all pixel intensities and divide it by the dimension of sliding window. This calculated threshold value is being compared with the proposed threshold value and the position of sliding window is returned as an error if calculated threshold value is greater than the proposed threshold value, otherwise sliding window will moves to next position. In this work, the proposed threshold values are as follows.

$$Threshold = \begin{cases} 1, & Leftboundary \\ 1, & Rightboundary \\ 1, & Topboundary \\ 1, & Bottomboundary \end{cases} \qquad (8)$$

Finally, the previous position of left and top edge is added with calculated error and the previous position of right and bottom edge is subtracted from calculated error to obtain the new position of left, right, top and bottom edges of the rectangular boundary box. At last, the proposed work draw edges of boundary box at newly calculated position.

## 4　Result and Analysis

All the images that has been used in this research work is taken from Unsplash and COCO dataset. An overview of all the steps with intermediate result that are produced in each step is shown in Fig. 4. This work starts with an image as an input, that is shown in Fig. 4(a). This input image is processed via YOLOv3 [21] algorithm and an

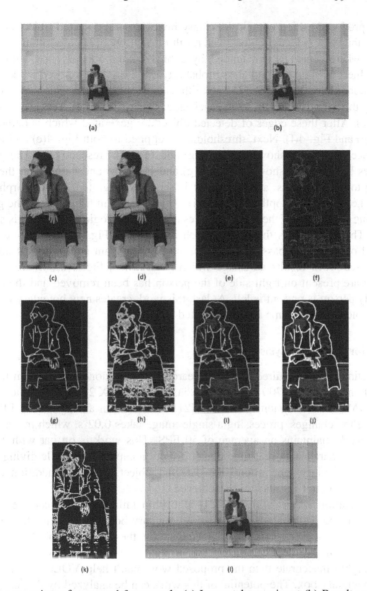

**Fig. 4.** An overview of proposed framework, (a) Image taken as input (b) Result produced by YOLOv3 (c) Region of Interest or ROI (d) RGB to grayscale (e) Applying edge detection i.e. Canny-wide (f) Applying edge detection i.e. Canny-auto (g) Applying threshold to Canny-wide i.e. Threshold-wide (h) Applying threshold to Canny-auto i.e. Threshold-auto (i) Blending Threshold-wide and Threshold-auto image (j) Preprocessed-image after applying morphological operator (k) Final-image where redundant edges are removed (l) Output produced by the proposed work (Color figure online)

output is produced which contain boundary boxes around detected object along with class probability of detected object. The result of YOLOv3 [21] algorithm is shown in Fig. 4(b), where object is surrounded by a blue color boundary box with class of detected object as "Person" and class probability of 92%. The proposed work, takes the output produced by YOLOv3 [21] algorithm and separate the region of interest by expanding the boundary boxes 2% on each side. This region of interest is demonstrated in Fig. 4(c). After these edges of detected object are generated which is demonstrated in Fig. 4(e) and Fig. 4(f). Next, thresholding is applied to both Fig. 4(e) and Fig. 4(f), and produced result are shown in Fig. 4(g) and Fig. 4(h) respectively. The proposed work takes both images shown in Fig. 4(g) and Fig. 4(h) and blend both the images according to their weights, and this result is shown in Fig. 4(i). Next, morphological operation i.e. dilation is applied to Fig. 4(i), which results in filling up all the gaps and highlighting the details of the edges. The result of morphological operation is shown in Fig. 4(j). This work takes the image which is shown in Fig. 4(j) as a result of morphological operator and pass it through proposed redundant edge removal algorithm. The proposed work results an image which is shown in Fig. 4(k), where redundant edges that are present on right side of the person has been removed and the region in which only person is present is left. At last, this work creates new boundary box which is of red color and the same is demonstrated in Fig. 4(l).

## 4.1 Performance Analysis

All the testing that is required for this research has been done on a system that has a configuration of Intel i7 9700 K CPU, Nvidia GeForce RTX 2080 Ti graphics card and 16 GB RAM. On this system, YOLOv3 [21] runs with an average of 52 FPS. After introducing the changes, processing a single image takes 0.02 s, which means that the proposed work maintains an average of 50 FPS. This work is on par with YOLOv3 [21] when compared with real-time object detection capabilities while giving an edge to improve boundary box around the detected object. With the addition of better hardware, even better results can be achieved.

In all situation where YOLOv3 [21] algorithm fails to detect accurate boundary box, this work helps the algorithm to get a boundary box which is much close to the ground truth. However, this work depends upon the result of the YOLOv3 [21] algorithm, if YOLOv3 [21] completely fails to detect an object or draws boundary box which is highly inaccurate then the proposed work can't help YOLOv3 [21] to make accurate boundary box. The potential of this work can be analyzed by the result shown in this section. Under different circumstances and with different objects, the results produced by the proposed framework are demonstrated in Fig. 5.

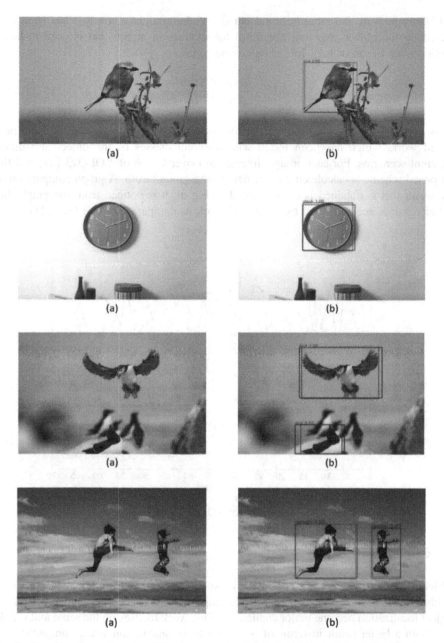

**Fig. 5.** Results obtained under different scenarios (a) Image taken as input (b) Final output where, blue color rectangular boundary box is created by YOLOv3 and red color rectangular boundary box is created by the suggested framework (Color figure online)

**IoU Comparison.** To measure the accuracy of the boundary box that has been predicted by the object detection algorithm the evaluation matric that is used is Intersection over Union or IoU. IoU is determined via.

$$IoU = \frac{Area\ of\ Overlap}{Area\ of\ Union} \qquad (9)$$

A comparison is made between the IoU of YOLOv3 [21] algorithm and the proposed work, which has been tested with different classes of the object and under different scenarios. For each image, Intersection over Union of YOLOv3 [21] and the proposed scheme is calculated with respect to the ground truth. A graph comparison of the result that is obtained is demonstrated in Fig. 6. It is noticed from the graph that better result is accomplished by suggested work as compared to YOLOv3 [21].

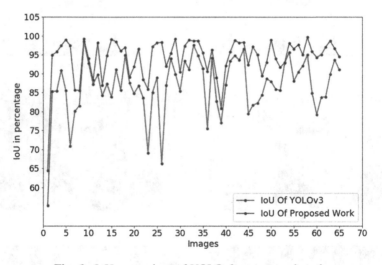

**Fig. 6.** IoU comparison of YOLOv3 vs proposed work

## 5   Conclusion

Object detection has become one of the most popular research topics in recent years. With its extensive use in every field of computer vision, accuracy and precision of object localization become major challenges. This work focuses on the same and is able to obtain a better result in terms of boundary box construction when compared with YOLOv3 algorithm. This work also proposes solution to address the problem that has been faced in previous works like drawing boundary boxes when too much redundant details or sharp objects is present in the image. However, since proposed work still depends on YOLOv3 for object detection, and if YOLOv3 fails to recognize an object or localize it very inaccurately then this work also suffers. The future work will look into the shortcomings of YOLOv3 algorithm and will try to resolve these problems.

# References

1. Druzhkov, P.N., Kustikova, V.D.: A survey of deep learning methods and software tools for image classification and object detection. Pattern Recogn. Image Anal. **26**, 9–15 (2016). https://doi.org/10.1134/S1054661816010065
2. Wojek, C., Dollar, P., Schiele, B., Perona, P.: Pedestrian detection: an evaluation of the state of the art. IEEE Trans. Pattern Anal. Mach. Intell. **34**, 743–761 (2012)
3. Lowe, D.G.: Distinctive image features from scale-invariant keypoints. Int. J. Comput. Vis. **60**(2), 91–110 (2004). https://doi.org/10.1023/B:VISI.0000029664.99615.94
4. Dalal, N., Triggs, B.: Histograms of oriented gradients for human detection. In: CVPR (2005)
5. Lienhart, R., Maydt, J.: An extended set of Haar-like features for rapid object detection. In: International Conference on Image Processing (2002)
6. Deng, J., et al.: ImageNet: a large-scale hierarchical image database. In: CVPR (2009)
7. Girshick, R., Donahue, J., Darrell, T., Malik, J.: Rich feature hierarchies for accurate object detection and semantic segmentation. In: CVPR (2014)
8. Girshick, R.: Fast R-CNN. In: International Conference on Computer Vision (2015)
9. Ren, S., He, K., Girshick, R., Sun, J.: Faster R-CNN: towards real-time object detection with region proposal networks. In: NIPS (2015)
10. Dai, J., Li, Y., He, K., Sun, J.: R-FCN: object detection via region-based fully convolutional networks. In: NIPS (2016)
11. Lin, T.-Y., Dollar, P., Girshick, R., He, K., Hariharan, B., Belongie, S.: Feature pyramid networks for object detection. In: CVPR (2017)
12. He, K., et al.: Mask R-CNN. In: ICCV (2017)
13. Erhan, D., et al.: Scalable object detection using deep neural networks. In: CVPR (2014)
14. Najibi, M., et al.: G-CNN: an iterative grid based object detector. In: CVPR (2016)
15. Yoo, D., Park, S., et al.: AttentionNet: aggregating weak directions for accurate object detection. In: CVPR (2015)
16. Redmon, J., Divvala, S., Girshick, R., Farhadi, A.: You only look once: unified real-time object detection. In: CVPR (2016)
17. Redmon, J., Farhadi, A.: YOLO9000: better faster stronger. In: CVPR (2016)
18. Liu, W., et al.: SSD: single shot multibox detector. In: Leibe, B., Matas, J., Sebe, N., Welling, M. (eds.) ECCV 2016. LNCS, vol. 9905, pp. 21–37. Springer, Cham (2016). https://doi.org/10.1007/978-3-319-46448-0_2
19. Fu, C.-Y., et al.: DSSD: Deconvolutional single shot detector. https://arxiv.org/abs/1701.06659 (2017)
20. Shen, Z., Liu, Z., Li, J., Jiang, Y.-G., Chen, Y., Xue, X.: DSOD: learning deeply supervised object detectors from scratch. In: ICCV (2017)
21. Redmon, J., Farhadi, A.: YOLOv3: an incremental improvement. https://arxiv.org/abs/1804.02767 (2018)
22. Uijlings, J.R.R., van de Sande, K.E.A., Gevers, T., Smeulders, A.W.M.: Selective search for object recognition. Int. J. Comput. Vis. **104**, 154–171 (2013). https://doi.org/10.1007/s11263-013-0620-5
23. Cortes, C., Vapnik, V.: Support vector network. Mach. Learn. **20**, 273–297 (1995). https://doi.org/10.1007/BF00994018
24. Blue, S.T., Brindha, M.: Edge detection based boundary box construction algorithm for improving the precision of object detection in YOLOv. In: 10th ICCCNT (2019)
25. Zhang, D., Zhang, P., Wang, L.: Cell counting algorithm based on YOLOv3 and image density estimation. In: 4th International Conference on Signal and Image Processing, (2019)

26. Zhang, X., Zhu, X.: Vehicle Detection in the aerial infrared images via an improved YOLOv3 network. In: 4th International Conference on Signal and Image Processing (2019)
27. Shi, T., Liu, M, Yang, Y., Wang, P., Huang, Y.: Fast classification and detection of marine targets in complex scenes with YOLOv3. In: OCEANS 2019, Marseille (2019)
28. Cui, H., Yang, Y., Liu, M., Shi, T., Qi, Q.: Ship detection: an improved YOLOv3 method. In: OCEANS 2019, Marseille (2019)
29. Qu, H., Yuan, T., Sheng, Z., Zhang, Y.: A pedestrian detection method based on YOLOv3 Model and Image enhanced by Retinex. In: 11th CISP-BMEI (2018)
30. Miao, F., Tian, Y., Jin, L.: Vehicle direction detection based on yolov3. In: 11th IHMSC (2019)

# Automatic Detection of Pneumonia from Chest X-Rays Using Deep Learning

Mriganka Nath$^{(\boxtimes)}$ and Chandrajit Choudhury$^{(\boxtimes)}$

National Institute of Technology Silchar, Silchar, Assam, India
mrinath123@gmail.com, chandrajit@ece.nits.ac.in

**Abstract.** In this work, we propose a novel algorithm using a Convolutional neural network (CNN) where learning is transferred to classify and detect the model presence of pneumonia from a collection of frontal-view chest X-ray image samples. Unlike traditional transfer learning methods where the predefined weights are solely used and the size of the last layer is changed to desired output size, we are fine-tuning the last layers of the loaded model which in our case is VGG16 over our dense network and then training the model, and hence classify the input images to detect if someone is suffering from pneumonia. With classification, we will also predict the severity of the disease giving the doctors to quickly make decisions for the treatment. The dataset used in our model has imbalanced data due to which, we utilized a variety of data augmentation techniques to boost the validation and train accuracy of the CNN model. Using the proposed method we achieve accuracy better than the state of the art.

**Keywords:** Computer vision · Convolutional Neural Network · Fine-tuning · Transfer learning

## 1 Introduction

Pneumonia is a great risk for many people, especially to the economically weak who lack a proper sanitation system and having high pollution rates in their area. According to WHO reports, 15% of all children below 5 years are killed by Pneumonia, taking life of 808694 kids in 2017 [1]. Nowadays chest X-ray is the best obtainable procedure to diagnose pneumonia [2], having a vital role in clinical care [3]. Detecting pneumonia in chest radiography can be challenging and which relies on the availability and the skill of radiologists. The appearance of pneumonia in X-ray images is often unclear and can overlap with other diseases. In this work, we introduce an algorithm that automatically detects pneumonia from frontal-view chest X-rays. In recent times, Deep learning algorithms involving Convolutional Neural Networks (CNNs) have become a standard solution for detecting of diseases and medical classification as compared to traditional computer vision techniques. We have used transfer learning while training our network which not only increases our accuracy but also decreases computational power and time. Transfer learning is useful when we are working with a dataset which is relatively small with respect to the pre-trained network we are working with. Although our base model, VGG16 have a lot of parameters to train but we have made our architecture excluding the fully-connected layer of the base model and trained our model over our

© Springer Nature Singapore Pte Ltd. 2020
A. Bhattacharjee et al. (Eds.): MIND 2020, CCIS 1240, pp. 175–182, 2020.
https://doi.org/10.1007/978-981-15-6315-7_14

dense architecture. We have frozen the first layers of the base model and unfreeze the others. Training both the newly-added classifier layers and last layers of the base model simultaneously allows us to "fine-tune" the higher-order feature representations in the base model in order to make them more relevant for the specific task. We will extract visualizations from the Convolutional layers to detect the severity and in which part of the lung, it is more severe. The classification task only needs 0.0036 s for the classification task. Automatic detection of diseases from chest X-rays would be very beneficiary for the medical world and it will help to implement proper healthcare to the section of the population with less access to it and live far places where there is no access to diagnostic imaging specialists and expert radiologists.

Here in Sect. 2, we introduce how deep learning is being used in different spheres of biomedical work and how are they making it easy for the detection of diseases. In Sect. 3 we propose our model which consist of the pre-trained model and our fully connected model and it also describes the different types of hyperparameters used. Section 4 discusses how was data being processed and thus giving the results. We also compare our results with other models. In Sect. 5 future work and scope of our work is discussed.

## 2    Related Works

Due to the availability of huge datasets, deep learning algorithms have improved exponentially and have outperformed medical experts in various medical imaging tasks such as skin cancer classification [4], hemorrhage identification [5] and diabetic retinopathy detection [6]. Automatic detection of diseases has received growing interests with their accuracy going up with new deep network models. The Chexnet [7] algorithm which has been developed at Stanford University, is a 121-layer convolutional neural network trained on ChestX-ray14 data, which is used to classify 14 chest disease, taking input from frontal-view chest x-rays. Along with predictions, their model shows heatmap of the images which gives us the information where the disease is mainly acting. The results achieved by them on their dataset are very high and exceeds the level of radiologists.

## 3    Proposed Method

### 3.1    Model

The overall architecture of the proposed CNN model consists of two major parts: the VGG16 layers and then the fully connected dense layer. This fully connected layer along with the last layer of our VGG 16 which is our base model is trained. The value of the parameters of the first few layers of the base model is not altered. We train the network until our model converges to give the necessary outputs (Fig. 1).

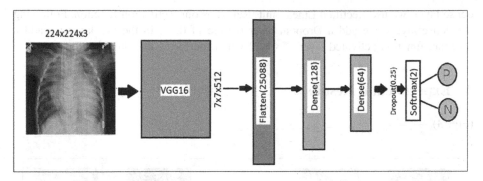

**Fig. 1.** The proposed architecture.

## 3.2 VGG16

In our proposed model The VGG layers are used as feature extractors. They work as our base layer. VGGNet is composed of 16 convolutional layers and is very captivating because of its very uniform architecture. Here we load the pre-trained network with weights trained with ImageNet [10]. However VGG16 network is a very big architecture and consists of 138 million parameters which are difficult to compute. So in our model, we load the network excluding the classification layers, which decreases the number of the parameters to 14 million, which makes the total number of layers to be 19. As we go higher up, the features learnt are increasingly more specific to the dataset on which the model was trained. So here we unfreeze the layers after layer number 15, which makes the total number of trainable parameters to almost 7 million (Fig. 2).

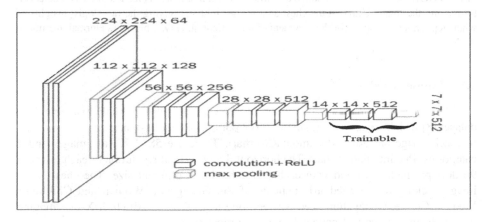

**Fig. 2.** VGG16 architecture

## 3.3 Fully Connected Layer

After the base model, we flatten the last layer of the base model, and then we follow with two dense networks of neuron numbers of 128 and 64 respectively. In both of the dense layer, we use Rectified Linear unit (ReLu) as our Activation function. Following the dense layers, we add a Dropout layer of rate of 0.25. In the last layer we add a Softmax function activated layer of size 2 which performs the classification task.

## 4  Experimental Results

(Fig. 3)

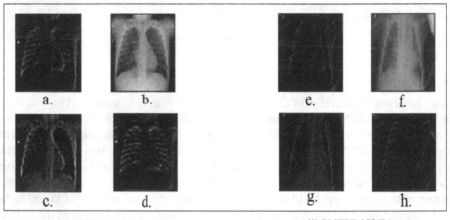

i) NORMAL case                                    ii) PNEUMONIA case

**Fig. 3.** Visualisation of the different feature maps on an input image by the Convolutional layers of the VGG16 net. Here we can notice that when Pneumonia image is feeded, the CNN detects it by making the image blurry in the chest area in the right side giving the radiologist insights of what steps should be taken for the treatment of the patient quickly, whereas in Normal, the image is clear.

### 4.1  Dataset Used

The dataset which we are working upon uses real data, and is publicly available. The dataset [8] which we used is organized into 2 parts (train and test) and contains subparts for each image category (Pneumonia/Normal). There are 5840 X-Ray images and 2 categories (Pneumonia/Normal). The horizontal and vertical resolution of each image is 96 dots per inch (dpi) and with each image having a different size. The chest X-ray images belong to the paediatric patients of the Guangzhou Women and Children's Medical Centre, Guangzhou aged between one to five years. All chest X-ray imaging was performed as part of patients' routine clinical care.

### 4.2  Data Splitting

In the original data, the total number of training images is 5216 and test images are 624 including both (Normal and Pneumonia) categories. Validation data is created from training data by randomly selecting 8 images from both classes, resulting in the size of validation data to 16. Hence the number of Training images goes to 5200. The size of each image is made equal to the dimension of $(224 \times 224 \times 3)$. The images are labeled as positive and negative examples to Pneumonia and Normal cases respectively (Fig. 4).

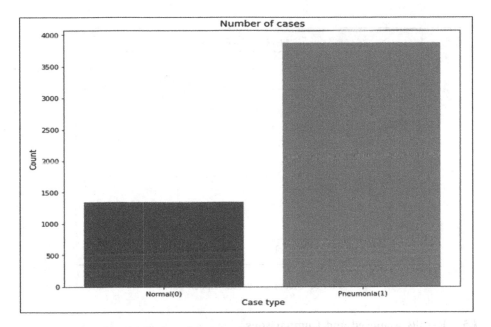

**Fig. 4.** Distribution of Training Pneumonia (right) and Normal data.

### 4.3 Data Augmentation

The training data is highly imbalanced. We have almost thrice the pneumonia cases as compared to the normal cases. To balance this data gap we propose data augmentation in the training data. At each iteration, we will take one augmentation technique and will apply that on the samples

- Horizontal flipping.
- Rotation of the image (between $-22$ to $22°$).
- Changing the brightness (1.2 to 1.5 times the original brightness).
- Scale to 80–120% of image height/width (each axis independently).
- Translate by $-20$ to $+20$ relative to height/width (per axis).
- Shear the image by $-16$ to $+16°$.

### 4.4 Training

The total number of weights in our model architecture is 18 million out of which 10 million parameters are trainable and the rest are freeze. The parameters are trained for 5 epochs, using Adam optimizer with the exponential decay rate for the 1st and 2ndmoment estimates. being 0.99 and 0.999 respectively. We train the model using mini-batches of size 16. We use an initial learning rate of $10^{-3}$ that is decayed by a factor of $10^{-5}$ and saving only the best weights after each epoch for the validation data. The training data have an average accuracy of 0.90 and validation data 0.933 (Figs. 5 and 6).

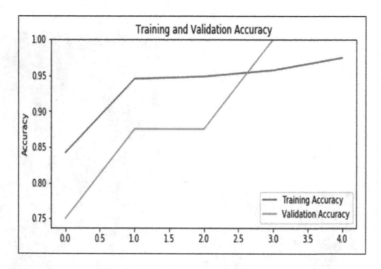

**Fig. 5.** Accuracy versus Epoch curve

## 4.5   Results Achieved and Comparisons

The accuracy of our model on the test dataset is 0.8667 with loss 0.9316. The recall and precision of our model are 0.99 and 0.83 respectively. The F1 score of the model is 0.90. The Area Under the Receiver Operating Characteristics (AUROC) curve is 0.8252 whereas in the CheXNet [7] paper where they created a model to classify various lung diseases using chest X-ray their AUROC for their pneumonia classification is 0. 7680.

Table 1 and Table 2 compare the results between different models. Methods in Table 1 consist of data different from our dataset whereas in Table 2 we are comparing same dataset as used in our model for testing.

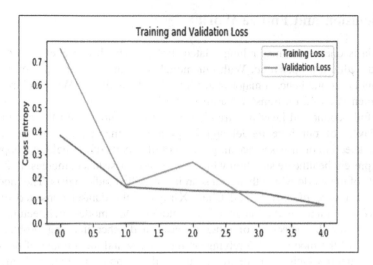

**Fig. 6.** Loss versus Epoch curve

**Table 1.** Comparisions between different models

| Methods | Validation accuracy | AUROC |
|---|---|---|
| A 121-layer Dense Convolutional Network (ChexNet [8]) | – | 0.7680 |
| The architecture in consists of convolution, max-pooling, and classification layers [11] | 0.93012 | – |

**Table 2.** Comparisions between different models over same Dataset

| Methods | Validation accuracy | Test accuracy | Precision | Recall | F1 score | AUROC |
|---|---|---|---|---|---|---|
| Depth Wise Convolution [11] | 0.819 | 0.826 | | | 0.874 | – |
| Our proposed model | 0.933 | 0.8667 | 0,83 | 0 99 | 0,90 | 0.8252 |

## 4.6  Platform Used

We made our model on Python language and have used Kaggle's cloud notebooks to train our model. Tensorflow and Keras frameworks are being used for training the data. The testing data which comprised of 624 images, each image requires 0.0036 s for the classification task. Since we are working on a large network, we are training our model using Graphics processing unit (GPU).

## 5 Conclusion and Future Work

Pneumonia is one of the major lung-related diseases which can even be fatal if not diagnosed within a proper time. With our model, we can detect if a person is having Pneumonia faster and hence a major factor for critical conditions. We develop a simple model which is based on transfer learning. We have used VGG16 as our base layer over our fully connected layer and training the network along with the parameters of the last layers of our base model and keeping the other parameters freeze. With automatic detection of diseases reaching the level of experts of the field, we hope that it helps the present healthcare situation which needs more assistance, increasing its access to the parts of the world where there is a scarcity of skilled radiologists. The model uses a dataset composed of only frontal Chest X-rays, if the dataset consisted of lateral images we can increase the range of our model. Our model architecture can be implemented for the detection of other diseases and other imaging problems. The performance of the model is also relying on the quality and the amount of the dataset. The dataset upon which we have made our model is not very big; with more data generated from medical institutes we can push the accuracy to the levels exceeding the skills of an expert radiologist. The model can be trained on different base models which have a complex and deep architecture with respect to VGG16 like ResNet, AlexNet and Inception which might give better results but requires more computational power and time.

## References

1. Pnemonia. https://www.who.int/news-room/fact-sheets/detail/pneumonia
2. WHO: Standardization of interpretation of chest radiographs for the diagnosis of pneumonia in children (2001)
3. Franquet, T.: Imaging of pneumonia: trends and algorithms. Eur. Respir. J. **18**(1), 196–208 (2001)
4. Andre, E., Brett, K., Roberto, A., et al.: Dermatologist-level classification of skin cancer with deep neural networks. Nature **542**(7639), 115–118 (2017)
5. Grewal, M., Srivastava, M.M., Kumar, P., Varadarajan, S.: Radiologist level accuracy using deep learning for hemorrhage detection in CT scans (2017)
6. Pranav, R., Awni, Y.H., Masoumeh, H., Codie, B., Andrew, Y.N.: Cardiologist-level ARR arrhythmia detection with convolutional neural networks (2017)
7. Rajpurkar, P., Irvin, J., Zhu, K., Yang, B., Mehta, H., Duan, T.: CheXNet: radiologist-level pneumonia detection on chest x-rays with deep learning. arXiv preprint arXiv:1711.05225 (2017)
8. https://data.mendeley.com/datasets/rscbjbr9sj/2
9. http://www.image-net.org/
10. Stephen, O., Sain, M., Maduh, U.J., Jeong, D.U.: An efficient deep learning approach to pneumonia classification in healthcare. J. Healthc. Eng. (2019). https://doi.org/10.1155/2019/4180949
11. https://www.kaggle.com/aakashnain/beating-everything-with-depthwise-convolution

# An Improved Accuracy Rate in Microaneurysms Detection in Retinal Fundus Images Using Non-local Mean Filter

N. Jagan Mohan[1]([✉])(iD), R. Murugan[1](iD), Tripti Goel[1](iD),
and Parthapratim Roy[2]

[1] Department of Electronics and Communication Engineering,
National Institute of Technology Silchar, Silchar 788010, Assam, India
jaganmohan427@gmail.com, murugan.rmn@gmail.com, triptigoel83@gmail.com
[2] Department of Ophthalmology, Silchar Medical College and Hospital,
Silchar 788014, Assam, India
parthapratim.smc@gmail.com

**Abstract.** Microaneurysms (MA) detection in diabetic patients is very important as it's the first phase in grading the Diabetic Retinopathy disease through retinal fundus images. This paper presented a method to improve the accuracy rate in MA detection using a Non Local Mean Filter (NLMF). MA is one of the small retinal features in fundus images and it is a very challenging task to segment it since it will be merged with other retinal parts and features. The noise has affected the overall performance of MA detection methods, hence this paper has proposed NLMF. The methodology starts firstly, the RGB fundus images are converted into green channel images, then the mask is generated for the green channel image and then the background noise is reduced by the NLMF approach. Secondly, the hidden features are extracted using the contrast-limited adaptive histogram equalization further if there is exists any noise, that is removed by the 2D Gaussian low pass filter. Finally, the filtered images are converted into binary images and then MAs are extracted using morphological top-hat transform. The proposed MA detection was examined using the available publicly accessible dataset such as e-Ophtha, Retinopathy Online Challenge (ROC) DIARETDB0 and DIARETDB1. The presented MA detection method has produced better accuracy with other state of the art methods.

**Keywords:** Retina · Microaneurysms · Diabetic retinopathy · Non local mean filter · Top-hat transform

## 1 Introduction

Diabetic retinopathy (DR) is an eye illness which is present in the patients suffering with diabetes. It is because of the harm of blood vessels in the retina

© Springer Nature Singapore Pte Ltd. 2020
A. Bhattacharjee et al. (Eds.): MIND 2020, CCIS 1240, pp. 183–193, 2020.
https://doi.org/10.1007/978-981-15-6315-7_15

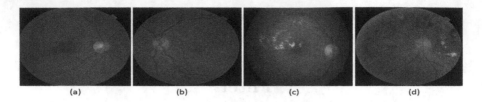

**Fig. 1.** DR stage (a) Normal (b) Mild (c) Moderate (d) Severe,  Source [3]

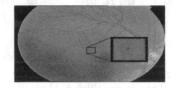

**Fig. 2.** Fundus image with MA, Source [10] (Color figure online)

causing obscured vision, may prompt vision failure if it left untreated [1]. It is the most well-known reason for visual deficiency in the working-age populace. With the expanding commonness of diabetes and also the maturing populace, it is normal for 333 million diabetic patients worldwide to need retinal evaluation every year in 2025 [2]. Mainly, the DR is devided into two major stages likely Non proliferative DR (NPDR), Proliferative DR (PDR) inturn NPDR is divided into mild, moderate and severe NPDR shown in Fig. 1 [3]. MA are the first clinical signs of DR. MA is the key imprint and the most punctual happening changes in the retina of a DR influenced individual. They are little, dull red, roundabout specks coming about because of swellings in retinal vessels shown in Fig. 2. The measurement of a MA may run from $10\,to\,125\,\mu$. Since MA's are first happening sores for DR, their localization can help in early DR recognition [4]. According to the state-of-the art, the MA detection methods proposed include the steps pre-processing, noise removal and segmentation. In most of the noise removal case, the authors [15–18] used median filtering. The drawback of median filtering is it produced low contrast in biomedical images. This paper contributes Non local mean filter which produces better contrast than median filter, which helps to detect MA accurately. The remaining parts of the paper organised as, in Sect. 2 relevant works are discussed, Sect. 3 presents methodology. The results and discussion fall in Sect. 4. In Sect. 5 conclusion is represented.

## 2    Related works

In DR screening, detection of MA helps to identify the stages of DR. The proposed MA detection algorithms produced less accuracy because the size of MA is very small and more over it presents with other retinal characteristics such as blood vessels, optic disk and macula. Kumar et al. [5] proposed a approach to reduce the non-MA candidates and an altered MA location strategy is introduced based on certain progressions to the filters in the strategy. The proposed strategy by Ganguly et al. [6] evaluates upper limit and lower edge of the red sores for the provided fundus image independently dependent on nearby image data. The importance of the versatile idea of this implemented calculation is that fundus-images procured from various cameras fluctuate in reliability and goals. Frangi filters are used to detect MA candidates for the first time in the method proposed by Srivastava et al. [7]. In this method each green channel image subdivided and filtered separately for MA detection. Purwita et al. [8] have used region filling operation to locate the MA's and removed the blood vessels using canny edge detection. Angadi et al. [9] illustrated dual tree complex discrete wavelet transform and log gabor feature extraction to detect MA. Retinal veins are wiped out utilizing minor and significant pivot properties and connection is performed on images with the Gabor highlights to recognize the MA. Antal et al. [10] presented a system that collects a few applicant extractors and pre-processing strategies to reinforce the location exactness of the individual methodologies. Ekatpure et al. [11] discussed the detection of MA by segmenting the blood vessels from the fundus image. In this method blood vessels are extracted using gaussian filter. Based on the stateof the art most of the authors used median filter in pre-processing and the segmentation. The accuracy rate is not upto the mark because in medical imaging the accuracy plays a vital role to diagnose or screening the disease. Hence we proposed a novel Non local mean filter in the pre-processing stage to increase the accuracy rate.

## 3   Methodology

This section describes a MA detection in retinal fundus images. The flow of proposed method includes green channel, masking, noise removal, histogram equalization and morphological processes. The work flow is shown in Fig. 3. The detailed description of every step is explained in the corresponding sub sections.

### 3.1   Green Component Estimation

The first step in the method is to extract the green channel image $(I_g)$. The green channel in the fundus image is separated from the RGB fundus image as shown in Eq. 1. The green channel provides detailed information than red and blue channels that is visually presented in Fig. 4. The blood vessels and optic disc have more contrast in $I_g$. The red, blue channel images have less features especially in biomedical images, hence we used $I_g$ for further processing.

$$I_g = \frac{G}{R + G + B} \tag{1}$$

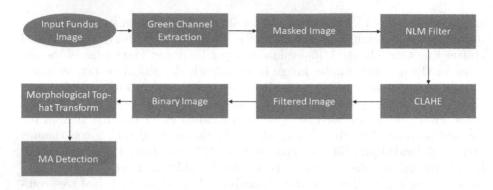

**Fig. 3.** Work flow of proposed methodology

## 3.2  Generating Mask

In $I_g$ image it is very important to exclude the background for further processing, hence we generated mask for $I_g$ for labelling the semi circled pixels for retinal ROI. The mask is done by selecting a threshold value for $I_g$ and with the help of morphological operations we removed unwanted pixels from the background as shown in Fig. 5.

## 3.3  Background Noise Removal Using Non Local Mean Filter

In the previous section we have removed the noise from non-background image of fundus and in this section we are going to sooth the noise from the background of the fundus image using Non Local Mean Filter (NLMF) [19]. Since the name suggests the NLMF calculates the mean of the pixel set, and Non Local means that it not only calculates the mean within a given size of local kernel, but it also looks at the mean in other non-local regions. The NLMF used to smooth the image by the average value of the set of pixels accompanying a target pixel. The NLMF takes an average of all pixels in the image measured by how close the target pixels are to be [14]. Estimated value $I_f$ is the weighted average of all pixels in the image $v(q)$ but the weight class depends on the similarity between the local and non-local pixels. In other words we may say that neighborhoods of similar pixels give greater weights. The NLMF mathematically written in Eq. 2.

$$I_f(p) = \frac{1}{N(p)} \int_\Omega v(q) w(p,q) dq \tag{2}$$

where $I_f(p) = $ filtered image at a given point $p$, $v(q) = $ unfilled image at $q$ point, $w(p,q) = $ weighting function, to decide how the image at $p$ is closely connected to image at $q$, and $N(p)$ is a factor used for normalisation and it is represented in Eq. 3.

$$N(p) = \int_\omega w(p,q) dq \tag{3}$$

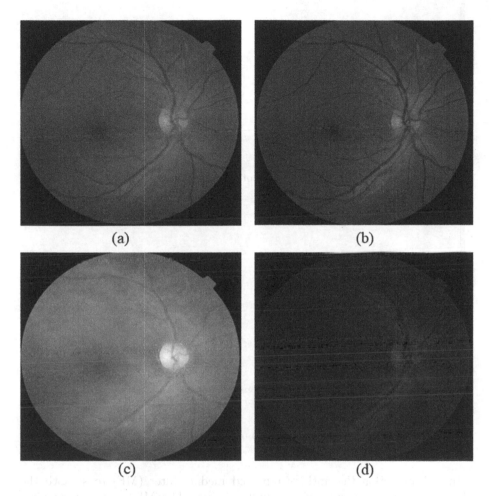

**Fig. 4.** (a) Fundus image (b) Green channel (c) Red channel (d) Blue channel (Color figure online)

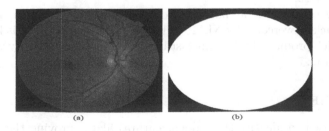

**Fig. 5.** (a) Green channel image (b) Generated mask

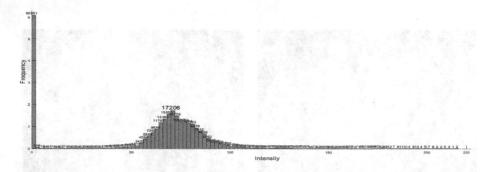

**Fig. 6.** Histogram of median filtering

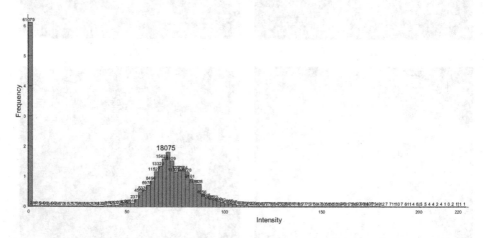

**Fig. 7.** Histogram of NLM filtering

In MA detection the authors reported median filter (MF) to smooth the noise from the background of the fundus image. The MF choose every pixel in the fundus image and its contrast only by illumination condition, where as NLMF choose all the pixel value in all conditions. The main drawback of the MF is it affect the overall contrast and background of the fundus image which is shown in Fig. 6.

From Fig. 6, we conclude that the median filter is limiting the intensity value. This drawback is overcome by NLMF. The performance of NLMF is better than the MF, which produces better contrast by spreading their intensity value which is shown in Fig. 7.

## 3.4   CLAHE

CLAHE is used to identify the hidden features like improving the contrast of the hidden blood-vessels in the fundus images. The measures in this approach are illustrated in Eq. 4. The enhanced fundus image using CLAHE is shown in Fig. 8(c).

$$PIX = [PIX_{max} - PIX_{min}] * P(f) + PIX_{min} \qquad (4)$$

where $PIX_{max}$ largest pixel value, $PIX_{min}$ lowest pixel value, $PIX$ is a calibrated pixel value, $P(f)$ is the cumulative probability distribution function (CDF). Here we Rayleigh distribution CDF function given in the Eq. 5.

$$R = P(f(\frac{x}{b})) = \int_0^x \frac{x}{b^2} e^{(-\frac{x^2}{2b^2})}) dx \qquad (5)$$

### 3.5 Noise Removal by 2D Gaussian Low Pass Filter from Enhanced Image

This section describes removing the noise from the enhanced image. We have used 2-D gaussian low pass filter (GLPF) for the removal of noise. The 2D GLPF is a correlation kernel and it is filtered with the intensity adjusted image. The filtered image is shown in Fig. 8(d).

### 3.6 MA Segmentation by Top-Hat Transform

This section extracts the features of MA from the fundus image. In ordered to highlight the MA from the enhanced filter image we have used morphological top-hat transform in which the image-opening operation with a structuring object with a size of 5 and then the Opened-image is deducted from the original image. The MA's with small size are extracted from the binary image in ordered to increase the accuracy. The results of the extracted MA features are shown in Figs. 8(e), 9(a) for e-Ophtha retinal database.

## 4 Results and Discussion

### 4.1 Dataset

The proposed methodology is tested on publicly available dataset such as e-ophtha [12], ROC [13], DIARETDB0 [20] and DIARETDB1 [21]. We have used a total of 700 fundus images for the detection of MA with 432 abnormal images and 268 normal images as depicted in Table 1.

**Table 1.** Database used for MA detection

| S.No | Dataset | Total images | Normal images | Abnormal images |
|------|---------|--------------|---------------|-----------------|
| 1 | e-Ophtha | 381 | 233 | 148 |
| 2 | DIARETDB0 | 130 | 20 | 110 |
| 3 | ROC | 100 | 10 | 90 |
| 4 | DIARETDB1 | 89 | 5 | 84 |
|   | Total | 700 | 268 | 432 |

## 4.2    Results

The algorithm suggested is developed on the MATLAB(2018b) prototype for the MA detection on each fundus image on desktop computer (Intel(R) Core(TM) i5-7500 CPU @3.40 GHz, 8 GB RAM). Firstly, the RGB fundus images are converted into green channel images. The mask is generated for the green channel image for reducing the number of false positive ones. In the next step the noise is reduced by the NLMF approach. Then the hidden features are extracted using the enhancement technique CLAHE. Further if there is exists any noise, that is removed by the 2D GLPF filtering method. Then, the filtered images are translated into binary and by using the morphological top-hat transform the MA's features are extracted. The Fig. 8(e) shows the results of the method proposed.

## 4.3    Performance Metrics

The effectiveness of the proposed MA detection method was reviewed by means of the Accuracy (Acc). In the proposed method we have applied noise removal techniques in the pre-processing stage to increase the Acc. The Acc obtained by the proposed method is 99% @The expression to calculate the Acc is given in Eq. 6.

$$Acc = \frac{Truepositives + Truenegatives}{FOVpixelcount} \tag{6}$$

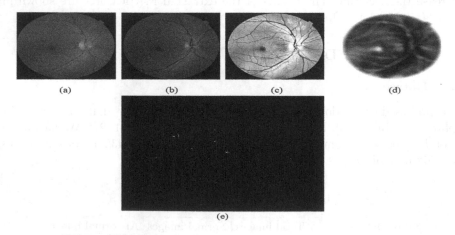

**Fig. 8.** Results for e-Ophtha database (a) Input image (b) Green channel image (c) CLAHE (d) Filtered image (e) Detected MA

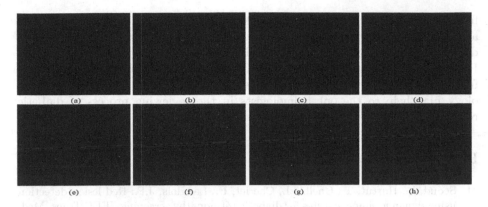

**Fig. 9.** Results of detected MA for the database (a–b) e-Ophtha (c–d) DB0 (c–f) ROC (g–h) DB1

## 4.4 Comparison

The proposed framework is more viable and effective than other frameworks, consider in past works as depicted in Fig. 9. Our framework consequently recognizes MAs from the fundus images compared to other methods proposed by Tasgaonkar et al. [15], Aishwarya et al. [16], Kamble et al. [17], Manohar et al. [18] as shown in Fig. 10 and henceforth encourages ophthalmologists to identify MA which is the clinical indication for DR detection. The obtained results are compared based on the e-Optha database as it is the largest dataset we have used.

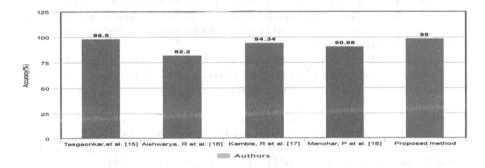

**Fig. 10.** Comparison of proposed method

## 5 Conclusion

This paper presented an improved microaneurysms detection through retinal fundus images using a sequence of image processing steps. The non-local mean filter has proposed to eliminate the background noise and to enhance the overall accuracy of the microaneurysms detection. The proposed microaneurysms detection process has been tested in the public database such as E-Ophtha, Retinopathy Online Challenge, DIARETDB0 and DIARETDB1. This proposed framework was more accurate with other existing systems. Hence this methodology may help to the ophthalmologists in the reviewing process of diabetic retinopathy and yet retinal image analysis.

# References

1. Seoud, L., Hurtut, T., Chelbi, J., Cheriet, F., Langlois, J.P.: Red lesion detection using dynamic shape features for diabetic retinopathy screening. IEEE Trans. Med. Imaging **35**(4), 1116–1126 (2015)
2. Reddy, G.N., Rao, K.D.G.: Microaneurysm identification using cross sectional profile analysis with optic disc removal. In: 2016 International Conference on Communication and Electronics Systems (ICCES), pp. 1–5. IEEE, October 2016
3. Murugan, R., Albert, A.J., Nayak, D.K.: An automatic localization of microaneurysms in retinal fundus images. In: 2019 International Conference on Smart Structures and Systems (ICSSS), pp. 1–5. IEEE, March 2019
4. Puranik, S.S., Malode, V.B.: Morphology based approach for microaneurysm detection from retinal image. In: 2016 International Conference on Automatic Control and Dynamic Optimization Techniques (ICACDOT), pp. 635–639. IEEE, September 2016
5. Kumar, P.S., Kumar, R.R., Sathar, A., Sahasranamam, V.: Automatic detection of red lesions in digital color retinal images. In: 2014 International Conference on Contemporary Computing and Informatics (IC3I), pp. 1148–1153. IEEE, November 2014
6. Ganguly, S., et al.: An adaptive threshold based algorithm for detection of red lesions of diabetic retinopathy in a fundus image. In: 2014 International Conference on Medical Imaging, m-Health and Emerging Communication Systems (MedCom), pp. 91–94. IEEE, November 2014
7. Srivastava, R., Wong, D.W., Duan, L., Liu, J., Wong, T.Y.: Red lesion detection in retinal fundus images using Frangi-based filters. In: 2015 37th Annual International Conference of the IEEE Engineering in Medicine and Biology Society (EMBC), pp. 5663–5666. IEEE, August 2015
8. Purwita, A.A., Adityowibowo, K., Dameitry, A., Atman, M.W.S.: Automated microaneurysm detection using mathematical morphology. In: 2011 2nd International Conference on Instrumentation, Communications, Information Technology, and Biomedical Engineering, pp. 117–120. IEEE, November 2011
9. Angadi, S., Ravishankar, M.: Detection and classification of microaneurysms using DTCWT and Log Gabor features in retinal images. In: Satapathy, S.C., Biswal, B.N., Udgata, S.K., Mandal, J.K. (eds.) Proceedings of the 3rd International Conference on Frontiers of Intelligent Computing: Theory and Applications (FICTA) 2014. AISC, vol. 328, pp. 589–596. Springer, Cham (2015). https://doi.org/10.1007/978-3-319-12012-6_65
10. Antal, B., Hajdu, A.: An ensemble-based microaneurysm detector for retinal images. In: 2011 18th IEEE International Conference on Image Processing, pp. 1621–1624. IEEE, September 2011

11. Ekatpure, S., Jain, R.: Red lesion detection in digital fundus image affected by diabetic retinopathy. In: 2018 Fourth International Conference on Computing Communication Control and Automation (ICCUBEA), pp. 1–4. IEEE, August 2018
12. Decencière, E., et al.: TeleOphta: machine learning and image processing methods for teleophthalmology. Irbm $34(2)$, 196–203 (2013)
13. Niemeijer, M., et al.: Retinopathy online challenge: automatic detection of microaneurysms in digital color fundus photographs. IEEE Trans. Med. Imaging $29(1)$, 185–195 (2009)
14. Zheng, J., et al.: Retinal image graph-cut segmentation algorithm using multiscale hessian-enhancement-based nonlocal mean filter. Comput. Math. Methods Med. **2013** (2013)
15. Tasgaonkar, M., Khambete, M.: Using differential morphological profiles for microaneurysm detection in diabetic retinal fundus images. In: 2016 International Conference on Signal and Information Processing (IConSIP), pp. 1–5. IEEE, October 2016
16. Aishwarya, R., Vasundhara, T., Ramachandran, K.I.: A hybrid classifier for the detection of microaneurysms in diabetic retinal images. The 17th International Conference on Biomedical Engineering. IP, vol. 61, pp. 97–103. Springer, Singapore (2017). https://doi.org/10.1007/978-981-10-4220-1_19
17. Kamble, R., Kokare, M.: Detection of microaneurysm using local rank transform in color fundus images. In: 2017 IEEE International Conference on Image Processing (ICIP), pp. 4442–4446. IEEE, September 2017
18. Manohar, P., Singh, V.: Morphological approach for retinal microaneurysm detection. In: 2018 Second International Conference on Advances in Electronics, Computers and Communications (ICAECC), pp. 1–7. IEEE, February 2018
19. Jin, Y., Jiang, W., Shao, J., Lu, J.: An improved image denoising model based on nonlocal means filter. Math. Prob. Eng. **2018** (2018)
20. Kauppi, T., et al.: DIARETDB0: evaluation database and methodology for diabetic retinopathy algorithms, vol. 73, pp. 1–17. Machine Vision and Pattern Recognition Research Group, Lappeenranta University of Technology, Finland (2006)
21. Kauppi, T., et al.: The DIARETDB1 diabetic retinopathy database and evaluation protocol. In: BMVC, vol. 1, pp. 1–10, September 2007

# Emotion Recognition from Periocular Features

Ekanshi Agrawal and Jabez Christopher[(⊠)] [iD]

Department of Computer Science and Information Systems, BITS – Pilani,
Hyderabad Campus, Hyderabad, Telangana, India
jabezc@hyderabad.bits-pilani.ac.in

**Abstract.** Image processing and Machine Learning approaches are used for face detection and emotion recognition. There are many features that could be extracted from a facial image, but the focus of this work is on identifying emotions by analyzing the features in the periocular region of the face; the region that consists of the features lying in the area of the immediate vicinity of the eyes. The work is broadly divided into two major modules: facial feature extraction and selection, and classifier training and evaluation. 327 labeled images are used to select seven features (periocular action units). Five classifiers are tested, and the Random Forest classifier provided the highest prediction accuracy at 75.61%, with the best performance observed for the happiness emotion label. The $k$-Nearest Neighbor classifier follows with a performance of 72% when augmented with Neighborhood Components Analysis. Statistical tests confirm that there is a significant difference between the performance of Random Forest classifier and SVM. The results of this work may serve as inputs for ensemble emotion recognition systems, and also as guidelines for enhancing works involving periocular-feature-based Facial Emotion Recognition systems.

**Keywords:** Facial expression recognition · Feature selection · Emotion classification · Periocular region · Facial Action Coding System

## 1 Introduction

An image is represented in the form of a matrix, with each entry signifying the intensity value of the corresponding pixel. Image processing is a large and deeply explored field of study and is used in computer vision systems such as face recognition and detection, and is a more mature and established field than that of computer vision. The core functionality of image processing systems involves pixel-wise transformations which maps input images to an output image. Digital image processing uses algorithms to perform these transformations, compressions, and decompressions on digital images. It is said to be a front-end system and a sub-process of computer vision procedures and considered to be the only empirical technology available for use in feature extraction, pattern recognition, and classification problems.

Face recognition and emotion classification systems generally require Machine Learning algorithms to be incorporated in them, providing them with the capacity to

© Springer Nature Singapore Pte Ltd. 2020
A. Bhattacharjee et al. (Eds.): MIND 2020, CCIS 1240, pp. 194–208, 2020.
https://doi.org/10.1007/978-981-15-6315-7_16

learn and acquire knowledge without being programmed explicitly. Machine learning is used for developing classification models that can be employed to deduce the correlation between facial muscle movements and emotions.

Emotion recognition is the mechanism of inferring human emotions mostly from facial expressions, and in some cases from gestures and verbal expressions. Emotions are automatically perceived by humans, due to our inherent abilities. However, computational methods for identifying emotions have been developed lately and are quickly gaining popularity. Computational processes of emotion interpretation take advantage of multi-faceted methodologies such as signal processing, computer vision, machine learning, among others. These processes involve processing human expressions in multiple ways, such as facial expressions, gestures, movements, in the form of audio, video, or text. Existing processing strategies for classification of certain forms of emotions could be typically categorized into three main classes, which are, Statistical, Knowledge-based, and hybrid methods. In this paper, the objective lies in recognition of emotions only through certain facial features from still images, and no instance of verbal, textual or gestural expressivity is taken into account. The Facial Action Coding System (FACS) is a system used to observe, identify, label, and quantify muscle movements on the face (named Action Units, or AU), that form an expression [1]. Emotions are mapped to combinations of AUs and their intensities to form a system known as the Emotional FACS [2]. Intensity scoring is done on a scale from A to E, A meaning only traces of an AU are detected, while E meaning the maximum possible intensity is detected. It consists of a list of main codes (pertaining to the entire face), head movement codes, eye movement codes, visibility codes, and other general behavior codes. It would be useful to note that the terms "action units" and "features" could be used interchangeably throughout this paper, the former being a term used for the latter in the dataset. More formally, action units represent the actions of individuals or groups of muscles used in the taxonomy of the human facial movements in the Facial Action Coding System. This work utilizes some of the main codes as well as a few of the behavioral codes, to detect expressions from the eye region [1].

Emotion recognition systems fail when the face is partially covered by a veil such as niqab, or due to a hand-to-face gesture. Hence, the emphasis of this paper lies in the determination of emotions from face images, focusing on the areas around the eyes, also known as the periocular region. The Periocular vicinity is thus the Region of Interest (RoI), and covers 12 action units. The entire face consists of 30 AUs; thus, intuitively, about 40% of an expression is conveyed by the periocular region. Further, studies pertaining to detection of emotions by the use of the vicinity of the eye alone, are very low in number and accessibility, essentially making it a less-trodden road. Apart from this, the fact that humans are capable enough to accurately deduce emotions shown on a partially visible face, is the motivation behind this work. This brings us to the basis of the reasoning of this RoI choice: figuring out how well a trained machine can recognize human expressions from a partially visible face. The key contribution of this work lies in analyzing the variation in performance of a few supervised machine learning strategies for the chosen region of interest – Periocular vicinity – in the face.

## 2  Literature Review

This section provides an insight into works in the fields of facial expression extraction and emotion recognition, including those in the periocular region. Information from these papers will be used for various purposes, at times regulated to fit the objective of this study.

Alonso-Fernandez et al. in their work, investigate the feasibility of recognizing expressions using the periocular region [3]. They have analyzed the performance of five image descriptors on a dataset of 1,574 images from 118 volunteers. The predictions were made with SVM classifiers and their approach attained an overall accuracy of 67–78% on the fusion of several of the five descriptors at a time. This level of accuracy still remains behind that when features of the entire face is used (83–96%). However, it should be noted that the studies that use full faces, use dynamic information, that is, they employ all the frames, right from the onset to the peak expression; this work employs an initial approach, based only on the apex expression frame. Nonetheless, it proves the feasibility of our choice of RoI for emotion recognition.

Kanade et al. presented their approach on a comprehensive database, developed for use in analysis of facial expressions [4]. Most experiments on facial recognition used relatively limited datasets, despite the fact the set of problems in the field of expression analysis requires inclusion of multiple dimensions. Some of these dimensions are the levels of description, distinction between spontaneous and deliberate, the transitions, test data reliability, orientation, image metadata, differences among subjects, among others. This paper presents the CMU-Pittsburgh AU-Coded Face Expression Image Database, including 2,105 image sequences, collected from 182 subjects of various racial backgrounds, with multiple tokens of FACS action unit coding.

Further improving the Cohn-Kanade Dataset, Lucey et al. brought about the Extended Cohn-Kanade Dataset (CK+), described as the complete dataset for the AU and emotion specifications of expressions. The extension was done after a wide study of limitations arising from the previously proposed dataset, including the fact that the emotion labels are not validated, while the AU are [5]. Apart from this, two more issues that arose were the lack of a common performance metric, and that the common databases do not have a set of standardized protocols. To address these, and a few other issues, the CK+ dataset increased the number of sequences by 22%, and that of the subjects by 27%. Sequences now have a revised set of validated emotion labels, and are fully FACS coded. Baseline results have been presented using Active Appearance Models (AAMs) and an SVM classifier that uses a leave-one-out cross validation model.

Vukadinovic and Pantic have studied a system for fully automated detection of twenty facial feature points, by experimenting the use of Gabor feature-based boosted classifiers [6]. The method used in their work was adapted from the Viola-Jones face detection system. The 20 regions of interest are examined further to detect feature points. Feature models are built from Gentle-Boost Templates, with both, Gabor-wavelet features and the gray level intensities. Using the Cohn-Kanade database as the test set, their approach achieved an average recognition accuracy of 93%.

A review of visual information-based Facial Emotion Recognition (FER) techniques is presented in [7]. The FER methods that are CNN-based, do not detect temporal variations in the face. Hence a hybrid approach is presented; this combines Long Short-term Memory (LSTMs) for temporal features for consecutive frames, and Convolution Neural Networks (CNNs) for spatial features. FER approaches that are based on deep learning, and use of networks that enable end-to-end learning were used. Further, metrics for the evaluation of FER based methods are instituted to establish a set of standardized metrics for comparison. Precision and Recall are the main metrics used for quantitative evaluation purposes.

Whitehill and Omlin, proposed a method to recognize FACS action units that utilizes Haar features, along with the Adaboost boosting algorithm [8]. Accuracy of recognition and the run-time for processing taken by this method is collated with the Gabor responses classifying with SVMs. The Haar and Adaboost method achieves similar accuracy as that of the Gabor and SVM method, and it performed at least two folds quicker in magnitude. These empirical results are based on runs on the CK facial expression database. The Haar features can be extracted from the Viola-Jones integral image, which is hypothesized to be an improvement.

The pioneers of the CK and the CK+ datasets, Lien et al. present a system to detect, track and classify action units. It uses three modules to extract features. Three AU combinations with analyzed in the brow region, with the highest classification accuracy of 92% among different methods [9]. The highest accuracy was obtained through Hidden Markov Models (HMM) for dense-flow extraction and tracking of facial-features. In the periocular vicinity, analysis was targeted at feature tracking accompanied by discriminant analysis. AU 5, 6 and 7 were classified only with 88% accuracy, as they are arduous to distinguish, even during manual FACS coding. Overall, the results from dense-flow-extraction with facial feature tracking showed the highest conformity with the manual FACS. Other methods used to experiment were HMM with feature tracking, and HMM with high gradient component detection.

In a recent work for recognizing expressions via an algorithmic periocular localization, a system that comprises of training a classifier on features extracted from labeled images, detecting multiple faces, localizing the periocular region for at least one face, extracting its features, and classifying the expression by querying the extracted representative features was developed; the classifier outputs an expression class [10]. To make the method more robust and dispose disturbances due to noise and movement, the sequential aspect of videos is utilized, which also helps in the validation of expressions, that is, those that last at least for a predetermined time. As an alternative, a statistical mode is employed where the most frequently occurring expression is determined as the valid one. The statistical method could analyze 60 sequential frames in 2 s, for a video at 30 frames per second.

There are several works that experiment on facial emotions involving many features (such as the mouth, nose, and the jawline, in addition to the eyes) [9, 11], but very few of them focus specifically on the periocular features [3, 10]. There are quite a few studies that focus on periocular feature extraction but do not use them for emotion recognition [12]. A reader interested in more recent research works and applications based on periocular region of the face can refer to [13–15].

## 3  Methods

The proposed system has two phases: first, face detection and feature extraction from a given image (with feature subset selection); second, analysis of classification approaches and parameter tuning, followed by selection of a classifier to obtain optimum performance. All experiments were implemented in Python 3.7. SciPy [16] for Wilcoxon signed-rank testing; Scikit-Learn [17] for classifier implementations; Matplotlib [18] and Seaborn for generating plots and confusion matrices; Pandas and NumPy libraries for handling data-frames. The schematic representation of the modules and components in the work is presented in Fig. 1.

### 3.1  Feature Extraction

For the purpose of extracting features, The CK+ dataset was used. This is generally considered to be a benchmark dataset for facial images used widely in FER (facial emotion recognition) and emotion detection systems. The dataset consists of 593 face images, taken from video sequences where subjects of varied racial backgrounds, show expressions ranging from neutral to a peak one. Out of these, 327 images are emotion labelled and proved to be of use to this study. The peak frame of the sequence is captured and used to identify the emotion. All images available in this set are grayscale images, and the expressions are posed. Keeping in view the robust and comprehensive dataset available, image processing procedures are not necessary here; this is because the dataset provides pre-processed imaged with well-defined AUs, as per the prototypic definition of the emotions, given with their corresponding intensities.

**Table 1.** Emotion labels

| Emotion | Label |
|---------|-------|
| Neutral | 0 |
| Anger | 1 |
| Contempt | 2 |
| Disgust | 3 |
| Fear | 4 |
| Happiness | 5 |
| Sadness | 6 |
| Surprise | 7 |

Eight emotions listed in Table 1 are recorded. In each of the facial images, the action units present and its respective intensity had been calculated and stored as a part of the dataset. Each set of action units corresponds to a different emotion and the degree to which it is perceived. The work presented in this paper focusses on building a similar correspondence between sets of AUs from the periocular area alone, and the emotion labels. Emotion coded files provided in the dataset consist of images that fit the prototypic definition of an emotion. Files corresponding to each image in the dataset hold the AU present in the image and the intensity of the AU detected, all in exponent notation, which is stored as floating-point numbers when the dataset is serialized.

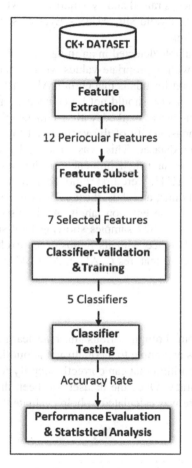

**Fig. 1.** System architecture

Since this system focuses only on a small part of the face, the presence and intensity of only those AUs which are found in our Region of Interest were considered; hence, during feature extraction only periocular features that are indeed relevant were extracted. This data was simultaneously serialized for ease of use, and stored as a table. The table consists of the relevant AUs as components of each image, which is an $n$-dimensional vector, where $n$ is the number of AUs taken into consideration, alongside the emotion label of the image. Thus, the feature extraction process resulted in a table that has columns denoting the features including the class label, that is the AUs and emotion label. Each row denotes an image in the dataset. The table, stored as a CSV file was used as an input to the classifiers.

## 3.2 Feature Subset Selection

Each expression has a unique set of action units that it comprises of. An entire face consists of 30 AUs; out of which the twelve action units in the periocular region, are as follows: AU1 - Inner brow raiser, AU2 - Outer brow raiser, AU4 - Brow lowerer, AU5 - Eyes widened, AU6 - Cheeks raised and eyes narrowed, AU7 - Lid tightened, AU41 - Upper eyelid drop, AU42 - Eyelid slit, AU43 - Eyes closed, AU44 - Eyes squinted, AU45 - Blink, AU46 - Wink.

AUs that were not available/detected in an image were marked with -1 for the time being and were replaced with appropriate values when it came to training classifiers, later in the study. The reason for this is that certain AUs that are detected in an image, but have no significant intensity, should not be counted as an absent AU. Thus, only absent AUs had a null intensity, marked with −1 to keep the CSV file completely numeric. Further, the dimensionality of the vectors had to be brought down to avoid overfitting to the training dataset. This was ensured by checking the correlation between the various features and their influence on the emotion labels. Action units AU46, AU44, AU42, and AU41, were first removed as none of the images had a non-null value for these action units, and thus, these AUs provided no useful input into the decision-making process for the emotion labels. AU43 also showed negligible influence, with only two out of the 327 samples showing faint signs of its existence, and showing absolutely no difference with its inclusion or exclusion. The final reduced feature-subset contained seven features (7 AUs): AU1, AU2, AU4, AU5, AU6, AU7, AU45.

## 3.3 Classification

The feature subset was run through various machine learning algorithms to classify images based on emotions and come to a conclusion about the accuracy of each, so as to decide on a suitable algorithm that can correctly identify (classify) the emotions and also achieve a good accuracy. Once the dataset had been divided into a training and testing set, a baseline score was calculated to help evaluate the performance of various classifiers.

### Baseline Score
The occurrences (normalized) of images of each emotion type in the training dataset is shown in Table 2. It can be concluded that any model chosen should give an accuracy score of over 25.3%, else it will be evident that it seems to be giving dissatisfactory results and is performing very poorly. Although, this does not mean that any classifier scoring better than the baseline is performing well, and will have to be checked on a label-basis to see what fraction of images belonging to each class it has classified correctly.

**Table 2.** Fraction of training examples in each class

| Emotion label | Occurrence |
|---|---|
| 7 | 0.253 |
| 5 | 0.211 |
| 3 | 0.180 |
| 1 | 0.137 |
| 6 | 0.085 |
| 4 | 0.076 |
| 2 | 0.055 |

## Validation and Training

Five classifiers had been used to relate facial images with the emotion they depict. They are as follows:

- Support Vector Machine/Classifier (SVM),
- Multinomial Naive Bayes (MNB) classifier,
- Random Forest classifier (RFC),
- $k$-Nearest Neighbours (KNN) classifier, and
- $k$-NN with Neighbourhood Components Analysis

Each classifier has one or more hyperparameters which may be adjusted to tune its performance. To pick the most suitable parameters, Grid Search with k-fold cross-validation was applied to a set of parameters (k = 5). Further, elements in the image-AU table that have no intensity (due to the absence) of an AU, were approximated by using the mean, median, or mode of the values of the intensity of that AU in the whole dataset. The measure (mean/median/mode) that worked best in each case was taken into consideration. Since the intensity data is given in floating point numbers, signifying continuity, one tends to incline towards the use of mean for replacement of nulls. However, all three measures had been tried here to observe what difference it made in the classification performance.

### Support Vector Machine

Replacing the nulls with mean, and supplying the following values in grid search for the parameters gamma ($\gamma$) and C (cost of misclassification) for the SVM: $\gamma \in \{0.1, 1, 2\}$ and $C \in \{0.5, 1, 2\}$.

The grid search algorithm gave the values of $\gamma = 1$ and C = 2 as the most suitable ones when using Radial Basis Function kernel. RBF kernel uses the equation given below, where $||x - x'||^2$ is the square of the Euclidean distance between two points ($x$ and $x'$):

$$K\left(x, x'\right) = exp\left(\frac{-||x - x'||^2}{2\sigma^2}\right)$$

The value of gamma ($\gamma$) is $\frac{1}{2\sigma^2}$

Using these parameters to train the SVM classifier on the training set, and then predicting labels for the test set, gave a score of 68.29%. Analyzing the values of $\gamma$ and C with random brute force approach, SVM achieved an accuracy of 64.63% at $\gamma = 2$ and any C value, and 63.41% at $\gamma = 0.1$ and C = 2. Applying the above process when absent values are replaced with either mode or median (as both mode and median are equal for each of the AU columns) gave a prediction score of a measly 35.41% at best. This is clearly not a suitable replacement for prediction of the absent values. Thus, the SVM classifier can correctly classify 68.29% of the images it is tested on.

*Multinomial Naïve Bayes Classifier*
The Multinomial Naive Bayes classifier seemed to perform relatively poorly. A grid search on the values of $\alpha$ (regularization/smoothing parameter for MNB) with prior probability fitting and 5-fold cross validation was conducted, on the following values: $\alpha \in \{0.001, 1, 5, 10, 15\}$.

$\alpha$ here contributes to the formation of the following estimator after the Laplacian smoothing $\widehat{\theta}_i = \frac{x_i + \alpha}{N + \alpha d}$; where $N = \sum_{j=1}^{d} x_j$ for $i$ ranging from 1 to $d$ ($d$ = no. of dimensions), where the uniform probability for each component becomes $\frac{1}{d}$. The estimator will lie between $\frac{x_i}{N}$ and $\frac{1}{d}$. When the missing values were predicted to be the mean values (of each AU), the optimal value for $\alpha$ was chosen by the grid-search to be 0.001, giving an unsatisfactory accuracy score of 32.92%. However, doing the same with median/mode in place of the absent values, gave 10 as the best $\alpha$ parameter and a score of 36.58%, which is better, yet highly unsatisfactory still. From this performance score of the MNB classifier, it can be said that the classifier fails in its presumption that each of the features in this use case are independent of each other. Intuitively, this deduction sounds appropriate to a good extent, as movements of muscle groups on the face cannot, biologically, be autonomous and free of any influence from that of other muscles around it. This biological factor is unfortunately something that cannot be eliminated from consideration when modelling for emotion classification.

*Random Forest Classifier*
Two measures were used for assessing the quality of a split: Gini impurity and Information gain (entropy-based). Parameters on which the grid search was conducted were the '$n$' (the number of trees in the forest) as well as the split quality metrics. The following two expressions define the two split metrics used: the Gini Impurity given by $\Sigma_{i=1}^{d} p_i(1 - p_i)$, and Entropy given by $\Sigma_{i=1}^{d} - p_i log(p_i)$. Thus, the grid search pipeline is: $n \in \{5, 10, 20, 70, 100\}$, criterion $\in \{gini, entropy\}$.

This process showed that the Gini split criterion with 20 trees in the forest gave the best prediction score of 75.61%. It was observed that the split quality measurement using information gain also gave the same result in this case. This was the case when absent data was approximated with the mean values of the corresponding columns. Trying the same with the null values replaced with the median/modes of the AUs, gave a low score of around 34%. Since this behavior was observed in all the classifiers tried, this approximation was not considered in the classifiers ahead, and only mean value approximations were used for the absent values.

*k-Nearest Neighbours Classifier*

The *k*-NN classification process using Euclidean distance measure (*L₂* norm) involved a search over the value of *k* (in the term *k-nearest*), where the number of neighbors were chosen using a grid-search pipeline process, with three-fold cross validation and values of $k \in \{5,7,10,20\}$

The grid search procedure returned 7 neighbors (k = 7) as the best parameter to be used with the Euclidean distance calculation. The Euclidean distance, used in the SVM classification previously as well, is calculated from the equation $dist(p,q) = \|p - q\| = \sqrt{\Sigma_{i=1}^{d}(q_i - p_i)^2}$. It is worth noting that all the points in the space were uniformly weighted when calculating the k-neighbors. Using the 7 nearest neighbors for classification gave a prediction performance score of 69.51%. Tweaking the value of k reported that, when the number of neighbors is set to any number from 7 up until 10, the accuracy seemed to remain the same, but plummeted when set to 11 or above. Using Neighborhood Components Analysis (NCA) usually works well in nearest neighbor classifiers, in that it helps improve the performance and classification accuracy. This method will be seen in the next section, as an addition to the k-nearest neighbor classifier which was used here.

*k-NN with Neighborhood Components Analysis*

The *k*-NN classification component of the experiment remains the same as the procedure followed above. NCA is used to improve the prediction accuracy of stochastic nearest-neighbor classifiers. Grid search parameters remained the same, but the NCA procedure was added to the pipeline and will be fit on the classifier that is already fitted on the *k*-NN training set. The NCA was set to undergo 50 iterations for optimization. This process returned 5 as the best value for k, from the grid-search and improved the prediction score of the nearest neighbor classifier to 71.95%, an improvement of about 2.5% from the 69.5% that was obtained when the *k*-NN classifier was applied alone. However, if the same number of neighbors as that used in the *k*-NN method above were employed here (that is, 7), the classification accuracy actually seemed to go down rather than getting better. Nonetheless, the addition of neighborhood components analysis has provided a promising improvement.

# 4   Results and Discussion

The preceding section analyzed the performance of the classification approaches based on trivial performance evaluation metrics. The relative performance of each of the classifiers is judged in this section using a statistical hypothesis test, followed by an analysis of the label-wise performances of the two best performing classifiers, namely, the Random Forest classifier and *k*-NN classifier with Neighborhood Components Analysis.

Table 3 presents the classification accuracy rate (Images Labelled Correctly) of each of the classification systems trained on the training set, sorted by the accuracy rate.

**Table 3.** Performance of classifiers

| Classifier | Parameters (tuned using grid-search) | Accuracy rate |
|---|---|---|
| RFC | n = 20, gini split | 75.61% |
| k-NN & NCA | k = 5, 50 NCA iterations | 71.95% |
| k-NN | k = 7 | 69.51% |
| SVM | $\gamma = 1, C = 2$ | 68.29% |
| MNB | $\alpha = 10$ | 36.58% |

It is quite evident that the Random Forest classifier seemed to provide a higher classification/labeling score, while k-Nearest Neighbor classifier along with NCA, comes second, correctly labelling close to 72% of the images with their emotion labels. Three of the classifiers have performed with similar accuracies, i.e., the k-NN with NCA, k-NN, and the SVM classifiers, with a difference lying in ±3% of each other. The Multinomial Naïve Bayes classification did not seem to work satisfactorily as compared to the other chosen classifiers, although it managed to cross the baseline score. This is hypothesized to be due to biological factors, although such factors will not be evaluated in this paper as they are out of the scope of this study. Due to the poor results, the Multinomial Naïve Bayes classifier will no longer be a part of the discussion ahead.

Relative performances of the classifiers were tested using a statistical hypothesis test, the Wilcoxon signed-rank test [19], which is a non-parametric version of the Student's t-Test. The reason for the choice of a non-parametric test is because the Wilcoxon Signed-Rank test does not assume the normal (Gaussian) distribution of samples, as opposed to the t-test. Normal distribution of training examples cannot be guaranteed in this case as the number of samples are only 327, which is quite a small number for such an assumption. The test was carried out on the four classifiers (excluding MNB) with k-fold cross validation (k = 20).

The null hypothesis here was that two classifiers tested against each other are not different significantly. The values in the correlation matrix in Fig. 2 signify the p-values obtained in the pairwise tests. The cutoff for significance was set to $\alpha = 0.05$. It is quite evident from the figure, that only in case of the RF and SVM classification techniques, the p value has been observed to be less than the value of $\alpha$. Thus, it can be said that the RF and SVM classifiers have significant differences (null hypothesis rejected), while the other classifiers have a similar prediction performance. This test goes hand in hand with the results presented in Table 3, where the RFC and SVM classification techniques show a significant difference in their accuracy measures, approximately 8 percent.

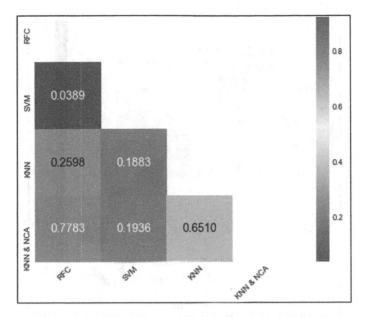

**Fig. 2.** Wilcoxon test correlation matrix

It is evident from the experiments performed using various classifiers and the parameters associated with each, that the best prediction score came out to be a little upwards of 75.61%, and was the result of the Random Forest Classification method. The following (normalized) confusion matrix gives an idea of the prediction score for each type of image in the training set, using the Random forest classifier.

From Fig. 3 it can be inferred that images labelled with the emotion 'Happy' were all correctly predicted, followed by 'surprise'. The lowest score seemed to be for disgust, with only one-third of its images labeled correctly. Apart from emotion labels disgust and fear, the other labels seemed to have been predicted with satisfactory accuracy. The classifier seems to have overestimated the number of contempt (label 2) images and underestimated the disgust-labeled images.

The second-best performance was given by the KNN classifier when augmented with the Nearest Components Analysis technique. The confusion matrix (Fig. 4) gives a visual overview of its prediction performance. Although the KNN classifier with NCA came a close second to the RFC method in terms of prediction performance, it clearly did not perform well per label. Contempt images had been predicted with zero accuracy.

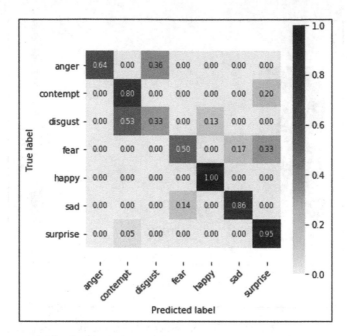

**Fig. 3.** Confusion matrix for predictions by the RFC

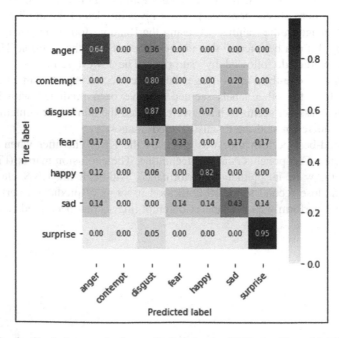

**Fig. 4.** Confusion matrix for predictions by the KNN classifier with NCA

From Fig. 4 it can be inferred that apart from the performance for label 3 (emotion: disgust), the accuracy for all the other emotion classes had either gone down or remained the same as that of RFC. Images belonging to the disgust class had been labelled with a higher accuracy by this classifier than that done by the RFC. Despite this, the performance of the k-Nearest Neighbors classifier, even with the help of Nearest Components Analysis, remains to be unsatisfactory when scrutinized for each class. It seemed to have wrongly estimated the number of images in each of the classes, with the number of contempt labelled images being grossly underestimated and most others, overestimated to some extent.

## 5 Conclusion

Analytic studies for emotion recognition in periocular images are far less in availability than those on full facial images. The periocular region proves to be a fit region of interest for emotion classification, as it contributes up to 40% in the display of an expression on the face (12 out of 30 possible AUs). This paper further studies the possibility of emotion labelling with a focus on this region alone; done by: extracting features, choosing a viable subset of features, and finding an algorithm for emotion classification. The proposed system can be used for a variety of applications, such as emotion detection for partially visible faces; faces covered due to veils such as niqab, pollution masks, or partially concealed due to hand-to-face gestures covering the region around the mouth.

### 5.1 Scope for Improvement

This venture has a wide potential for improvement. The dataset used here is not substantially sized, and can be expanded further in order to avail and take advantage of more training examples for the classifiers. Further, the metadata of the CK+ dataset mentions the existence of faces with neutral expressions, which is emotion label 0. However, no such labelled images were actually present in the database of the labelled faces. This led the system to completely lack the understanding of neutral expressions, and thus, in case a neutral expression is fed to the system, it will be recognized as some other expression, bringing down the performance. This brings us to another possible improvement, which is to include a wider selection of emotions and prototype them, just like the ones available in the CK+ dataset and used in this project, and form a labelled dataset of such images as training examples.

The subset selection could be improved by using wrapper algorithms that make sure we minimize the cohesion between the features. However, this seems to be quite difficult since the human biological features, or the muscle groups in the taxonomy of the face, often depend on each other extensively. Nevertheless, any deduction cannot be made without running a trial. Further, a greater number of classification methods can be tried, so as to include various other techniques to help with validation of results obtained so far and provide a better comparison, and possibly coming up with a solution that is a hybrid of two or more techniques.

# References

1. Ekman, P., Friesen, W.: Facial Action Coding System: A Technique for the Measurement of Facial Movement. Consulting Psychologists Press, Palo Alto (1978)
2. Friesen, W., Ekman, P.: EMFACS-7: emotional facial action coding system, p. 1. University of California, San Francisco (1983). Unpublished manuscript
3. Alonso-Fernandez, F., Bigun, J., Englund, C.: Expression recognition using the periocular region: a feasibility study. In: 14th International Conference on Signal-Image Technology & Internet-Based Systems (SITIS), pp. 536–541 (2018)
4. Kanade, T., Cohn, J.F., Tian, Y.: Comprehensive database for facial expression analysis. In: Proceedings of the Fourth IEEE International Conference on Automatic Face and Gesture Recognition (Cat. No. PR00580), pp. 46–53. IEEE, March 2000
5. Lucey, P., Cohn, J.F., Kanade, T., Saragih, J., Ambadar, Z., Matthews, I.: The extended Cohn-Kanade dataset (CK+): a complete dataset for action unit and emotion-specified expression (2010)
6. Vukadinovic, D., Pantic, M.: Fully automatic facial feature point detection using Gabor feature based boosted classifiers. In: IEEE International Conference on Systems, Man and Cybernetics, vol. 2, pp. 1692–1698 (2005)
7. Ko, B.: A brief review of facial emotion recognition based on visual information. Sensors **18**(2), 401 (2018). https://doi.org/10.3390/s18020401
8. Whitehill, J., Omlin, C.W.: Haar features for FACS AU recognition. In: 7th International Conference on Automatic Face and Gesture Recognition, pp. 5–pp, April 2006
9. Lien, J.J.J., Kanade, T., Cohn, J.F., Li, C.C.: Detection, tracking, and classification of action units in facial expression. Robot. Auton. Syst. **31**(3), 131–146 (2000)
10. Shreve, M.A., Mongeon, M.C., Loce, R.P., Bernal E.A., Wu, W.: Method and system for automatically recognizing facial expressions via algorithmic periocular localization. Patent and Trademark. U.S. Patent 9,600,711, Washington, DC (2017)
11. Majumder, A., Behera, L., Subramanian, V.: Emotion recognition from geometric facial features using self-organizing map. Pattern Recogn. **47**(3), 1282–1293 (2014)
12. Borza, D., Danescu, R.: Eye shape and corners detection in periocular images using particle filters. In: International Conference on Signal Image Techonology & Internet Based Systems (SITIS), pp. 15–22, November 2016
13. Kumari, P., Seeja, K.R.: Periocular biometrics: a survey. J. King Saud Univ.-Comput. Inf. Sci. (2019)
14. Umer, S., Sardar, A., Dhara, B.C., Rout, R.K., Pandey, H.M.: Person identification using fusion of iris and periocular deep features. Neural Netw. **122**, 407–419 (2020)
15. Liu, X., Vijaya Kumar, B.V.K., You, J., Jia, P.: Adaptive deep metric learning for identity-aware facial expression recognition. In: Proceedings of the IEEE Conference on Computer Vision and Pattern Recognition Workshops, CVPRW, July 2017, pp. 522–531 (2017)
16. Jones, E., Oliphant, T., Peterson, P., et al.: SciPy: open source scientific tools for Python (2001). http://www.scipy.org/
17. Pedregosa, F., et al.: Scikit-learn: machine learning in Python. JMLR **12**, 2825–2830 (2011)
18. Hunter, J.D.: Matplotlib: a 2D graphics environment. Comput. Sci. Eng. **9**(3), 90–95 (2007)
19. Wilcoxon, F.: Individual comparisons by ranking methods. Biom. Bull. 80–83 (1945)

# A Comparative Study of Computational Intelligence for Identification of Breast Cancer

Divyue Sharma[✉], Parva Jain[✉], and Dilip Kumar Choubey[✉]

School of Computer Science and Engineering (SCOPE),
Vellore Institute of Technology, Vellore 632014, Tamil Nadu, India
tomchi.sharma305@gmail.com, parva98@gmail.com,
dilipchoubey_1988@yahoo.in, dilip.choubey@vit.ac.in

**Abstract.** Breast cancer is a type of invasive cancer that occurs in women. Breast cancer accounts for 18% of all cancer related deaths among women according to World Health Organization. After Lung Cancer, breast cancer is the leading cause of death of women in India. Due to inaccessibility, especially in rural areas, it is impossible for everyone to get diagnosed in time. If breast cancer is detected at an early stage, the doctor will be aided in suggesting an efficient way to proceed with the treatment of the patient, thus reducing the mortality rate and medical expenses. So, in this paper a comparative study on machine learning and computational intelligence techniques has been performed to optimize the process and achieve better accuracy and precision. The focus of this review article is to survey several articles existing on breast cancer majorly on Wisconsin dataset which is obtained from UCI repository. This review article has been concluded with suggestions for future directions.

**Keywords:** Machine learning · Soft computing · KNN · CNN · Naive Bayes · K-means · Logistic Regression · SVM (Support Vector Machine) · Random Forest

## 1 Introduction

Breast cancer is one of the most common types of diseases to affect women. Breast cancer accounts for 18% of all cancer related deaths among women according to World Health Organization (WHO; 2018) [28]. One of the reasons for such a high mortality rate is that screening and diagnosis process for breast cancer is not a very fast process. Hence creating a machine learning model to help diagnose breast cancer early, easily and quickly can help decrease the mortality rate significantly. After a tumour is confirmed one can implement soft computing techniques to figure out if the tumour is malignant or benign. This will help the doctor recommend different types of treatments based the condition of the tumour. A benign tissue is one that does not invade it's surrounding tissue, meanwhile a malignant tumour is one that may have started spreading to surrounding tissue. For a benign tumour the treatment can range from removing particular lymph nodes or only the tumour, whereas the treatment for malignant tumour could go as far as to remove both breasts.

© Springer Nature Singapore Pte Ltd. 2020
A. Bhattacharjee et al. (Eds.): MIND 2020, CCIS 1240, pp. 209–216, 2020.
https://doi.org/10.1007/978-981-15-6315-7_17

The rest of the paper is signified as follows: Sect. 2 contains Literature review, Summary of Existing Work is included in Sect. 3, Sect. 4 contains Discussion and Future Direction

## 2 Literature Review

Polat and Sentürk [12] used three steps to detect breast cancer. The first task was to use MAD normalization to normalize the features. In the second part, k-means clustering was used for weighting the normalized features. Then they used AdaBoostM1 classifier on the weighted to classify the data and predict the existence of breast cancer. Lu et al. [9] used computer vision along with machine learning techniques to perform image processing, area segmentation, feature extraction and classification on images of histograms. Sharma et al. [6] used three prediction techniques namely k-Nearest-Neighbours, Naive Bayes and Random Forest on the Wisconsin Breast Cancer data set and compared the results between the prediction models. Sharma et al. [15] used classifiers such as Logistic Regression, Support Vector Machine and k-Nearest Neighbours on the Wisconsin Breast Cancer dataset to predict whether the tumour is benign or malignant and compared the accuracy between the three classifiers. Osareh and Shadgar [10] have used principal component analysis for feature selection before using k-Nearest Neighbours, Support Vector Machine and Probabilistic Neural Networks to classify the tumour as malignant or benign. Islam et al. [11] used Support Vector Machine and k-Nearest Neighbours along with 10-fold cross validation to improve the accuracy of classifying malignant and benign breast tumours. Gupta and Gupta [19] used Linear Regression, Random Forest, Multi-Layer Perceptron and Decision trees to classify between malignant and benign tumours of the breast. Nemissi et al. [3] proposed a single hidden layer neural network with a new approach to the activation function of the neurons. Khuriwal and Mishra [8] have proposed a deep learning algorithm neural network for the diagnosis of breast cancer. They have applied a pre-processing algorithm on the Wisconsin Breast cancer database and then split the data into two: testing purpose and training dataset. Bharat et al. [2] have used Support Vector Machine (SVM) on the Wisconsin Breast Cancer dataset. They have also performed several algorithms such as K-nearest neighbours, Naives Bayes and CART and compared the accuracy of each algorithm. Sultan et al. [5] have used image processing techniques such as grayscale histograms on doppler ultrasound images and then applied linear regression for breast cancer diagnosis. Amrane et al. [21] have used classification machine learning techniques on WBCD and checked performance based on extended metrics including not only accuracy, precision and recall but also area under the ROC curve. In a similar manner, Choubey et al. [13, 14, 17, 18, 24, 25] and Bala et al. [26, 27] have explained elaborately many soft computing, data mining and machine learning techniques for the classification of diabetes and thunderstorm respectively. Bazazeh and Shubair [7] performed a comparison between Bayesian Network, Random Forest and Support Vector Machine algorithms and concluded that Bayesian network gave the best result. Bhat et al. [4] have developed an algorithm such that research on breast cancer can be done using the adaptive resonance theory. The classification of breast is done on the basis of ART 1 and this algorithm is then stored in a cloud platform and through an interface a clinician is given access to the cloud and algorithm. Khuriwal and Mishra [20] proposed to use MIAS mammograph database to train the convolutional neural network deep learning algorithm. They have divided the procedure in three different parts, first they have collected data and set for the pre-processing algorithm on data. Then they have split data into two: training set and testing set. At last they have achieved an accuracy of 98% after performing on a trained dataset.

# 3 Summary of Existing Work

Multiple research articles on breast cancer have been reviewed and the following information has been gathered in Table 1 notably, Data Set, Techniques Used and Tools Used, Purpose, Advantages, Issues and Accuracy.

**Table 1.** Summary of existing work for breast cancer

| Authors and ref. no. | Data set | Techniques used and tools used | Purpose | Advantages | Issues | Accuracy |
|---|---|---|---|---|---|---|
| Polat and Sentürk [12] | Combria dataset | K-means, adaboostm1 classifier | AdaBoostM1 classifier is used for solving the binary classification problem. K-means clustering is used normalized dataset | Uses normalization and weighting to find more accurate results | Relatively small dataset | 91.37% |
| Lu et al. [9] | MITOS, AMIDA13, Camelyon16, MIAS, DDSM, INbreast | Adaboost, m Random Forest, IP | Random forest, uses bagging as an ensemble model and Adaboost is a boosting ensemble model | Uses many different datasets | No consistent dataset | 98.8% |
| Sharma et al. [6] | Wisconsin Breast Cancer | Random forest, kNN, Naive Bayes and Python Jupyter notebook | They show a comparison between naïve bayes, random forest and kNN algorithms on WDBC dataset | Accuracy for all three models is higher than 94% | Better ML techniques can further be implemented | 95.9% |
| Sharma et al. [15] | Wisconsin Breast Cancer | SVM Logistic regression, kNN | Linear SVM is used here, which is able to maximize functional margin. LR is used here to describe data relationship between dependent and independent variable kNN is used to predict the class | Found results for prognostic and diagnostic data separately | – | 96.89% |
| Osareh and Shadgar [10] | Dataset of fine needle aspirate of breast lesions | SVM, kNN, PNN | SVM can deal with classification and regression problems. PNN is proposed to reduce the computational time taken by CNN. kNN is used for classification | Unique dataset that does not have a lot of work done on it | The dataset is very specific and has few features | 98.8% |

(*continued*)

**Table 1.** (*continued*)

| Authors and ref. no. | Data set | Techniques used and tools used | Purpose | Advantages | Issues | Accuracy |
|---|---|---|---|---|---|---|
| Islam et al. [11] | Wisconsin Breast Cancer | SVM, kNN and Python Spyder | A model using support vector Machine and K-Nearest Neighbour has been proposed and 10-fold technique is used to split data into 10 chunks | Proposed model is more accurate than existing SVM models | This work compares existing SVM models with proposed kNN model | 99.68% |
| Gupta and Gupta [19] | Wisconsin Breast Cancer | DT, SVM, k-NN, MLP, 10-fold cross validation and Anaconda 2.7 python IDE | They used Multi-Layer Perceptron, k-Nearest Neighbours, Decision tree and Support vector machine on WBCD and then performed a comparative study | The comparative analysis of four widely used machine learning techniques are performed | – | 98.12% 10-fold cross validation |
| Khuriwal and Mishra [8] | Wisconsin Breast Cancer | CNN | CNN is used and some additional processes are added unit of bias, additional hidden layer, and after calculating activation function, a final output is generated | Uses convoluted neural network which has been used very rarely | – | 99.67% |
| Amrane et al. [21] | University of California breast cancer dataset | Naive Bayes, KNN | Naive Bayes is used on data that directly influence each other to determine the model. To predict the property of data, kNN is used | Unique dataset that does not have a lot of work done on it | Relatively Small dataset | 97.51% |
| Khuriwal and Mishra [20] | MIAS | CNN | CNN was used with sigmoid function as activator to classify the tumours from mammograms | 98% accuracy has been achieved while working on 12 features only | Limited dataset | 98% |
| Bayrak et al. [1] | Wisconsin Breast Cancer | SVM, ANN | SVM is used 10-fold cross validation and in ANN, Multi-layer perceptron and voting perceptron are used for classification | The best performance has been obtained by SVM technique with the highest accuracy | Comparison among the known algorithms | 97.13% |
| Bharat et al. [2] | Wisconsin Breast Cancer | k-NN, Naives Bayes, CART, SVM | The author uses all four techniques before and after standardization of values to compare the performance | KNN technique has given the best results | – | 99.1% |
| Nemissi et al. [3] | Wisconsin Breast Cancer | Extreme learning machine, Genetic Algorithm | A neural network is created and different sigmoid functions are used on different neurons to provide a better result | ELM is faster, it can be used with non-differential activation | – | 97.28% |

(*continued*)

**Table 1.**  (*continued*)

| Authors and ref. no. | Data set | Techniques used and tools used | Purpose | Advantages | Issues | Accuracy |
|---|---|---|---|---|---|---|
| Bhat et al. [4] | Wisconsin, Local Hospital | Adaptive Resonance Theory (ART) and MATLAB | Adaptive Resonance Theory (ART) is a neural network architecture that generates suitable weights by clustering the pattern space | Use of Feature selection process to reduce the time and improve the accuracy | Less accuracy obtained when compared to others | 83.82% |
| Sultan et al. [5] | Doppler Ultrasound images | Logistic Regression classifier | Logistic regression is run on the values derived from image processing of ultrasound results | ML with multi modal ultrasound | Unreliable dataset | 89% |
| Bazazeh and Shubair [7] | Wisconsin Breast Cancer | SVM, Random Forest and Bayesian Networks | SVM divides the data into a hyperplane to classify. Random Forest is a culmination of many decision trees. Bayesian Network is a system that uses probability to classify | SVM has shown relatively high performance as compared to the other methods | Comparison among the known algorithms | 99.1% |
| Saleh et al. [16] (2016) | Wisconsin Breast Cancer | SVM, Random Forest and Bayesian Networks | Used decision trees, random forest, K-nearest neighbour, SVM, and Gaussian process classifiers, combined with testing different and novel biomarkers | LAPTM4B expression level is more indicative than its counter alleles | – | 97.1% |
| Adel et al. [22] | Elastogram and B-mode images | Image Processing, Principal component analysis, SVM | image processing to extract features from images, principal component analysis for pre-processing and SVM for classification | SVM is helpful in making decision by building a generic and robust model. | Average error produces is higher when compared with others | 94.12% |

# 4   Discussion and Future Direction

In Table 2, Existing work and Future work of some of the existing research papers has been discussed in tabular form. Existing Work shows the work which has already been done by researchers and Future work explains about the possible gaps in research that can be filled with future work.

**Table 2.** Discussion in future direction for breast cancer

| Authors and ref. no. | Existing work | Future work |
|---|---|---|
| Bharat et al. [2] | SVM used here is applicable when the class variable number is binary that is 1 or 0 | Scientists came up with the idea of multiclass SVM. Fine tuning of the parameters must be done to attain better results with better accuracy. For further purposes it can be implemented on cloud |
| Khuriwal et al. [8] | Used Convolution Neural Network and compared the results to conventional machine learning algorithms | In the future convolutional neural networks can be used with the dataset of images |
| Gupta et al. [19] | The comparative study between Multi-Layer Perceptron, K- Nearest Neighbour, Decision Tree and Support Vector Machine is performed | More metrics can be used in the future in order to obtain a more descriptive and diverse comparisons between the algorithms |
| Bhat et al. [4] | By taking the vigilance parameter as 0.5 and ratio of the data is taken as 90% for training and 10% for testing | Use of Feature selection process in order to improve the accuracy and time performance |
| Khuriwal and Mishra [20] | Trained a convoluted neural network model using features extracted from mammography images | The image processing and CNN can be used with real images dataset which might lead to an improved model in terms of accuracy |
| Sultan and Schultz [5] | ML with multi modal ultrasound including greyscale and doppler can achieve high sensitivity and specificity for breast cancer diagnosis | Identification of cases that can cause weak learning can enhance the diagnosis. Implementation and further validation of ML with multimodal modal approach using a larger dataset can have a potential to reduce unnecessary biopsies of breast |
| Saleh et al. [16] | Classifiers used are known and famous for good performance measure and stability | Features like RANKL T643C allele and LAPTM-4BT gene allele increases the accuracy of classification which suggests that their existence is introducing noise to the classification |
| Sharma et al. [6] | The comparison of ML techniques showed here are Random Forest, kNN and Naives Bayes. KNN have significantly shown better f1 score and accuracy | The early diagnosis of cancer can be shown by training a lot more data to get an accurate result if the cancer is malignant or benign |
| Khuriwal et al. [20] | The deep learning method CNN is used for dataset classification and after implementation, 98% accuracy has been achieved while working on 12 features only | Trying to implement the algorithm to new features with real image dataset in order to achieve best result and accuracy |

In this paper, several research papers have been reviewed based on computational Intelligence techniques proposed for the detection of breast cancer. Most of the researchers have performed this task on Wisconsin dataset and have achieved higher accuracy over time. Thus, the accuracy obtained is between 83%–99%, which varies for different datasets. So, authors are planning to propose an efficient and effective method based on Wisconsin dataset. Authors have also discussed what gaps these researches leave us with to work on in the future. In the existing research articles, Feature selection techniques enables us to save storage capacity and reduce computation time and increase accuracy and ROC. The purpose of this study was to realize the gaps in cancer classification and will follow it up with different methods of implementation in our future research work.

# References

1. Bayrak, E.A., Kırcı, P., Ensari, T.: Comparison of machine learning methods for breast cancer diagnosis. In: Scientific Meeting on Electrical-Electronics & Biomedical Engineering and Computer Science (EBBT), Istanbul, Turkey, pp. 1–3 (2019)
2. Bharat, A., Pooja, N., Reddy, R.A.: Using machine learning algorithms for breast cancer risk prediction and diagnosis. In: 3rd International Conference on Circuits, Control, Communication and Computing (I4C), Bangalore, India, pp. 1–4 (2018)
3. Nemissi, M., Salah, H., Seridi, H.: Breast cancer diagnosis using an enhanced extreme learning machine based-neural network. In: International Conference on Signal, Image, Vision and their Applications (SIVA), Guelma, Algeria, pp. 1–4 (2018)
4. Bhat, J.A., George, V., Malik, B.: Cloud computing with machine learning could help us in the early diagnosis of breast cancer. In: Second International Conference on Advances in Computing and Communication Engineering, Dehradun, pp. 644–648 (2015)
5. Sultan, L.R., Schultz, S.M., Cary, T.W., Sehgal, C.M.: Machine learning to improve breast cancer diagnosis by multimodal ultrasound. In: IEEE International Ultrasonics Symposium (IUS), Kobe, pp. 1–4 (2018)
6. Sharma, S., Aggarwal, A., Choudhury, T.: Breast cancer detection using machine learning algorithms. In: International Conference on Computational Techniques, Electronics and Mechanical Systems (CTEMS), Belgaum, India, pp. 114–118 (2018)
7. Bazazeh, D., Shubair, R.: Comparative study of machine learning algorithms for breast cancer detection and diagnosis. In: 5th International Conference on Electronic Devices, Systems and Applications (ICEDSA), Ras Al Khaimah, pp. 1–4 (2016)
8. Khuriwal, N., Mishra, N.: Breast cancer diagnosis using deep learning algorithm. In: International Conference on Advances in Computing, Communication Control and Networking (ICACCCN), Greater Noida, UP, India, pp. 98–103 (2018)
9. Lu, Y., Li, J.-Y., Su, Y.-T., Liu, A.-A.: A review of breast cancer detection in medical images. In: IEEE Visual Communications and Image Processing (VCIP), Taichung, Taiwan, pp. 1–4 (2018)
10. Osareh, A., Shadgar, B.: Machine learning techniques to diagnose breast cancer. In: 5th International Symposium on Health Informatics and Bioinformatics, Antalya, pp. 114–120 (2010)
11. Islam, M., Iqbal, H., Haque, R., Hasan, K.: Prediction of breast cancer using support vector machine and K-nearest neighbors. In: IEEE Region 10 Humanitarian Technology Conference (R10-HTC), Dhaka, pp. 226–229 (2017)

12. Polat, K., Sentürk, U.: A novel ML approach to prediction of breast cancer: combining of mad normalization, KMC based feature weighting and AdaBoostM1 classifier. In: 2nd International Symposium on Multidisciplinary Studies and Innovative Technologies (ISMSIT), Ankara, pp. 1–4 (2018)

13. Choubey, D.K., Paul, S., Sandilya, S., Dhandhania, V.K.: Implementation and analysis of classification algorithms for diabetes. Curr. Med. Imaging Rev. (2018, in Press)

14. Choubey, D.K., Kumar, P., Tripathi, S., Kumar, S.: Performance evaluation of classification methods with PCA and PSO for diabetes. Netw. Model. Anal. Health Inform. Bioinform. **9** (2020). Article number: 5. https://doi.org/10.1007/s13721-019-0210-8

15. Sharma, A., Kulshrestha, S., Daniel, S.: Machine learning approaches for breast cancer diagnosis and prognosis. In: International Conference on Soft Computing and its Engineering Applications (icSoftComp), Changa, pp. 1–5 (2017)

16. Saleh, D.T., Attia, A., Shaker, O.: Studying combined breast cancer biomarkers using machine learning techniques. In: IEEE 14th International Symposium on Applied Machine Intelligence and Informatics (SAMI), Herlany, pp. 247–251 (2016)

17. Choubey, D.K., Tripathi, S., Kumar, P., Shukla, V., Dhandhania, V.K.: Classification of diabetes by kernel based SVM with PSO. Recent Patents Comput. Sci. (2019, in Press)

18. Choubey, D.K., Kumar, M., Shukla, V., Tripathi, S., Dhandhania, V.K.: Comparative analysis of classification methods with PCA and LDA for diabetes. Curr. Diabetes Rev. (2020, Accepted)

19. Gupta, M., Gupta, B.: A comparative study of breast cancer diagnosis using supervised machine learning techniques. In: Second International Conference on Computing Methodologies and Communication (ICCMC), Erode, pp. 997–1002 (2018)

20. Khuriwal, N., Mishra, N.: Breast cancer detection from histopathological images using deep learning. In: 3rd International Conference and Workshops on Recent Advances and Innovations in Engineering (ICRAIE), Jaipur, India, pp. 1–4 (2018)

21. Amrane, M., Oukid, S., Gagaoua, I., Ensari̇, T.: Breast cancer classification using machine learning. In: 2018 Electric Electronics, Computer Science, Biomedical Engineerings' Meeting (EBBT), Istanbul, pp. 1–4 (2018)

22. Adel, M., Kotb, A., Farag, O., Darweesh, M.S., Mostafa, H.: Breast cancer diagnosis using image processing and machine learning for elastography images. In: 8th International Conference on Modern Circuits and Systems Technologies (MOCAST), Thessaloniki, Greece, pp. 1–4 (2019)

23. Choubey, D.K., Paul, S.: GA_RBF NN: a classification system for diabetes. Int. J. Biomed. Eng. Technol. (IJBET) **23**(1), 71–93 (2017)

24. Choubey, D.K., Paul, S.: Classification techniques for diagnosis of diabetes: a review. Int. J. Biomed. Eng. Technol. (IJBET) **21**(1), 15–39 (2016)

25. Choubey, K., Paul, S.: GA_MLP NN: a hybrid intelligent system for diabetes disease diagnosis. Int. J. Intell. Syst. Appl. (IJISA) **8**(1), 49–59 (2016)

26. Bala, K., Choubey, D.K., Paul, S.: Soft computing and data mining techniques for thunderstorms and lightning prediction: a survey. In: International Conference of Electronics, Communication and Aerospace Technology (ICECA 2017), 20–22 April, 2017, vol. 1, pp. 42–46. IEEE (2017)

27. Bala, K., Choubey, D.K., Paul, S., Lala, M.G.N.: Classification techniques for thunderstorms and lightning prediction-a survey. In: Soft Computing-Based Nonlinear Control Systems Design, pp. 1–17. IGI Global (2018)

28. World Health Organization: WHO position paper on mammography screening. WHO Library (2018)

# Segmentation of Blood Vessels from Fundus Image Using Scaled Grid

Rajat Suvra Nandy[1(✉)], Rohit Kamal Chatterjee[2], and Abhishek Das[1]

[1] Aliah University, Newtown, Kolkata 700156, West Bengal, India
rajatsuvranandy@yahoo.co.in, adas@aliah.ac.in
[2] Birla Institute of Technology, Mesra, Ranchi 835215, Jharkhand, India
rkchatterjee@bitmesra.ac.in

**Abstract.** This paper proposes an automated technique to segment the retinal blood vessels from funduscopic images. An Adaptive Line Structuring Element (ALSE) [12] is used for initial segmentation, but the process introduces large number of noisy objects accompanying the vessel structure. Fortunately, these noisy objects are relatively isolated structures in comparison to the blood vessels. So, a suitably Scaled Grid can be used to delimit the noisy objects from its neighborhood. When an object falls fully inside a block of the grid, it is considered as a noise and is eliminated. But the objects which passes over the boundary of a block are preserved. The scale of the grid is iteratively increased to identify eventually the all isolated objects and are eliminated without any loss of the actual vessel's structure. To measure the performance, Accuracy, Sensitivity and Specificity are calculated and compared with the recently found algorithms proposed in the literature.

**Keywords:** Adaptive Line Structuring Element · Medical image processing · Retinal image · Diabetic Retinopathy · Mathematical morphology

## 1 Introduction

An Ophthalmoscope or Fundoscope is used to visualize the anatomical structure of retina, including blood vessels and the optic nerve, for diagnosis and prognosis of retinal pathologies. Change in the characteristics of blood vessels, such as the diameter, tortuosity or branching angles, are the indication of ophthalmic diseases. The success of treatment for Diabetic Retinopathy or other ophthalmic disorders is dependent on the timely monitoring of the changes in retinal anatomy. Many recent studies in medical literature [1, 2] finds high correlation of the coronary and cardiovascular diseases with morphological changes in retinal blood vessels. The manual scanning of retinal images to detect pathological changes entails specialized training and skill and hence is an expensive process in terms of time and cost. A better alternative is to find out a reliable and automated method to segment the retinal blood vessels that could help in early detection of morphological variations in the fundus vasculature. In last decade, a significant amount of research effort was directed towards automated detection of pathological changes in blood vessels of retina. A detailed review related to retinal vessel segmentation can be found in [3]. Those approaches can be classified into two

© Springer Nature Singapore Pte Ltd. 2020
A. Bhattacharjee et al. (Eds.): MIND 2020, CCIS 1240, pp. 217–227, 2020.
https://doi.org/10.1007/978-981-15-6315-7_18

wide categories: the supervised methods and the unsupervised or rule-based methods. The rule-based methods can also be categorized into techniques based on morphological image processing [4, 10, 12, 13], matched filtering [5], model-based algorithms [6] and multiscale analysis [7]. The supervised segmentation approach [8, 9], utilize training and test images to classify the blood vessels from its noisy background based on selected features.

This paper proposes an unsupervised technique to extract retinal vasculature from fundus image using adaptive mathematical morphological operations. In [12], the authors proposed a novel mathematical morphology based method to extract the vessel structure using Adaptive Line Structuring Elements (ALSE). By rotating a straight line shaped Structuring Element and collecting the maximum response at each pixel with increasing size of the line at each step, the vessel's structure with minimum loss can be extracted. The rationale behind this process is that, a curved line can be approximately represented by a set of connected straight lines of assorted sizes. This approach efficaciously extracts the vessel's structure but faces two major difficulties when practically applied for segmentation of retinal blood vessels. Firstly, fundoscopic images, in general, contains large number of noisy pixels and many pathological objects that are similar in appearance in terms of intensity and shape and sometime in close proximity with blood vessels. ALSE confoundingly match these unwanted objects as blood vessels, and as a consequence, extracts them. Secondly, by increasing the size of the Line Structuring Element (LSE), the curved shape of the blood vessels is lost and isolated linear artifacts are created from finer arterioles and venules. In this paper our aim is to address and rectify the above-mentioned shortcomings faced by the ALSE process. By efficacious selection of noise elimination technique, this paper presents a novel unsupervised method to segment blood vessel structure for both physiological and pathological fundoscopic images.

There are three significant observations that can help us in overcoming the shortcomings of ALSE process. (i) The length (or scale) of the line structuring element must be limited to a convenient size so that the curvature of the vessels is preserved and that small-scale vessels are not dislodged from their continuous structure. Requirement of this observation is that the number of iterations in ALSE process must be kept small. Small size of the LSE can preserve vessel shape and structure but is unable to eliminate noisy and unwanted objects from the resultant image. To overcome this problem, we have our second observation. (ii) Most noise and other pathological objects are isolated and discontinuous from the main vessel structure in a limited scale of observation. So, all isolated discontinuous objects in limited scale can be safely eliminated without any harm to the main vessel structure. Lastly, (iii) objects that are in close proximity to the main vessel structure and similar (but not same) in color can be isolated by suitable contrast stretching algorithms. Following this, these isolated objects can be treated in the same manner as described in second observation.

For practical implementation of the above mentioned observations, following steps are adopted in succession:

(A) Preprocessing of the gray scale image by eliminating small scale noisy objects and bridging the small gaps present in the vessels by mathematical morphological operations.

(B) Constructing and applying an ALSE process, by limiting the size of the structuring element, which does not deform the shape of the vessels, but, extracts the full vessel structure with noise. A suitable adaptive threshold is used to convert the resultant image into a binary image.

(C) A Scaled Grid starting with a minimum size is placed on the binary image found in the last step. Any object that falls fully inside a block of the grid are eliminated but objects that falls on the boundary of a grid are preserved. The size of the grid is iteratively increased, and the same procedure is followed to eliminate the unwanted noisy objects.

The final binary image contains a clear view of the blood vessels of the retinal image, without loss of information.

Rest of this paper is organized as follows: Sect. 2 describes the details of ALSE process and the proposed Scaled Grid-Based noise elimination algorithm. Section 3 explains the experimental results and comparison of the performance of our algorithm with other methods proposed in the literature and finally in Sect. 4 the conclusion is drawn.

## 2 Proposed Algorithm

### 2.1 Preprocessing of Retinal Image

In the color (RGB) fundus image ($I_{RGB}$), the Green channel (G) has maximum contrast compared to the other channels and the Blue channel (B) has got very low contrast with maximum noise. On the other hand, the retinal image is generally saturated by the Red channel (R). Hence, maximum importance is applied over the Green channel (G) to convert the RGB image into a gray level fundus image ($I_{gray}$) and the following Eq. (1) is used:

$$I_{gray} = 0.31 \times R + 0.69 \times G + 0 \times B \tag{1}$$

Kundu et al. [12] and others [10] observed that the diameter of all the retinal blood vessels range from 3 to 7 pixels in fundus images. Accordingly, objects having size 3 pixels or less are eliminated form $I_{gray}$ using a morphological Top-Hat operation as shown in Eq. (2) below. In Eq. (2), the morphological opening ($\gamma_{S_{d3}}$) followed by the closing ($\varphi_{S_{d8}}$) operations are done using disc shaped structuring element having diameters 3 and 8 pixels respectively. The resultant image ($I_{rst}$) retains the objects of size larger than 3 pixels and bridges the small gaps present between the finer vessels.

$$I_{rst}(x,y) = \varphi_{S_{d8}}\left(\gamma_{S_{d3}}\left(I_{gray}(x,y)\right)\right) - I_{gray}(x,y) \tag{2}$$

### 2.2 Segmentation of Retinal Vessels Structure from Background

For initial segmentation of the blood vessels from $I_{rst}$, mathematical morphological operations are applied with an Adaptive Line Structuring Element (ALSE). ALSE has two parameters, Size or Span ($i$) and Angle ($\theta°$). The ALSE ($S_{\theta°}^i$) is a one-dimensional array of numbers having length '$i$' pixels, and value 1. The position of the middle pixel of $S_{\theta^\circ}^i$ is taken as center and the orientation of ALSE is given by the angle $\theta^\circ$. Now, for each pixel of $I_{rst}$ a *morphological opening* is employed using $S_{\theta^\circ}^i$ as a *structuring element*, for a specific length, $i$, starting from 3 pixels and with an angle $\theta^\circ$. Angle $\theta^\circ$ is increased from 0° to 180°, with successive increment of 9°. After a complete 180° rotation, the maximum response ($I^i(x, y)$) of each pixel is collected. In each iteration the length, '$i$', of ALSE ($S_{\theta^\circ}^i$) is increased by 1 pixel, starting from 3 pixels up to 7 pixels (as the diameter of vessels are in between 3 pixels to 7 pixels). Value of length, '$i$', higher than 7 pixels can distort the original vessel's structure as mentioned in the introduction, and that was a drawback of Kundu et al. [12].

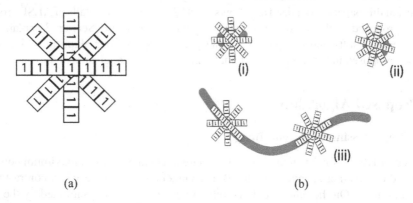

**Fig. 1.** (a) Rotation of ALSE ($S_{\theta^\circ}^7$) with size 7 pixels and value of each pixel is one. (b) (i) and (ii) where $S_{\theta^\circ}^7$ does not match with the pixels, it is not considered as vessel's structure and so eliminated. (b) (iii) where $S_{\theta^\circ}^7$ matches with image pixels, it is considered as vessels structure and hence preserved.

The above mentioned operations are precisely given by Eq. (3) and (4) and Fig. 1 explains the working of *ALSE* algorithm as discussed above.

$$I^i = max\left(\gamma_{s_{180^\circ}^i}(\ldots\ldots\ldots(\gamma_{s_{27^\circ}^i}(\gamma_{s_{18^\circ}^i}(\gamma_{s_{9^\circ}^i}(\gamma_{s_{0^\circ}^i}(I_{rst}))))))\right) \tag{3}$$

$$I^{i+1} = \gamma_{s_{\theta^\circ}^{i+1}}(I^i) \tag{4}$$

## 2.3    Enhancement of Vessel's Structure Using Difference of Gaussian

When the resultant image ($I^7$) of vessel structure is segmented, it is accompanied with numerous amounts of noisy pixels. Some of these noisy pixels are close to the vessels with almost similar gray levels. To separate these noisy pixels from the neighboring vessels by increasing the contrast, Difference of Gaussians (DoG) is applied. The DoG acts as a band pass filter that preserves spatial information but gains contrast between vessels and neighboring noise.

For applying DoG, grayscale retinal image ($I^7$) is convolved with the Gaussian kennel of two different variance, $\sigma_1^2$ and $\sigma_2^2$ respectively and the difference is taken between the two convolved images, as shown in Eq. (5).

$$\Gamma_{\sigma_1,\sigma_2}(x,y) = I^7 * \left( \frac{1}{2\pi\sigma_1^2} e^{-(x^2+y^2)/2\sigma_1^2} - \frac{1}{2\pi\sigma_2^2} e^{-(x^2+y^2)/2\sigma_2^2} \right) \tag{5}$$

$$\text{Where } \Gamma_{\sigma_1,\sigma_2} : \{X \subseteq \mathbb{R}^n\} \to \{Z \subseteq \mathbb{R}\}$$

### 2.4   Elimination of Background Noise Using Scaled Grid

At this stage, a local threshold is applied on the resultant image ($\Gamma_{\sigma_1,\sigma_2}$) to separate vessel structure from the background, and the binary image thus produced is denoted by $I_{binary}^r$. It is done by dividing the image ($\Gamma_{\sigma_1,\sigma_2}$) into number of blocks and then the Otsu's threshold [15] is applied to each of these blocks.

The main difficulty in extracting the vessel structure in retinal image is the similarity of gray levels between the blood vessels and noise. Though the application of DoG separates the noise in the neighborhood of vessel structure, numerous noisy pixels and small objects remain persistent.

An interesting property of these noisy pixels is that, compared to the blood vessels they are small isolated structures. Hence a suitable boundary can isolate each noisy structure from its neighborhood. For this purpose, a sequence of virtual grids, $I_{grid}^i$ are superimposed on the binary image, $I_{binary}^r$. The sides of each square block in the grid, $I_{grid}^i$ starts with $i = 3$ pixels and increases gradually. One-Pixel thick boundary of each block is set to one and inside is kept as zero.

Now, the $i^{th}$ grid $I_{grid}^i$ is superimposed (logically multiplied) on the image $I_{binary}^r$ to get the parts of the object which falls on the boundary. Let, the overlapped image thus formed, be denoted by $I_{boundary\_obj}^i$, as shown in Eq. (6).

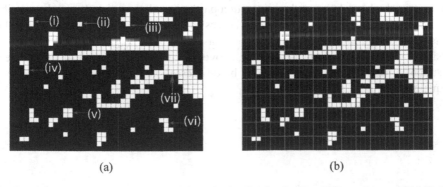

(a)                                          (b)

**Fig. 2.** (a) Part of a Fundus image, (i)–(vi) the isolated noises having different shapes and (vii) the vessel's parts which is continuous. (b) $3 \times 3$ pixels window grid image ($I_{grid}^3$) superimposed on image 2(a), where the boundary of each window is represented by red color. (Color figure online)

The isolated objects inside the boundary of a block are considered as a noise, and are required to be eliminated. To detect the objects that falls fully inside the boundary (isolated objects) and the objects which continues to the next block by passing over the boundary, a sequence of logical operations are applied.

Step 1: The complement of the grid ($I^i_{\sim grid}$) is taken and it is superimposed on $I^r_{binary}$ and the resultant image, $I^i_{iso}$, contains all objects falling inside a block.

Step 2: A morphological dilation is applied on each resultant block or window of $I^i_{iso}$, using a disk shaped Structuring Element ($s_{r1}$) with radius 1 pixel and the dilated image ($\delta I^i_{iso}$) is formed.

Step 3: The dilated image ($\delta I^i_{iso}$) is superimposed again on the $I^i_{boundary\_obj}$ and the resultant image ($I^i_{iso \wedge boundary\_obj}$) contains all the objects falls inside a block and continues over the boundary to the adjacent block.

Step 4: If the boundary of a block of the image $I^i_{iso \wedge boundary\_obj}$, contains non zero value, it means that this is the continuation of same object of the two adjacent windows. So, these continuous objects are preserved. But, if the boundary of the window doesn't contain any non-zero value, it is considered to be an isolated object, so it can be treated as noise and this window is filled with '0'. So, in this procedure, noisy isolated objects are eliminated. The above process is shown in Eqs. (7), (8), and (9).

$$I^i_{boundary\_obj} = I^r_{binary} \wedge I^i_{grid} \tag{6}$$

$$I^i_{iso} = I^r_{binary} \wedge I^i_{\sim grid} \tag{7}$$

$$\delta I^i_{iso} = I^i_{iso} \oplus S_{r1} \tag{8}$$

$$I^i_{iso \wedge boundary\_obj} = \delta I^i_{iso} \wedge I^i_{boundary\_obj} \tag{9}$$

The above described method retains the parts of the vessel structure which are present on the boundaries of the grid with a particular window size. It may be possible that a large noisy object is considered as vessel's part for a small window size, but when the size of window is gradually increased, then the large noises also fully fall inside a window and eliminated by the above procedure. At the end of this process, resultant image contains only retinal blood vessel structure. Above technique is explained in Fig. 2 and Fig. 3.

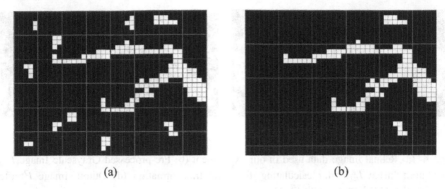

**Fig. 3.** (a) $5 \times 5$ pixels window grid image $(I_{grid}^5)$ superimposed on image 2(b), where the isolated objects which had fallen fully inside a window are eliminated. (b) $7 \times 7$ pixels window grid image $(I_{grid}^7)$ superimposed on image 3(a), where the isolated objects which had fallen into $5 \times 5$ pixels window grid are eliminated.

## 3   Experiment

### 3.1   Results and Discussions

The proposed algorithm is tested on the freely available Drive database [14]. This database contains Forty of Funduscopic images and for every image there is a corresponding mask and manually segmented ground truth image, having size $584 \times 565$ pixels.

Figure 4(b) shows the converted gray scale image $I_{gray}$, after applying Eq. (1) on the original RGB image $(I_{RGB})$. Next, the Top-Hat transformation is applied on $I_{gray}$ using Eq. (2) and the resultant image $I_{rst}$ is formed, as shown in Fig. 4(c). It contains large quantity noise very similar to the intensity of vessels. Now, to segment the vessel's structure from background an Adaptive Line Structuring Element (ALSE) is used on $I_{rst}$ with the help of Eq. (3) and (4) and the output image $I^7$ is shown in Fig. 4 (d). Following this, to increase the contrast between the vessel's structure and neighboring noise, a DoG is applied on $I^7$ and the output image $(\Gamma_{\sigma_1,\sigma_2})$ as shown in Fig. 5 (a). Next Otsu's threshold is applied locally on $\Gamma_{\sigma_1,\sigma_2}$ to segment the vessels from the background. Figure 5(b) shows the output binary retinal image $(I_{binary}^7)$.

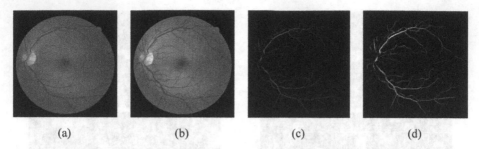

**Fig. 4.** (a) Retinal image data used in our experiment (b) Pre-processed Grayscale Image $I_{gray}$ (c) Output Image $I_{rst}$, after calculating Top- Hat transformation (d) Output image $I^7$ after applying the ALSE on $I_{rst}$ with $S^7_{\theta^\circ}$

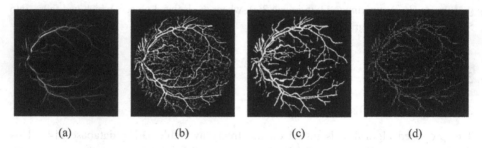

**Fig. 5.** (a) Output Image $\Gamma_{\sigma_1,\sigma_2}$, after applying DoG on $I^7$ (b) Binary retinal image $I^7_{binary}$, after applying locally Otsu's threshold on $\Gamma_{\sigma_1,\sigma_2}$ (c) The resultant image ($\delta I^7_{iso}$), which is formed after dilation is applied on of $I^7_{iso}$ using the $s_{r1}$ (d) output image $I^7_{iso\wedge boundary\_obj}$, which contains the common boundary objects of $\delta I^7_{iso}$ and $I^7_{boundary\_obj}$

To calculate the isolated objects of $I^7_{binary}$, the complimented grid image ($I^7_{\sim grid}$) is overlapped (logically AND) on $I^7_{binary}$ and the resultant image $I^7_{iso}$, is dilated by $s_{r1}$ to form $\delta I^7_{iso}$ (see Fig. 5(c)). The Fig. 5(d) shows the resultant image $I^7_{iso\wedge boundary\_obj}$, which is formed after the dilated image $\delta I^7_{iso}$ is superimposed on the $I^7_{boundary\_obj}$. This resultant image ($I^7_{iso\wedge boundary\_obj}$) contains only the parts of the image $I^7_{binary}$, which are the common boundary objects of $\delta I^7_{iso}$ and $I^7_{boundary\_obj}$.

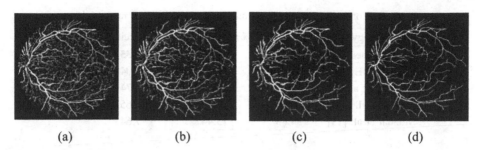

    (a)                    (b)                    (c)                    (d)

**Fig. 6.** Binary image After removing noise by the grids of block or window size (a) 3 × 3 pixels (b) 5 × 5 pixels (c) 7 × 7 pixels and (d) 9 × 9 pixels.

After calculating the non-zero boundary information, we consider the adjacent blocks as part of the vessel's structure and those blocks remain untouched, and others are filled with zero. Again, the size of the window is increased and the same procedure is followed, until no isolated structures appear in the image. After applying different sized grids (3 × 3 pixels to 9 × 9 pixels), the resultant images are shown in the Fig. 6 (a), 6(b), 6(c) and 6(d), where the noiseless vessel's structure is found after the block or window size is 9 × 9 pixels (see Fig. 6(d)).

### 3.2 Performance Measurement

The performance of our algorithms is measured on the DRIVE data set, where the segmented image is compared with the given ground truth image. The following measures are found, when the comparison is done with respect to each pixel: A segmented vessel pixel is considered as a true positive (TP) measure, if it is a part of both the vessel pixel and the given ground truth, otherwise it is consider as a false positive (FP), if it is a part of background pixel in the given ground truth image; also a background pixel of the segmented image is considered as true negative (TN) if is a part of the background in the given ground truth image, otherwise it is consider as a false negative (FN). To compare the performance of our proposed technique with existing technique, we calculated the Accuracy (*Accu*), Sensitivity (*Sen*) and Specificity (*Spf*). which are defined as follows:

$$Accu = \frac{TP + TN}{TP + TN + FP + FN}, \quad Sen = \frac{TP}{TP + FN} \quad \text{And} \quad spf = \frac{TN}{TN + FP}$$

The performance measures, Accuracy (*Accu*), Sensitivity (*Sen*) and Specificity (*Spf*) of our proposed technique, are calculated on all the images of DRIVE database and the average value of these measures are compared with the latest existing methodology which is presented in Table 1.

**Table 1.** Comparison of the performance with the existing methodology

| Methodology | Accuracy (%) | Sensitivity (%) | Specificity (%) |
|---|---|---|---|
| Our proposed method | **95.21** | 72.83 | **98.35** |
| B-COSFIRE [11] | 94.42 | **76.55** | 97.04 |
| Samanta et al. [10] | 58.21 | 54.66 | 62.74 |
| Kundu et al. [12] | 92.75 | 67.47 | 95.65 |
| Mondal et al. [13] | 94.63 | 73.44 | 97.64 |

## 4    Conclusion

In this paper, a novel technique is proposed to segment the vessel's structure from retinal or fundoscopic image. No new objects or structures have been introduced in the fundus image after using the morphological operators, which are anti-extensive by nature. Elimination of noise using scaled grid is a less time consuming and more efficient method. The Accuracy, Specificity and Sensitivity of the output images are measured with respect to the ground truth images given in DRIVE database (manual-1 and manual-2). The average Accuracy, Sensitivity and Specificity of our proposed method are 95.21%, 72.83% and 98.35% respectively. The results of this method are potentially better than the others previously proposed unsupervised techniques. The experimental results prove that our proposed mathematical morphology and uniform grid-based technique is very efficient to extract the structure of both the large and small vessels simultaneously. This technique can enhance the vessel's structure and suppress the noise without changing its original structure. So, using this method, low contrasted vessels are also detected accurately.

## References

1. Wong, T.Y., Klein, R., Sharrett, A.R., et al.: Retinal arteriolar narrowing and risk of coronary heart disease in men and women **287**(9), 1153–1159. JAMA: J. Am. Med. Assoc. (2002). http://jama.amaassn.org/content/287/9/1153.abstract
2. Gelman, R., Martinez-Perez, M.E., Vanderveen, D.K., et al.: Diagnosis of plus disease in retinopathy of prematurity using retinal image multiscale analysis. Invest. Ophthalmol. Vis. Sci. **46**(12), 4734–4738 (2005)
3. Fraz, M.M., Barman, S.A., Remagnino, P., et al.: Blood vessel segmentation methodologies in retinal images – a survey. Comput. Methods Prog. Biomed. **108**, 407–433 (2012)
4. Fraz, M.M., Barman, S.A., Remagnino, P., et al.: An approach to localize the retinal blood vessels using bit planes and centerline detection. Comput. Methods Prog. Biomed. **108**(2), 600–616 (2011)
5. Hoover, A.D., Kouznetsova, V., Goldbaum, M.: Locating blood vessels in retinal images by piecewise threshold probing of a matched filter response. IEEE Trans. Med. Imaging **19**(3), 203–210 (2000)
6. Al-Diri, B., Hunter, A., Steel, D.: An active contour model for segmenting and measuring retinal vessels. IEEE Trans. Med. Imaging **28**(9), 1488–1497 (2009)

7. Sofka, M., Stewart, C.V.: Retinal vessel centerline extraction using multiscale matched filters, confidence and edge measures. IEEE Trans. Med. Imaging **25**(12), 1531–1546 (2006)
8. Ricci, E., Perfetti, R.: Retinal blood vessel segmentation using line operators and support vector classification. IEEE Trans. Med. Imaging **26**(10), 1357–1365 (2007)
9. Lupascu, C.A., Tegolo, D., Trucco, E.: FABC: retinal vessel segmentation using AdaBoost. IEEE Trans. Inf. Technol. Biomed. **14**(5), 1267–1274 (2010)
10. Samanta, S., Saha, S.K., Chanda, B.: A simple and fast algorithm to detect the fovea region in fundus retinal image. In: Second International Conference on Emerging Applications of Information Technology, pp. 206–209. IEEE Xplore (2011)
11. Azzopardi, G., Strisciuglio, N., Vento, M., Petkov, N.: Trainable COSFIRE filters for vessel delineation with application to retinal images. Med. Image Anal. **19**(1), 46–57 (2015)
12. Kundu, A., Chatterjee, R.K.: Morphological scale-space based vessel segmentation of retinal image. In: Annual IEEE India Conference (INDICON), pp. 986–990 (2012)
13. Mondal, R., Chatterjee, R.K., Kar, A.: Segmentation of retinal blood vessels using adaptive noise island detection. In: Fourth International Conference on Image Information Processing (ICIIP), pp. 1–5 (2017)
14. http://www.isi.uu.nl/Research/Databases/DRIVE/. Accessed 30 June 2012
15. Otsu, N.: A threshold selection method from gray-level histogram. IEEE Trans. Syst. Man Cybern. **9**(1), 62–66 (1979)

# Head Pose Estimation of Face:
# Angle of Roll, Yaw, and Pitch
# of the Face Image

Jitendra Madarkar$^{(\boxtimes)}$ and Poonam Sharma

Computer Science and Engineering, VNIT, Nagpur, Maharashtra, India
jitendramadarkar475@gmail.com

**Abstract.** Face recognition has achieved immense success in near-frontal images, but in case of pose variation, it remains an unsolved problem for better efficiency. Many researchers have proposed different approaches for pose-invariant face recognition (PIFR) but still, need to explore more. Pose estimation is useful in pose-invariant face recognition and computer vision. PIFR needs a proper pose estimation to achieve better performance. The head pose estimation can be beneficial for synthesized and reconstruction of the frontal face image. In this paper, we have proposed a geometric approach to estimate the angle of roll, yaw, and pitch of the face image. This estimation will be useful to improve the correlation with frontal images and also it will help to reconstruct a frontal face image. Also, an estimated angle can be used to improve the performance of face recognition. . . .

**Keywords:** Face detection · Pose variation · Yaw · Biometric · Roll · Pitch · Head pose estimation

## Abbreviations

| | |
|---|---|
| PIFR: | Pose-invariant face recognition |
| NIFR : | Near-frontal face recognition |
| MSE: | Mean squared error |
| EGM: | Elastic Graph Matching |
| $(E_{lx}, E_{ly})$: | Co-ordinate of left eye |
| $(N_x, N_y)$: | Co-ordinate of nose tip |
| $(M_{lx}, M_{ly})$: | Co-ordinate of left mouth corner |

## 1 Introduction

Since the last three decades, face recognition is one of the most popular research areas in computer vision. In today's era, the face recognition application has been used all over the world for security purpose. Several face recognition based biometric system are deployed in the home and corporate offices for an authentication purpose. Surveillance cameras have been deployed in several public places

© Springer Nature Singapore Pte Ltd. 2020
A. Bhattacharjee et al. (Eds.): MIND 2020, CCIS 1240, pp. 228–242, 2020.
https://doi.org/10.1007/978-981-15-6315-7_19

such as railway stations, airports, and traffic signals to monitor the activities of the traffic. The main motivation of the face recognition application is to recognize the test image from the given labeled dataset. Accuracy of the face recognition on frontal images has achieved immense success but to obtain frontal images in the real-world scenario is an unrealistic task. Face recognition have several challenges such as illumination, occlusion, noise, corrupted, low resolution, expression, pose variation and undersampled. Several challenges of face recognition have been resolved by researchers but still, issues like low resolution, pose variation, and undersampled need to be explored more. Existing face recognition algorithms have been achieved remarkable success in near-frontal face recognition (NFFR) [16] but these algorithms did not solve the issue of PIFR [17]. In this paper, we targeted the issue of head pose estimation in three ways such as the angle of a roll, yaw, and pitch, illustrated in Fig. 1.

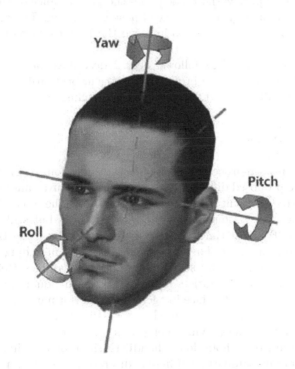

**Fig. 1.** Different pose variation of human face

A pose variation changes the appearance of a face in a 2D image and also hide some portion of the face. When some portion of the face is invisible then it is difficult to extract a discriminative feature of the face. In real-time scenarios, the relative position of the face with respect to the camera may not be fixed, hence the image may capture from different viewpoints. Pose variation caused more differences in samples of the same object rather than the sample of the same pose of another object. The same pose samples have more similarities than other pose images. The pose variation degrades the performance of face recognition due to self-occlusion and nonlinear variation. The feature extraction and classification process of face recognition play a significant role. A classification mostly depends on the discriminative features and for better features needs a good quality of images. Even a small variation can make a lot of differences, hence it affects the performance of face recognition. The performance of PIFR can be improved by doing the preprocessing on face images, the preprocessing can bring rotated face images into a frontal pose or make a correlation with yaw and pitch variation images.

Generally three types of deviation occurred in face images i.e. roll, pitch, and yaw. This paper targets the aforementioned pose variation issue and proposed three different approaches as follows: Estimate the angle of 1. Roll 2. Yaw 3. Pitch of the face image. A pose variation degrades the performance of face recognition, which can be overcome by a proper head pose estimation. The prior knowledge of pose estimation can be a help to improve the performance of pose-invariant face recognition.

The paper is organized as follows: Sect. 2 describes the reviews of related work. Section 3 introduced the proposed approach. Section 4 illustrated experimentation and result and Sect. 5 describes the conclusion.

## 2   Related Work

Pose estimation is a preprocessing step of face recognition. In the recent decade, researchers have proposed different approaches to pose-invariant face recognition (PIFR), but its requirement is proper pose estimation. The researchers have been working on head pose estimation for the last 2 decades but still, this topic has more challenges. The first time, the pose is estimated by using the appearance template matching method. The appearance template matching compares test image with the given training set of different pose samples (templates) with the corresponding pose annotation. [1] have used mean squared error (MSE) to compare two templates of the face image. But its performance is affected by the different resolution of images. [2] used a normalized cross-correlation method to resolved resolution issues, which correlates with different image resolutions. These aforementioned methods do not handle the issue of a roll image and require a number of training samples for different discrete poses. As a number of templates increases in the training set, it directly leads to high computational cost. These two problems can be solved by [3] using a support vector machine, which detects and localize the face and used a support vector as a feature to compare the images. A template matching compares the two images on the assumption of pairwise similarity which is improper for high-resolution images and leads to high erroneous. To reduce the pose estimation error of the pairwise similarity problem, many researchers used image transformation and distance metrics. For example, the Laplacian-of-Gaussian filter and Gabor wavelet [4] and [5]. Transformation techniques are invariant to shift and appearance errors. Appearance template matching is not fruitful for pose estimation due to the aforementioned problems and these problems are resolved by [3] and [6]. The author proposed a clustering mechanism where each cluster has a number of same pose samples or called detector and it is trained by the supervised learning algorithm. Clustering mechanism need not require to do separate head detection and localization step. Each cluster is trained by supervised learning could manage to ignore appearance variation which is not useful in pose estimation, even it can work on high-low resolution images. If the number of the cluster increases for different pose then the training burden also increases and need a substantial amount of samples. All the previous methods have been used pixel base metric to compare any two images but in reality, two image feature can not lie on the same coordinates, it means two faces local features varies in their location. Flexible mechanism or Elastic bunch graph (EBG) [7] can overcome the problem of pixel base metric. Elastic bunch graph has the potential to represent a nonrigid or deformable mechanism and stores a bunch of facial point descriptors at each node. To compare a bunch graph to a new face image, the graph is placed over the image and completely deformed to find the minimum distance between the feature at every graph node location. This process is called Elastic Graph Matching (EGM). [8, 9] used EGM to estimate pose variation. For pose estimation, different bunch graphs are created for respective discrete pose and these bunch graphs compared with the test image. To gain better pose estimation requires a number of different bunch graphs for each discrete pose, so its comparison becomes computationally expensive. Nonlinear regression methods have been used to estimate head pose but some regression tool faces the challenge for the large dimensionality of the image. Support Vector regressors (SVRs) have shown better performance using a dimensional reduction method PCA [13] and [14]. The Multilayer perceptron [6], locally linear map (LLM) [15] neural network most widely used for head pose estimation. The neural network is fast and more accurate but prone to error because of poor head localization.

Some mechanism has been developed to estimate pose variation based on geometric facial landmarks. Accurate local landmark point detection is the first priority in this type of pose estimation methods. Eyes, nose, chin, and mouth plays a big role to estimate the pose in the geometric based method. These landmarks effects and location of the face in relation to the standard contour of the face gives strong perception about pose variation. [10] said in his article that the head pose variation relies on the deviation of the head bilateral symmetry and the angle at the nose point. [11] have estimated pose using five facial landmarks such as the outside corner of the eyes and mouth, the tip of the nose. The face is symmetric in nature, and facial symmetric axis founded by joining a line in between the midpoint of the mouth and midpoint of the mouth. [12] used a different set of five landmark point (tip of the nose and inner and outer point of eyes) to estimate the pose. Horprasert assumes that all four landmarks point lies on the same plane. side pose or yaw can be determined using the size of the left eye and right eye, pitch or direction can be determined by the distance between horizontal eye-line and tip of the nose, the roll can be determined by the angle eye-line with the horizontal axis.

The proposed approached has used same facial landmarks that used in [12] but we have added extra facial landmarks i.e. left and right mouth corner in our methods. Here we estimate the angle of deviation.

# 3    Proposed Work

The proposed approach estimates the angle of the face: roll, yaw, and pitch of the face image using facial landmarks. The geometric representation of the face always estimates the proper estimation of the pose. Eyes, nose, and mouth are the most significant landmarks of the face to estimate the angle of deviation and these facial landmarks changes their location with respect to the pose variation.

## 3.1    Find the Angle of Roll

In the rotation images, features of the image remain the same as a frontal view but the position of the features changes to its relative position. The main goal of this approach is to estimate an appropriate angle so that the face image can bring back in frontal view by rotating face image with the estimated angle. For rotation, three landmarks are extracted such as the left retina, right retina, and nose tip. From Fig. 2, Line $L1$ and $L2$ be the line between nose and eyes. Let $(E_{lx}, E_{ly})$ be the coordinates of the left eye, $(E_{rx}, E_{ry})$ be the co-ordinate of the right eye and $(N_x, N_y)$ be the co-ordinate of the nose tip. The line $L1$ and $L2$ make the angle with reference to the x-axis and y-axis respectively. In the case of the frontal face, the angle between (x-axis, $L1$) and (x-axis, $L2$) will be the same. Similarly, the angle between (y-axis, $L1$) and (y-axis, $L2$) will be the same. When the face is rotated then the angle of Line $L1$ and $L2$ with respect to the x-axis as well as y-axis also changes. This deviation can help to find the angle of rotation. where $R_\alpha$ is an angle between Line $L1$ and X-axis, $R_\beta$ is an angle between Line $L2$ and X-axis, $R_\alpha$' is an angle between Line $L1$ and Y-axis, $R_\beta$' is an angle between Line $L2$ and Y-axis (Fig. 3).

$$slope = (E_{ly} - N_y)/(E_{lx} - N_x)$$
$$R_\alpha = tan^{-1}(slope) \tag{1}$$

$$RollAngle = (R_\alpha + R_\beta)/2 \tag{2}$$

## 3.2    Estimate the Angle of Yaw

The yaw variation hides some portion of the face image. The face is symmetric in structure, it means the left and right side of the nose has a similar feature. If the face has yaw variation, then it loses the discriminative feature from the one side of the face. In this approach, the main aim is to estimate the deviation

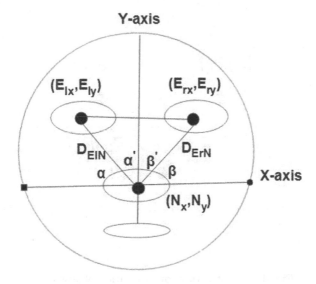

**Fig. 2.** Face structure for estimation of roll image

**Fig. 3.** Roll image, rotated image and crop image

---

**Algorithm 1.** Estimate the angle of roll.

---

1: First detect the facial landmarks.

2: Extract the coordinate of facial landmarks.

3: Calculate the angle with reference to x-axis and y-axis.

4: Estimate rotated angle $(R_\alpha + R_\beta) / 2$ or $(R_\alpha' + R_\beta') / 2$.

5: Rotate the face image with the estimated angle using an interpolation method.

6: Crop the image in a given input image size.

7: End

---

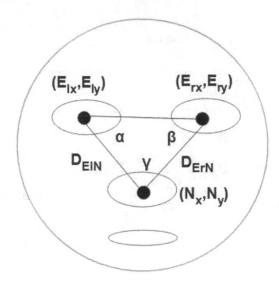

**Fig. 4.** Face structure for estimation of yaw angle

angle of the face with respect to the focusing camera. Three facial landmarks have been taken into consideration for estimation of yaw variation with reference to the frontal image.

The euclidean distance metric is used to measure the distance of $D_{ElN}$ and $D_{ErN}$ by Eq. 3 (Fig. 4).

$$D_{ElN} = \sqrt{(N_x - E_{lx})^2 + (N_y - E_{ly})^2}$$
$$D_{ErN} = \sqrt{(N_x - E_{rx})^2 + (N_y - E_{ry})^2}$$
(3)

where, $D_{ElN}$ = distance between the retina of the left eye and the nose tip, $D_{ErN}$ = distance between the retina of the right eye and the nose tip, $\alpha$ is an angle at the left retina, $\beta$ is an angle at the right retina, and $\gamma$ is an angle at the nose tip. The ratio of $(D_{ElN}/D_{ErN})$ is 1 for all frontal face images and ratio changes due to the variation of yaw in the images. The ratio varies with respect to the head deviation of every degree and this ratio can be used to determine deviation angle in yaw images, but its accuracy remains up to deviation of 25° but beyond it, the ratio doesn't work. To estimate beyond 25° of deviation, the angle at nose tip and the angle at both retinae play an important role to estimate the head pose. The angle at the left retina, right retina and tip nose calculated by Eq. 3, and these angle changes as yaw of face changes. The angle at the left and right retina used to estimate the angle of yaw, if the angle at the left retina is higher than the angle of the right retina then it considers that the face deflected toward the left side or left pose (Fig. 5).

$$u = [E_{ly} - N_y \quad E_{lx} - N_x] \quad v = [E_{ry} - N_y \quad E_{rx} - N_x]$$
$$\theta = dot(u \quad v)/(norm(u) * norm(v)) \tag{4}$$
$$Y_\gamma = cos^{-1}(\theta)$$

---

**Algorithm 2.** Estimate the Angle of yaw.

---

1: First detect the facial landmark (nose tip, the retina of eyes).

2: Extract the coordinate of landmarks.

3: Measure the distance of $D_{ElN}$ and $D_{ErN}$ using equation 3.

4: Estimate the ratio $r = D_{ElN}/D_{ErN}$.

    **if** $r > 1$ **then**
|     left side pose
    **end**
    **if** $r \leq 1$ **then**
|     Right side pose
    **end**
    **if** $r == 1$ **then**
|     Frontal
    **end**

5: Estimate the angle $Y_\alpha$, $Y_\beta$, and $Y_\gamma$ using equation 4.

    **if** $Y_\alpha \geq Y_\beta$ **then**
|     Left side pose
    **end**
    **if** $Y_\alpha \leq Y_\beta$ **then**
|     Right side pose
    **end**
    **if** $Y_\alpha == Y_\beta$ **then**
|     Frontal
    **end**

6: End

---

**Fig. 5.** Face samples to estimate the yaw angle.

## 3.3 Estimate the Pitch Angle of the Face Image

In this subsection, we proposed an Algorithm 3 to estimate pitch angle by considering three facial landmarks such as the nose tip, left and right corner of

---

**Algorithm 3.** Estimate the angle of pitch.

---

1: First detect the facial landmark(tip of the nose, left mouth corner, and right mouth corner).

2: Extract the coordinates of the landmark.

3: Calculate the angle $P_\alpha$, $P_\beta$, and $P_\gamma$ using equation 5.

       **if** $P_\beta \geq 80$ **then**
|      downward direction
       **end**

       **if** $P_\beta \leq 80$ **then**
|      Upward direction
       **end**

       **if** $P_\beta == 80$ **then**
|      Frontal
       **end**

4: End.

---

the mouth or the left and right corner of the eyes. If we join these three facial landmarks by line it creates a triangular shape and the angle at nose landmark plays a crucial role to decide the direction (upward/downward) of the face in the image. The face structure as shown in Fig. 7 to estimate the pitch angle. In the case of the downward direction, the distance between nose and mouth reduces, so the angle at the nose landmark becomes large. Similarly, in the case of the upward direction the distance between nose and mouth increases, so the angle at the nose landmark becomes small. The same way we can use eye landmarks instead of the mouth corner to estimate the pitch angle. The face samples are shown in Fig. 6.

$$u = [M_{ly} - N_y \quad M_{lx} - N_x] \quad v = [M_{ry} - N_y \quad M_{rx} - N_x]$$
$$\theta = dot(u \quad v)/(norm(u) * norm(v)) \tag{5}$$
$$P_\beta = cos^{-1}(\theta)$$

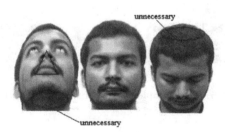

**Fig. 6.** Upward and downward direction face images

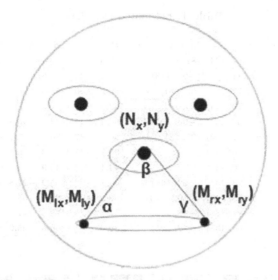

**Fig. 7.** Face structure for estimation of pitch

# 4    Experimentation and Results

The experimentation carried out on a publicly available database such as GT [18] for estimation of the angle of roll images. We have captured face images in the unconstrained environment for estimation of pitch and yaw but for estimation of yaw images captured at every 5° of rotation of the camera. The proposed approached has used different facial landmarks (retina of eyes, nose tip, outer eyes corner and both mouth corner) to estimate the angle of deviation of the face image with respect to the frontal face. The coordinates of facial landmarks are extracted manually. The experimental results have shown a proper estimation of roll, yaw and pitch angle.

## 4.1    Estimate the Angle of Roll

Here, estimate the roll angle by extracting three facial landmarks (left retina, right retina, and nose tip) that have been taken into consideration. First, calculate the slope between two facial landmarks (nose and retina) and used an inverse trigonometric function to calculate the angle with respect to X-axis and Y-axis. The rotated angle estimated by Eq. 1 and 2. The result has illustrated in Table 1 and the pictorial representation depicted in Fig. 8.

**Table 1.** Estimated roll angles

| | Retina left eye | Nose | Retina right eye | $R_\alpha$ | $R_\beta$ | $R_\alpha'$ | $R_\beta'$ | Rotated angle |
|---|---|---|---|---|---|---|---|---|
| 1 | (−30, 101) | (−51, 124) | (82, 85) | 47.6 | −51.5 | 42.4 | −38.5 | 2 |
| 2 | (44, 98) | (−61, 137) | (−94, 113) | 66.4 | −36 | 23.6 | −54 | −15 |
| 3 | (−43, 110) | (−71, 132) | (94, 99) | 38.2 | −55.1 | 51.8 | −34.9 | 8 |
| 4 | (−45, 104) | (−76, 124) | (93, 85) | 32.8 | −66.4 | 57.2 | −23.6 | 17 |
| 5 | (−32, 102) | (−57, 140) | (−93, 105) | 56.7 | −44.2 | 33.3 | −45.8 | −6 |
| 6 | (33, 89) | (−57, 122) | (95, 93) | 54 | −37.3 | 36 | −52.7 | −8 |
| 7 | (48, 98) | (−70, 149) | (−104, 117) | 66.7 | −43.3 | 23.3 | −46.7 | −12 |
| 8 | (−38, 108) | (−70, 139) | (94, 92) | 44.1 | −62.9 | 45.9 | −27.1 | 9 |
| 9 | (−42, 116) | (−73, 137) | (−92, 101) | 34.1 | −62.2 | 55.9 | −27.8 | 14 |
| 10 | (−53, 104) | (−73, 140) | (−102, 120) | 60.9 | −34.6 | 29.1 | −55.4 | −13 |
| 11 | (53, 95) | (−71, 138) | (−98, 113) | 67.3 | −42.8 | 22.7 | −47.2 | −12 |
| 12 | (−40, 112) | (−68, 135) | (−92, 101) | 39.4 | −54.8 | 50.6 | −35.2 | 8 |

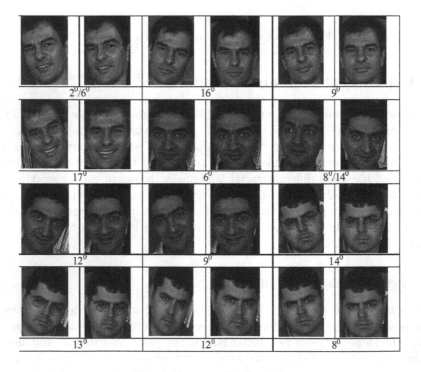

**Fig. 8.** Estimated roll angles

## 4.2   Estimate the Angle of Yaw

Here, we estimate the angle of yaw by extracting three facial landmarks from the face image and measure the distance between the nose tip and retina of each eye using Euclidean distance, and then estimate the ratio using Eq. 3. The ratio $(D_{ElN}/D_{ErN})$ decides the head pose side and estimate the exact angle deviation up to 25° but to estimate the angle beyond 25° the aforementioned ratio does not give a proper estimation. To measure the deviation beyond 25° in yaw images, the angle at the retina of eyes and tip nose plays a significant role to estimate head pose. The result has illustrated in Table 2.

**Table 2.** Estimated yaw angle at every 5° of rotation

| Pose variation $\theta°$ | $D_{ElN}$ | $D_{ErN}$ | $(D_{ElN}/D_{ErN})$ | $Y_\alpha$ | $Y_\beta$ | $Y_\gamma$ |
|---|---|---|---|---|---|---|
| Frontal (0°) | 46.8 | 43.3 | 1.08 | 45 | 45 | 90 |
| 5° | 47.5 | 39.7 | 1.2 | 42.5 | 50 | 87.5 |
| 10° | 49 | 37.2 | 1.32 | 40 | 55 | 85 |
| 15° | 50 | 35.5 | 1.41 | 38.5 | 60 | 82.5 |
| 20° | 54.1 | 32.2 | 1.68 | 35 | 65 | 80 |
| 25° | 51.6 | 26.2 | 1.97 | 31 | 74 | 75 |
| 30° | 52.4 | 27.7 | 1.9 | 29 | 83 | 68 |
| 35° | 55.5 | 28 | 1.98 | 27 | 92 | 61 |
| 40° | 53 | 28.2 | 1.88 | 25 | 101 | 54 |
| 45° | 55 | 47.8 | 1.15 | 23 | 107 | 47 |

## 4.3   Estimate the Angle of Pitch

Here, we can decide the direction (upward/downward) or pitch of the face image. We estimated the angle of the pitch in two ways: first way to considering the three facial landmarks (both eyes and nose tip) and a second way to consider both mouth corner and nose tip facial landmark. The experimentation carried out on several images and encoded the standard angle value for different direction variation. The angle at nose point dictates the pitch variation. $P_\alpha$ = the angle at left mouth corner, $P_\beta$ = angle at the nose, and $P_\gamma$ = angle at the right mouth corner. The results have shown in Fig. 9.

## 4.4   Result Analysis

1. On frontal view face images, the isosceles triangle is created from three facial landmarks such as nose tip and both mouth corner, the angle at nose tip could be in between of 65°–75° but in case of pitch, downward direction the angle at nose tip is increases and upward direction it decreases.

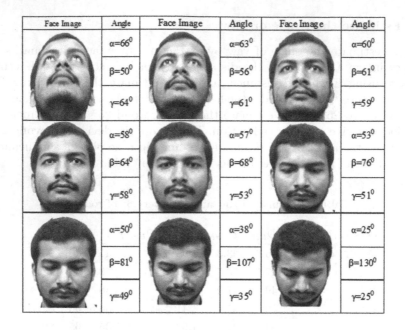

| Face Image | Angle | Face Image | Angle | Face Image | Angle |
|---|---|---|---|---|---|
| | $\alpha=66^0$ | | $\alpha=63^0$ | | $\alpha=60^0$ |
| | $\beta=50^0$ | | $\beta=56^0$ | | $\beta=61^0$ |
| | $\gamma=64^0$ | | $\gamma=61^0$ | | $\gamma=59^0$ |
| | $\alpha=58^0$ | | $\alpha=57^0$ | | $\alpha=53^0$ |
| | $\beta=64^0$ | | $\beta=68^0$ | | $\beta=76^0$ |
| | $\gamma=58^0$ | | $\gamma=53^0$ | | $\gamma=51^0$ |
| | $\alpha=50^0$ | | $\alpha=38^0$ | | $\alpha=25^0$ |
| | $\beta=81^0$ | | $\beta=107^0$ | | $\beta=130^0$ |
| | $\gamma=49^0$ | | $\gamma=35^0$ | | $\gamma=25^0$ |

**Fig. 9.** Estimated pitch angle

2. In case of yaw, up to 25° deviation we estimate the angle by the ratio of distances and which measure from the left retina to nose tip and right retina to nose tip respectively. For frontal view face images, the ratio of distances should be 1. The results of yaw variation have shown in Table 2.
3. Beyond 25° of deviation of yaw angle is estimated with the help of angle at nose tip and its decreases with yaw variation, the result has shown in Table 2. For left side variation the angle at right retina increases and vice versa.
4. In frontal view images, the angle at nose tip will be 90° and angle at retinae of eyes will be 45°.
5. Roll angle is estimated by the difference of two angle which is measure by the co-ordinate of retinae and nose tip.

## 5 Discussion

In this study, we have estimated the angle of three different head pose variations: roll, yaw, and pitch with the help of Euclidean distance and trigonometric. The existing methods did not provide the proper estimation of the deviation angle. This estimation of angle might provide the concrete structure of the head and it will be beneficial for the application like face recognition, driver inattention. This information also useful to construct a 2-D face model and can be correlated with frontal view face images.

# 6 Conclusions

In this paper, estimates the angle of roll, yaw, and pitch of the face image using geometric properties of the facial landmark. Five facial landmarks such as the tip of the nose, the retina of eyes and both mouth corners have been taken into consideration to estimate the head pose. The euclidean distance and trigonometric concept have used to measure the distance and estimate the angle. The experimentation carried out on publicly available GT databases and images captured by ourselves. The experimental result shows a proper estimation of the head pose. Facial landmarks are difficult to detect in less reliable an environment such as occlusion, facial expression and large variation in the head pose. The estimation of head poses useful for pose-invariant face recognition and field of computer vision.

## Declaration

**Acknowledgements.** The work was supported by Visvesvaraya PhD scheme, Govt of India.

**Funding.** This study was funded by the Ministry of Electronics and Information Technology (India) (Grant No. MLA/MUM/GA/10(37)B).

**Competing interests.** The authors declare that they have no competing interests.

## References

1. Beymer: Face recognition under varying pose. In: 1994 Proceedings of IEEE Conference on Computer Vision and Pattern Recognition, pp. 756–761 (1994). https://doi.org/10.1109/CVPR.1994.323893
2. Niyogi, S., Freeman, W.T.: Example-based head tracking. In: Proceedings of the Second International Conference on Automatic Face and Gesture Recognition, pp. 374–378. https://doi.org/10.1109/AFGR.1996.557294
3. Huang, J., Shao, X., Wechsler, H.: Face pose discrimination using support vector machines (SVM). In: Proceedings of the Fourteenth International Conference on Pattern Recognition, vol. 1, pp. 154–156 (1998). https://doi.org/10.1109/ICPR.1998.711102
4. Sherrah, J., Gong, S., Ong, E.-J.: Understanding pose discrimination in similarity space. In: 10th British Machine Vison Conference, pp. 523–532. BMVA Press (1999)
5. Sherrah, J., Gong, S., Ong, E.J.: Face distributions in similarity space under varying head pose. Image Vis. Comput. **19**, 154–156 (2001). https://doi.org/10.1016/S0262-8856(00)00096-2
6. Zhang, Z., Hu, Y., Liu, M., Huang, T.: Head pose estimation in seminar room using multi view face detectors. In: Stiefelhagen, R., Garofolo, J. (eds.) CLEAR 2006. LNCS, vol. 4122, pp. 299–304. Springer, Heidelberg (2007). https://doi.org/10.1007/978-3-540-69568-4_27
7. Lades, M., et al.: Distortion invariant object recognition in the dynamic link architecture. IEEE Trans. Comput. **42**, 300–311 (1993). https://doi.org/10.1109/12.210173

8. Lades, M., et al.: Determination of face position and pose with a learned representation based on labelled graphs. Image Vis. Comput. **15**, 665–673 (1997). https://doi.org/10.1016/S0262-8856(97)00012-7

9. Wu, J., Trivedi, M.M.: A two-stage head pose estimation framework and evaluation. Pattern Recogn. **41**, 1138–1158 (2008). https://doi.org/10.1016/j.patcog.2007.07.017

10. Wilson, H.R., Wilkinson, F., Lin, L.-M., Castillo, M.: Perception of head orientation. Vis. Res. **40**, 459–472 (2000). https://doi.org/10.1016/S0042-6989(99)00195-9

11. Gee, A., Cipolla, R.: Determining the gaze of faces in images. Image Vis. Comput. **12**, 639–647 (1994). https://doi.org/10.1016/0262-8856(94)90039-6

12. Horprasert, T., Yacoob, Y., Davis, L.S.: Computing 3-D head orientation from a monocular image sequence. In: Proceedings of the Second International Conference on Automatic Face and Gesture Recognition, pp. 242–247 (1996). https://doi.org/10.1109/AFGR.1996.557271

13. Li, Y., Gong, S., Liddell, H.: Support vector regression and classification based multi-view face detection and recognition. In: Proceedings of the Fourth IEEE International Conference on Automatic Face and Gesture Recognition (Cat. No. PR00580), pp. 300–305 (2000). https://doi.org/10.1109/AFGR.2000.840650

14. Li, Y., Gong, S., Sherrah, J., Liddell, H.M.: Support vector machine based multi-view face detection and recognition. Image Vis. Comput. **22**, 413–427 (2004)

15. Rae, R., Ritter, H.J.: Recognition of human head orientation based on artificial neural networks. IEEE Trans. Neural Netw. **9**, 257–265 (1998). https://doi.org/10.1109/72.661121

16. Madarkar, J., Sharma, P., Singh, R.: Improved performance and execution time of face recognition using MRSRC. In: Das, K.N., Bansal, J.C., Deep, K., Nagar, A.K., Pathipooranam, P., Naidu, R.C. (eds.) Soft Computing for Problem Solving. AISC, vol. 1048, pp. 597–607. Springer, Singapore (2020). https://doi.org/10.1007/978-981-15-0035-0_49

17. Sharma, P., Yadav, R.N., Arya, K.V.: Pose-invariant face recognition using curvelet neural network. IET Biom. **3**, 128–138 (2014). https://doi.org/10.1049/iet-bmt.2013.0019

18. Nefian, A.V.: Georgia tech face database. http://www.anefian.com/research/face_reco.htm

# Enhancing and Classifying Traffic Signs Using Computer Vision and Deep Convolutional Neural Network

Satish Kumar Satti, K. Suganya Devi$^{(\boxtimes)}$, Prasenjit Dhar, and P. Srinivasan

National Institute of Technology, Silchar, Assam, India
sskumar789@gmail.com, suganyanits@gmail.com

**Abstract.** We are well aware of the importance of traffic signs and road rules in our day-to-day lives. Ignorance of traffic signs and rules may lead to various road mishaps. Technology has been trying to develop "smarter cars" that are able to automatically recognize the traffic signs and understand roadways leading to a safe drive. Within these smart cars "driver alert" system is an important feature for knowing the roadway (especially the traffic signals) to alert drivers. Recognizing the traffic signs at night is still a challenging task for researchers. This can be tried to overcome by various Deep Learning models by employing Computer Vision. In this work, the data set is trained with a Convolutional Neural Network and analyzed using the Deep Learning technique on the Keras framework. Our proposed model achieved a state-of-the-art performance of 99.66% and 96.86% accuracy on the training and testing datasets respectively ...

**Keywords:** Traffic sign · Computer vision · CNN · Deep Learning · Real time transportation

## 1 Introduction

As per the insights are given by the Government of India, around 400 mishaps happened consistently. As reported by the World Health Organization survey report, car accidents incur 3% of the absolute total output of a nation. Therefore it is the sincere responsibility of every citizen to realize the importance of these traffic signs along with the rules. These traffic signs help us to avoid dangerous situations and even accidents. While following the traffic signs, we can limit the number of road accidents to a huge extent. There are various traffic signs and each has its own meaning and significance. These have been divided into three categories viz, Mandatory traffic signs; Cautionary traffic signs and Informative traffic signs.

### 1.1 Traffic Signs that Are Compulsory

The main classification of traffic signs in this category is the obligatory signs that guarantee the smooth running of the traffic out and about. These signs

© Springer Nature Singapore Pte Ltd. 2020
A. Bhattacharjee et al. (Eds.): MIND 2020, CCIS 1240, pp. 243–253, 2020.
https://doi.org/10.1007/978-981-15-6315-7_20

ensures that the vehicles running on the road adhere to the guidelines mentioned. Violation of any of these obligatory traffic sign is an offense under the law of Roadways and Transport. Some of the traffic signs in this category are shown in Fig. 1:

**Fig. 1.** Compulsory traffic signs

## 1.2    Traffic Signs that Are Cautionary

A complete set of 40 cautionary traffic signs have been introduced by the Roadways and Transport division. The aim of these cautionary signs are meant for the drivers and pedestrians out there to warn them of any upcoming diversion or turns or crossings etc. so that they can take their required moves accordingly. The list of cautionary signs are depicted in Fig. 2.

## 1.3    Traffic Signs that Are Informative

This category of traffic signs comprises of information given on traffic signboards in the form of symbols to be known by the driver while on the road or about to park or blowing a horn depicted in Fig. 3. These signboards may contain information about a number of scenarios such as:

1. The distance remaining to cover in order to arrive at some particular location or landmark.
2. Alternative routes to the particular location (if present).
3. Whereabouts on the cautionary traffic signs are shown including schools, universities, work environments, clubs, open spots, cafes, etc.

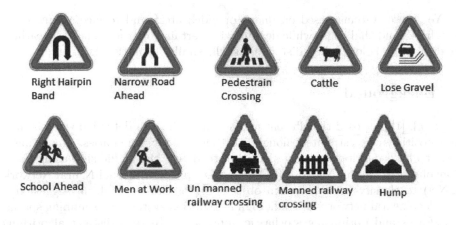

**Fig. 2.** Cautionary traffic signs

**Fig. 3.** Cautionary traffic signs

Technology has tried to develop "smarter vehicles" capable of automatically detecting traffic signs and knowing roads leading to safe driving. The driver alert system is an important feature within these smart cars to know the roads around them to help and protect the driver. Detection of traffic signs has been evolving as a traditional issue in computer vision for smart vehicles. The detection mechanism is observed as a preliminary step for the recognition of these signs that provide useful information such as providing direction alerts for self-driving cars (including driver assistance systems). Detection of these traffic signs have been recently gaining additional importance from various systems due to their ability to distinct landmarks for mapping and location. Unlike the natural landmarks with irregularities in their appearance (such as corner or edge points), the traffic signs have uniform appearances specified by strict regulations which may include various forms, intensities and patterns, etc. Dynamic traffic sign appearance makes it easier in identifying and matching traffic signs under different conditions. This becomes a primary reason for choosing the traffic signs as landmarks for the reconstruction of road maps.

Detection and recognition of traffic signs based on image or video were evolved by employing features to a wide variety of classifiers such as vector support, random forests, neural networks, decision fusion, reasoning module, prototype matching methods, etc.

Yet these systems based on image or video are found to face a number of drawbacks and challenges while dealing with certain conditions such as weather, shadow, light, color fading, distortion, slight similarity in the signs, etc.

## 2   Background

Lee et al. [1] proposed the efficient method of traffic sign detection where traffic sign positions are estimated along with their precise boundaries. Zhu, Yingying, et al. [2] developed a new algorithm to detect the traffic sign using Fully Convolutional Neural Network (FCN) and Deep Convolutional Neural Network (CNN) to classify the traffic sign objects. Arcos-García et al. [3] suggested a new deep neural network for traffic sign recognition system by examining spatial transforms and optimizing stochastic approaches. In this, distinct algorithms for the optimizing the adaptive and non-adaptive stochastic gradient descent are assessed. Subsequently, multiple blends of Spatial Transformer Networks are examined in the foremost neural network at different positions. The proposed method shows 99.71% recognition accuracy in the German traffic sign data. Mannan et al. [4] proposed a new model called Gaussian Mixture Model to detect the traffic signs which are degraded with poor contrast, color, etc. Zhang et al. [5] proposed novel student and teacher lightweight networks to classify the traffic signs. To learn features $1 \times 1$ conv and dense layer is used by teacher network. In student network a 6 layered end to end architecture is used to deploy the model in mobile devices. Wali et al. [9] used Malaysian traffic sign data-set to develop an automatic traffic sign recognition and detection system. In this model initially the data set was pre-processed then detect and recognise the traffic sign. Support vector machine classifier is used to classify the Malaysian traffic signs and it outperforms with the accuracy 95.1%. Liu et al. [11] suggested Deconvolution region dependent neural network (DR-CNN) to detect from the large image the small size traffic sign. This method initially adds a deconvolution layer and a normalization layer to the convolution layer output. It concatenates the characteristics of the various layers into a fused feature map to provide sufficient information for the identification of small traffic signs. We propose a two-stage adaptive classification loss function for regional proposal networks (RPNs) and fully connected neural networks within DR-CNN to enhance training effectiveness and differentiate hard-negative samples from easy-positive ones. Han et al. [12] Proposed an approach for the identification of small traffic signs in real-time based on updated Faster-RCNN. In this model a small area proposal generator used to extract the characteristics of small traffic signs and combined Faster-RCNN's revised architecture with Online Hard Examples Mining (OHEM) to make the system more robust to identify small traffic signs in the region.

## 3    Methodology

---

**Algorithm 1:** Training the CNN to predict the traffic signs

Step 1: Load the Traffic Sign Data set from disk;
Step 2: Apply pre-processing techniques on the images(resizing image,
De-noise, and contrast improvement on data-set);
Step3: Apply Region Of Interest(ROI) on the images;
Step4: Train the network model(CNN) with our pre-processed traffic sign
data-set;
Step5: Testing the trained model with the input image and check whether
it predicts the image class or not;

---

The pictorial representation for this algorithm is shown in Fig. 4.

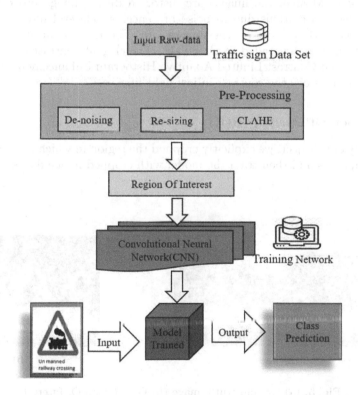

**Fig. 4.** Training and Testing (prediction) the model

### 3.1    Dataset

In any research the first and foremost task is to collect essential data sets. The
German Traffic Sign Recognition Benchmark (GTSRB) [7] is one of the publicly

available data-sets which we will use to train our custom traffic sign classifier. Comprising of a total of 43 different traffic sign labels, this data-set has a total of 51839 images of different traffic signs such as stop signs, warning signs, etc. For us, the traffic signs were pre-cropped, indicating that the annotators/creators of the data-set manually labelled the signs in the photos and extracted for us the Region of Interest (ROI) traffic sign, thus simplifying our project.

### 3.2    Pre-processing

The GTSRB data-set poses a number of challenges—low resolution or poor contrast images. Such images are pix-elated which is even difficult to be identified by the human eye. So in order to train our classifier for such challenging datasets we need to devise a powerful pre-processing technique [6] to enhance the input image quality. Most of the images are distorted during image processing due to atmospheric conditions due to noise presence. A bilateral filter was added to quash the noise present on the images [10]. The images captured with the camera at night are degraded to poor light. The elegant contrast enhancement technique called Contrast Limited Adaptive Histogram Enhancement (CLAHE) is applied to improve the contrast in low light images.

### 3.3    Region Of Interest (ROI)

To simplify our project, we explicitly cropped the region in which the traffic sign actually appears and then train the model with cropped image dataset (Fig. 5).

(a)                                    (b)

**Fig. 5.** (a) Ground truth image (b) Our Region Of Interest

### 3.4    Training Network Model

With a view to train our network model the pre-processed Traffic sign dataset is fed into pre-trained Convolutional Neural Network (CNN) [8]. CNN has three significant highlights that help to decrease the system multifaceted nature and for effective training of the various categorized layers. Dissimilar to the customary neural system network augmentation, the convolution activity of the CNNs lean towards sparse interaction i.e the neurons of one layer are not associated with every one of the neurons in the first layer. Rather, it deals with making the bit littler than the information and utilizing it for the entire picture. CNN chips away at a similar parameter for more than one capacity in the model. Every individual from the piece is utilized at each position of the input. This property of the CNN is called parameter sharing and makes the system straightforward by adapting just one lot of parameters rather than a different set for every area. Another significant property of CNN is comparability sharing. As per this property, at whatever point input is changed in the system, the yield additionally changes in a similar way. Because of the nearness of these three properties, the heap on the system engineering is diminished somewhat and this makes the CNNs work superior to the next Deep Learning designs. CNN has three significant highlights that help to decrease the network complexity and allow the hierarchical layers to be trained effectively. How the image features are extracted and how the image is classified is shown in Fig. 6

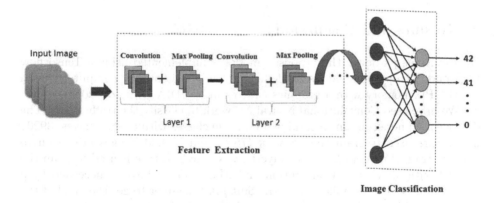

**Fig. 6.** Feature extraction and classification

### 3.5   Prediction

Now load the sample input images from the disk and pre-process them in the identical way as we did to train the data. Pre-processing the input images is found to be absolutely critical, including image resizing, contrast enhancement using CLAHE and scaling them from 0 to 1. We also need to pre-process the test data in the same manner as the training data. Now load the trained model from the disk and provide modeling for the pre-processed sample images to predict the class label. The projected label image class is shown in Fig. 7.

**Fig. 7.** Predicted output with the image class labels

# 4    Results and Discussion

On the Keras platform, the proposed model is implemented using a Tensorflow back end. The python code is implemented on a Windows 10 computer with a 5 GB GPU memory with a graphics card from NVIDIA Quadro P2000.

We have used Convolutional Neural Network to classify the traffic signs. The dataset used here contains a total of 43 unique classes with 51839 images. 39209 images are used to train the network (75%) and 12,630 images are taken to test the trained model (25%). Six layered CNN architecture is used to train the dataset with alternative Convolution and Max Pooling Layers succeeded by a Fully Connected Layer followed by the Soft max classifier to get the label of the image class. The CNN working model is depicted in Fig. 8.

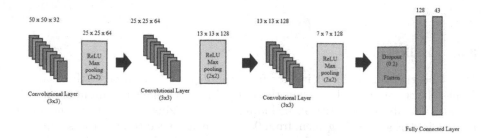

**Fig. 8.** Working model of Convolutional Neural network

The Fig. 8 shows that, the input image is resized to $50 \times 50$ pixels and set the batch size to 128 with 20 epochs and total $303,675$ parameters are trained with this model. The precision, Recall, FI- score and support is measured for some sample input images and same is shown in the Table 1.

**Table 1.** Precision, Recall, FI- score and support for sample traffic sign images.

| Label name | Precision | Recall | FI- score | Support |
|---|---|---|---|---|
| Class 1 | 0.95 | 0.99 | 0.97 | 62 |
| Class 3 | 0.96 | 0.97 | 0.97 | 755 |
| Class 5 | 1.00 | 0.96 | 0.97 | 660 |
| Class 6 | 0.99 | 0.97 | 0.95 | 451 |
| Class 7 | 0.99 | 0.98 | 1.00 | 481 |
| Class 8 | 1.00 | 0.96 | 0.98 | 660 |
| Class 10 | 0.99 | 1.00 | 0.99 | 720 |
| Class 11 | 1.00 | 1.00 | 1.00 | 270 |
| Class 16 | 0.98 | 0.93 | 0.97 | 210 |
| Class 18 | 0.98 | 0.99 | 0.98 | 150 |
| Class 23 | 0.75 | 0.60 | 0.67 | 60 |
| Class 28 | 0.69 | 1.00 | 0.81 | 90 |
| Class 31 | 0.93 | 0.94 | 0.94 | 150 |
| Class 35 | 0.99 | 0.96 | 0.96 | 270 |
| Class 37 | 0.97 | 1.00 | 0.98 | 210 |
| Class 40 | 0.98 | 1.00 | 0.99 | 120 |

Our CNN architecture was able to achieve an accuracy of 96.86%. The training and testing of value_accuracy and value_loss graphs are shown in Fig. 9.

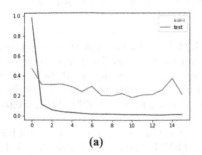
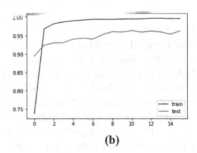

(a)                    (b)

**Fig. 9.** (a) Training and testing value loss (b) Training and testing value accuracy

# 5    Conclusion

Deep learning techniques alone are not adequate to achieve reasonable predictive precision. Along with deep learning, they may also use computer vision techniques to improve prediction accuracy. Initially, pre-processing techniques such as bilateral filters were applied to remove noise, CLAHE was applied to improve contrast in low-light images on traffic sign dataset and then specifically crop traffic sign information from the ground-truth image using the region-of-interest technique for quicker processing. In this paper, a convolutionary neural network model with 6 layers is used to automatically identify the traffic signs. This model is implemented on alternative convolutionary and max layers of the pool. To train the Convolutionary Neural Network, 39209 image samples with a size of $50 \times 50$ are considered. Traffic sign recognition is analyzed using the Keras framework's Deep Learning methodology. This model runs epochs of 20 and batch size of 128. This experiment is based on image samples of 12,630 and predicts the traffic sign class with a precision of 96.86%. So far no data set for Indian traffic signs is identified. Build a data set for Indian traffic signs in the future, and develop a new model that will train on data set proposals.

# References

1. Lee, H.S., Kim, K.: Simultaneous traffic sign detection and boundary estimation using convolutional neural network. IEEE Trans. Intell. Transp. Syst. **19**(5), 1652–1663 (2018)
2. Zhu, Y., et al.: Traffic sign detection and recognition using fully convolutional network guided proposals. Neurocomputing **214**, 758–766 (2016)
3. Arcos-García, Á., Alvarez-Garcia, J.A., Soria-Morillo, L.M.: Deep neural network for traffic sign recognition systems: an analysis of spatial transformers and stochastic optimisation methods. Neural Netw. **99**, 158–165 (2018)
4. Mannan, A., et al.: Classification of degraded traffic signs using flexible mixture model and transfer learning. IEEE Access **7**, 148800–148813 (2019)
5. Zhang, J., et al.: Lightweight deep network for traffic sign classification. Ann. Telecommun. 1–11 (2019). https://doi.org/10.1007/s12243-019-00731-9
6. Satti, S.K., et al.: An efficient noise separation technique for removal of Gaussian and mixed noises in monochrome and color images. https://doi.org/10.35940/ijitee.I1122.0789S219
7. Stallkamp, J., Schlipsing, M., Salmen, J., Igel, C.: The German traffic sign recognition benchmark: a multi-class classification competition. In: Proceedings of the IEEE International Joint Conference on Neural Networks, pp. 1453–1460 (2011)
8. Yamashita, R., Nishio, M., Do, R.K.G., et al.: Convolutional neural networks: an overview and application in radiology. Insights Imaging **9**, 611–629 (2018). https://doi.org/10.1007/s13244-018-0639-9
9. Wali, S.B., et al.: An automatic traffic sign detection and recognition system based on colour segmentation, shape matching, and SVM. Math. Probl. Eng. **2015**, 1–11 (2015)
10. Satti, S.K., Murthy, R.V., Srinivasan, P.: Efficient technique for removal of white and mixed noises in gray scale images. Int. J. Innov. Eng. Manag. Res. **8**(09), 22–36 (2019)

11. Liu, Z., et al.: Small traffic sign detection from large image. Appl. Intell. **50**(1), 1–13 (2020)
12. Han, C., Gao, G., Zhang, Y.: Real-time small traffic sign detection with revised faster-RCNN. Multimedia Tools Appl. **78**(10), 13263–13278 (2019)

# Diabetic Retinopathy Detection on Retinal Fundus Images Using Convolutional Neural Network

Adarsh Pradhan$^{(\boxtimes)}$ (iD), Bhaskarjyoti Sarma (iD), Rahul Kumar Nath (iD),
Ajay Das (iD), and Anirudha Chakraborty (iD)

Department of Computer Science and Engineering, Girijananda Chowdhury
Institute of Management and Technology, Azara, Guwahati, India
adarsh@gimt-guwahati.ac.in,
bhaskarjyotisarma85@gmail.com,
rahulnath847@gmail.com, ajay999das@gmail.com,
imanirudhachakraborty64@gmail.com

**Abstract.** Diabetic retinopathy is a serious eye disease that occurs due to diabetes mellitus, also commonly known as diabetes, and it has grown as the most common cause of blindness in the present world. It is a disease in which the blood vessels behind the retina are damaged. At first, it shows no symptoms, but with time, it eventually leads to blindness. Early diagnosis of diabetic retinopathy can prevent vision loss in patients. The method proposed here for the detection of diabetic retinopathy disease is based on a convolutional neural network that categorizes the fundus images of patients according to the severity level of diabetic retinopathy. The input images are collected from the Kaggle diabetic retinopathy dataset, and various preprocessing steps such as cropping, resizing, grayscaling, CLAHE and Min-Max normalization are performed. Precision, recall and Kappa score values of our model are highly affected, due to the unequal distribution of dataset.

**Keywords:** Diabetic retinopathy · Convolutional neural network · Fundus images · CLAHE · Kappa score

## 1 Introduction

Diabetes, also known as diabetic mellitus (DM), is a growing disease worldwide. The World Health Organization statistics show that the count of people suffering from DM is going to reach 439 million by 2030 [1]. One of the major complications caused by DM is diabetic retinopathy (DR), which is now a major cause of blindness. Diabetic retinopathy is a severe eye disease caused due to high sugar level content in blood, which results in damage caused to the blood vessels behind the retina [2, 3]. This is usually followed by swelling and leakage. At the advanced stage, the retina starts producing tiny new blood vessels that might bleed, causing vision blockage leading to permanent vision loss. The earliest signs of retinal damage are shown by the formation of microaneurysm followed by hard exudates, soft exudates, hemorrhages, macular edema, etc. Several screening tools are used for diabetic retinopathy detection, such as

A. Bhattacharjee et al. (Eds.): MIND 2020, CCIS 1240, pp. 254–266, 2020.
https://doi.org/10.1007/978-981-15-6315-7_21

Optical Coherence Tomography (OCT) or fundus image examination [4]. Here we use fundus images for the detection of Diabetic Retinopathy (DR) stages. We use the Kaggle diabetic retinopathy dataset, which is of size 82 GB and consists of 35,126 RGB retinal images. It consists of several stages of DR as shown from Figs. 1, 2, 3, 4 and 5, where a clinician has rated each image on a scale of 0 to 4, where, 0 signifies No DR (Fig. 1), 1 signifies Mild DR (Fig. 2), 2 signifies Moderate DR (Fig. 3), 3 indicates Severe DR (Fig. 4) and 4 indicates Proliferative DR (Fig. 5). The images are first pre-processed and then fed to the CNN model for training, validation and testing.

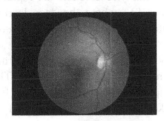

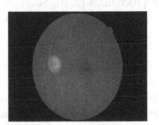

**Fig. 1.** No DR (Stage 1)            **Fig. 2.** Mild DR (Stage 2)

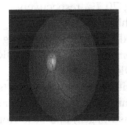

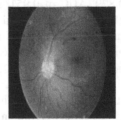

**Fig. 3.** Moderate DR (Stage 3)    **Fig. 4.** Severe DR (Stage 4)    **Fig. 5.** Proliferative DR (Stage 5)

Early detection and regular screening for DM can reduce the effect of DR, but it's not cost-efficient [5]. Also, highly skilled technicians are required for the examination of the fundus image, which is not quite possible, especially in rural areas where the rate of diabetes is high. So, this has led to the need for creating new automated detection tools that can help tackle the problem relating to diabetes. We propose to address the problem using a CNN based method that can train on the fundus images and classify them to the different stages of DR. The proposed CNN architecture consists of 13 layers, as shown in Fig. 12. The first two convolutional layers have 32 filters of size 3 * 3, which are followed by the ReLu layer and the max-pool layer. The third convolutional layer is as same as before, except it has 64 filters of size 3 * 3. The last set consists of a fully connected layer having 64 nodes and ReLu as activation function followed by a dropout layer with a dropout ratio of 0.5, which is ultimately followed by another fully connected layer of 5 nodes with softmax as an activation function. Finally, precision, recall and Kappa score values are evaluated to examine the performance of our model.

## 2 Related Work

We have seen that earlier methods were divided into feature extraction and classification category. Methods like SVM, K-NN, etc., are still useful for classification. However, the complexity and computation time are much higher because it depends upon manual procedures [2, 6]. So, to extract features, many researchers are replacing these two-step methods with deep learning techniques [2], where the deep learning method that they have used are based on some architectures like AlexNet, ResNet-50 etc. [2].

Zhiguang and Jianbo Yang [2] proposed the model that includes regression activation mapping which shows the area of the desired region in the fundus image. They have also illustrated that by using the global average pooling layer instead of the fully connected layer in their Net-5 architecture, a good kappa score can be acquired and training speed can be increased.

Xianglong Zeng et al. [7] have developed a system that classifies the fundus images with or without DR which takes fundus images of both eyes as input and calls novel Siamese-like CNN model based on Inception V3 architecture and achieved kappa score of 0.829, AUC of 0.951, sensitivity and specificity of 82.2%, 70.7% respectively. In another proposed method [6], they have used three steps which are pre-processing, retinal segmentation, and image classification. They have used U-Net for retinal segmentation, which significantly improved the output of classifying 5 stages of DR namely - No DR, Mild DR, Moderate NPR, Severe NPR, PDR.

In another paper [8], they have used Inception-V3 architecture, which extracts multilevel features from the fundus images and the model is trained by taking different sizes of datasets giving an accuracy of 67% (for 10,000 fundus images) and 88% (for 40,000 fundus images). Also, based upon different hyperparameters, they have obtained different accuracies; for instance, they have taken different number of training epochs like 100 and 200, where they got the accuracy of 70% and 88%, respectively, and concluded that the accuracy of the model could be increased by training the model for more number of epochs, though after a certain point, further number of epochs did not change the accuracy of the model.

In [16], they have proposed a method to divide the EyePacs datasets into two sections one for left eye and other for right eye, then train them individually using the CNN model. They obtained an accuracy of 63.6% and 66.4% respectively.

In [5], Xiaoliang Wang et al. applied different types of deep neural architectures to classify DR in five stages. They have used the EYEPACS dataset to train 166 fundus images on AlexNET, VGG16, InceptionNet, giving the accuracy of 37.43%, 50.03%, 63.23% respectively, with InceptionNet architecture giving the highest accuracy among the three. In [9], Gen-Min Lin et al. showed that the use of entropy images increased the accuracy of their model by 4.3%, where the accuracy of 81.80% on original fundus images increased to 86.10% for the entropy images.

## 3   Proposed Method

Figure 6 gives a brief description of the CNN based method that we have employed for the detection of Diabetic Retinopathy (DR) detection.

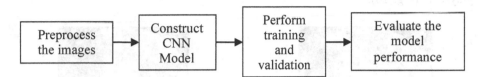

**Fig. 6.** CNN based method for DR detection

### 3.1   Preprocessing

In the preprocessing step, we have performed Cropping, Resizing, Grayscaling, Histogram Equalization and Normalization to standardize the high-resolution fundus images as illustrated below.

**Cropping.** All the fundus images in the dataset are cropped by a percentage in such a way that most of the unwanted black pixels are removed without cutting off the region of interest. Here we have cropped by 10% from the left and the right side and by 0.5% from the top and the bottom side of the original image (Fig. 7) to obtain the cropped image (Fig. 8).

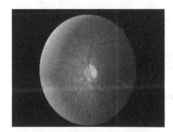
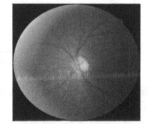

**Fig. 7.** Original image                **Fig. 8.** Cropped image

**Resizing.** The Kaggle dataset contains high-resolution images and training those images in the convolutional neural network requires a system with a high-end configuration. Therefore, in order to reduce the network's training time, we resized the cropped image to $256 \times 256$ using bilinear interpolation method.

**Grayscaling the Images.** In an image, one color pixel is made with three colors, namely, red, green and blue (RGB), having a total bit size of 24, which is represented by three arrays. In a grayscale image, the grey pixel is represented by only one dimension with a bit size of 8, therefore converting RGB to grayscale helps us to reduce the computation time for the model and also grayscale image takes less space than RGB image. So, after we crop the original image (Fig. 9), we convert it to grayscale (Fig. 10).

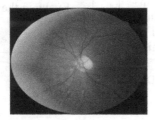

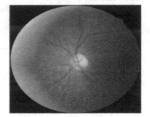

**Fig. 9.** Cropped image                **Fig. 10.** Grayscale image

**Histogram Equalization and Normalization.** Contrast Limited Adaptive Histogram Equalization is performed over ordinary AHE in order to minimize the over-amplification of noise in near contrast regions [10]. Histogram equalization equalizes the contrast level in higher and lower contrast portions of the image and enhances edges. As shown in Fig. 12, CLAHE is applied to the image in Fig. 11. The resized images that are in RGB format are converted to grayscale image, applied CLAHE, and then Min-Max normalization is performed in order to scale the image values within a range of 0 and 1. Using Eq. 1 we can rescale an image's pixel intensities within a range [0,1]:

$$x' = \frac{x - \min(x)}{\max(x) - \min(x)} \tag{1}$$

where $x$ is the original value and $x'$ is the new normalized value.

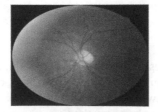

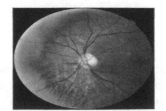

**Fig. 11.** Grayscale image                **Fig. 12.** CLAHE image

## 3.2   Convolutional Neural Network

In recent years, the deep learning algorithms which imitate the operations of the human cerebral cortex have been found of excellent use [11], and one of the vastly used deep learning algorithms for image processing is a convolutional neural network, also known as ConvNet or CNN. CNN can automatically extract local features of an image by applying a set of weights called filters and applied multiple filters to extract different features [2]. There are many CNN architectures like AlexNet (which has 8 layers and can process 61 million parameters), VGG (19 layers), GoogleNet (22 layers and can process 5 million parameters), ResNet (152 layers) and in all these CNN networks they have many hidden layers, and as the layers go deeper, more features are extracted for classification [12].

**Convolution Layer.** The convolutional layer contains a set of filters that are used to extract features. When these filters are convolved with the input volume, it produces feature maps containing convoluted values, computed by the convolution operation occurring between an array of inputs and filters. A convolution operation is a matrix dot product between an array of the input volume and a set of filters. A convolution layer can have multiple filters in the network, and with these filters, one can extract features from low-level to high-levels in an image during each training cycle [12, 13].

**Pooling Layer.** The pooling layer is applied to downsample the input volume received from the previous layers. There are different methods that can be used, such as Average pooling, Max pooling and Global pooling. Max pooling is one of the standard techniques where it calculates the maximum value from a small region say n*n of the input image and store it in the output map. This max-pooling process continues until it moves across every region of the input volume to generate a max-pooling map [6, 12, 13].

**Fully Connected Layer.** Before giving the input to the fully connected layer for classification, the output from the previous layer is flattened [13]. The backpropagation technique used in the fully connected layer is responsible for the precision of the weights, where each node or neuron receives those weights to determine the most appropriate labels. Finally, the output results from each node are used to make the classification decision.

**ReLU Layer.** ReLU is the commonly used activation function to add non-linear properties to the inputs from the previous convolution layer. Here the Relu function transforms all the weighted sum of inputs to the maximum of either 0 or the input itself, i.e., it changes all the negative activations value to zero [6, 13].

**Dropout Layer.** Overfitting is the problem where our model learns too many patterns from our training sets such that it fails in classifying new datasets. That's why the dropout layer is used to prevent the model from overfitting, where it randomly drops out some of the hidden nodes during the training process [11], and as a result, this layer provides some improvements in the accuracy of the model [12, 13].

**Softmax Layer.** This layer uses the softmax activation function to transform all inputs received from the fully connected layer in the range of 0 to 1, where each output from the softmax layer sums up to 1 forming a probability distribution. The softmax layer is basically used for multiclass classification by calculating probabilities for different classes [14]. The formula for softmax is shown in Eq. 2:

$$\sigma(z)_i = \frac{e^{z_i}}{\sum_{j=1}^{K} e^{z_j}} \tag{2}$$

where i → 1…, K and input vector (z) → $(z_1, z_2…, z_K) \in R^K$.

### 3.3   CNN Architecture

The CNN architecture that we have used consists of 13 layers, as shown in Fig. 13. The first two sets of the layer are the convolution layer, where 32 filters convolve across the image to produce 32 feature maps, then the Relu layer is respectively applied to each feature map for non-linearity, and lastly, the max-pool layer is used to reduce the spatial representation of the feature map. In the third sets of layers, we again use a convolutional layer where 64 filters are used, which is again followed by Relu and max-pool layer.

In the last set of layers, it consists of one fully connected layer of 64 nodes, followed by one dropout layer where the dropout ratio is 0.5, and ultimately it is followed by another fully-connected layer with five nodes and one softmax layer which gives us the final classification outputs.

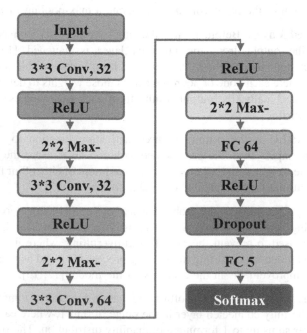

**Fig. 13.**  CNN architecture

## 3.4 Training Algorithm

We applied Stochastic Gradient Descent with Nesterov Momentum, an optimization algorithm that speeds up training and improves the rate of convergence towards the global minimum of the cost function significantly. Stochastic Gradient Descent differs slightly from regular gradient descent, where it looks for a single mini-batch instead of the whole dataset to calculate the cost and minimize the loss or minimize the global cost function of the network. Nesterov Momentum helps in guiding the gradient always towards the right direction of minimum loss despite the momentum pointing towards the wrong direction as the gradient is not computed from the current position. The rule for updating Stochastic Gradient descent with Nesterov Momentum is shown in Eqs. 3 and 4 [15]:

$$v_t = \mu v_{t-1} - \eta \nabla l(\theta + \mu v_{t-1}) \tag{3}$$

$$\theta_t = \theta_{t-1} + v_t \tag{4}$$

where,

't' $\rightarrow$ the number of iterations
'$\mu$' $\rightarrow$ the momentum parameter
'$\nabla$' $\rightarrow$ the gradient
'l' $\rightarrow$ the loss function
'$\eta$' $\rightarrow$ the learning rate.

## 3.5 Hyperparameter Tuning

To optimize our model, we have performed tuning of some hyper parameters in the training period. As the performance of any machine learning model is susceptible to its hyperparameters, we, therefore, experimented those by performing training with a small dataset. Having observed the effects, we came up with the values that showed better results, as shown in Table 1. We tuned the initial learning rate to 0.01 with a decay of $10e^{-6}$, which reduces the learning rate after every batch. The batch size was determined in such a way that after every epoch, the learning rate decreases by 10%, as decreasing the learning rate prevents from overshooting the global minimum of the cost function. Also, the momentum for the optimization algorithm was set to 0.9. The update schedule for the learning rate is (Eq. 5):

$$L_t = L_{t-1} * \frac{1}{1 + (D * t)} \tag{5}$$

where,

L $\rightarrow$ Learning Rate
t $\rightarrow$ No. of batch iteration
D $\rightarrow$ Learning Rate Decay

**Table 1.** Hyperparameters values

| Hyperparameters | Values |
|---|---|
| Initial learning rate | 0.01 |
| Learning rate decay | $10\ e^{-6}$ |
| SGD momentum | 0.9 |
| Batch size | 70 |
| Number of epochs | 15 |

# 4 Experimental Design and Data

## 4.1 Dataset

For our proposed model, we have used the EYEPACS dataset, which we collected from the Kaggle website (https://www.kaggle.com/c/diabetic-retinopathy-detection). It contains 35,126 RGB retinal images captured by fundus camera, which are labelled and categorized by the clinicians in five different classes from 0 to 4 depending upon their severity where each class corresponds to different stages of DR as shown above from Figs. 1, 2, 3, 4 and 5. The class distribution of the dataset provided by Kaggle is highly imbalanced which can be seen in Table 2.

**Table 2.** Class distribution of original datasets

| Class | Name | No. of images | Percentage |
|---|---|---|---|
| 0 | No DR | 25810 | 73.48% |
| 1 | Mild DR | 2443 | 6.96% |
| 2 | Moderate DR | 5292 | 15.07% |
| 3 | Severe DR | 873 | 2.48% |
| 4 | Proliferative DR | 708 | 2.01% |

## 4.2 Implementation and Results

Using Open Source Computer Vision (OpenCV) Library, we have performed all the preprocessing steps such as cropping, resizing, greyscaling, CLAHE and Min-Max normalization. After preprocessing, we have divided the whole dataset into 80% as the training set, 15% as the validation set, and the remaining 5% as the testing set. We have fed the training and validation dataset into our model that has been built using Keras API and TensorFlow Library for training the network. In a Windows 10 platform having a system configuration of 16 GB RAM and Intel i7-4790 k 4th generation processor, training of the network has been performed for 15 epochs, as more epochs demand more computational power and high time consumption.

**Evaluation Metrics.** The accuracy of the model alone cannot evaluate the classifier perfectly, as in this case the distribution of the classes is highly imbalanced. Therefore, for the evaluation of the performance of our trained model accuracy, confusion matrix, Precision & Recall, and Kappa Score are computed [13].

Accuracy is the score of correctly predicted observations over total observations. The model managed to get a training accuracy of 93.13% but scores about 85.68% accuracy on the testing dataset, which might be due to overfitting as the dataset is highly imbalanced.

The confusion matrix represents the True Positives (TP), True Negatives (TN), False Positives (FP), and False Negatives (FN) values for all the classes. In Fig. 14, a confusion matrix has been shown representing true labels on the vertical co-ordinates and predicted labels on the horizontal co-ordinates.

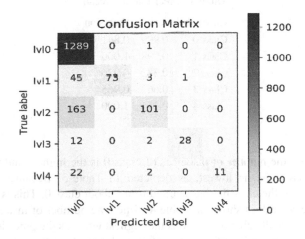

**Fig. 14.** Confusion matrix

As mentioned above, we have taken 5% of the dataset for testing purpose, shown in Table 3. In the confusion matrix, we see that out of 1290 images of class 0, 1289 images are correctly classified and 1 image is falsely classified. Similarly, for class 1, 73 images are correctly predicted and the rest 49 images are incorrectly predicted.

**Table 3.** No of testing images

| No of testing images | Class label |
| --- | --- |
| 1290 | Class 0 |
| 122 | Class 1 |
| 264 | Class 2 |
| 43 | Class 3 |
| 35 | Class 4 |

Using Eqs. 6 and 7, we compute Precision & Recall from the confusion matrix. Precision represents the portion of relevant occurrences among retrieved occurrences, whereas Recall is the portion of the relevant occurrences that are retrieved.

$$Precision = \frac{TP}{TP + FP} \tag{6}$$

$$Recall = \frac{TP}{TP + FN} \tag{7}$$

**Table 4.** Precision and recall

| Class label | Recall | Precision |
|---|---|---|
| Class 0 | 0.999 | 0.841 |
| Class 1 | 0.598 | 1.000 |
| Class 2 | 0.382 | 0.926 |
| Class 3 | 0.667 | 0.965 |
| Class 4 | 0.314 | 1.000 |

In the dataset, the number of instances of class 0 is the highest and the number of instances of class 4 is the lowest, as depicted in Table 3. Because of this highly imbalanced dataset, the classifier has learned more about class 0. This is evident in the precision and recall values shown in Table 4. Since the number of instances of class 0 is the highest, the recall value of class 0 is the highest whereas the precision value is the lowest. Similarly, the number of instances of class 4 is the lowest, so the recall value of class 4 is the lowest, whereas the precision value is the highest.

Cohen's Kappa Score compares the judgment produced by various raters; i.e., how much similarity exists in the judgments. In our case, one of the raters is the ground truth or the true labels, and the other corresponds to our classifier i.e., the predicted labels. Kappa score(K) can be evaluated by Observed Accuracy ($p_o$) and Expected Accuracy ($p_e$) as shown in Eq. 8.

$$Kappa\,Score(K) = \frac{p_o - p_e}{1 - p_e} \tag{8}$$

The model gained a Kappa Score of 0.584.

## 5 Conclusion and Future Scope

In this paper, we use a CNN model to classify various stages of Diabetic Retinopathy (DR) from the fundus images. We use the Kaggle diabetic retinopathy dataset, and perform various preprocessing steps such as cropping, resizing, grayscaling and use CLAHE and Min-Max normalization for further image enhancement. 80% of the dataset is used for training, 15% for validation and 5% for testing. Multiple metrics are used to evaluate and examine the performance of our model. The Kaggle diabetic retinopathy dataset is highly disproportionate, and it becomes evident by the results of precision and recall values that we acquired. The Kappa Score is also found to be of moderate value. One of our future goals would be to minimize this problem by upscaling the dataset and by using various regularization techniques. Also training in high end system with a greater number of training epochs could further enhance the performance of the network.

We are currently planning to build the Graphical user Interface (GUI) for this project where one can feed the retinal fundus image and have the image classified as DR or non-DR. A detection model of such kind would be highly beneficial to people in rural areas where they may not have instant access to doctors.

**Acknowledgments.** This work is supported by Assam Science and Technical University, under TEQIP III program of Ministry of Human Resource Development, India, funded by World Bank.

# References

1. Kaveeshwar, S.A., Cornwall, J.: The current state of diabetes mellitus in India. Austr. Med. J. **7**(1), 45–48 (2014). https://doi.org/10.4066/AMJ.2013.1979
2. Wang, Z., Yang, J.: Diabetic retinopathy detection via deep convolutional networks for discriminative localization and visual explanation. ArXiv abs/1703.10757 (2017)
3. Wang, X., Lu, Y., Wang, Y., Chen, W.: Diabetic retinopathy stage classification using convolutional neural networks. In: IEEE International Conference on Information Reuse and Integration (IRI), pp. 465–471 (2018). https://doi.org/10.1109/IRI.2018.00074
4. Mookiah, M.R.K., Acharya, U.R., Chua, C.K., Lim, C.M., Ng, E.Y.K., Laude, A.: Computer-aided diagnosis of diabetic retinopathy: a review. Comput. Biol. Med. **43**(12), 2136–2155 (2013). https://doi.org/10.1016/j.compbiomed.2013.10.007
5. Williams, R., Airey, M., Baxter, H., et al.: Epidemiology of diabetic retinopathy and macular oedema: a systematic review. Eye **18**, 963–983 (2004). https://doi.org/10.1038/sj.eye. 6701476
6. Burewar, S., Gonde, A.B., Vipparthi, S.K.: Diabetic retinopathy detection by retinal segmentation with region merging using CNN. In: IEEE 13th International Conference on Industrial and Information Systems (ICIIS), pp. 136–142 (2018). https://doi.org/10.1109/ ICIINF3.2018.8721315
7. Zeng, X., Chen, H., Luo, Y., Ye, W.: Automated diabetic retinopathy detection based on binocular siamese-like convolutional neural network. IEEE Access **7**, 30744–30753 (2019). https://doi.org/10.1109/ACCESS.2019.2903171
8. Kanungo, Y.S., Srinivasan, B., Choudhary, S.: Detecting diabetic retinopathy using deep learning. In: 2nd IEEE International Conference on Recent Trends in Electronics, Information & Communication Technology (RTEICT), pp. 801–804 (2017). https://doi. org/10.1109/RTEICT.2017.8256708
9. Lin, G.-M., et al.: Transforming retinal photographs to entropy images in deep learning to improve automated detection for diabetic retinopathy. J. Ophthalmol. (2018). https://doi.org/ 10.1155/2018/2159702

10. Ma, J., Fan, X., Yang, S.X., Zhang, X., Zhu, X.: Contrast limited adaptive histogram equalization based fusion for underwater image enhancement. Int. J. Pattern Recogn. Artif. Intell. **32**(07) (2018). https://doi.org/10.1142/S0218001418540186
11. Chauhan, R., Ghanshala, K.K., Joshi, R.C.: Convolutional neural network (CNN) for image detection and recognition. In: First International Conference on Secure Cyber Computing and Communication (ICSCCC), pp. 278–282 (2018). https://doi.org/10.1109/ICSCCC.2018. 8703316
12. Doshi, D., Shenoy, A., Sidhpura, D., Gharpure, P.: Diabetic retinopathy detection using deep convolutional neural networks. In: International Conference on Computing, Analytics and Security Trends (CAST), pp. 261–266 (2016). https://doi.org/10.1109/CAST.2016.7914977
13. Ghosh, R., Ghosh, K., Maitra, S.: Automatic detection and classification of diabetic retinopathy stages using CNN. In: 4th International Conference on Signal Processing and Integrated Networks (SPIN), pp. 550–554 (2017). https://doi.org/10.1109/SPIN.2017. 8050011
14. Kouretas, I., Paliouras, V.: Simplified hardware implementation of the softmax activation function. In: 8th International Conference on Modern Circuits and Systems Technologies (MOCAST), pp. 1–4 (2019). https://doi.org/10.1109/MOCAST.2019.8741677
15. Ruder, S.: An overview of gradient descent optimization algorithms. ArXiv, abs/1609.04747 (2016)
16. García, G., Gallardo, J., Mauricio, A., López, J., Del Carpio, C.: Detection of diabetic retinopathy based on a convolutional neural network using retinal fundus images. In: Lintas, A., Rovetta, S., Verschure, P., Villa, A. (eds.) ICANN 2017. LNCS, vol. 10614. Springer, Cham (2017). https://doi.org/10.1007/978-3-319-68612-7_72

# Medical Image Fusion Based on Deep Decomposition and Sparse Representation

K. Vanitha[1]([⊠]), D. Satyanarayana[2], and M. N. Giri Prasad[1]

[1] JNTUA College of Engineering, Ananthapuramu, Anantapur, India
vanithakamarthi@gmail.com
[2] RGM College of Engineering and Technology, Nandyal, India

**Abstract.** In this paper, a new fusion algorithm for combining multimodal sensor brain images based on deep decomposition and sparse representation is presented. Firstly, the extraction of detail and base parts is done by using deep decomposition method. Next, the base parts are merged according to maximum fusion strategy to produce final base image. Then detail parts are applied with laplacian pyramid to obtain their high pass and low pass frequency bands. The low and high pass bands are merged using sparse representation and absolute rule. The above fused bands are applied with inverse laplacian pyramid, final detail image is produced. Final fused image is produced by adding final detail and base images. Our method not only preserves the source information but also reduces halo artifacts, pixel distortion. Experimental results reveal that our method gives the better results compared with existing methods.

**Keywords:** Multimodal medical image fusion · Deep decomposition · Laplacian pyramid · Sparse representation

## 1 Introduction

Images from single imaging system don't give inclusive information concerning the region of interest in medical imaging. Physicians take the information reflected from medical images of human organs to understand the lesion. CT, MRI, PET and SPECT are necessary for clinical practices, which gives anatomical and functional data. For proper treatment, doctors require the data of above mentioned multimodalities into one image. So merging of multimodalities is carried out by the process of image fusion. The detailed literature of different fusion algorithms are available in [1–3]. To avoid the drawbacks of decomposition level of multi-scale transform [2–4], edge preserving [5–8] based methods, dictionary learning of sparse representation [9–11], selection of membership function of fuzzy [12], training of neural networks [13, 14], a novel decomposition method is used in this paper. The decomposition based on latent low rank representation LatLRR called DDLatLRR is used to decompose input images into detail, base parts [15, 16]. The base and detail parts are merged by maximum rule and combination of laplacian pyramid and sparse representation. The fused image provides data which is very useful for doctors for further process. The main innovations of proposed decomposition are providing more salient parts, preserving details, extraction of global and local structural data from source images. The remaining sections of this

© Springer Nature Singapore Pte Ltd. 2020
A. Bhattacharjee et al. (Eds.): MIND 2020, CCIS 1240, pp. 267–277, 2020.
https://doi.org/10.1007/978-981-15-6315-7_22

paper are organized as follows. The related theories and proposed fusion method are explained briefly in Sect. 2, 3 respectively. The obtained results are analyzed in Sect. 4, finally concluded in Sect. 5.

## 2  Preliminaries

The description of deep decomposition (DD) and sparse representation (SR), which are used in the proposed fusion framework, is given in detail as follows.

### 2.1  Deep Decomposition Based on Latent LRR (DDLatLRR)

Based on latent low rank representation (LatLRR) [15], the deep decomposition is developed so called DDLatLRR [16]. In this decomposition, LatLRR is used to learn the project matrix 'L' from the training data and explained in detail in [15]. Firstly, patches are formed by dividing source images and then vectors are formed by reshuffling using the P (.) operator. Then, project matrix L is used to calculate the detail parts as follows:

$$I_d^k = L * P(I_k) \tag{1}$$

where I = $(I_1, I_2)$, L = project matrix, P(.) = operator, k = 1,2.
    Then the corresponding base part is obtained as follows:

$$I_b^k = I_k - I_d^k \tag{2}$$

### 2.2  Sparse Representation (SR)

The representation of signal 'a' by linear combination of atoms in the over complete dictionary is Sparse representation, whose sparse coefficients are obtained as follows:

$$\min_X \|X\|_0, s.t. \|A - DX\|_2^2 \le \varepsilon \tag{3}$$

    Where D is dictionary, X is a sparse coefficient vector; $\|X\|_0$ = nonzero entries number in X; $\varepsilon$ = representation error. In our fusion method, dictionary is trained by K-SVD method, which uses orthogonal matching tracking optimization (OMP) for estimation of sparse coefficient [8].

# 3   Block Diagram

See Fig. 1.

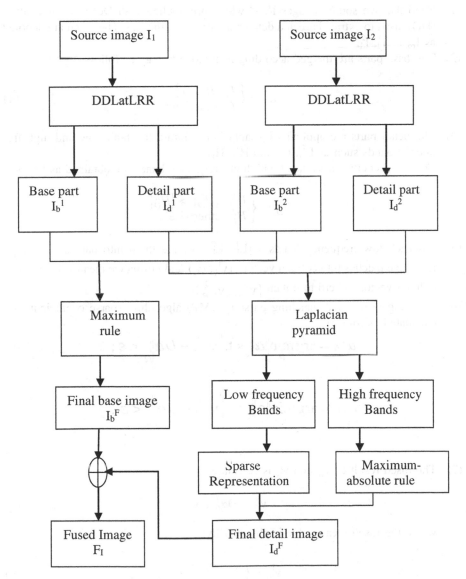

**Fig. 1.** Schematic diagram of the proposed MIF framework

## 4  Proposed Method

The multimodalities of medical images are merged using the procedure, explained step by step as follows.

(1) Read the two source images $I^1$, $I^2$ which are applied with Deep decomposition (DD), used to extract base and detail parts by using the Eqs. (1–2) and are denoted as $I_b^1$, $I_b^2$, $I_d^1$, $I_d^2$.

(2) The base parts are merged according to fusion strategy as follows:

$$I_b^F = \begin{cases} I_b^1, & I_b^1 > I_b^2 \\ I_b^2, & \text{otherwise} \end{cases} \tag{4}$$

(3) The detail parts are applied with laplacian pyramid to obtain low and high frequency bands such as $L_D^1$, $L_D^2$ and $H_D^1$, $H_D^2$.

(4) The fused coefficients related with high frequency bands are obtained as follows:

$$H_D^F = \begin{cases} H_D^1, & |H_D^1| > |H_D^2| \\ H_D^2, & \text{otherwise} \end{cases} \tag{5}$$

(5) For each low frequency bands $= [L_D^1, L_D^2]$, divide them into patches $\{p_A^j, p_B^j\}$, rearrange patches into column vectors $\{v_A^j, v_B^j\}$ and normalize mean value of each column vector to zero to obtain $\{v^{\wedge j}_A, v^{\wedge j}_B\}$.

(6) By using orthogonal matching pursuit (OMP) algorithm, sparse coefficients are calculated as follows:

$$\alpha^j{}_A = \arg\min_\alpha \|\alpha\|_0 \text{ s.t.} \left\| v^{\wedge j}_A - D\alpha \right\|_2 < \varepsilon\,; \tag{6}$$

$$\alpha^j{}_B = \arg\min_\alpha \|\alpha\|_0 \text{ s.t.} \left\| v^{\wedge j}_B - D\alpha \right\|_2 < \varepsilon\,, \tag{7}$$

and $\alpha_F^j$ is selected as maximum of $\alpha_A^j$, $\alpha_B^j$.

(7) The fused result of $v_A^j$ and $v_B^j$ is calculated by:

$$v_F^j = D\alpha_F^j + \bar{v}_F^j.1 \tag{8}$$

where the fused mean value is obtained by:

$$\bar{v}_F^j = \begin{cases} \bar{v}_A^j, & \alpha_A^i \geq \alpha_B^i \\ \bar{v}_B^j, & \text{otherwise} \end{cases} \tag{9}$$

(8) The above process is carried out iteratively for all patches and is averaged to obtain final low frequency fused result $L_D^F$.

(9) The above fused coefficients are applied with laplacian pyramid to reconstruct the final detail image $I_d^F$.

(10) The fused image is given as:

$$F_I = I_d^F + I_b^F \tag{10}$$

## 5  Experimental Results

The efficacy of proposed method is demonstrated by conducting experiment on four pairs of multimodal images which are taken from med Harvard site [18] and are shown in Fig. 2. All these source images are accurately registered and their size is $256 \times 256$ pixels. The five methods such as LP-SR [9], ASR [10], CSR [11], LatLRR [15] and CSMCA [17] are considered for comparison and fused images are shown in Figs. 3(a–f), 4, 5 and 6(a–f). Evaluation of fusion quality metrics such as ENT, information metrics $Q_{TE}$, $Q_{NCIE}$, $Q_{MI}$, metrics based on image features $Q_P$, $Q_G$ and $Q_W$, $Q_S$, $Q_{ABF}$, NFMI which are described in detail [19]. The overall information of an output image can be measured by EN, $Q_{MI}$ and NFMI. With respect to source images, $Q_s$ gives the structural similarity, $Q_{TE}$ is tsallis entropy, $Q_{NCIE}$ is nonlinear correlation information entropy, $Q_P$ measures features of fused image, and $Q_G$ measures the edge transfer to a fused image.

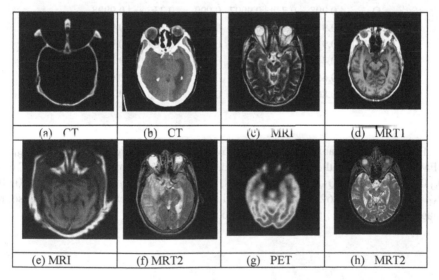

| (a)  CT | (b)  CT | (c)  MRI | (d)  MRT1 |
| (e) MRI | (f) MRT2 | (g)  PET | (h)  MRT2 |

**Fig. 2.** (a–e) CT & MRI (b–f) CT & MRT2 (c–g) MRI & PET (d–h) MRT1 & MRT2

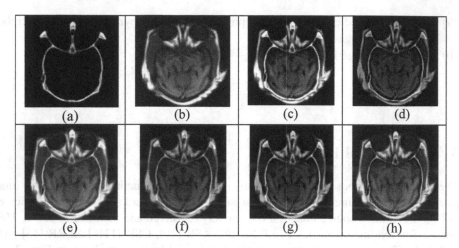

**Fig. 3.** (a) CT (b) MRI (c) LP-SR (d) ASR (e) CSR (f) LatLRR (g) CSMCA (h) Proposed method

**Table 1.** Quantative analysis of fusion techniques for CT and MRI

| Metrics | LP-SR | ASR | CSR | LatLRR | CSMCA | PROPOSED |
|---------|-------|-----|-----|--------|-------|----------|
| ENT | 6.045 | 6.177 | 6.737 | 6.492 | 4.571 | **6.760** |
| $Q_G$ | 0.759 | 0.703 | 0.525 | 0.614 | 0.626 | **0.846** |
| $Q_P$ | 0.524 | 0.563 | 0.503 | 0.541 | 0.542 | **0.595** |
| $Q_W$ | 0.998 | 0.724 | 0.997 | 0.998 | 0.667 | **0.999** |
| $Q_S$ | 0.998 | 0.744 | 0.9997 | 0.999 | 0.736 | **0.9998** |
| $Q_{ABF}$ | **0.913** | 0.899 | 0.904 | 0.908 | 0.893 | 0.906 |
| NFMI | **0.911** | 0.903 | 0.903 | 0.899 | 0.909 | 0.905 |
| $Q_{MI}$ | 0.442 | 0.501 | 0.645 | 0.605 | 0.474 | **0.666** |
| $Q_{TE}$ | **0.652** | 0.567 | 0.626 | 0.619 | 0.543 | 0.621 |
| $Q_{NICE}$ | 0.806 | 0.807 | 0.811 | 0.809 | 0.806 | **0.813** |

From the above Table 1, for all the above mentioned metrics except $Q_{TE}$, $Q_{ABF}$ and NFMI are bolded for the proposed method. The metrics of proposed are as ENT 6.76, $Q_G$ 0.846, $Q_P$ 0.595, $Q_W$ 0.999, $Q_S$ 0.9998, $Q_{ABF}$ 0.906, $Q_{NICE}$ 0.813 and NFMI 0.905, $Q_{MI}$ 0.666 and $Q_{TE}$ 0.621. Thus, our algorithm preserve the detail and texture of source images and suppresses artifacts to the maximum extent.

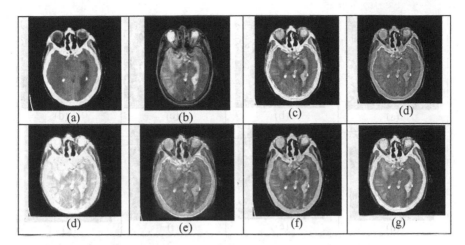

**Fig. 4.** (a) CT (b) MRT2 (c) LP-SR (d) ASR (e) CSR (f) LatLRR (g) CSMCA (h) Proposed

**Table 2.** Quantative analysis of fusion techniques for CT and MRT2

| Metrics | LP-SR | ASR | CSR | LatLRR | CSMCA | Proposed |
|---|---|---|---|---|---|---|
| ENT | 4.574 | 4.538 | 4.304 | 5.675 | 4.671 | **5.979** |
| $Q_G$ | 0.432 | **0.703** | 0.321 | 0.335 | 0.599 | 0.275 |
| $Q_P$ | 0.347 | 0.399 | 0.303 | 0.262 | **0.494** | 0.356 |
| $Q_W$ | 0.444 | 0.813 | 0.983 | **0.996** | 0.792 | 0.994 |
| $Q_S$ | 0.486 | 0.868 | 0.999 | 0.999 | 0.876 | **0.9998** |
| $Q_{ABF}$ | 0.048 | 0.824 | **0.853** | 0.842 | 0.777 | 0.836 |
| NFMI | 0.872 | **0.872** | 0.858 | 0.847 | 0.876 | 0.866 |
| $Q_{MI}$ | 0.658 | 0.646 | 0.631 | 0.649 | **0.680** | 0.653 |
| $Q_{TE}$ | 0.502 | 0.469 | 0.862 | 0.377 | 0.322 | **0.863** |
| $Q_{NICE}$ | 0.805 | 0.805 | 0.805 | 0.808 | **0.807** | 0.8067 |

From the above Table 2, it is perceived that the proposed method has the highest values for metrics ENT, $Q_s$ and $Q_{TE}$. However, our method is visually good as it provides more salient information which is very much required for doctors in clinical practices.

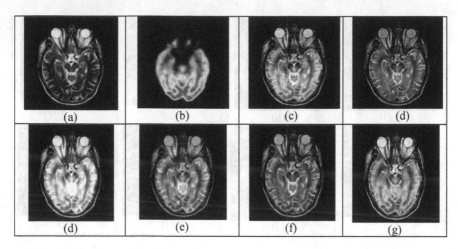

**Fig. 5.** (a) MRI (b) PET (c) LP-SR (d) ASR (e) CSR (f) LatLRR (g) CSMCA (h) Proposed

**Table 3.** Quantative analysis of fusion techniques for MRI and PET

|  | LP-SR | ASR | CSR | LatLRR | CSMCA | Proposed |
|---|---|---|---|---|---|---|
| ENT | 4.317 | 4.052 | 5.025 | 5.24 | 3.792 | **5.659** |
| $Q_G$ | 0.432 | 0.737 | 0.406 | 0.58 | **0.836** | 0.358 |
| $Q_P$ | 0.393 | 0.542 | 0.423 | 0.42 | **0.731** | 0.463 |
| $Q_W$ | 0.452 | 0.833 | 0.992 | 0.99 | 0.892 | **0.997** |
| $Q_S$ | 0.507 | 0.902 | 0.9997 | 0.99 | 0.915 | **0.9998** |
| $Q_{ABF}$ | 0.045 | 0.855 | 0.871 | 0.87 | **0.913** | 0.875 |
| NFMI | 0.8519 | 0.8518 | 0.859 | 0.85 | **0.899** | 0.863 |
| $Q_{MI}$ | 0.609 | 0.611 | 0.666 | 0.63 | 0.548 | **0.669** |
| $Q_{TE}$ | 0.312 | 0.320 | 0.719 | 0.37 | 0.412 | **0.734** |
| $Q_{NICE}$ | 0.8059 | 0.805 | 0.807 | 0.8 | 0.805 | **0.808** |

From the Table 3, it is observed that the quality metrics except $Q_G$, $Q_P$, $Q_{ABF}$ and NFMI are highest for proposed method and high accuracy is attained. The output image gives the details of disease by which the doctors are able to diagnose accurately.

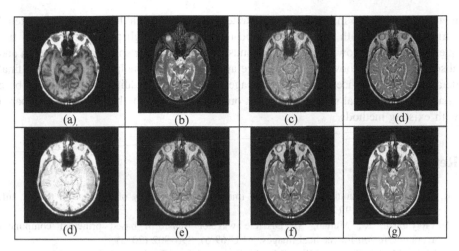

**Fig. 6.** (a) MRT1 (b) MRT2 (c) LP-SR (d) ASR (e) CSR (f) LatLRR (g) CSMCA (h) Proposed

**Table 4.** Quantative analysis of fusion techniques for MRT1 and MRT2

|            | LP-SR | ASR   | CSR   | LatLRR | CSMCA | Proposed |
|------------|-------|-------|-------|--------|-------|----------|
| ENT        | 4.565 | 4.035 | 4.127 | 5.072  | 4.088 | **5.7018** |
| $Q_G$      | 0.480 | **0.754** | 0.295 | 0.344 | 0.743 | 0.2753 |
| $Q_P$      | 0.355 | 0.491 | 0.331 | 0.300  | **0.524** | 0.4286 |
| $Q_W$      | 0.497 | 0.814 | 0.989 | 0.997  | 0.825 | **0.9977** |
| $Q_S$      | 0.543 | 0.873 | 0.999 | 0.999  | 0.835 | **0.9999** |
| $Q_{ABF}$  | 0.046 | **0.855** | 0.834 | 0.823 | 0.852 | 0.8537 |
| NFMI       | 0.865 | 0.862 | 0.858 | 0.843  | 0.864 | **0.8658** |
| $Q_{MI}$   | 0.755 | 0.738 | 0.731 | 0.684  | **0.758** | 0.7256 |
| $Q_{TE}$   | 0.338 | 0.319 | 0.711 | 0.379  | 0.316 | **0.7254** |
| $Q_{NICE}$ | 0.808 | 0.807 | 0.808 | 0.808  | 0.808 | **0.8095** |

It is observed from the above results, that our method has the highest values for all the metrics for ENT 5.7018, $Q_w$ 0.9977, $Q_s$ 0.9999, NFMI 0.8658, $Q_{TE}$ 0.7254 and $Q_{NICE}$ 0.8095. The remaining metrics such as $Q_G$, $Q_P$, $Q_{ABF}$ and $Q_{MI}$ are slightly less compared to CSMCA and ASR methods. But the visual quality of our method is more with respect to details, salient information (Table 4).

## 6 Conclusion

A new fusion algorithm for combining multimodal sensor brain images based on deep decomposition and sparse representation is presented. Firstly, the extraction of detail and base parts is done by using deep decomposition method. Next, the base parts are merged according to maximum fusion strategy to produce final base image. Then detail parts are applied with laplacian pyramid to obtain their high pass and low pass frequency bands. The low and high pass bands are merged using sparse representation and absolute rule. The above fused bands are applied with inverse laplacian pyramid, final detail image is produced. Final fused image is produced by adding final detail and base images. Experimental results reveal that our method gives the better results compared with existing methods.

# References

1. James, A.P., Dasarathy, B.V.: Medical image fusion: a survey of the state of the art. Inf. Fusion **19**(1), 4–19 (2014)
2. Vijayarajan, R., Muttan, S.: Discrete wavelet transform based principal component averaging fusion for medical images. AEU **69**(6), 896–902 (2015)
3. Li, H., Manjunath, B.S., Mitra, S.K.: Multisensor image fusion using the wavelet transform. Graph. Models Image Process. **57**(3), 235–245 (1995)
4. Bhatnagar, G., Wu, Q.M.J., Liu, Z.: Directive contrast based multimodal medical image fusion in NSCT domain. IEEE Trans. Multimedia **15**(5), 1014–1024 (2013)
5. Vanitha, K., Satyanarayana, D., Giri Prasad, M.N.: A new hybrid medical image fusion method based on fourth-order partial differential equations decomposition and DCT in SWT domain. In: 2019 10th International Conference on Computing, Communication and Networking Technologies (ICCCNT), Kanpur, India, pp. 1–5 (2019)
6. Bavirisetti, D.P., Dhuli, R.: Fusion of infrared and visible sensor images based on anisotropic diffusion and Karhunen-Loeve Transform. IEEE Sensors J. **16**(1), 203–209 (2016)
7. Li, S., Kang, X., Hu, J.: Image fusion with guided filtering. IEEE Trans. Image Process. **22**, 2864–2875 (2013)
8. Yang, B., Li, S.: Multifocus image fusion and restoration with sparse representation. IEEE Trans. Instrum. Meas. **59**(4), 884–892 (2010)
9. Liu, Y., Liu, S., Wang, Z.: A general framework for image fusion based on multi-scale transform and sparse representation. Inf. Fusion **24**, 147–164 (2015)
10. Liu, Yu., Wang, Zengfu: Simultaneous image fusion and denosing with adaptive sparse representation. IET Image Process. **9**(5), 347–357 (2015)
11. Liu, Y., Chen, X., Ward, R., Wang, Z.J.: Image fusion with convolutional sparse representation. IEEE Sig. Process. Lett. **23**(12), 1882–1886 (2016)
12. Tirupal, T., Chandra Mohan, B., Srinivas Kumar, S.: Multimodal medical image fusion based on yager's intuitionistic fuzzy sets. Iranian J. Fuzzy Syst. **16**(1), 33–48 (2019)
13. Liu, Y., Chen, X., Cheng, J., Peng, H.: A medical image fusion method based on convolutional neural networks. In: Proceedings of 20th International Conference Information Fusion, pp. 1–7 (2017)
14. Xia, J., Chen, Y., Chen, A., Chen, Y.: Medical image fusion based on sparse representation and PCNN in NSCT domain. Comput. Math. Methods Med. **2018**, 2806047 (2018)
15. Li, H., Wu, X.J.: Infrared and visible image fusion using Latent Low-Rank Representation arXiv:1804.08992 (2018)

16. Li, H., Wu, X.J.: Infrared and visible image fusion using a novel deep decomposition method. arXiv preprint arXiv:1811.02291 (2018)
17. Yu, L., Chen, X., Ward, R.K., Wang, Z.J.: Medical image fusion via convolutional sparsity based morphological component analysis. IEEE Sig. Process. Lett. **26**(3), 485–489 (2019)
18. www.med.harvard.edu/AANLIB/
19. Zheng, L., et al.: Objective assessment of multi resolution image fusion algorithms for context enhancement in night vision: a comparative study. IEEE Trans. Pattern Anal. Mach. Intell. **34**(1), 94–107 (2012)

# Rice Plant Disease Detection and Classification Using Deep Residual Learning

Sanjay Patidar, Aditya Pandey(✉) ⓘ, Bub Aditya Shirish ⓘ,
and A. Sriram

Department of Computer Science & Engineering,
Delhi Technological University, New Delhi, India
aditya00p00@gmail.com

**Abstract.** In the present scenario, India's economy highly depends upon the farming output and agricultural productivity. Hence, identifying and detecting diseases in the crops or plants become profoundly important, as it is very natural for plants out there in the fields to get attacked by certain specific bacterial or fungal diseases. If not taken care of at the earliest, this may prove to be a disaster for the product quality and quantity, or one may say productivity overall. For better efficiency at this goal, Machine Learning concepts can definitely be helpful, rather than just by visual sightings and recognition. The following research presents a paradigm for the detection and classification of diseases in rice plants, one of the major crops of the Indian staple diet, using the images of tainted rice plants. Three diseases were mainly focused on namely Bacterial leaf blight, Brown spot, and Leaf smut. The Rice Leaf Disease Dataset, from the UCI Machine Learning Repository, was used. To classify the images into desired disease classes, Residual Neural Network was used which is found to be a speedy, highly efficient technique and gives better results than the plain Convolutional Neural Network and other classifiers such as the Support Vector Machines, by not letting the model to reach saturation level for larger data or deeper networks. We achieved an accuracy of about 95.83% on the dataset.

**Keywords:** Machine learning · Residual Neural Network · Convolutional Neural Network · Detection · Classification · Diseases · Rice plants

## 1 Introduction

India is a renowned agricultural country as agriculture is one of the biggest sectors contributing to its economy. Approximately 70% of the population of India relies upon farming [1]. Farming is a necessary means of livelihood for 58% of the rural people dependent on it. One of the essentials foods of the Indian staple diet is Rice [2]. About 10 to 15% of the production in all over Asia is destroyed by Rice diseases [3]. The government and various private sector levels are carrying out research for increasing farming output and preventing hazards. Due to illiteracy among young farmers, they are unable to detect and cure the diseases in rice crops such as Leaf blast, Brown spot, Sheath blight and Leaf scald [4]. Various parts of plants like stem, seed, leaf and root are significantly affected by diseases caused by viruses, nematodes, fungi and bacteria

© Springer Nature Singapore Pte Ltd. 2020
A. Bhattacharjee et al. (Eds.): MIND 2020, CCIS 1240, pp. 278–293, 2020.
https://doi.org/10.1007/978-981-15-6315-7_23

at any stage of plant growth. Hence, it is essential to detect and classify diseases on a timely basis for a cure.

## 1.1 Machine Learning Based Architecture of Plant Disease Detection System

The general architecture of detecting and classifying the diseases in plants on the basis of images is shown in Fig. 1. The method of acquiring diseased leaf images is known as Image Acquisition. The plant disease detection system generally consists of two parts namely Image pre-processing and Machine Learning [5]. The images are either taken from the fields or acquired from known dataset repository available on the internet. Firstly, the image pre-processing task is carried out to process the images, on which further, the Machine learning techniques are applied to classify the image based on the various image features into the disease classes.

Image pre-processing consists of various operations like noise removal, image segmentation, image resizing, flipping of images, background removal, extraction of features, etc. [6]. Some of these may not be required every time. Their usage varies on the basis of the type of dataset. Machine Learning basically includes the selection of features and the classification of images using a certain classifier. Machine Learning evaluation metrics including precision, recall, accuracy and confusion matrix, carry out the evaluation of the system.

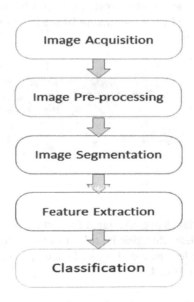

**Fig. 1.** General architecture of plant disease detection system based on machine learning

## 1.2 Selected Diseases

In India, rice crops suffer from various kinds of diseases. However, this paper mainly focuses on detecting and classifying three very common diseases namely: Bacterial Leaf Blight, Brown Spot, and Leaf Smut [4]. The following section briefly describes the properties of these diseases-

**Leaf Smut.** Mainly, it affects the plants' leaves. The appearance of minute, angular, sooty, dull patches on the leaves confirms its presence and is of reddish-brown color. It is caused by a fungus caused by Entyloma oryzae. It is shown in Fig. 2.

**Fig. 2.** Leaf smut [14]

**Brown Spot.** This also affects the plants' leaves primarily. It is generally observable in all parts of India. In the initial stage, it appears as a tiny and light-colored circular-shaped spot. Later, when these spots merge, they form brown colored and dark-toned linear spots. This is followed by the shrinking of the leaves with a yellowish tinge on them. It is shown in Fig. 3.

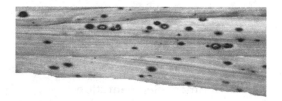

**Fig. 3.** Brown spot [14]

**Bacterial Leaf Blight.** Plant leaves are again the victims of its attack. At later stages, it may appear on the entire leaf, changing its color to yellow. Airflow and irrigation water are its main carriers. The lesions are elongated enough to several inches, once spread throughout. It is shown in Fig. 4.

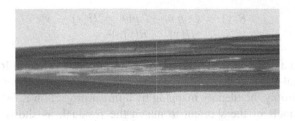

**Fig. 4.** Bacterial leaf blight [14]

## 1.3 Machine Learning Classifiers

**SVM Classifier.** It is used for data analysis and recognition. It is quite helpful for carrying out classification and regression analysis. A hyperplane is created by this linear model trainer, grouping the data in the separation created between the closest training points and the hyperplane according to the features extracted.

**Convolutional Neural Network.** An algorithm based on Deep Learning, which acquires input image, assigns weights to the various aspects and distinguishes them from each other. This method requires very little pre-processing when compared to other classifiers. Also, the convolutional nets have the strength to grasp filters and characteristics.

They are made up of a sequence of convolutional layers and spatial pooling layers fitted one after the other. The linear convolutional filters are followed by non-linear activation functions in the convolutional layer which is used to extract the feature maps. The local features, which are derived from the pixels spatially adjacent, are aggregated using the spatial pooling layer.

**Residual Neural Network.** It is a kind of Artificial Neural Network that is constructed based on the pyramidal cells of the cerebral cortex. This is achieved by making use of skip connections jumping over some of the layers. These are typically double or triple layer skips that possess in between nonlinearities (ReLU) and batch normalization. The skip weights are learned using an extra weight matrix, called Highway nets. It is very helpful in avoiding the barrier of gradients vanishing with deeper nets

*Residual Block.* Let, for an input y, we have an ideally mapped value f(y) obtained by learning (from the dotted-line box in Fig. 5), which is to be used as an input to the activation function. The left image shows the Regular CNN block. If we want to skip layers, we would rather just retain the input x. Since now we return y+f(y), the dotted line box should only parameterize the deviation from the identity. To optimize, f(y) is set as zero. The right image shows the Residual block.

A Residual block needs two 3X3 convolutional layers which have the same number of output channels. Each of the layers precedes a batch normalization layer and a ReLU activation function. The input is added to the final ReLU activation function directly, skipping the two convolution operations. The output of both the convolution operations is of the same shape as that of the input so that they can be added together.

For a true distribution, say H(y), the residual R(y) is given as-

$$R(y) = Output - Input = H(y) - y$$
$$H(y) = R(y) + y$$
(1)

The layers in a plain network learn the true output H(x), while in Resnet, the layers learn the residual R(y). If the output channels of the shortcut are not the same as the residual, we multiply the identity mapping by a linear projection K, which expands the number of channels of the shortcut to match the residual, as shown in the equation below. The $K_s$ term in the equation can be implemented with $1 \times 1$ convolutions, which introduces certain additional parameters to the model.

$$H(y) = f(y, K_i\}) + K_s y$$
(2)

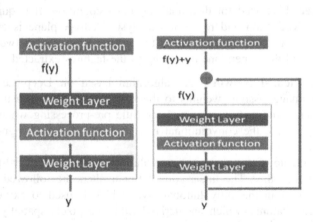

**Fig. 5.** Regular CNN block (left) vs residual block (right)

The following paper is divided into sections. Section 2 puts light into the previous work which has already been done in the field of plant disease detection and classification. The proposed work, the methodology and implementation details are discussed in Sect. 3, followed by the experiments and results in Sect. 4. The Conclusion and Future work are presented in Sects. 5 and 6 respectively.

## 2  Literature Survey

The research work is directed at different levels for enhancing the productivity of the farming field in various sections like weed cure, selection of seeds, water analysis and soil inspection. This segment provides a review of the research carried out by using various image processing and machine learning techniques for the identification of diseases in plant leaves.

Prajapati et al. [7] utilized the SVM classifier on rice diseased leaves. In image preprocessing, they removed the background and resized the images. For segmentation of the diseased part of the leaves, they used centroid feeding based K-mean clustering to allow precise feature extraction. On the basis of color, texture and shape, the features were extracted. For multi-class classification, the support vector machine was used to get 93.33% accuracy on the training dataset and 73.33% accuracy on the test dataset. 83.80% and 88.57% accuracy was achieved on 5 and 10-fold cross-validations.

Jayanti et al. [8], utilized ANN classifier on rice diseased leaves. Noise removal is done in the image pre-processing step. To detect edges in diseased parts of the leaves, Fuzzy C-mean clustering was performed. Texture and SURF techniques were used to extract important features, on which Artificial Neural Network was applied to classify the disease. Satisfactory classification results were obtained through this method.

Atabay et al. [9], utilized deep residual learning to train CNN from scratch on images of tomato leaves from the PlantVillage dataset. The outcome demonstrated that the proposed model outflanks the VGG model which is pre-trained on the ImageNet dataset in terms of both the time for re-training and accuracy. The model had 97.53% top 1 accuracy and 99.89% top 3 accuracy.

Liang et al. [10], utilized CNN for the rice blast recognition model, to classify 2902 negative and 2906 positive sample. The assessment results show that the features extracted from CNN were more selective and constructive than the features extracted from Haar-WT (Wavelet Transform) or local binary patterns histograms (LBPH). The CNN+SVM achieved an accuracy of 95.82% whereas LBPH+SVM achieved an accuracy of 82.59%.

Kumbhar et al. [11], utilized CNN for cotton leaf disease detection. The dataset had 513 training and 207 testing images. The image was acquired and resized into shape 128*128. The image is then passed through 3 hidden layers, in which pooling, extraction of features and flattening layer are moreover performed. CNN achieved 80% accuracy on the training dataset and 89% accuracy on the testing dataset.

Jayasripriyanka K et al. [12], utilized a support vector machine classifier on thousands of soybean images collected from PlantVillage dataset. In the pre-processing step, the background is removed and the color space division of the testing image is done. In segmentation, to split up infected and healthy leaf regions, k mean clustering technique is used. In feature extraction, various combinations of color and texture features are examined to design a performance-oriented system. Finally, SVM was applied to obtain an accuracy of 90%.

Durmuú et al. [13], utilized AlexNet and then SqueezeNet, the two different deep learning architectures on the leaves of the tomato plant from the PlantVillage dataset. It had ten different classes. AlexNet had 95.65% accuracy whereas SqueezeNet had an accuracy of 94.3%.

## 3 Proposed Work

Here, we present our proposed work for the detection of diseases in rice plants. In our work, we will be focusing mainly on detecting three types of rice diseases namely- Leaf smut, Bacterial leaf Blight and Brown spot. Here, we would not dive deep into the image pre-processing and segmentation steps, rather we would be concentrating our interest in improving the accuracy of classification the pre-processed images into their respective disease classes.

We use the "Rice Leaf Disease Dataset" from the UCI Machine Learning Repository [14], which contains the rice plant leaf images with only the three types of diseases we need to deal with, 40 images for disease class.

For the classification task, we have used the technique of **Residual Neural Networks**. The vanishing gradient problem and the curse of dimensionality are common in plain Convolutional Neural nets, if they are sufficiently deep, which leads to saturation of accuracy at one point and eventual degradation with the number of layers increases. This degradation problem is dealt with by skipping the training of a few layers, i.e. skipping connections or using the residual connections. These are known as identity shortcut connections as they are relied upon to learn the identity function directly. This type of neural network is called the Residual Neural Network.

In our research, we have made use of the 34-layer Residual Neural Network for the multi-class classification to get **95.83%** accuracy on the given dataset, and our methodology proves out to be more efficient with improved accuracy to perform disease detection on the rice plants.

### 3.1  Methodology

The method of computer vision and machine learning are intensively used in agricultural research and play a vital role in the protection of plants from diseases and as a result, increases productivity. The images of the diseased plants are taken through the camera; hence image pre-processing and segmentation techniques are required to detect the diseased parts of the leaves. The methodology of the proposed work is depicted in the above flow chart (Fig. 6).

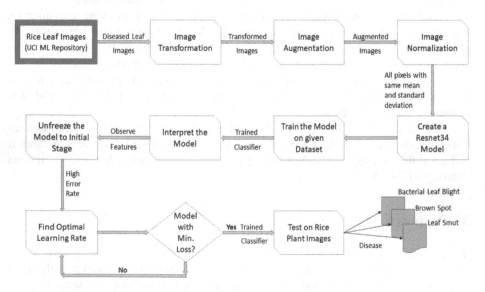

**Fig. 6.** Implementation flowchart

**Image Acquisition.** Here, the raw image is taken from the given dataset as input.

**Image Preprocessing.** A transformation function is used to add variations in the images, for example, flipping the images vertically. Also, a normalization function is used over the data so that all the pixels have the same mean and standard deviation values, hence helping the model to learn faster and easier.

### Creating the Residual Neural Network

*Resnet Architecture:* The first two layers of the Resnet comprises of a $7 \times 7$ convolution layer with 64 output channels and a stride of 2 and a $3 \times 3$ max pooling layer with a stride of 2. A batch normalization layer is added after each convolutional layer. After the first two layers, we have a trail of 4 modules of comparable behavior. The modules use several residual blocks. The pattern followed in each module is the same. Each module performs $3 \times 3$ convolution with a fixed feature map dimension (64, 128, 256, 512) respectively, bypassing the input after every 2 convolutions. In the entire module, the dimensions of width and height remain constant (Table 1).

**Table 1.** Resnet-34 architecture.

| Layer name | Output size | 34-layer Resnet |
|---|---|---|
| conv1 | $112 \times 112$ | $7 \times 7$, 64, stride 2 |
| conv2_x | $56 \times 56$ | $3 \times 3$ max pool, stride 2 <br> $\begin{bmatrix} 3 \times 3, & 64 \\ 3 \times 3, & 64 \end{bmatrix} \times 3$ |
| conv3_x | $28 \times 28$ | $\begin{bmatrix} 3 \times 3, & 128 \\ 3 \times 3, & 128 \end{bmatrix} \times 4$ |
| conv4_x | $14 \times 14$ | $\begin{bmatrix} 3 \times 3, & 256 \\ 3 \times 3, & 256 \end{bmatrix} \times 6$ |
| conv5_x | $7 \times 7$ | $\begin{bmatrix} 3 \times 3, & 512 \\ 3 \times 3, & 512 \end{bmatrix} \times 3$ |
|  | $1 \times 1$ | Average pool, 1000-d fc, softmax |
| FLOPS |  | $3.6 \times 10^9$ |

**Training the Model.** A CNN learner model is created using Resnet-34 architecture. This learner is used to train the model on the given dataset and then tested to measure the accuracy. Features such as top_losses, most_confused, etc. are observed in order to interpret the results of the model.

**Fine Tuning.** In order to achieve better accuracy and improve the parametric values, the model is unlearnt to its initial stage and trained again for different learning rates in the chosen range. If a minimum loss is recorded, we proceed with that learning rate to test for the accuracy else repeat the above step.

**Disease Classification.** After the application of Resnet, based on the highest probability of occurrence, the images of leaves are classified into disease classes using the Softmax layer.

### 3.2 Optimization in the Methodology

The concept of 'Cyclical Learning Rates for Training Neural Networks' [15] is used for optimizing the model. **Cyclical Learning Rates (CLR)**, is utilized to diminish the requirement of finding the best values and schedule for the global learning rates to be used in the experiment. The learning rate is varied between considerable boundary values rather than just decreasing the learning rate monotonically or exponentially. This pattern of training the model with cyclical learning rates gives out results with better accuracy than what it was when the learning rate was fixed. This is achieved in fewer iterations as well. Although, increasing learning rates may impact the neural network negatively in the short run but prove out to have a very positive impact in the long run.

### 3.3 Implementation Details

Spyder 3.3.0 IDE is used as a standard platform for the overall development of the system. Spyder provides us with various unique features such as debugging, analysis, advance editing along with data exploration, data visualization and interactive execution. A 64-bit Windows operating system is used for running Anaconda application that provides us with Spyder. A computer having NVIDIA 1050TI Graphics Card and 16 GB RAM is used for fast execution.

For building RNN, Python 3.7 is used. For basic Python processing, libraries like Numpy and Panda are used. Python OS module helps in directory related functionality such as creating, deleting and changing the current working directory, etc. Dataset is stored in the directory, to be accessed through Python. For various computer vision related functionality, a module called fast.ai vision is used. It makes image preprocessing tasks much quicker and easier. Resnet34, which is applied to our dataset, is imported through the fast.ai module. Utilizing libraries permits us to broaden the functionalities for utilizing it on a bigger database. The training and test datasets are in the ratio of 70:30 of the original dataset. Also, cross-validation is carried out to improve the accuracy.

## 4    Experiments and Results

### 4.1    Dataset

The "Rice Leaf Disease Dataset" from the UCI Machine Learning Repository [14], is used for training and testing our model. This dataset contains images for three diseases namely- Leaf Smut, Bacterial Leaf Blight and Brown Spot. Originally, the dataset available was formed by images of the infected leaves captured after separating them manually into the disease classes. There are about 40 images of each disease class mentioned.

## 4.2 Experimental Analysis

We have presented the use of Residual Neural Network on image classification tasks as a more efficient and improved technique compared to Convolutional Neural Networks (CNN), Support Vector Machine (SVM) etc. The experiments in our analysis were divided into two stages – Image Preprocessing and Machine Learning Techniques. Our focus was solely on the machine learning techniques to develop a model which could give a better classification accuracy on the Rice Leaf Dataset.

**Loss vs Learning Rate.** In our model, we have tried to achieve a minimum error rate or maximum accuracy. This was achieved by fine-tuning our model, i.e. resetting the model to the pre-trained stage and again training the model with a different learning rate so that we can find the most appropriate learning rate for the model to function more accurately. The graph of the process of achieving this shown in Fig. 7.

We set a range for the value of learning rate which was from 1e-06 to 1e-01. From the graph between loss and the learning rate, we can clearly observe that initially, the loss decreased non-uniformly as the learning rate was increased slowly from 1e−06 to 1e−05. Near 1e−05, we observe a slight increase in the loss but we continue to test for other rates. From 1e−05 to 1e−03 we see, there is a clear decline of the loss with a minimum loss near 1e−03 and then again thereafter, the loss starts to increase rapidly for values greater than 1e−03 till 1e−01. Therefore, we found our best learning rate to be approximately 1e−03.

The major improvement was the optimization technique being used. Cyclical Learning Rates were used and resulted in a marked improvement in the training time and the overall accuracy of the model. The use of CLR has resulted in quicker computation time due to lesser number of iterations being required to find the most optimal learning rate and for the model to converge, an additional benefit over previous works.

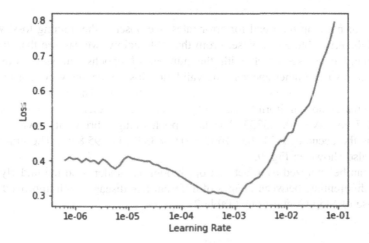

**Fig. 7.** Loss vs learning rate

**Training Loss, Validation Loss and Error Rate.** Having obtained an optimal learning rate, we also observe the training and validation losses with the number of batches processed for our model. As we can see from the graph below (Fig. 8), the training loss initially increased a bit for the first batch-processed. The reason for this could be slight overfitting by the model since the dataset has only 120 images altogether for training and testing. But, the training loss starts to decline non-uniformly thereafter, which is logically analyzed as with increasing number of processed batches, our model becomes more learned and hence, the training loss must decline. Noticing the trend for the validation loss, it initially decreases for six batches, then has a slight increase for the next three batches and then starts to decline again thereafter.

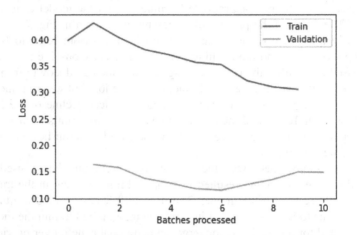

**Fig. 8.** Training and validation loss vs number of batches processed

Now, for noticing the trend for error rates, we observe the training loss, validation loss and the error rate epoch wise. From the table below, we can see that the training loss initially decreases much with the number of epochs but slows down in its decrement towards higher epochs. The validation loss decreases very sharply until the first three epochs, and then it decreases slowly till the end. The error rate, on the other hand, decreases non- uniformly for the first 7 epochs but then it becomes constant for the next 7 epochs to 0.083333. The last epoch though, brings it down to 0.41667, giving us the accuracy of $1-0.041667 = 0.9583330$, i.e. 95.83%. The graph for this trend is also shown in Fig. 9.

This can be analyzed as a fact that our model has understood the underlying trend and can differentiate between images of different rice diseases with improved accuracy by the use of Skip Connections (Table 2).

**Table 2.** Training loss, validation loss and error rate epoch wise

| Epoch | Train-loss | Valid-loss | Error-rate | Time (secs) |
|-------|-----------|-----------|-----------|-------------|
| 0 | 2.163581 | 1.796214 | 0.750000 | 00:10 |
| 1 | 1.916766 | 1.215812 | 0.625000 | 00:09 |
| 2 | 1.803676 | 0.799141 | 0.375000 | 00:09 |
| 3 | 1.657866 | 0.759994 | 0.291667 | 00:10 |
| 4 | 1.437835 | 0.826733 | 0.250000 | 00:10 |
| 5 | 1.306667 | 0.740503 | 0.125000 | 00:10 |
| 6 | 1.211296 | 0.606699 | 0.083333 | 00:10 |
| 7 | 1.149749 | 0.568663 | 0.083333 | 00:09 |
| 8 | 1.095029 | 0.531142 | 0.083333 | 00:10 |
| 9 | 1.069771 | 0.475884 | 0.083333 | 00:10 |
| 10 | 1.012833 | 0.439210 | 0.083333 | 00:11 |
| 11 | 0.989074 | 0.384781 | 0.083333 | 00:09 |
| 12 | 0.919315 | 0.340389 | 0.083333 | 00:10 |
| 13 | 0.884251 | 0.300628 | 0.083333 | 00:10 |
| 14 | 0.848599 | 0.277654 | 0.041667 | 00:10 |

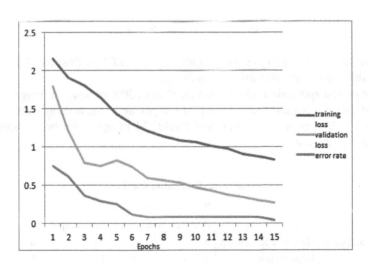

**Fig. 9.** Training loss, validation loss and error rate vs number of epochs.

Our system hence overcomes the problem of vanishing gradients and the curse of dimensionality, which often occurs with deeper plain convolutional networks, to achieve an accuracy of 95.83%.

### 4.3   Performance Measures of Disease Classes

The performance of three disease classes is compared using various statistical performance metrics. Quantitative metrics such as Recall, Precision and Accuracy are used.

**Accuracy.** The principle indicator is accuracy, the higher the metric value, the better is the evaluation by a classifier.

$$Accuracy = (TP + TN)/(TP + FP + TN + FN) \tag{3}$$

**Precision.** Precision answers the proportion of positive indication that is actually correct.

$$Precision = (TP)/(TP + FP) \tag{4}$$

**Recall.** Recalls answers the proportion of actual positive which was identified correctly.

$$Recall = (TP)/(TP + FN) \tag{5}$$

Where TP, TN, FP and FN are the number of cases of True Positive, True Negative, False Positive and False Negative respectively.

The train-test-split ratio is chosen as 0.3. That is, 30% of data, 36 images at random are in test dataset whereas the remaining 84 images are in the training dataset. The test dataset had 9 images with bacterial leaf blight, 14 images with brown spot and 13 images with leaf smut.

**Table 3.**  Confusion matrix

|              |                      | Predicted class       |            |           |
|--------------|----------------------|-----------------------|------------|-----------|
|              |                      | Bacterial leaf blight | Brown spot | Leaf smut |
| Actual class | Bacterial leaf blight | 9                     | 0          | 0         |
|              | Brown spot           | 0                     | 13         | 1         |
|              | Leaf smut            | 0                     | 1          | 12        |

As shown in confusion matrix (Table 3), all 9 images of bacterial leaf blight were predicted correctly, out of 14, 13 of brown spot were predicted correctly and 1 was wrongly predicted as leaf smut and lastly, out of 13 images for the leaf smut, 12 were predicted correctly and 1 was wrongly predicted as brown spot. Hence, in our dataset with 120 images, the classifier had 100% accuracy in predicting bacterial leaf blight,

92.86% accuracy in predicting brown spot and 92.31% accuracy in predicting leaf smut. The reason behind confusion between the leaf smut and the brown spot is the fact that both classes of diseases have regions or spots of brown color.

The precision value for the bacterial leaf blight is 1.0, for the brown spot is 0.93 and for the leaf smut is 0.92. The recall value for the bacterial leaf blight is 1.0, for the brown spot is 0.93 and for the leaf smut is 0.92.

The Fig. 10. shows the predicted results are in the format: Predicted/Actual/Loss/Probability:

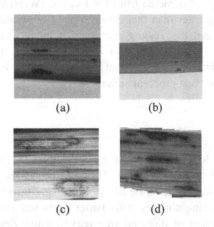

(a)                        (b)

(c)                        (d)

**Fig. 10.** Predicted results: (a) brown spot/leaf smut/2.16/0.12 (b) brown spot/brown spot/0.03/0.97 (c) leaf smut/brown spot/1.46/0.23 (d) leaf smut/leaf smut/0.01/0.99

### 4.4 Comparison of Proposed Model with Other Prevailing Methods

The analysis of our model is better than other machine learning models, such as the Convolutional Neural Network and Support Vector Machine, in our problem is shown in Table 4. This comparison is done after applying all the stated models on our Rice Plant Disease Dataset one by one.

**Table 4.** Comparison of performance of proposed model with other prevailing methods

| Performance measures | RNN | CNN | SVM |
|---|---|---|---|
| Time taken (secs) | 10 | 14 | 21 |
| Type 1 error | 0.06 | 0.11 | 0.15 |
| Type 2 error | 0.06 | 0.05 | 0.03 |
| Accuracy | 95.83% | 92.48% | 73.33% |
| Recall | 0.94 | 0.84 | 0.69 |
| Precision | 0.94 | 0.90 | 0.77 |
| F-measure | 0.94 | 0.87 | 0.73 |

The comparison is done on the basis of the different performance measures. The Tuning time taken by the models for prediction and classification suggests that RNN is superior in terms of efficiency through complex enough to implement, followed by CNN and finally SVM. In SVM, since picking the right kernel is important, the model consumes more time to tune.

The Type 1 error or the "False Positive" rate is the lowest for the RNN model when compared to the other two. Though our model exceeds in the Type 2 error or the "False Negative" rate minutely over the other two models, overall, in case of larger datasets containing healthy images also, our model turns out to have better-distinguishing properties. And this is well depicted from the Recall, Precision and F-measure values on the table, all being greater than that of the other two models.

Last but not the least, the Testing Accuracy achieved for our RNN model, i.e. 95.83% outsmarts CNN and SVM, who have accuracies of 92.48% and 73.33% respectively when applied on our Rice Plant Disease Dataset. Hence, we find that RNN is considerably better for our problem statement.

## 5   Conclusion

There could be a huge loss in the domain of agriculture if rice plant diseases are not detected and dealt with at an early stage. This can be achieved by building an auto-mated system that provides notification of disease, using information technologies and Computer Machine learning abilities. This paper proposes a successful model for the detection and classification of diseased rice leaves using Residual Neural Network. Three diseases viz. Leaf Smut, Bacterial leaf Blight and Brown Spot, were detected by our system, built on a dataset having 120 images (40 for each disease class). The Residual Neural Network had 34 layers to classify the images of rice leaf diseases. The model could take an input image and classify the image by detecting its disease with minimal error. The significant steps and representation of the proposed model are presented in this paper. Our work achieved an efficient accuracy of 95.83%.

## 6   Future Work

Our framework can be stretched out to some other crops having the accessibility of enough huge datasets for that yield. A number of different diseases can be incorporated for detection. A framework, additionally, can be used to execute equipment utilizing IoT for image catching in the fields. The web interface can likewise include a gathering for farmers to have a discussion in regards to the ongoing trend they are experiencing in different diseases.

# References

1. Agriculture Economics and Importance of Agriculture in National Economy. http://agriinfo. in/?page=topic&superid=9&topicid=185. Accessed 23 Nov 2015
2. Agriculture Sector in India. http://www.ibef.org/industry/agriculture-india.aspx. Accessed 23 Nov 2015
3. Gianessi, L.P.: Importance of pesticides for growing rice in South and South East Asia, pp. 30–33 (2014)
4. Rice Production (Peace Corps): Chapter 14 - Diseases of rice. http://www.nzdl.org. Accessed 23 Nov 2015
5. Shruthi, U., Nagaveni, V., Raghvendra, B.K.: A review on machine learning classification techniques for plant disease detection. In: 5th International Conference on Advanced Computing & Communication Systems (ICACCS). IEEE, Coimbatore (2019)
6. Shah, J.P., Prajapati, H.B., Dabhi, V.K.: A survey on detection and classification of rice plant diseases. In: IEEE International Conference on Current Trends in Advanced Computing (ICCTAC), pp. 1–8. IEEE, Bangalore (2016)
7. Prajapati, H.B., Shah, J.P., Dabhi, V.K.: Detection and classification of rice plant diseases. J. Intell. Decis. Technol. 11(3), 357–373 (2017). IOS Press 2017
8. Jayanthi, G., Archana, K.S., Saritha, A.: Analysis of automatic rice disease classification using image processing techniques. Int. J. Eng. Adv. Technol. (IJEAT) 8(3S), 2249–8958 (2019)
9. Atabay, H.A.: Deep residual learning for tomato plant leaf disease identification. J. Theor. Appl. Inf. Technol. 95(24), 6800–6808 (2017)
10. Liang, W., Zhang, Z., Zhang, G., Cao, H.: Rice blast disease recognition using a deep convolutional neural network. Sci. Rep. 9, 2869 (2019). https://doi.org/10.1038/s41598-019-38966-0
11. Kumbhar, S., Nilawar, A., Patil, S., Mahalakshmi, B., Nipane, M.: Farmer buddy-web based cotton leaf disease detection using CNN. Int. J. Appl. Eng. Res. 14(11), 2662–2666 (2019). ISSN 0973-4562
12. Jayasripriyanka, K., Gaayathri, S., Vinmathi, M.S., Jayashri, C.: Semi-automatic leaf disease detection and classification system for soybean culture. Int. Res. J. Eng. Technol. (IRJET) 06, 1721–1724 (2019)
13. Saleem, M.H., Potgieter, J., Arif, J.M.: Plant disease detection and classification by deep learning (2019). https://www.mdpi.com/journal/plants, https://doi.org/10.3390/plants8110468
14. Shah, J.P., Prajapati, H.B., Dabhi, V.K.: Rice leaf diseases data set https://archive.ics.uci. edu/ml/datasets/Rice+Leaf+Diseases. Accessed 14 Mar 2019
15. Smith, L.N.: Cyclical learning rates for neural networks arXiv:1506.01186v6 [cs.CV] (2017)

# Flood Detection Using Multispectral Images and SAR Data

Tanmay Bhadra[1]([⊠]) [iD], Avinash Chouhan[2] [iD], Dibyajyoti Chutia[2] [iD], Alexy Bhowmick[1] [iD], and P. L. N. Raju[2]

[1] Assam Don Bosco University, Guwahati, Assam, India
tanmaylbhadra@gmail.com
[2] North Eastern Space Applications Centre, Umiam, Meghalaya, India

**Abstract.** Remote sensing imagery analysis is a very crucial task in regard to climate or disaster monitoring. Satellite images can capture the ground surface conditions and give a huge amount of information in a single image. In recent days, with the availability of multi-temporal satellite data, monitoring of flood events have become pretty easy. It gives accurate and real time flood information. Flood is one of the most disastrous natural disasters in Assam, India. It is necessary to predict or monitor flood events to minimise the overall damage caused due to floods. There are many scientific approaches which have been made operational in flood monitoring related activities. However Deep Learning based approaches are not yet fully exploited so far to monitor and predict flood events. We propose flood detection in real-time with the help of multispectral images and SAR data using Deep Learning technique Convolutional Neural Network (CNN). The satellite images are from Sentinel-2 and the SAR data are from Sentinel-1. The CNN was trained with 100 images for 100 iterations. CNN has shown excellent performance in image-oriented tasks like classification, segmentation and feature extraction. Recently Deep learning techniques are used extensively on remote sensing data due to their high resolution and the former's extensive computing capability. The study area comprises of 2 districts namely Barpeta and Kamrup of Assam, India. We have obtained an accuracy of 80% in detecting flood. Based on our result, deep learning may be vigorously explored in various other disaster detection or monitoring activities.

**Keywords:** Flood detection · Deep learning · Sentinel · Multispectral image · SAR image

## 1 Introduction

Detection of disaster is one of the highest priority activities when it comes to disaster management because it affects human life and various types of tangible properties. It is very important for the disaster management team to predict or detect the disaster beforehand for the safety of the people living nearby. Flood is one of the most destructive types of disasters on earth. As we know 75% of earth's surface is covered by water, but when this water surface area tends to increase, it enters areas that are used by humans or on which humans depend for their livelihood. This, in turn, creates a

© Springer Nature Singapore Pte Ltd. 2020
A. Bhattacharjee et al. (Eds.): MIND 2020, CCIS 1240, pp. 294–303, 2020.
https://doi.org/10.1007/978-981-15-6315-7_24

chaotic situation, people have to move along with their belongings, family, etc. leaving behind the immovable property to higher grounds, having less clarity of when the disaster will move on. Prediction of such type of disaster provides great help to the common people but it isn't an easy task to predict a disaster. Climatic conditions can be very dynamic, due to which flood occurrence's time and location prediction are very complex. Hence, today's flood prediction systems are data specific. Earlier studies mainly focus on detecting changes that have occurred due to the disaster, manually adjust image processing techniques as image algebra, post-classification comparison and object-based change detection method [1]. Machine learning has also been implemented to increase the accuracy of detection, improve the efficiency of feature extraction [3].

The task of image acquisition can be done in different ways like ground cameras, Unmanned aerial vehicles (UAV), satellite images, etc. [5]. Images from the ground camera can have a good amount of noise whereas long-range UAV incur costs along with charging duration, weather condition, range capability, etc. Social media images have also been experimented upon but it's non-scalability i.e. small region images added up to its disadvantages [8]. As known to all of us remote sensing/satellite images help us in recording multi-scale information of an area. A good amount of analysis of such images is very important for many applications like urban planning, military monitoring, disaster management, etc. Such images are very high in dimensions which adds to the challenges while analysis. Recently Deep learning techniques have achieved new heights in classification and segmentation problems. As mentioned the remote sensing images due to its high dimensions, require a good amount of processing power along with capable algorithms.

Detection of flood in real-time from the satellite image will be very useful for the disaster management authorities. Normally flood is predicted on a prior basis to alert the people living nearby and concerned government authorities to take necessary precautions. But this process requires data beforehand like rainfall data, an increase in water level due to the release of dams, etc. Obtaining such type of data incurs cost along with proper, regular data [4, 5]. The main motive of this paper is to provide a system to detect flood instead of predict flood, with the help of satellite images that are freely available from many reliable sources. The trained model only needs a satellite image to detect the presence of flood in the image. Such a system can also be used to detect an increase/decrease in the area of water bodies if tuned to detect new water bodies.

## 2 Convolutional Neural Network (CNN)

Since the beginning of Artificial Intelligence, the concept of Neural Network has always been a center of attraction for the researchers. A model that mimics the real-life brain is enough for any researcher to jump into it. Since the introduction of artificial neural networks in 1943, despite having limitations like proper computing facilities, appropriate algorithms, etc. it has always been a key area for researchers for various fields [6]. When we go further into the hierarchy of Neural Networks we get Deep

Learning which is also considered as a type of Machine Learning. Hubel and Wiesel in 1968 published a paper that is based on a cat's visual cortex [1].

In contrast to Artificial Neural Network (ANN) which has a single layer, CNN has a number of layers placed in sequence. In detail, it consists of an input layer, many convolutional layers, pooling layers, fully connected layer and finally an output layer. But the three layers namely convolutional, pooling and fully-connected form the base of any CNN architecture [7]. Apart from the input and the output layer the rest of the layers are termed as hidden layers. CNN's are mostly used for image classification and recognition due to its high accuracy. Facebook, Google are few among the many who are using CNN for various face, image-related activities [1].

CNN was used in various types of problems. Starting from object recognition tasks, human pose estimation, in natural language processing some of its implementations are text classification, emotion analysis, text translation, etc. (Fig. 1).

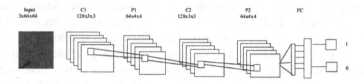

**Fig. 1.** CNN architecture

## 2.1 Convolutional Layer

A convolutional layer (CL) is the first layer that reads the input image directly. In simple words, it extracts features from the input image. It consists of filters that convolve on the input image to extract out its features. Whenever an input is received by the CL, it convolves each filter over the related dimensionality of the input. If the filter is a 2 × 2 filter, then the central element of the filter will be placed over the input in such a way that the filter fits in the input and then the product is calculated element-wise and added along with the nearby pixel. Here, it must be noted that the value and the size of the filter plays a vital role in processing the input. Each CL is followed by an Activation function, ReLU (Rectified Linear Unit) mostly used to remove negative values. Other activation functions include are Sigmoid, Leaky ReLU, etc. [2] (Fig. 2).

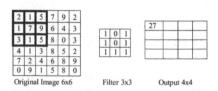

**Fig. 2.** Visual representation of a convolutional layer with filter size 3 × 3

The input image can be of multiple dimensions, in our case it's a three-dimensional (3D) layer a × b × c, where a, b are the height and width of the image respectively and c is the number of bands.

## 2.2 Pooling Layer

The main objective of a pooling layer (PL) is the reduction of the spatial size of our representation and thus reduce the number of parameters and computing complexity of the model. Each activation map in the input is operated by the pooling layer, which scales its dimensionality. Such operation of a pooling layer on the image doesn't impact small changes in value. Thus it is a fit for working with image, as a small change in the image will have less effect and will yield the same result.

Due to the capability of reducing dimensions, it is also known for its destructive nature. The PL uses the max-pooling layer for general purpose with a filter size of 2 × 2 and stride of 2 × 2. Also, overlapping pooling which consists of a filter size of 3 × 3 and stride of 2 × 2 is also a sub variation of the max-pooling layer. Having a filter size greater than 3 is not advisable due to the destructive nature of the PL. However, apart from the max-pooling layer, the General pooling layer also exists such as the average pooling layer (calculates the average value) and L2-norm pooling [2].

## 2.3 Fully Connected Layer

The main objective of a Fully Connected Layer (FCL) is to take results from the CL or PL and then classify them based on the labels. Normally the outcome from the CL/PL is flattened to a single vector which comprises of the values, each representing a probability of a feature belonging to a particular class/label [1].

## 3 Study Area

For this work, Barpeta and Kamrup districts of Assam state of India were selected. The Barpeta district lies in 26° 19' 49.5156" N Latitude and 91° 0' 14.5836" E Longitude and Kamrup district lies in 26° 19' 60.00" N Latitude and 91° 14' 60.00" E Longitude. Barpeta district topography varies from low-lying plains to highland having small hillocks. The river Brahmaputra flows in an east to west direction transversing the whole Southern part of the district. Beki, Manah, Pohumara, Bhelengi are few among the districts through which the tributaries of this river flows in a North to South direction. Kamrup district majorly has 7 rivers - Brahmaputra, Puthimari, Bornoi, Nona, Kulsi, Pagladiya, Kalajal. Every year during May-August generally flood occurs in the low lying areas of the district.

## 4 Methodology

As per the current scenario, most researchers implement machine/deep learning techniques to detect floods post occurrence. Flood classification, flood aftermath are some of the conclusions deduced. Such types of conclusions are generally used to analyze the condition after a flood, like conditions of the road, which areas are being impacted, etc. [8]. To enhance the potential of this work (prediction using deep learning) we implemented CNN to detect the change in the water bodies. We obtain satellite images from EarthExplorer for both training and testing purposes. Training images include images of the selected area pre-occurrence of the flood i.e. during January, February, March. Generally, the selected area of study has rainfall little or more for the rest of the year, so images from the rest of the year were used for testing purposes. All the images contain the same geospatial information but differ in the time accumulated.

We have started with the accumulation of data for our work. All data used here are Sentinel data. Multispectral data are from Sentinel-2 and SAR data from Sentinel-1. Multispectral data has been downloaded from earthexplorer whereas SAR data has been downloaded from ASF data search. Along with it, shapefiles of the water bodies are also used which were manually created using QGIS 3.0 based on the input images. The objective of using the shapefiles is to gain information about the water bodies. With the help of shapefile and satellite images, we train our CNN model about water bodies in non-flooded conditions. All the downloaded data are from the same area which covers 2 districts namely- Barpeta and Kamrup of Assam, India. Below is a basic workflow diagram of our work (Fig. 3).

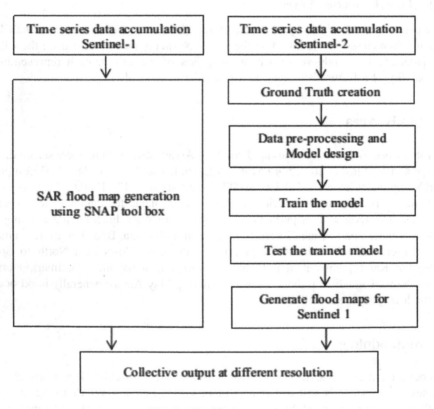

**Fig. 3.** Workflow structure

The main focus of our research is to learn the changes in water bodies from an early stage. So, that in future when input is given with a flooded water body it can easily detect the occurred change. In simple words, we detect flood from pre-flooded images along with the help of post-flooded ones.

## 4.1    Data

In remote sensing there is no standard dataset available for flood. Various study area require it's own set of images. However there are many remote sensing dataset available like Brazilian Coffee, SIRI-WHU, NWPU-RESISC45 [10] etc. but they are used for other purposes like scene classification, object detection etc., having less relevance in the field of disaster. Below is the description of the data set used in our work (Table 1):

**Table 1.** Dataset description,

| Training data set | 100 images |
|---|---|
| Testing data set | 10 images |
| On average single image size | 5490 * 5490 (pixels) |

Pre-disaster, post-disaster and ground truth data are of the same size and dimensions. By ground truth, it is meant the original condition of the area which is derived from the shapefiles mentioned earlier (Table 2).

**Table 2.** Experimental setup for our computer.

| Version | Intel® Xeon(R) CPU E5-2630 v4 @ 2.20 GHz × 20 |
|---|---|
| OS type | Ubuntu 16.04-64bit |
| RAM | 16 GB |

## 4.2    Data Processing

In order to train our CNN model, features and labels are created for the given dataset. Features mean tiles which consist of the bands of the image (here 3 bands, RGB). They have the form 64 * 64 * 3, 64 being the tile size and 3 for the number of bands. Labels are of the form of bitmaps where pixels in the satellite image which represent water are indicated by 1. This process can also be treated as the pre-processing step for each image.

The activity of assigning 1 to every pixel representing water in bitmaps is done with the help of the shapefile. Our Shapefiles contain only water polygons, thus bitmaps are easily created with the help of these shapefiles. The satellite images due to projection do not form a perfect rectangle and due to this, the remaining space on the edge is blacked out. When the Geotiff image is overlayed with the shapefile, it also overlays the features for the blacked-out parts. This results in feeding non-empty labels for empty features to the classifier. Therefore, we remove the tiles on the edges which are blacked out. This is done by checking our tile and if it contains a black pixel, if not we append it to the bitmap. Once done, we have all the water features from the satellite image. We burn it into a new raster image and get a black and white image with water features in white and the rest in black (Fig. 4).

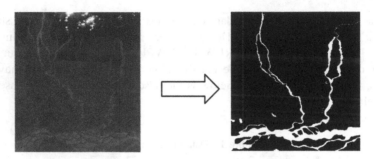

**Fig. 4.** Segregating water from rest of the image. Original image (left) segregated image (right)

While passing the features and labels to our training model they are in the form of a list in triples. Each triple consists of the tile, information about the source image it came from and its position in the source image. For training purposes we only need the tile, hence we extract only the tile from the triples. A simple normalization is also performed on the features in order to bring all the pixel values within a particular range.

### 4.3    Training and Testing Phase

In the training phase, the main focus is on learning features of the flood. The features have already been extracted and labeled in the data processing phase. A total of 100 full tile RGB images were trained for 100 epochs in our described system. Every single image is processed by dividing it into various tiles, each of size 64. Once our model is trained it consists of features and labels about water bodies. Below is the description of the parameters used for the CNN model (Table 3):

**Table 3.**  CNN parameters

| Layer (type) | Shape |
| --- | --- |
| conv2d_1 (Conv2D) | (20, 20, 64) |
| activation_1 (Activation) | (20, 20, 64) |
| max_pooling2d_1 (MaxPooling2D) | (5, 5, 64) |
| conv2d_2 (Conv2D) | (2, 2, 128) |
| activation_2 (Activation) | (2, 2, 128) |
| flatten_1 (Flatten) | (512) |
| dense_1 (Dense) | (4096) |
| activation_3 (Activation) | (4096) |

In the testing phase, the input images (flooded or non-flooded) are provided to the model. The model is tested with unseen images of flood/non-flood. The flood is detected by first identifying the water surfaces in the input image and then subtracting them from the ground truth images. This in result leaves behind the extra or flooded water surfaces indicating flood. The model description and its corresponding weights are stored in the local system as.json and.hdf5 file respectively so that they can be used for other analysis related purposes.

## 5 Results

The accuracy of our model is 80% on test data whereas it is 95% when tested on the training data. All the results which includes the accuracy, precision, recall values, F score are stored in the local system so that later it can be used for analysis or as a reference to compare with other models/architecture. The precision value obtained by using the combination of this architecture and model is 0.83 whereas the recall value is 0.80. The F score value obtained is 0.81 (Figs. 5 and 6).

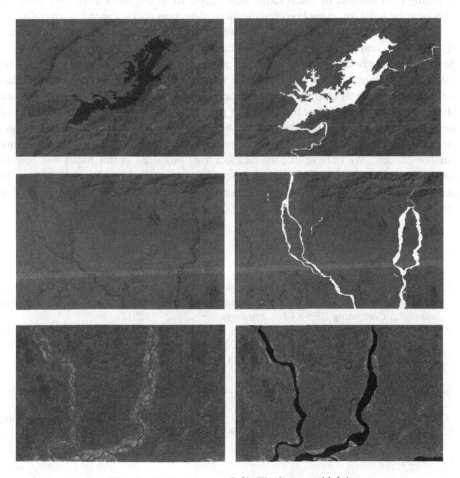

**Fig. 5.** Original image (left), Final output (right)

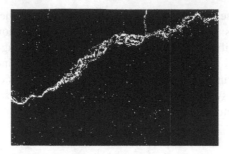

**Fig. 6.** SAR image flood mapping using SNAP tool box

## 6 Conclusion and Future Work

This paper shows a Deep learning model implementation on how to detect floods. The images, architecture used are of moderate level. But with high level images like including more number of bands rather than simple RGB and more advanced, complex architectures a lot of complex classification, detection tasks can be accomplished. Compared to the existing methodologies where the change is detected post occurence of the disaster, and improve it's accuracy with the help of Machine learning techniques, the proposed methodology can detect an increase in water area at a early stage. This will help the concerned authorities to take a look at the situation of the area and plan accordingly for the upcoming disaster (if any). Many existing methodologies do use Machine learning techniques but only as a post disaster activity to detect the effected areas. In regard to Deep learning approaches, [9] have used CNN on ImageNet and Places dataset but only to classify flood and detect it's aftermath, but these are not satellite datasets. We believe that the methodology proposed in this paper will help in many disaster mitigation activities. It also aims to motive budding researchers to explore and/or fuse various methods, algorithms and domains to gain progressive results in their respective problems.

## References

1. Amit, S.N.K.B., Aoki, Y.: Disaster detection from aerial imagery with convolutional neural network. In: 2017 International Electronics Symposium on Knowledge Creation and Intelligent Computing (IES-KCIC), Surabaya, pp. 239–245 (2017)
2. Xinni, L., Fengrong, H., Kamarul Hawari, G., Mohamed, I.: A review of convolutional neural networks in remote sensing image. In: ICSCA 2019: Proceedings of the 2019 8th International Conference on Software and Computer Applications, pp. 263–267, February 2019
3. Mosavi, A., Ozturk, P., Chau, K.: Flood prediction using machine learning models: literature review. Water **10**, 1536 (2018)
4. Gebrehiwot, A., et al.: Deep convolutional neural network for flood extent mapping using unmanned aerial vehicles data. Sensors. **19**(7), 1486 (2019)

5. Loretta, I., Dan, P.: Flooded areas evaluation from aerial images based on convolutional neural network. In: Geoscience and Remote Sensing Symposium IGARSS 2019, IEEE International, pp. 9756–9759 (2019)
6. O'Shea, K., Nash, R.: An introduction to convolutional neural networks, CoRR abs/1511.08458 (2015)
7. Mahind, R., Patil, A.: A review paper on general concepts of artificial intelligence and machine learning. Int. Adv. Res. J. Sci. Eng. Technol. (IARJSET) 4(4), 79–82 (2017)
8. Said, N., et al.: Natural disasters detection in social media and satellite imagery: a survey. Multimed. Tools Appl. 78(22), 31267–31302 (2019). https://doi.org/10.1007/s11042-019-07942-1
9. Said, N., et al.: Deep learning approaches for flood classification and flood aftermath detection. In: MediaEval, October 2018
10. Shafaey, M.A., Salem, M.A.-M., Ebied, H.M., Al-Berry, M.N., Tolba, M.F.: Deep learning for satellite image classification. In: Hassanien, A.E., Tolba, M.F., Shaalan, K., Azar, A.T. (eds.) AISI 2018. AISC, vol. 845, pp. 383–391. Springer, Cham (2019). https://doi.org/10.1007/978-3-319-99010-1_35

# Handwritten Character Recognition Using KNN and SVM Based Classifier over Feature Vector from Autoencoder

Dibyakanti Mahapatra$^{(\boxtimes)}$ [iD], Chandrajit Choudhury$^{(\boxtimes)}$, and Ram Kumar Karsh$^{(\boxtimes)}$

National Institute of Technology Silchar, Silchar 788010, Assam, India
dibyakanti_mahapatra@yahoo.in,
{chandrajit,ram}@ece.nits.ac.in

**Abstract.** Optical character recognition system is a necessity for the field of man-machine interaction. Handwritten character recognition is a subset of OCR technique by which computer classifies the handwritten alphabets as well as digits. In this work, we present four methods using a vanilla Autoencoder and a Convolutional Autoencoder. For classification purpose we have used KNN, SVM based classifiers such as hybrid KNN-SVM and v-SVM. We evaluated our proposed models on different handwritten scripts such as EMNIST, Devanagari Handwritten Character, and Kannada-MNIST. Autoencoders are generally used to reduce the dimension of the dataset in a non-linear manner and hence extract features for efficient data representation. Baseline of our approach has been different combination of deep learning based feature extraction methods with classifiers. Our developed CNN models consists of less number of layers yet achieved results comparable to other state-of-the-art. A detailed justification for differences in accuracy of our proposed models are discussed in the main article.

**Keywords:** Handwritten character recognition · Autoencoder · KNN-SVM · v-SVM

## 1 Introduction

With the aggressive development of technology, difference between physical world and digital world is getting prominent hurdle for mankind. The need to transfer the records present in physical world, i.e. in written documents, to digital world is growing day by day. Recently to meet this challenge, the problem of handwritten character recognition has gained a lot of attention from the research community. The advent of Deep Learning especially with Neural Networks made this challenge simpler in case of the digits and alphabets considered separately. However in case of entire English character set, i.e. digits, small and capital letters taken together, the task of automatic handwritten character recognition is a tough task to do.

There exists, in broad sense, two types of handwritten character recognition technique: *online* and *offline*. In online methods the data are recorded by a digital pen on an electronic surface. In the latter method, the data are stored in the image format through

© Springer Nature Singapore Pte Ltd. 2020
A. Bhattacharjee et al. (Eds.): MIND 2020, CCIS 1240, pp. 304–317, 2020.
https://doi.org/10.1007/978-981-15-6315-7_25

a scanner after the writing process is over. Offline method is more challenging due to presence of noise and outliers during the process of capturing the images in digital format. Handwritten character recognition by offline method has been one of the challenging research areas in the field of image processing and pattern recognition in recent years. Main motivation behind our work is to produce electronic documents from physical handwritten documents so that it can be easily retrieved and contents can be accessed from anywhere around the world. This recognition technique has prospective applications for different areas such as

a. Conversion of Handwritten documents into digital format without much engagement of human workforce.
b. Recognizing important keywords from handwritten documents.

The challenges of recognition of handwritten characters in offline method originate not only from noises in the electronic recording process but also from style of writing of different persons. By style of writing we mean the orientation of his/her palm, fingers, wrist and the pressure applied on the nib of the pen/pencil. The hand orientation decides the tilt and direction of the written characters. The pressure applied on and the quality of pen/pencil decides the width and smoothness of the curves of those characters. Above all any person's handwriting may change depending on the situation and place where the writing is being done. All these factors make the same character written by different or same person different. We propose two models for tackling the problems of off-line character recognition. In first approach we use a fully connected vanilla Autoencoder and in second, we use a Convolutional Autoencoder (CAE) for extraction of features. Our initial investigation with Autoencoders suggested that the feature representation at latent layer are not quite clusterable. To make data more clusterable, output of CAE is mapped to target images which are one good quality image per class, selected manually from the dataset. By this Autoencoders develop capability of mapping character images to more recognizable form.

In this work we, instead of feature engineering, depend on the features extracted by Autoencoder [1] for recognition. The features extracted by the hidden layer i.e. middlemost layer of Autoencoders are fed to a hybrid KNN-SVM [2] classifier for final classification. We also used a v-SVM [3] classifier on those latent layer features for classification. To validate robustness of our proposed models, we used EMNIST-Balanced [4], Kannada-MNIST [5] and Devanagari Handwritten character [6]. Handwritten character samples from above mentioned datasets are shown in Fig. 1.

**Fig. 1.** Character images from Devanagari, EMNIST and Kannada Datasets (left to right)

This paper is organized in the following manner: Sect. 2 gives a brief idea about the history of research in this field, Sect. 3 describes the proposed method. The experimental results, discussion about the results and their comparison with the state-of-the-art are presented in Sect. 4 and finally, in Sect. 5 we conclude our work.

## 2 Literature Survey

There are many recognition methodologies available for handwritten characters. Continuous persuasion of researchers to improve the recognition accuracy have resulted in combination of various feature extraction and classification techniques and these combinations have evolved as better than any single classifier. If we track the historical timeline of handwritten character recognition there are mainly three well-established paths taken by the fraternity: Template Matching, Statistical Techniques and Neural Networks. Template matching means finding similarity between two feature vectors obtained from images. Template Matching can be done in four ways. First method is Direct Matching proposed by Gadder et al. 1991 [7] which was applied to only numerals. This work laid the foundation of the template matching technique. This method [7] is a two-stage template matching technique, based on combination of multiple information, including match strength and K Nearest Neighbor measurement between two metrics. Second one is Deformable templates [8] by Anil K Jain, Zhong Y., & Lakshmanan, S. where two images are matched by changing the shape accordingly to fit to the edges. Third one is 'Elastic Matching' proposed by C Tappert [9], matches an input image to several letter prototypes. Last one is Relaxation Matching technique (Xie 1988) [10] which was first applied on Chinese handwritten characters due to its high number of characters and recognition complexity. It follows the procedure of matching between a mask character and the input object pattern. There are popular statistical methods such as structural/statistical feature based vector (SSFBV) [11] which works on linear discrimination technique. Here statistical features such as moments, n-tuples are used. This helps to find inter and intra class differences of the dataset. The Quadratic Discriminant Classifier has been used by Hailong Liu. and Xiaoqing Ding [12] for handwritten character recognition. In this work [12] gradient based features like Directional element feature (DEF) process the information about the direction of character strokes and quadratic classifier like Modified Quadratic Discriminant Function (MQDF) is used for classification. MQDF works on probabilistic model which assumes that the prior probability is equal for all the classes. Recently Neural Networks (NN) have found huge ground in application to this field. One of the earliest attempts to achieve accurate recognition of characters using NN was reported by Seong-Whan Lee [13]. It [13] uses a simple three layer neural network with five independent sub networks. It applies Genetic Algorithm in combination with back-propagation algorithms and obtains optimized initial weights. However these proposed algorithms are not sufficient for the recognition of complete dataset of handwritten alphabets and digits taken together. In the original work of EMNIST [4], authors have proposed two separate models for recognition such as - a three layer Extreme Learning Machines (ELM) network and other one is Online Pseudo Inverse Update Method (OPIUM) classifier where exact pseudo-inverse of output weights are calculated iteratively. OPIUM based classifier were trained and tested over a range of hidden layers whereas ELM network does not contain any hidden layer and works as a linear classifier. They were able to report accuracy of 78.02% ± 0.09% for EMNIST-Balanced using OPIUM. In case of ELM linear classifier the accuracy was reported to be 50.93% for EMNIST-Balanced. Ghadekar P, Shubham Ingole and Dhruv Sonone [17] used hybrid DWT-DCT to extract features from handwritten characters and classified the images based on those features using KNN and SVM separately. They reported accuracy of 89.51% and 97.74% for EMNIST-letters and EMNIST-digit respectively using SVM classifier which performed better in terms of accuracy and computation time compared to KNN. Dufourq and Bassett presented EDEN [18], a deep network where they applied neuro-evolution algorithm that combines Genetic Algorithm and deep neural networks to explore the search space of neural network architectures obtaining an accuracy of 88.3% on EMNIST-Balanced. An early attempt to apply deep learning in EMNIST was done by Peng and yin [15]. They proposed Markov Random Field based CNN and reported accuracy of 90.29%, 95.44% and 99.75% for EMNIST-Balanced, EMNIST Letters and EMNIST-Digits respectively. MRF-CNN [15] model is based on multi-level-logistic MRF models with parameter β specified on a fifth-order neighborhood system and by changing the parameter β, different distributions can be modelled. Sample image generation, filtering by MRF filters and passing the image through CNN is the baseline of their method. TextCaps [16] proposed by Jayasundara V et al. is based on capsule network and makes use of a CNN with three convolution, two capsule layers and achieves accuracy of 90.46% on EMNIST-Balanced. First idea of Autoencoder used for dimensionality reduction can be traced back to 'Auto-Association by Multilayer Perceptron and Singular Value Decomposition' [1] by H. Boulard and Y. Kamp. Multilayer Perceptron (MLP) consists of input and output layer of $n_i$ and $n_o$ units respectively with one or more multiple hidden layers which is determined by weighted sum of preceding layers and then passing through an activation function. In the original Kannada-MNIST [5] paper the authors have used an off-the-self CNN to classify the characters and reported accuracy of 97.13%. Creators of Devanagari Handwritten Characters [6] dataset tested two different neural network architecture. First one is very deep network consisting 13 layers and obtained accuracy of 98.47% over validation data. Second model is from LeNet family which has comparatively shallower architecture with less number of layers and obtained accuracy of 98.27% over validation data. From the works reported here we find that the task of recognizing EMNIST-Balanced characters is still an open-end challenge majorly because of the confusion created while considering alphabets and digits together for classification. The script of Kannada and Devanagari pose challenges due to the diversity in amount of shear and spacing between the strokes in the written characters. In this paper we present a novel yet simple method for recognition of the complete dataset of handwritten alphabets and digits comparable to the state-of-the-art.

The proposed work is based on following classifiers:

a. KNN-SVM
b. ν-SVM

First instance of Nearest Neighbor classifier based on Euclidean distance can be found in a research article by TM Cover [14]. SVM classification based on maximum margin was first coined in the article by Bernhard E. Boser [20]. In our application we have used a hybrid KNN-SVM [2] classifier as well as ν-SVM [3] for classification purpose.

## 3 Proposed Method

**Method Set-1 Using Autoencoder**

In the first set of work we used an Autoencoder's latent layer representation for classification of the data. To make the latent layer representation easily classifiable by the classifier, we trained the Autoencoder to map all the images of a certain class to a single target image of that class. Our results suggests that this enables the Autoencoder to encode the images in the latent layer in a clusterable form so that the decoder decodes the latent layer representation to the same image for all the images in a particular class. For this classification we used two separate methods ν-SVM and KNN-SVM, the corresponding results are tabulated in Table 1 and Table 2.

**Method Set-2 Using Convolutional Autoencoder**

In the second set of method we followed the same methodology as in method 1, but replaced the Autoencoder with a Convolutional Autoencoder. The results suggest that the later method performs better.

In our experiment we found that the method of forcing the latent representation to be more clusterable by mapping the images of same class to a single image makes the network overfit. This hampers the classification performance in the test case. To stop the network from overfitting we used data-augmentation, as discusses in Sect. 3.2.

Here we discuss the step-wise techniques that we have used in our method.

### 3.1 Preparing Target Data

One good quality handwritten character per class is chosen from all datasets and saved separately as target images for all datasets. The target images are selected in such a way that there is as less confusion as possible between characters to minimize the chances of a mistake. The images from train and validation sets are mapped to the target images of the respective classes. So for given images of a particular character the target image for the Autoencoder is one particular user defined image.

### 3.2 Data Augmentation

From the below Fig. 2 it is evident that different angular orientation of handwritten characters with vertical axis affects overall recognition task. Rotation of each image in a range of $-20°$ to $+20°$ with a step size of $4°$ and saving in 11 differently-angled instance of each image helps us to improve overall recognition accuracy. The step size of $4°$ suits best and it is determined after trial and error.

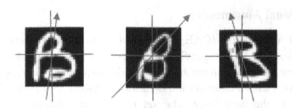

**Fig. 2.** Angular orientation of characters of EMNIST-Balanced

### 3.3 Autoencoder

Autoencoder has been used here as a technique of dimensionality reduction of image features. Autoencoder has multiple hidden layers and the output is calculated by weighted sum of the preceding layers and then passing the result through an Activation function such as sigmoid function in our case. It is desired to have the encoded data of lower dimension for better classification purpose. Thus for hidden layer representation it can be expressed as following:

$$H_k = F(W_k X_k + b_k) \tag{1}$$

Where $W_k$ is the input weight matrix, $X_k$ is input vector and $b_k$ is biases. The Non-linear activation function $F$ is operated component-wise and generates high order moments of each input vector. Our aim is to find desirable weight matrix $W_k$ by minimizing the MSE. RMSprop optimizer is used in the Sequential Autoencoder with parameters as Learning rate = 0.0001 which corresponds to the optimization used for MLP training. Architecture of a vanilla Autoencoder is shown in the following Fig. 3 which have been used in our application. It contains 784 input as well as output nodes. The next layer contains 512 and middlemost layer is of 256 units from which features are taken for classification task. We have used ReLu activation function in all layers except the final layer. For final layer we have used sigmoid activation function.

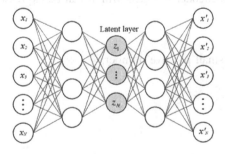

**Fig. 3.** Architecture of Autoencoder model

## 3.4  Convolutional Autoencoder

A Convolutional Autoencoder (CAE) is a type of artificial neural network which learns efficient data encoding in unsupervised manner. It receives input directly from the dataset and process the information through successive layers. Convolutional Autoencoder makes use of Convolution operation between input signal and a filter and result is passed to the next layer. The set of the input images $I = \{I_1, I_2 ... I_D\}$ is convolved with a bank of filters $\{f_1, f_2 ... f_m\}$ and passed through an activation function. The activation maps after convolutional layer are obtained as:

$$O_m = a\left(\sum_{d=1}^{D} \sum_{u=-2k-1}^{2k+1} \sum_{v=-2k-1}^{2k+1} \left(f_m(u,v)I_d(i-u,j-v) + b_m\right)\right) \qquad (2)$$

Where $a$ is the non-linear activation function, in our case we have used ReLu. Detailed architecture of the CAE used in our experiments is shown in the Fig. 4 and Fig. 5. Every convolutional operation is followed by a Maxpooling layer which reduces the number of parameters by selecting the maximum value out of the all elements in the kernel. Final encoded latent layer is of dimension $256 \times 1$. After three dense layers, four successive layers of deconvolution and up-sampling, reconstructed images of same size of the input is obtained back. Deconvolution is the same operation as convolution with filters performed in the decoder layers. Decoder architecture is shown in Fig. 5. For perfect reconstruction of the image we need to minimize the loss function, mean squared error, in our experiment. The classification task is based on the cost function which helps the model to put the images to right class or wrong class. It can be expressed mathematically as

$$\frac{1}{N} \sum_{i=1}^{N} \sum_{c=1}^{C} 1_{y_i \epsilon c_c}\left(logP_{model}[y_i \epsilon c_c]\right) \qquad (3)$$

Whereas $1_{y_i \epsilon c_c}$ is the indicator function of the $i^{th}$ observation belonging to $c^{th}$ category. $P_{model}[y_i \epsilon c_c]$ is the probability predicted by the model for the $i^{th}$ observation belongs to $c^{th}$ category, N being total no. of samples. The activation function used for the Convolutional Autoencoder is ReLU which can be expressed mathematically as:

$$a(x) = \max(x, \epsilon) \qquad (4)$$

Where $\epsilon$ is a very small positive number.

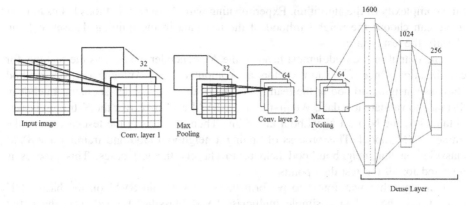

**Fig. 4.** Encoder architecture of CAE

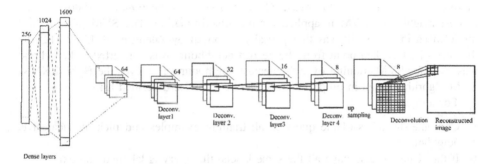

**Fig. 5.** Decoder architecture of CAE

## 3.5   ν-SVM

The ν-support vector classification [3] introduces parameter $\nu \in (0, 1]$ in SVM. ν is an upper limit on the number of support vectors and that lie on the wrong side of the hyperplane. It allows us to set a level by imposing a soft margin during the classification. We have varied value of the ν to obtain best results. For implementing this classifier we have used MATLAB library libSVM [3].

## 3.6   KNN-SVM

Both SVM and KNN can classify images separately but both have their drawbacks which can be improved using hybrid KNN-SVM classifier. Major drawbacks of KNN is that it slows the process of classification as the dataset grows in size. Moreover in our experiments we saw poor performance of KNN using the above obtained feature vectors from Autoencoder. The reason behind that is even though the feature vector is a compressed representation of the data it may not be scattered enough to be classifiable by KNN. In case of SVM we found that different neighbourhoods of the training data require different kernels for classification however that kind of modelling increases the time complexity of the algorithm. Experimenting with these two methods led us to infer if we can choose the neighbourhood of the test data in the training dataset and can classify the test dataset.

The output of the middlemost layer of the Autoencoder is taken as the features for classification. Once the feature vectors are computed using Autoencoder, our method chooses a neighbourhood in the feature vectors of the training dataset using Euclidean distance to validate test data. We first train a v-SVM classifier over the K-training cases obtained by the Nearest Neighbour algorithm. Then we classify the test case using the trained SVM model. This process of finding a neighbourhood and training a v-SVM classifier on that neighbourhood help us to classify the test cases. This process is repeated for all the test data-points.

Our algorithm was found to perform better as we train SVM on the basis of K nearest neighbour than a simple multiclass SVM classifier trained over the entire dataset. Here we use the Nearest Neighbour as an initial classification. The nearest neighbour algorithm reduces the training dataset to much smaller size as well as much more relevant to the present test case. Once the search has been narrowed down to the nearest neighbours, SVM is applied for fine discrimination. The SVM-KNN hybrid model used in this work was first partially proposed by Zhang et al. [2]. In [2] the distance of a test data point from the nearest neighbours was converted to kernel and was used for SVM training over the nearest neighbours. However the Hybrid KNN-SVM algorithm, used in proposed work can be stepwise described as:

For a query,

a. Compute distances of the query to all training examples and pick the nearest K neighbours;
b. If the K neighbours have all the same labels, the query is labelled and exit;
c. Else, train a multiclass SVM on the nearest neighbours only.
d. Use the resulting classifier to label the query.

## 4   Results and Discussion

We first used EMNIST-Balanced dataset where each image is of resolution $28 \times 28$. This dataset is divided into train and test dataset of sizes 112,800 and 18,800 respectively of 47 different labels. The image set was augmented by their rotated version with a rotation range of $-20°$ to $20°$.

### 4.1   Autoencoder

We tried to classify the latent layer representation of the Autoencoder using a multiclass v-SVM but the best result that could be achieved was of 81% using a Gaussian kernel with kernel spread of 0.5 and $v = 0.01$. KNN-SVM was applied with a value of K = 1500 and an accuracy of 88.35% was achieved for the EMNIST-Balanced dataset (alphabets and digits combined). We could run testing and classification of latent layer features using KNN-SVM and v-SVM in our Desktop with Intel i5 processor and 8 GB RAM on MATLAB 2018a. Autoencoder models were built and trained in cloud based

GPU systems provided by Google CoLab. A brief comparison of the accuracy of recognition of the proposed algorithm with the other state-of-the-art- methods is given in the below Table 1.

## 4.2 CAE

We trained the CAE on the training images of the EMNIST balanced and the details of the training process are presented in Fig. 7. We observe that highest accuracy of 89.02% achieved on EMNIST-Balanced by using CAE and v-SVM combination with Gaussian kernel of spread of 0.3, v = 0.001. We also tested the performance of KNN-SVM classifier with K = 1500 for the CAE latent representations. Using KNN-SVM we achieved an accuracy of 83.67%.

**Table 1.** Accuracy comparison of EMNIST-Balanced

| Methods | Accuracy (%) |
|---|---|
| Linear classifier [4] | 50.93 |
| OPIUM [4] | 78.02 ± 0.09 |
| **Proposed Method 1 (Autoencoder + v-SVM)** | **81** |
| **Proposed Method 2 (CAE + KNN-SVM)** | **83.67** |
| CNN (2Conv +1 Dense) [19] | 87.18 |
| EDEN [18] | 88.3 |
| **Proposed Method 3 (Autoencoder + KNN-SVM)** | **88.35** |
| **Proposed Method 4 (CAE + v-SVM)** | **89.02** |
| MRF-CNN [15] | 90.29 |
| Text-Caps [16] | **90.46** |

Inspired by the best performance of the CAE and v-SVM we tested it on other two handwritten character datasets such as Devanagari Handwritten [6] and Kannada MNIST [5]. Devanagari dataset contains training images of 78,200 and test images of 13,800 whereas Kannada-MNIST dataset consists of 60,000 train, 10,000 test images. Results on these datasets are shown in Table 2 and compared with state-of-the-art [5, 6]. Performance of CAE as training progresses is shown in Fig. 7 and 8.

**Table 2.** Accuracy comparison of Devanagari and Kannada datasets

| Methods | Devanagari | Kannada |
|---|---|---|
| Off-the-shelf CNN [5] | – | **97.13%** |
| Deep CNN [6] | **98.47%** | – |
| **Proposed Method 4 (CAE + v-SVM)** | **86.67%** | **95.3%** |

The latent layer clustered features of EMNIST-Balanced, Devanagari Handwritten Character and Kannada MNIST, as encoded by the CAE are projected in the dominant three dimensions and shown in Fig. 6. The plots support our claim of clusterable representation of the data in feature space.

**Fig. 6.** Clustering of latent layer representation of EMNIST, Devanagari and Kannada characters (from left to right)

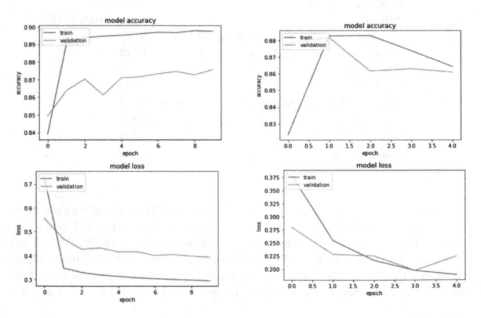

**Fig. 7.** Performance of CAE vs. epochs for EMNIST (left) Devanagari (right)

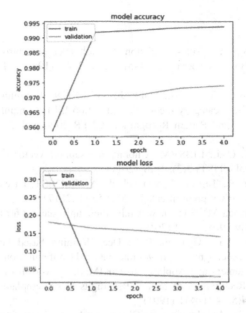

**Fig. 8.** Performance of CAE vs. epochs for Kannada

Training and testing variation with epochs in CAE for different dataset are shown in the Fig. 7 and 8. Here validation plot indicates the performance of the models on test data present in the datasets. The training of the models is not related to the validation performance, as evident from few plots where training continues even after reaching highest validation performance. The values stated above are the highest validation accuracy achieved.

## 5   Conclusion

In this work, we investigated four different methods for handwritten character recognition and we have obtained results which are comparable to the state-of-the art. Highest obtained accuracy for EMNIST-Balanced, Devanagari Handwritten and Kannada-MNIST is **89.02%**, **86.67%** and **95.3%** respectively. CNN models used in our experiment, have less number of layers and yet achieved accuracy comparable to state-of-the-art methods. Another important observation is that machine learning based classifiers such as KNN-SVM and v-SVM performed very well on latent layer features obtained from Autoencoders. We plan to extend our works in other application areas such as - detection of forge signatures or abnormality in finger movement due to neurodegenerative disorders.

# References

1. Bourlard, H., Kamp, Y.: Auto-association by multilayer perceptrons and singular value decomposition. Biol. Cybern. **59**(4–5), 291–294 (1988). https://doi.org/10.1007/BF00332918
2. Zhang, H., Berg, A.C., Maire, M., Malik, J.: SVM-KNN: discriminative nearest neighbor classification for visual category recognition. In: 2006 IEEE Computer Society Conference on Computer Vision and Pattern Recognition, CVPR 2006, vol. 2, pp. 2126–2136. IEEE (2006)
3. Chang, C.-C., Lin, C.-J.: LIBSVM: a library for support vector machines. ACM Trans. Intell. Syst. Technol. (TIST) **2**(3), 1–27 (2011)
4. Cohen, G., Afshar, S., Tapson, J., van Schaik, A.: EMNIST: an extension of MNIST to handwritten letters. arXiv preprint arXiv:1702.05373 (2017)
5. Prabhu, V.U.: Kannada-MNIST: a new handwritten digits dataset for the Kannada language. arXiv preprint arXiv:1908.01242 (2019)
6. Acharya, S., Pant, A.K., Gyawali, P.K.: Deep learning based large scale handwritten Devanagari character recognition. In: 9th International Conference on Software, Knowledge, Information Management and Applications (SKIMA), pp. 1–6. IEEE (2015)
7. Gader, P., et al.: Recognition of handwritten digits using template and model matching. Pattern Recogn. **24**(5), 421–431 (1991)
8. Jain, A.K., Zhong, Y., Lakshmanan, S.: Object matching using deformable templates. IEEE Trans. Pattern Anal. Mach. Intell. **18**(3), 267–278 (1996)
9. Tappert, C.C.: Cursive script recognition by elastic matching. IBM J. Res. Dev. **26**(6), 765–771 (1982)
10. Xie, S.L., Suk, M.: On machine recognition of hand-printed Chinese characters by feature relaxation. Pattern Recogn. **21**(1), 1–7 (1988)
11. Heutte, L., Paquet, T., Moreau, J.-V., Lecourtier, Y., Olivier, C.: A structural/statistical feature based vector for handwritten character recognition. Pattern Recogn. Lett. **19**(7), 629–641 (1998)
12. Liu, H., Ding, X.: Handwritten character recognition using gradient feature and quadratic classifier with multiple discrimination schemes. In: Eighth International Conference on Document Analysis and Recognition, ICDAR 2005, pp. 19–23. IEEE (2005)
13. Lee, S.-W.: Off-line recognition of totally unconstrained handwritten numerals using multilayer cluster neural network. IEEE Trans. Pattern Anal. Mach. Intell. **18**(6), 648–652 (1996)
14. Cover, T.M., Hart, P.: Nearest neighbor pattern classification. IEEE Trans. Inf. Theory **13**(1), 21–27 (1967)
15. Peng, Y., Yin, H.: Markov random field based convolutional neural networks for image classification. In: Yin, H., et al. (eds.) IDEAL 2017. LNCS, vol. 10585, pp. 387–396. Springer, Cham (2017). https://doi.org/10.1007/978-3-319-68935-7_42
16. Jayasundara, V., Jayasekara, S., Jayasekara, H., Rajasegaran, J., Seneviratne, S., Rodrigo, R.: TextCaps: handwritten character recognition with very small datasets. In: IEEE Winter Conference on Applications of Computer Vision (WACV), pp. 254–262. IEEE (2019)
17. Ghadekar, P., Ingole, S., Sonone, D.: Handwritten digit and letter recognition using hybrid DWT-DCT with KNN and SVM Classifier. In: 2018 Fourth International Conference on Computing Communication Control and Automation (ICCUBEA), pp. 1–6. IEEE (2018)
18. Dufourq, E., Bassett, B.A.: Eden: evolutionary deep networks for efficient machine learning. In: Pattern Recognition Association of South Africa and Robotics and Mechatronics (PRASA-RobMech), pp. 110–115 (2017)

19. Cavalin, P., Oliveira, L.: Confusion Matrix-Based Building of Hierarchical Classification. In: Vera-Rodriguez, R., Fierrez, J., Morales, A. (eds.) CIARP 2018. LNCS, vol. 11401, pp. 271–278. Springer, Cham (2019). https://doi.org/10.1007/978-3-030-13469-3_32
20. Boser, B.E., Guyon, I.M., Vapnik, V.N.: A training algorithm for optimal margin classifiers. In: Proceedings of the Fifth Annual Workshop on Computational Learning Theory. ACM (1992)

# A ConvNet Based Procedure for Image Copy-Move Forgery Detection

Ayush Kumar[(✉)] and Badal Soni[ID]

National Institute of Technology Silchar, Silchar, Assam, India
ayushkumarnits@gmail.com, badal@nits.ac.in
http://www.nits.ac.in/

**Abstract.** Copy-Move forgery is one of the popular image tempering procedure. In which the forger modifies the original image by creating multiple instances of some objects within the image itself. Recently, several deep convnet methods have been applied in the classification of images, forensic images, image hashing retrieval, and so on, showing better performance than the traditional method. In this paper, a new architecture of deep learning is proposed for image copy-move forgery detection. This architecture includes VGG16 as the first layer, then RPN for proposing a set of regions and an "object" score for each region and RoI for finding interested area. Both original and forged area in this method is being localized. Through intensive experiments on multiple datasets, we demonstrate that the proposed model is very effective and robust against a number of known attacks. Which outperforms other state-of-the-art image copy-move forgery detection approaches.

**Keywords:** Convolution Neural Network · Deep learning · Region of interest · Copy-move · SIFT · SURF

## 1 Introduction

Over the past decade, with the advent of continuous new technologies in computer vision, users have become very trivial in manipulating images quickly. The number of digital images has increased exponentially due to social media such as Facebook, Instagram, Twitter, Whatsapp, etc. and the development of smart devices such as smartphones. Likewise, applications like Adobe Photoshop, Gimp, Affinity Photo and mobile apps like Snapseed, Pixlr, and digital image processing tools have evolved significantly and made it very easy for users to manipulate images quickly.

In recent years, a variety of social problems and loses have created due to image forging. Most of these images are copy-move because it becomes impossible to identify the forged area by the human perceptual system. Hence, in digital image forensics, probably CMFD is one of the most active fields of research. Since the copied part of the image is from the same image, the color characteristics, noise frequency, gray-scale distance, and all other characteristics are compatible

© Springer Nature Singapore Pte Ltd. 2020
A. Bhattacharjee et al. (Eds.): MIND 2020, CCIS 1240, pp. 318–330, 2020.
https://doi.org/10.1007/978-981-15-6315-7_26

with the rest of the image. So many research has been done in this area, and they all could be broadly divided into two categories such as Key-point based [24] and Block-based [16]. In key-point based, SIFT and SURF are widely used for feature extraction. Key-point based method also performed very well but the problem with this method is that if the tampered area with less entropy or the surface is smooth, that can not be detected. The block-based method divides the gray-scaled image into overlapping blocks and tries to extract features from them.

To handle this problem, we proposed a new architecture using deep learning techniques. The extraction of features from an image is done via a set of convolution filters of pretrained VGG16 [22] neural network where a back-propagation technique is used to learn the gradients. Then on the generated feature map, RPN has been used for proposing a set of regions and an object score for each region. After that non-maximum suppression (NMS) has been used for selecting only those regions whose IoU is greater than 0.9 and RoI for finding interested area in the image. Both original and forged area in this method is being localized.

The remainder of the paper is structured as follows. Section 2 addresses the works concerned with the identification of image manipulation so far. Section 3 discusses the background. The implementation and experimental results are defined in Sect. 4 and 5. Finally, we are summarizing and ending the paper in Sect. 6.

## 2   Related Work

CMFD research work started in the early 2000s [10] and [12]. During that period, most of the research work focused on the cloning of plain region. An approach for detecting and localizing the spliced images by Lyu et al. [16]. Owing to camera or post-processing sensors, they showed the irregularities of local noises. By being inspired by the fact that image forging can change an image's texture micro-patterns. In [17], Steerable Pyramid Transform (SPT) and Local Binary Pattern (LBP) were used to detect texture distortions in faked images. The advanced detection quality on the [9] CASIA dataset has been achieved so far. Badal et al. [24] used SIFT and DBSCAN (density-based clustering algorithm). They first detected SIFT features from the image and matched using generalized two nearest neighbors (2NN) procedure. They then used a clustering algorithm based on density to improve the results of detection. A reader can refer to [23] and [1] to know more about the existing methods.

In recent years, to extract complex statistical features and to efficiently learn hierarchical representations from high-dimensional sensory inputs, deep neural networks, such as Convolution Neural Network (CNN) [15], Deep Belief Network [2] and Deep Auto Encoder [14] have shown very high capacity. They have a very high generalization ability across a wide range of tasks related to computer vision (CV), involving image classification [13], speech recognition [25], etc. More lately, in passive image forensics, applications of deep learning-based approaches have been found. CNN was used by Jiansheng et al. [6] to detect median filters. Ying et al. [4], however, showed that for image tampering detection, directly applying conventional deep learning frameworks did not show the robustness because forged images and their authentic ones are closely resembled each other not only optically but also statistically. For this reason, as an input to the deep auto-encoder, wavelet features of images are adopted by them. Motivated by related observations, Bayar et al. [7] used an adaptive filter in front of the CNN network and also had very high accuracy even when one of the attacks was implemented through median filtering, Gaussian blurring, white Gaussian additive noise and resampling. J. Ouyang et al. [10] trained the AlexNet [13] model with forged images but got very less accuracy on handcrafted real scenario CMFD [12] dataset.

To obtain higher performance and improved efficiency in detecting the copy-move forged image in our paper we have implemented manipulation detection using deep learning in Keras using Tensor-flow as back-end.

## 3    Background Knowledge

In the proposed system, a ConvNet known as VGG16, Region Proposal Network (RPN), Region of Interest Align (RoIAlign), and at the end Fully connected layers for generating bounding boxes and convolution layer for generating masks have been used.

**Convolution Layer**
A convolution layer mainly performs two operations such as the first Convolution and then pooling.

**Convolution:** Convolution is the first layer that acts as a feature extractor from an input image. It converts all the pixels in its respective fields into a single value. The mathematical operation, that is performed between two inputs such as image tensor and a kernel, is bitwise matrix multiplication then the addition of all those values.

$$f(m, c, b) = \sum_{ij}(m_{ij} * c_{ij}) + b \tag{1}$$

where $*$ denotes convolution, $m$ denotes a region of size i*j of an image, $c$ is a convolution kernel and $b$ is the bias parameter.

**Non Linearity (ReLU):** ReLU (rectified linear unit) is an activation function. That performs non-linear operation. The output of ReLU function is

$$f(n) = \begin{cases} n & \text{if } n \neq 0 \\ 0 & \text{Otherwise} \end{cases}$$

**Pooling Layer:** Generally, convolution neural networks have a very large number of neurons which make learning problems more complex. Pooling layers therefore help to reduce the representation size, speed up the computation and make some of the features that detect somewhat more robust. It also makes the model slightly invariant to transformations. There are so many pooling operators. Some of them are max-pooling, avg-pooling. Max-pooling is as follows:

For e.x: If matrix size $=$ n $*$ n Kernel size $=$ k $*$ k Padding $=$ p Stride $=$ s

Then, for overlapping regions, the output of a pooling layer is

$$\lfloor (n - k + 2 * p)/(s + 1) \rfloor * \lfloor (n - k + 2 * p)/s + 1) \rfloor \tag{2}$$

## Dropout

Dropout is a regularization technique that helps in preventing over-fitting in a neural network. It ignores a set of neurons during a particular forward or backward pass in the training phase. In this study, a dropout of 0.5 has been used because it will prevent the inter-dependencies among the neurons which results in the reduction of over-fitting.

## VGG16

VGG16 [22] contains 16 layer architectures, out of which there are 13 convolution layers, 5 max pooling layers, 3 fully connected layers and one output layer called soft-max layer. To better understand the VGG16 layer, it has been shown below (Fig. 1):

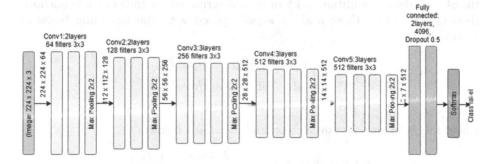

**Fig. 1.** VGG16 CNN model.

## Region Proposal Network

It [20] is a small fully convolution network that takes in a feature map and outputs a set of regions and an "objectness" score for each region. Each point of the feature map is considered as an anchor. From each anchor, k Anchor boxes are generated of standard length and of aspect ratios of 1:1, 1:2 and 2:1 (Fig. 2).

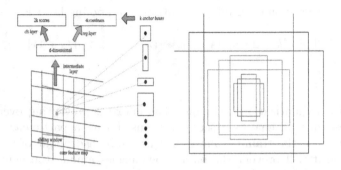

**Fig. 2.** Left figure is the RPN and right one is the 9 anchor-boxes generated for three different aspect ratios and three different scales.

The regressor output specifies a predicted bounding-box (x, y, w, h), the classification sub-network output is a probability p which indicates whether the predicted box contains an object or whether it is from the context (no object).

Each anchor box is compared with the ground truth. Only those anchor boxes are selected which has an IoU overlap with the ground-truth higher than the threshold value. In addition, a k* value is determined for each of these anchors, showing how much these anchors superimposed with the bounding boxes of ground-truth.

$$k^* = \begin{cases} 1 & \text{if } IoU > threshold \\ -1 & \text{if } IoU < threshold \\ 0 & \text{otherwise} \end{cases}$$

where IoU is intersection over union and is defined below:

$$IoU(Anchor, \ GT_{box}) = \frac{Anchor \ \cap \ GT_{box}}{Anchor \ \cup \ GT_{box}}$$

where $GT_{box}$ is ground-truth box.

**RoIAlign**

[11] A region of interest are samples identified within a dataset for a specific purpose. If an output of N × N is desired, the proposed region is split into a grid of N × N. Since each region includes the exact same number of pixels, we can have fractional pixels sometimes. Then each cell of the grid is split into four sub-cells. Bilinear interpolation operation is performed to get a single value for each subregion, or four values for each cell. These values are shown in the fourth image. Finally, we perform a simple max-pooling on the bilinear interpolated values, taking the maximum value per cell to reach an N × N output. This output is then passed through the fully connected layers for bounding-box regression, and through the small Fully Convolution Network (FCN) that makes up our masking head (Fig. 3).

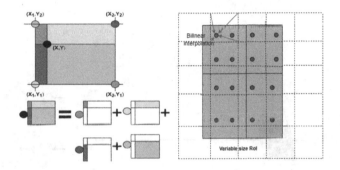

**Fig. 3.** Bilinear interpolation in RoIAlign (Color figure online)

At the black spot, the bilinear interpolated value is the sum of the values of each of the four colors multiplied by the areas of their respective rectangles, divided by the total area. The nearest 4 pixel values at each blue dot (represented in the figures on the previous page with a red one) are selected and multiplied by their respective areas.

## 4   Proposed Methodology

In this section, we describe our end-to-end system for copy-move image manipulation detection. It is trained on a large dataset which contains numerous forgery examples to create a robust model. A deep ConvNet architecture known as VGG16 has been used to generate feature maps. For each point of the feature map, RPN generates k anchor boxes and an object score for each region. Since hundreds of anchor boxes will be generated for a single feature map. As the method of generating proposals should have high recall, at this stage we kept loose constraints. However, it is cumbersome to process these many proposals throughout the classification network. So, to find the most probable localized area we used the threshold value as 0.9. Hence NMS selects only those regions whose IoU is greater than 0.9. Because IoU operation is being performed between an anchor-box and ground-truth.

Then each bounding-box is divided into four grid cells. Then each grid cell is divided into four subcells. Bilinear interpolation is performed to get a single value for each sub-cell. For each RoI, p number of m × m masks are predicted where p is the number of classes. Then these p number of m × m masks goes to two sub-networks. One of the network is fully connected layer that generates bounding box. And the other network is convolution layer that generates mask for the desired area. Optimization of stochastic gradient descent (SGD) is used to optimize the proposed model with an 0.99 momentum and a 0.001 weight decay. Using SGD with momentum helps speed up the gradient vectors in the right direction, resulting in faster convergence.

Schematic diagram of the proposed model (Fig. 4):

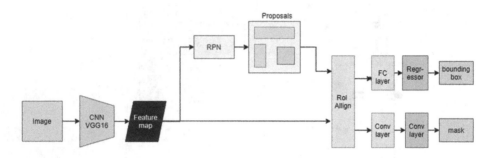

**Fig. 4.** Proposed ConvNet model for image manipulation detection.

1. In the first step, copy-move images with the ground-truth are given as input to the convolution layer of a pre-trained VGG16 ConvNets to generate feature maps.
2. Then for each point of the feature map, k anchor-boxes and scores for each box are generated by region proposal network. Non-maximum suppression removes all those boxes with IoU less than 0.9.
3. RoIAlign operation is performed on each anchor-boxes generated by RPN.
4. The output of RoIAlign is given as input to the convolution layer for bounding-box regression and through the small Fully Convolution Network (FCN) that makes up our masking head.

---

**Algorithm 1.** Image Copy-Paste Forgery Detection

---

1: Input: Manipulated image(img)
2: Output: location of both source and target regions
3: **procedure** COPY-MOVE(img)
4:  $\quad$ x $\leftarrow$ *img*
5:  $\quad$ **for** $i \leftarrow 0$ *to* 1 **do**
6:  $\quad\quad$ **for** $j \leftarrow 0$ *to* 1 **do**
7:  $\quad\quad\quad$ y $\leftarrow features(x)$ $\qquad\qquad\qquad$ ▷ Using Convolution layer
8:  $\quad\quad\quad$ y $\leftarrow features(y)$
9:  $\quad\quad\quad$ y $\leftarrow non - linear(y)$ $\qquad\qquad$ ▷ Using ReLU layer
10: $\quad\quad\quad$ y $\leftarrow invariant(y)$ $\qquad\qquad$ ▷ Using Max-pooling layer
11: $\quad\quad$ **end for**
12: $\quad$ **end for**
13: $\quad$ **for** $i \leftarrow 0$ *to* 2 **do**
14: $\quad\quad$ **for** $j \leftarrow 0$ *to* 2 **do**
15: $\quad\quad\quad$ z $\leftarrow features(y)$
16: $\quad\quad\quad$ z $\leftarrow features(z)$
17: $\quad\quad\quad$ z $\leftarrow non - linear(z)$
18: $\quad\quad\quad$ z $\leftarrow invariant(z)$
19: $\quad\quad$ **end for**
20: $\quad$ **end for**
21: $\quad$ p $\leftarrow proposals(z)$ $\qquad\qquad\qquad\qquad$ ▷ Using RPN layer
22: $\quad$ q $\leftarrow RPN_{prob}(p) + RPN_{box}(p)$
23: $\quad$ r $\leftarrow (IoU > 0.9)(z)$ $\qquad\qquad\qquad$ ▷ Using NMS layer
24: $\quad$ s $\leftarrow classifier\text{-}set(r) + regressor\text{-}sct(r)$ $\quad$ ▷ Using RoIAlign layer
25: $\quad$ s $\leftarrow features(s)$
26: $\quad$ bounding-box + mask $\leftarrow features(s)$
27: **end procedure**

---

## 5 Experimentation Results and Discussions

For the performance evaluation of our proposed model, we first built an experimental database of original and tampered images. The database consists of 27000 images. The proposed model has been implemented in Keras deep learning framework using Tensor-flow as back-end. All the training and testing was done on Google colab with 12 GB GPU. After the extensive experiment, we found that the model is able to identify the location of the original and forged area in the image.

**A. Datasets:** The experiment has been conducted on MICC-F2000 [2], UCID [21], CMFD [7], CoMoFoD [26], CVIP [3], MICC-F220 [2], OXFORD flower [18] and COCO [5]. MICC-F2000, CMFD, CoMoFoD, CVIP, MICC-F220 datasets contain 700, 110, 7266, 5393, 920 tampered images respectively. UCID, OXFORD flower and COCO datasets contain 862, 8189 and 3560 (initial 3560 images were selected) images respectively. Since UCID, Oxford flower and COCO datasets contain more challenging images because they have more textured regions but they had only pristine images. So, on the UCID, Oxford flower and COCO datasets, we created copy-move images by copying one portion of the image of any size and then paste it onto the other region in the same image. Only on 3560 images, we manually created forged images from COCO dataset. Most specifically, none of existing datasets provide ground-truth boxes for source and target copies. For training the model, we created ground-truth boxes on all the images using VGG16-annotator tool.

Therefore, to build the train and test datasets, 27000 copy-move forged images were selected. Furthermore, the dataset was divided into the ratio of 80:20. That means the train dataset contains 21600 images and test dataset contains 5400 images. Out of 27000 forged images, 12611 images were created manually by simply performing a copy-move operations on UCID and oxford flower and COCO images datasets.

**B. Performance appraisal:** The efficiency of the proposed system is evaluated by measuring the bounding-box and mask losses. Training and validation losses are defined as $L = L_{box} + L_{mask}$ where $L_{box}$ is the loss of the bounding box and $L_{mask}$ is the loss of the mask. Loss of the bounding box is calculated using smooth loss of L1, and loss of the mask is calculated using binary cross-entropy. The result shows that pre-trained VGG16 network on the ImageNet dataset is outperforming the other state-of-the-art techniques.

$$L = L_{bounding\_box} + L_{mask} \tag{3}$$

where,

$$L_{1;smooth}(m) = \begin{cases} 0.5\,\mathrm{m}^2 & \text{if } |m| \leq 1 \\ |m| - 0.5 & \text{Otherwise} \end{cases}$$

$$Cross\_entropy\ loss = (-1/J) \sum_{i=1}^{J} [y_i log\ p_i + (1 - y_i)log(1 - p_i)] \tag{4}$$

where, J is the number of points, $p_i$ is the predicted value and $y_i$ the actual value.

The performance of the model is also checked in terms of Precision, Recall and F1-score.

$$Precision = \frac{TP}{TP + FP}$$

$$Recall = \frac{FP}{FP + TN}$$

$$F1score = 2 * \frac{Precision * Recall}{Precision + Recall}$$

Where, TP: Images which are defined as manipulated are actually manipulated. FP: Images which are defined as manipulated are actually pristine. TN:

**Table 1.** Precision, Recall and F1-score values for proposed model

| Method | Precision | Recall | F1-score |
|---|---|---|---|
| Pun et al. [19] | 0.5439 | 0.5390 | 0.8327 |
| Dnon et al. [8] | 0.6963 | 0.8042 | 0.8835 |
| **Proposed** | 0.92 | 0.86 | 0.89 |

Images which are defined as pristine are actually pristine. FN: Images which are defined as pristine are actually manipulated.

**C. Experimental results and Analysis:** For training the proposed model, we use the image datasets of the CVIP group, OXFORD flower, UCID, CoMoFoD, CMFD, MICC-F2000, MICC-F220 and COCO. Our proposed model achieves a training loss and test loss of .0978 and .1127 respectively after 80 epochs. It means the model is not over-fitting. Accuracy in terms of precision, recall and f1-score is shown in the Table 1 (Fig. 5).

**Fig. 5.** First row corresponds to original images and second row is their corresponding localized region of original and forged images. These images are from the test dataset.

We have also tested on CASIA v2.0 dataset which was not part of the training and test dataset. The test loss on CASIA v2.0 dataset is 0.1448. This proposed model is able to recognize the real scenario tampered images with a very high accuracy than the other up-to-date copy-move forgery detection approaches.

The detection result on the CASIA CMFD dataset is shown in the below table. From the CASIA dataset, We sampled 190 copy-move images to compare with the other methods where the accuracy is the ratio of corrected samples to the opt-in samples.

The MICC-F8 dataset that contains 8 challenging manipulated images with high resolution. All these images are manipulated at multiple locations in real scenario. Manipulations like shifting, rotation, translation, and their compositions are present in the dataset. The Recall is 100% on this dataset (Figs. 6 and 7) (Table 2).

**Fig. 6.** First row corresponds to original images and second row is their corresponding localised region of original and forged images. These images are from CASIA v2.0 dataset.

**Table 2.** Performance analogy of detection result on CASIA CMFD dataset

| Methods | Datasets number of images(copy-move) | Correct | Accuracy(%) |
|---|---|---|---|
| BusterNet [27] | CASIA v2.0(190) | 146 | 76.84 |
| Proposed | CASIA v2.0(190) | 162 | 85 |

**Fig. 7.** First row corresponds to original images and second row is their corresponding localized region of original and forged images. These images are from MICC-F8 dataset.

## 6    Conclusions and Future Work

A new ConvNet based image copy-move forgery detection method has been proposed in this paper. Through intensive experiments on multiple datasets, we demonstrate that the proposed model shows very high accuracy on the test dataset. Which outperforms other advanced approaches to the detection of copy-move image forgery. This proposed model is robust against most of the well-known attack like image resizing, rotation, translation, and their compositions, etc. It is also noted that very few papers in CMFD have employed deep learning techniques for localizing both source and the target regions. Future work may suggest generalizing the model into other forgery of images such as splicing forgery or retouching of images. This can be achieved by tuning the model using datasets which contain examples of forgery of this kind.

# References

1. Abd Warif, N., et al.: Copy-move forgery detection: survey, challenges and future directions. J. Netw. Comput. Appl. **75**, 259–278 (2016)
2. Amerini, I., Ballan, L., Caldelli, R., Del Bimbo, A., Serra, G.: A SIFT-based forensic method for copy-move attack detection and transformation recovery. IEEE Trans. Inf. Forensics Secur. **6**, 1099–1110 (2011)
3. Ardizzone, E., Mazzola, G.: A tool to support the creation of datasets of tampered videos. In: Murino, V., Puppo, E. (eds.) ICIAP 2015. LNCS, vol. 9280, pp. 665–675. Springer, Cham (2015). https://doi.org/10.1007/978-3-319-23234-8_61
4. Bayar, B., Stamm, M.: A deep learning approach to universal image manipulation detection using a new convolutional layer, pp. 5–10, June 2016
5. Caesar, H., Uijlings, J., Ferrari, V.: COCO-Stuff: thing and stuff classes in context. In: 2018 IEEE Conference on Computer Vision and Pattern Recognition (CVPR). IEEE (2018)
6. Chen, J., Kang, X., Liu, Y., Wang, Z.: Median filtering forensics based on convolutional neural networks. IEEE Sig. Process. Lett. **22**, 1849–1853 (2015)
7. Christlein, V., Riess, C., Jordan, J., Riess, C., Angelopoulou, E.: An evaluation of popular copy-move forgery detection approaches. IEEE Trans. Inf. Forensics Secur. **7**, 1841–1854 (2012)
8. Dnon, D.: Copy-move forgery detection and localization using a generative adversarial network and convolutional neural-network. Information **10**, 1–26 (2019)
9. Dong, J., Wang, W., Tan, T.: CASIA image tampering detection evaluation database, pp. 422–426, July 2013
10. Fridrich, J., Soukal, D., Lukás, J.: Detection of copy-move forgery in digital images. Int. J. Comput. Sci. Issues **3**, 55–61 (2003)
11. He, K., Gkioxari, G., Dollár, P., Girshick, R.: Mask R-CNN, March 2017
12. Ke, Y., Sukthankar, R., Huston, L.: An efficient parts-based near-duplicate and sub-image retrieval system, pp. 869–876, January 2004
13. Krizhevsky, A., Sutskever, I., Hinton, G.E.: ImageNet classification with deep convolutional neural networks. In: Pereira, F., Burges, C.J.C., Bottou, L., Weinberger, K.Q. (eds.) Advances in Neural Information Processing Systems 25, pp. 1097–1105. Curran Associates, Inc. (2012). http://papers.nips.cc/paper/4824-imagenet-classification-with-deep-convolutional-neural-networks.pdf
14. Larochelle, H., Bengio, Y., Louradour, J., Lamblin, P.: Exploring strategies for training deep neural networks. J. Mach. Learn. Res. **1**, 1–40 (2009). https://doi.org/10.1145/1577069.1577070
15. Lecun, Y., Bottou, L., Bengio, Y., Haffner, P.: Gradient-based learning applied to document recognition. Proc. IEEE **86**, 2278–2324 (1998)
16. Lyu, S., Pan, X., Zhang, X.: Exposing region splicing forgeries with blind local noise estimation. Int. J. Comput. Vis. **110**, 202–221 (2013). https://doi.org/10.1007/s11263-013-0688-y
17. Muhammad, G., Al-Hammadi, M.H., Hussain, M., Bebis, G.: Image forgery detection using steerable pyramid transform and local binary pattern. Mach. Vis. Appl. **25**(4), 985–995 (2013). https://doi.org/10.1007/s00138-013-0547-4
18. Nilsback, M.E., Zisserman, A.: Automated flower classification over a large number of classes, pp. 722–729, December 2008
19. Pun, C.M., Yuan, X., Bi, X.L.: Image forgery detection using adaptive over-segmentation and feature points matching. IEEE Trans. Inf. Forensics Secur. **10**, 1705–1716 (2015). https://doi.org/10.1109/TIFS.2015.2423261

20. Ren, S., He, K., Girshick, R., Sun, J.: Faster R-CNN: towards real-time object detection with region proposal networks. IEEE Trans. Pattern Anal. Mach. Intell. **39**, 1137–1149 (2015). https://doi.org/10.1109/TPAMI.2016.2577031
21. Schaefer, G., Stich, M.: UCID: an uncompressed color image database, vol. 5307, pp. 472–480, January 2004
22. Simonyan, K., Zisserman, A.: Very deep convolutional networks for large-scale image recognition. arXiv:1409.1556, September 2014
23. Soni, B., Das, P., Thounaojam, D.: CMFD: a detailed review of block based and key feature based techniques in image copy-move forgery detection. IET Image Process. **12**, 167–178 (2017)
24. Soni, B., Das, P., Thounaojam, D.: Keypoints based enhanced multiple copy-move forgeries detection system using density-based spatial clustering of application with noise clustering algorithm. IET Image Process. **12**, 2092–2099 (2018)
25. Swietojanski, P., Ghoshal, A., Renals, S.: Convolutional neural networks for distant speech recognition. IEEE Sig. Process. Lett. **21**, 1120–1124 (2014)
26. Tralic, D., Zupancic, I., Grgic, S., Grgic, M.: CoMoFoD - new database for copy-move forgery detection, September 2013
27. Wu, Y., Abd-Almageed, W., Natarajan, P.: BusterNet: detecting copy-move image forgery with source/target localization. In: Ferrari, V., Hebert, M., Sminchisescu, C., Weiss, Y. (eds.) ECCV 2018. LNCS, vol. 11210, pp. 170–186. Springer, Cham (2018). https://doi.org/10.1007/978-3-030-01231-1_11

# A Novel Invisible Watermarking Approach for Double Authentication of Image Content

R. Vidhya and M. Brindha$^{(\boxtimes)}$

CSE, National Institute of Technology, Tiruchirappalli, Tiruchirappalli, India
vidhu.cs111@gmail.com, brindham@nitt.edu

**Abstract.** Nowadays, digital watermarking approaches are proposed for content authentication of digital images. Digital watermarking is a technique that is used to embed watermarks into a digital image. In this work, a novel double authentication mechanism is proposed to ensure the authenticity of image content based on the hash function and signature value. The suggested technique is capable of finding malicious image manipulation even if simple image processing operations have unintentionally corrupted them. Using the hash function, the difficulty level of finding embedded bits is increased and this scheme also withstands any kind of attacks. Moreover, the proposed technique is simple which is based on modifying a single pixel value in the host image itself using the surrounding pixels i.e., neighboring pixels. Experimental results are shown to illustrate the system's capability to detect unauthorized image alteration.

**Keywords:** Watermarking · Hash function · Authentication

## 1 Introduction

Over the past few years, the usage and delivery of multimedia information, such as videos and images, has incremented promptly over internet and computer networks. Using digital image editing tools, the multimedia information can be easily manipulated and altered. Accordingly, content authentication and image integrity verification are very crucial under this situation. To assure content authentication and integrity of image, two approaches [22] are widely utilized (i) signature (ii) watermarking. In signature-based method, image signature information is acquired using cryptographic methods such as hash functions, which are kept either in individual file or the regions defined by user [10]. Within these approaches, integrity verification is carried out by checking the preserved(stored) signature value with the image signature produced. From the outcome of the comparison, any alteration in an image can be verified. The flaw of signature-related methods, is, they will not be able to identify or locate the manipulated places of altered images. On the other side, visible watermarking techniques like

© Springer Nature Singapore Pte Ltd. 2020
A. Bhattacharjee et al. (Eds.): MIND 2020, CCIS 1240, pp. 331–342, 2020.
https://doi.org/10.1007/978-981-15-6315-7_27

insertion of logo or user related information in the original image are also done. Cox et al. [6] briefly discussed about the applications of watermarking like owner identification, authentication, broadcast monitoring and proof of ownership. Also the properties involved in the watermarking techniques like fidelity, robustness, computational cost, tamper resistance and false positive rate are also discussed.

There are three approaches mainly considered in digital watermarking (i) robust (ii) fragile (iii) semi-fragile. In this, for copyright protection and identification of ownership related applications, robust watermarking approaches are involved to overcome intentional or unintentional attacks [4,23]. On the other side, for tamper and forgery detection, and authentication of content, fragile and semi-fragile approaches are preceded. Fragile watermarks can be lost or corrupted easily if the watermarked image has a tiny change [14,18,19] whereas semi-fragile approaches [5,16] are developed to be vigorous against unintentional functions, like JPEG compression. The main intention here is to overcome intentional attacks.

Fragile watermarking approach is classified into two categories: transform and spatial domains (i.e., based on modification done). Here, in transform domain approaches, the watermarks are inserted at frequency coefficients of host images and highly utilized methods for inserting co-efficients are Discrete Cosine Transform (DCT) [12,24] and Discrete Wavelet Transform (DWT) [1,3]. In the second (spatial) approach, the watermarks are inserted into the host image by directly changing the pixels i.e., LSB method is the easiest and highly popular approach in spatial domain methods [15]. Regarding the application requirements, fragile methods should have major features such as imperceptibility, reliability, blind detection, and data payload. Imperceptibility refers to invisible watermark in an image and it should not be seen by the human. The image fidelity describes that the embedding phase of a watermark should not reduce the perceivable nature of the initial image. The total number of bits inserted into the host image refers to the data payload. Blind detection means extraction of watermarks and identification of manipulators in the absence of initial host image. Moreover, many of the fragile approaches apply watermarks without the knowledge of content of image like binary sequence or logo. In many watermark embedding approaches, very small blocks are utilized and this type of embedding is added into huge amount of data resulting in reduced quality of watermarked image.

Researchers have studied to develop the fragile methods of watermarking of images in recent years. In [7] a novel fragile watermarking approach is proposed which is based on hash functions to obtain high visual quality watermarked images. Hsu et al. [8] use DCT-based technique for embedding and extracting the watermark into images. [14] suggested a reversible watermarking procedure for authentication of images using DWT region in order to attain good reliability and tamper detection. Qianli and Cai [17] implemented a digital watermarking for gray scale images which utilizes DWT and DCT approaches to preserve the copyright of digital media efficiently. Amit Kumar Singh [20], proposed a hybrid watermarking technique for the protection of patient identity in medical applications. Abdelhakim et al. [2] suggested an efficient block based watermarking procedure for image authentication which uses DCT. Moreover, self watermarked image which depends on DCT is proposed by [21], and in this the watermark is acquired by the most five significant digits of pixel. Nazari et al., [13] suggested a new watermarking approach which is basically related on block features of original image. Li et al., [9] suggested a double authentication using semi fragile approach which follows a ring structure and ring based watermark is generated by chaos. This watermark is embedded into mid-frequency bands. Yang et al., [25] recommended a novel approach to reconstruct the tamper image using vector quantization indexing method to increase the quality of watermarked image.

The main contributions of the suggested method are given as follows,

(i) A novel invisible watermarking scheme is proposed in this paper for providing double authentication of digital image content.
(ii) The positions (i.e., pseudo random number is generated) for embedding the watermark is computed from Rabin cryptosystem. For an unauthorized person, the difficulty level is high for detecting the position which is equal to factorization problem that is hard to break.
(iii) The watermark is embedded at any location of a pixel, and not in LSB. Due to this reason, the embedded watermark is more robust and preserves good image quality than any other methods.
(iv) Moreover, the suggested scheme considers the sum of the surrounding pixels as one more signature for double authentication purpose.

The rest of the paper is organized as follows: Sect. 2 describes about the preliminaries used in watermarking method and the proposed watermarking approach is explained in Sect. 3. Sections 4 provides the analytical experiments of the proposed watermarking technique and the paper concludes in Sect. 5.

## 2   Preliminaries

The study behind the recommended watermarking method is explained in this section.

### 2.1   Watermarking

Watermarking method is applied for authentication of images at the receiver side. Watermarking is an embedding of feature(data) with secret information that can be retrieved by a receiver . This can be classified into two types i) visible watermarking ii) invisible watermarking. Visible watermarking is visually seen by everyone like company logo (it specifies the company ownership). In Invisible watermarking , the image after watermarked looks same as the original image and by extraction and detection algorithm, the watermark can be determined. The general insertion procedure presumed in the watermarking is given in Fig. 1. This process is observed for authentication of the suggested encryption method and the recommended invisible watermarking procedure is described in the consequent section.

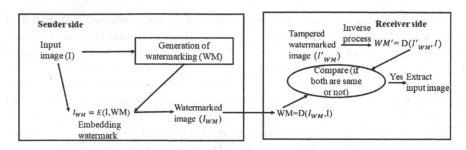

**Fig. 1.** Architecture of watermarking process

## 2.2    One-Way Hash Function (OHF)

The idea of one-way hash function is described here. OHF is a group of functions $f : x \to y$ which is having the unique features [11]:

(i) The function $f$ is easily calculated and the process of choosing a member is random and somewhat simple.
(ii) The inversions of the functions are computationally hard. In other words, given a value $x$, to generate the one more value $x \neq x'$ is computationally hard and it meets $f(x) = f(x')$ for a arbitrarily chosen $f$.
(iii) For any size, the functions are applied and the produced output are all of equal size.
     For the past few years, the hash functions are applied for the cryptographic applications such as access control, user authentication, key management, and other functions.

## 2.3    Rabin's Cryptosystem

Rabin's cryptosystem is a asymmetric approach which is based on the factorization of integers. Moreover, the difficulty level of this approach is high. For encrypting a message $Me'$, calculate $Ci' = (Me')^2 mod n$, where $n = p'q'$ and $p'$ and $p'$ are the large primes.
For decrypting a message:
Using Chinese remainder theorem, the original message is obtained

$$Me'_1 = Ci'(p' + 1)/4 \bmod n \tag{1}$$

$$Me'_2 = p' - Ci'(p' + 1)/4 \bmod n \tag{2}$$

$$Me'_3 = Ci'(q' + 1)/4 \bmod n \tag{3}$$

$$Me'_4 = q' - Ci'(q' + 1)/4 \bmod n \tag{4}$$

One among $Me'_1$, $Me'_2$, $Me'_3$, and $Me'_4$, is similar to message. In the suggested approach, the Rabin method is utilized for finding the position to insert a bit of the watermark. The positions are taken randomly, hence it is difficult to extract the watermark and its position embedded in image.

# 3  Proposed Watermarking Approach

Here a novel and very simple watermarking technique is described. A novel double authentication of image content which is based on One-Way Hash Function (OWHF) and signature to the average of the surrounding pixels (i.e., spatial domain) is clearly explained here. Normally, a plain image $\hat{P}i$ of size is expressed as $i' \times j'$, where $i'$ and $j'$ denotes the rows and columns respectively. Two phases are involved in suggested watermarking procedure i.e., embedding the watermark and extraction of watermark phase. Embedding of watermark phase starts with computing the positions using Rabin's cryptosystem to embed the watermark and the signature value is computed for providing double authentication. Let us assume, that the user of the host image generated a private key $(k')$ of length of 512 bits using hash function. The procedure associated in embedding of watermark is explained as follows:

Step 1: The enormous prime numbers of $p'$ and $q'$ are randomly selected and parameter $n = p'.q'$ is measured, where $p'$ and $q'$ remain secret, and n is public. The length of both $p'$ and $q'$ is 256 bits.

Step 2: Use the following enciphering procedure to get two secret seeds $X'$, $Y'$.

$$X' = \hat{P}i^{k'} \bmod n \tag{5}$$

$$Y' = \hat{P}i^{(k')^2} \bmod n \tag{6}$$

where $X'$ and $Y'$ have a length of 512 bits.

Step 3: Compute the positions $(U_{x'}, U_{y'})$ using the following equations (i.e., Rabin cryptosystem):

$$U_{x'} = (X')^2 \bmod n \tag{7}$$

$$U_{y'} = (Y')^2 \bmod n \tag{8}$$

where $U_{x'}$, $U_{y'}$, and $n$ have a length of 512 bits.

Step 4: Generate the insertion (embedding) position $(x', y')$ and this is expressed as follows:

$$x' = U_{x'} \bmod i' \tag{9}$$

$$y' = U_{y'} \bmod j' \tag{10}$$

where $i'$, $j'$ are the size of the original image.

Step 5: The bit of the watermark is embedded into the position of $(x', y')$ defined from step 4.

Step 6: Generate the next position $U_{x'}$, $U_{y'}$ using the following expressions,

$$U_{x'} = U_{x'}^2 \bmod n \tag{11}$$

$$U_{y'} = U_{y'}^2 \bmod n \tag{12}$$

Step 7: Untill all bits of watermark is enclosed into the original image the steps 4, 5, 6 are repeated.

For double authentication, the same embedding position is generated from step 4 and it is utilized for adding one more signature to the original image.

From the image size, the minimum length(number) of bits required to denote the location of a pixel is determined. For example, for a $256 \times 256$ image, 16 bits are needed to represent a pixel, 8 bits for the row index and 8 bits for the column index. If the number of rows or columns are not a power of 2, the log of the next highest power of 2 is to be taken. Hence, the number of bits to represent the signature i.e. the location of the bit whose value are changing is equivalent to the following.

$$\lceil \log_2 c \rceil + \lceil \log_2 r \rceil \tag{13}$$

A signature value is taken to denote the position of a pixel. The signature consists of the row index appended with the column index. The value of the pixel at that location is newly set to the average of the values of the surrounding pixels. The average value is calculated accordingly if the pixel is an edge or corner pixel. The obtained image is a watermarked image. The signature or location can be selected differently for different images so as to easily identify in case of copyright violation.This is considered to be invisible watermarking as the change in the image is very small and is not noticeable for regular and large sized images.

The procedure for proposed second watermarking for double authentication is illustrated in Fig. 2. In that, the input image is taken and then the size of the image is obtained. From the size, the number of bits needed to express the rows and columns are attained. Using that, suitable signature value is acquired and this value is applied to the bit at the location that is specified by the signature to the average of the neighboring pixel values of the location. The results obtained for the proposed invisible watermarking technique is given in Fig. 3. From this obtained results, it is proven that the quality of the acquired watermarked image is not degraded.

## 3.1   Extraction of Watermarking

For extracting the watermark, the input (i.e., watermarked image) is given, and the watermarking embedding procedures are symmetrical to the extraction process.

Step 1: Compute the set of secret seeds $X'$, $Y'$ from Eqs. (5) and (6).
Step 2: Compute the positions $(U_{x'}, U_{y'})$ from Eqs. (7) and (8).

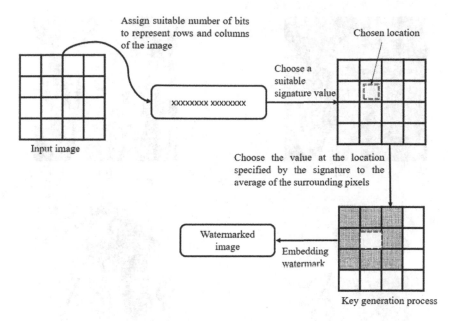

**Fig. 2.** Block schematic of proposed watermarking

Step 3: From that, the number of digits needed to obtain the watermark is found and then the neighboring pixels are taken to find the sum. The extracted sum is compared with the cover image and if both are same then the original image is not tampered from the attacker. The image of size $256 \times 256$ is taken for the simulation, assume that the pixel at the $4^{th}$ row and $4^{th}$ column has been chosen for obtaining the watermark. Hence, in this case, the signature is 00000100 00000100. From this, the second watermark for double authentication is extracted then using hash function, the inserted bits (i.e., first inserted watermark) are retrieved from following steps.

Step 4: The positions used for embedding the first watermark is computed using Eqs. (9) and (10).

Step 5: Extract the bits of the watermark using the positions. Similarly, compute the next positions $U_{x'}$, $U_{y'}$ using Eqs. (11) and (12).

Step 6: To extract all watermarks, steps 3 and 4 are repeated.

## 4   Performance Analysis

The quality metrics are used for checking the imperceptibility of the suggested technique is explained clearly in this section.

### 4.1   Quality Assessment Test for Watermarked Image

The recommended watermarking approach is tested using different test images and from the obtained results it is shown that the image visual quality is still

**Fig. 3.** Results for proposed watermarking process (a–b) Cover image (c–d) Water-marked image

maintained. The quality change before and after watermark cannot be perceived by the human eye. For evaluating invisibility of watermark and robustness, two performance metrics are utilized (i) Peak Signal-to Noise ratio *(PSNR)* (ii) Root Mean Square Error *(RMSE)*. These two metrics are defined as follows:

Using RMSE, the original image $I$ and watermarked $In$ is compared and this is expressed as,

$$RMSE = \frac{1}{\sqrt{m'n'}} \sum_{\overline{ii}=0}^{m'-1} \sum_{\overline{jj}=0}^{n'-1} \left\| I(\overline{ii},\overline{jj}) - In(\overline{ii},\overline{jj}) \right\|^2 \tag{14}$$

The ratio among the $I(E_{maxi})$ maximum possible energy and the potential (power) of the corrupted image $In$ from watermarking is known as PSNR. The mathematical formulation is as follows:

$$PSNR = 20 \log_{10} \frac{E_{maxi}}{RMSE} \tag{15}$$

RMSE values for different sample images are provided in Table 1. From this , PSNR is computed and this is given Table 1. From Table 1, it is inferred that the PSNR value is above 42 dB for all samples which insists that the suggested method is having high quality of watermarked image.

The superiority of the suggested approach is compared with the existing watermarking approaches provided in [1,7,9,21,25]. The listed approaches in Table 2 possess the potential to restore the original image without any loss of information. Moreover, the suggested approach acquired an average PSNR which is superior than other approaches provided in Table 2 except [7]. The approach provided in [7] has high PSNR compared with the proposed one but the same hash function is used which needs further improvement. Moreover, this method is utilized for identifying the tampered blocks instead of finding the tampered pixel. In [1], embedding code for authentication is done without considering the high number of blocks in an image as this approach is utilized for histogram-shifting design. The embedding values for authentication is done for random locations on images which preserves the watermarked images with high quality.

Table 1. RMSE and PSNR values for different test images

| S. no | Images | RMSE | PSNR |
|---|---|---|---|
| 1 | Lena | 0.81 | 49.96 |
| 2 | Cameraman | 0.94 | 48.66 |
| 3 | Couple | 0.86 | 49.44 |
| 4 | Zelda | 0.89 | 49.14 |
| 5 | Clown | 0.98 | 48.57 |
| 6 | Boat | 1.07 | 47.54 |
| 7 | Clock | 1.15 | 46.91 |
| 8 | House | 1.29 | 45.91 |
| 9 | Aerial | 1.39 | 45.27 |
| 10 | Male | 1.51 | 44.55 |

Table 2. Performance comparison of suggested approach using PSNR (dB) with other watermarking approaches

| S. no | Watermarking approaches | PSNR |
|---|---|---|
| 1 | Ref. [1] | 48.826 |
| 2 | Ref. [25] | 40.72 |
| 3 | Ref. [9] | 34.9 |
| 4 | Ref. [21] | 39.31 |
| 5 | Ref. [7] | 57.196 |
| 6 | Suggested approach | 49.96 |

## 4.2  Structural Similarity Measure (SSim)

For evaluating the resemblance among pair of images, SSim metric is utilized. The SSim index provides a complete associated metric; in other words, it is an image quality measurement dependent on distortion-free image as a reference. On different windows of an image, the SSim metric is measured. Two windows $x'$ and $y'$ of general size $M \times N$ are calculated as

$$SSim = \frac{(2\mu_{x'}\mu_{y'} + c_1')(2\sigma_{x'y'} + c_2')}{(\mu_{x'}^2 + \mu_{y'}^2 + c_1')\sigma_{x'}^2\sigma_{y'}^2 + c_2')} \tag{16}$$

where, $\mu_{x'}$, $\mu_{y'}$ are the average of $x'$ and $y'$ respectively;
$\sigma_{x'}^2$, $\sigma_{y'}^2$ are the variance of $x'$ and $y'$ respectively;
$\sigma_{x'y'}$ is the covariance of $x'$ and $x'$
$c_1' = (k_1'Li)^2$, $c_2' = (k_2'Li)^2$, $Li$ is the dynamic length (range) of the pixel-values and $k_1' = 0.01$, $k_2' = 0.03$. The corresponding SSim index represents a decimal value of $-1$ to $1$, and value close to $1$ can be reached only for two similar data sets and for this it is referred as perfect structural similarity. From Table 3, it is seen that the SSIM values are almost nearer to 1. It indicates that the proposed invisible watermarking attains high robustness.

**Table 3.** SSim values for different test images

| S. no | Images | SSim value |
|-------|--------|------------|
| 1 | Lena | 0.8432 |
| 2 | Cameraman | 0.7346 |
| 3 | Couple | 0.8256 |
| 4 | Zelda | 0.8513 |
| 5 | Clown | 0.7772 |
| 6 | Boat | 0.8722 |
| 7 | Clock | 0.8457 |
| 8 | House | 0.7662 |
| 9 | Aerial | 0.7952 |
| 10 | Male | 0.8331 |

## 5  Conclusion

An efficient technique is proposed for double authentication of image content based on one way hash function and signature value. Using private key, 512 bits are randomly inserted in to the original image and the positions are defined from

Rabin cryptosystem (Pseudo random number is generated). After this, for double authentication, a single pixel value is modified in the same location and this signature value is generated from the neighbouring pixels. Using this location, the signature is generated and this is enclosed into the original image itself. The ability to detect this location by unauthorized users is very difficult. Uncovering the watermark is done by user defined column and row indices. Watermark is inserted into the same row and column index but not the least significant digits. Experimental outcomes show that watermarked image has acquired a good visual quality, using the proposed method.

# References

1. A reversible image authentication scheme based on fragile watermarking in discrete wavelet transform domain. AEU - Int. J. Electron. Commun. **70**(8), 1055–1061 (2016)
2. Abdelhakim, A., Saleh, H.I., Abdelhakim, M.: Fragile watermarking for image tamper detection and localization with effective recovery capability using k-means clustering. Multimed. Tools Appl. **78**(22), 32523–32563 (2019). https://doi.org/10.1007/s11042-019-07986-3
3. Abdulrahman, A.K., Ozturk, S.: A novel hybrid DCT and DWT based robust watermarking algorithm for color images. Multimed. Tools Appl. **78**(12), 17027–17049 (2019). https://doi.org/10.1007/s11042-018-7085-z
4. Ali, M., Ahn, C.W., Pant, M.: An efficient lossless robust watermarking scheme by integrating redistributed invariant wavelet and fractional fourier transforms. Multimed. Tools Appl. **77**(10), 11751–11773 (2018). https://doi.org/10.1007/s11042-017-4815-6
5. Ali, S.A., Jawad, M.J., Naser, M.A.: A semi-fragile watermarking based image authentication. J. Eng. Appl. Sci. **12**(6), 1582–1589 (2017)
6. Cox, I.J., Miller, M.L., Bloom, J.A.: Watermarking applications and their properties. In: Proceedings of the International Conference on Information Technology: Coding and Computing, pp. 6–10. IEEE (2000)
7. Gul, E., Ozturk, S.: A novel hash function based fragile watermarking method for image integrity. Multimed. Tools Appl. **78**(13), 17701–17718 (2019). https://doi.org/10.1007/s11042-018-7084-0
8. Hsu, C.T., Wu, J.L.: Hidden digital watermarks in images. IEEE Trans. Image Process. **8**(1), 58–68 (1999)
9. Li, C., Zhang, A., Liu, Z., Liao, L., Huang, D.: Semi-fragile self-recoverable watermarking algorithm based on wavelet group quantization and double authentication. Multimed. Tools Appl. **74**(23), 10581–10604 (2014). https://doi.org/10.1007/s11042-014-2188-7
10. Lu, C.S., Liao, H.Y.: Structural digital signature for image authentication: an incidental distortion resistant scheme. IEEE Trans. Multimed. **5**(2), 161–173 (2003)
11. Merkle, R.C.: One way hash functions and DES. In: Brassard, G. (ed.) CRYPTO 1989. LNCS, vol. 435, pp. 428–446. Springer, New York (1990). https://doi.org/10.1007/0-387-34805-0_40
12. Moosazadeh, M., Ekbatanifard, G.: A new DCT-based robust image watermarking method using teaching-learning-based optimization. J. Inf. Secur. Appl. **47**, 28–38 (2019)

13. Nazari, M., Sharif, A., Mollaeefar, M.: An improved method for digital image fragile watermarking based on chaotic maps. Multimed. Tools Appl. **76**(15), 16107–16123 (2016). https://doi.org/10.1007/s11042-016-3897-x

14. Nguyen, T.S., Chang, C.C., Yang, X.Q.: A reversible image authentication scheme based on fragile watermarking in discrete wavelet transform domain. AEU-Int. J. Electron. Commun. **70**(8), 1055–1061 (2016)

15. Parekh, M., Bidani, S., Santhi, V.: Spatial domain blind watermarking for digital images. In: Pattnaik, P.K., Rautaray, S.S., Das, H., Nayak, J. (eds.) Progress in Computing, Analytics and Networking. AISC, vol. 710, pp. 519–527. Springer, Singapore (2018). https://doi.org/10.1007/978-981-10-7871-2_50

16. Patel, H.A., Divecha, N.H.: A feature-based semi-fragile watermarking algorithm for digital color image authentication using hybrid transform. In: Bhatia, S.K., Mishra, K.K., Tiwari, S., Singh, V.K. (eds.) Advances in Computer and Computational Sciences. AISC, vol. 554, pp. 455–465. Springer, Singapore (2018). https://doi.org/10.1007/978-981-10-3773-3_44

17. Qianli, Y., Yanhong, C.: A digital image watermarking algorithm based on discrete wavelet transform and discrete cosine transform. In: 2012 International Symposium on Information Technology in Medicine and Education (ITME), vol. 2, pp. 1102–1105. IEEE (2012)

18. Qin, C., Ji, P., Wang, J., Chang, C.C.: Fragile image watermarking scheme based on VQ index sharing and self-embedding. Multimed. Tools Appl. **76**(2), 2267–2287 (2017). https://doi.org/10.1007/s11042-015-3218-9

19. Qin, C., Wang, H., Zhang, X., Sun, X.: Self-embedding fragile watermarking based on reference-data interleaving and adaptive selection of embedding mode. Inf. Sci. **373**, 233–250 (2016)

20. Singh, A.K.: Improved hybrid algorithm for robust and imperceptible multiple watermarking using digital images. Multimed. Tools Appl. **76**(6), 8881–8900 (2016). https://doi.org/10.1007/s11042-016-3514-z

21. Singh, D., Singh, S.K.: DCT based efficient fragile watermarking scheme for image authentication and restoration. Multimed. Tools Appl. **76**(1), 953–977 (2017). https://doi.org/10.1007/s11042-015-3010-x

22. Sreenivas, K., Kamkshi Prasad, V.: Fragile watermarking schemes for image authentication: a survey. Int. J. Mach. Learn. Cybern. **9**(7), 1193–1218 (2017). https://doi.org/10.1007/s13042-017-0641-4

23. Verma, V.S., Jha, R.K., Ojha, A.: Significant region based robust watermarking scheme in lifting wavelet transform domain. Expert Syst. Appl. **42**(21), 8184–8197 (2015)

24. Wu, X., Li, J., Tu, R., Cheng, J., Bhatti, U.A., Ma, J.: Contourlet-DCT based multiple robust watermarkings for medical images. Multimed. Tools Appl. **78**(7), 8463–8480 (2019). https://doi.org/10.1007/s11042-018-6877-5

25. Yang, C.W., Shen, J.J.: Recover the tampered image based on VQ indexing. Sig. Process. **90**(1), 331–343 (2010)

# Remote Sensing Signature Classification of Agriculture Detection Using Deep Convolution Network Models

G. Rohith$^{(\boxtimes)}$ ⓘ and Lakshmi Sutha Kumar ⓘ

Department of Electronics and Communication Engineering,
National Institute of Technology-Puducherry,
Karaikal, Puducherry 609609, India
rohith.giridharan@gmail.com, lakshmi@nitpy.ac.in

**Abstract.** Categorical signature classification plays a vital role in environmental monitoring, disaster response, etc. In view of Geographical expansions, manual identification of the object is time consuming and task of classification is difficult owing to limited trained images. Conventional categorical signature classification using Machine learning techniques requires higher level of abstract features. Deep learning is a successful technique that is widely used in extracting minute level multiple features of the object representation for automatic learning of the data representation. In this paper, performance analysis of the state of the art eight pre trained Convolutional Neural Networks (CNN) networks (Alexnet, Resnet34, Resnet 50, Resnet-101 Resnet-152, VGG-16, VGG-19 and Densenet-121) are tested for the benchmarked datasets (UC Merced and EUROSAT Datasets). Common signature between the datasets like Agriculture, Residential, River and salt lake is considered with the objective of search of the agriculture in an area composed of residential, river and lake. It is concluded from the results that the use of more number of images to train for the search of particular dataset and the use of shallow CNN network increase the accuracy, precision, recall and F-Score, closer to unity (one). Densenet-121 performs better when compared to other CNN networks for both the datasets with an accuracy of 99.67% (EUROSAT) and 97.05% (UC Merced) respectively. Hence, Densenet-121 is recommended for the search of the particular object in a remote sensed scene and classification into respective labels.

**Keywords:** Categorical signature · Convolution Neural Networks (CNN) · Densenet-121 · Remote sensed image

## 1 Introduction

Remote sensing signature classification is a prominent technique of feature exploitation with application in the agriculture identification, urban management, identification of target, thematic information etc. Signature classification is the process of the classifying the remote sensed images into different classes in supervised or unsupervised manner. It segregates the image into different classes based on set of semantic intra class variability and low interclass distance between the labels [1]. In general, the task of

© Springer Nature Singapore Pte Ltd. 2020
A. Bhattacharjee et al. (Eds.): MIND 2020, CCIS 1240, pp. 343–355, 2020.
https://doi.org/10.1007/978-981-15-6315-7_28

classifying the image into different classes is attributed by abstraction, pixels, objects and scene with global or local features like color, texture and shape features for categorizing the image into the respective class labels [2]. Traditional methods of classification like K Means, Maximum likelihood are based on spectral characteristics with low accuracy [3]. These methods were overcome by introducing geometric information with Machine Learning (ML) algorithms like Support Vector Machine, Random Forest and Neural Networks yielding higher accuracy [3]. However, ML methods extract global or local features like color, texture and shape features which are difficult to categorize into the respective class labels [4]. Inspired from ML, Deep Learning (DL) aims to construct a multilevel neural network that extracts feature from each neuron layer, with set up complex mapping relations between low level features and high-level semantics [4]. Deep learning model attempts to learn minute features with high level of abstraction [5]. The attempt of finding the minute difference in features for categorical classification requires CNN activated high level representation, well annotated remote sensing dataset, deep CNN model and limited dataset [6]. But practically, with limited remote sensing trained dataset fed to the deep CNN, it is difficult to arrive at prominent solution in classifying the remote sensed scenes with high accuracy [7]. Contrary to this; a deeper architecture trained by large scale dataset may lead to more hypotheses for remote sensing classifications [7]. A balance between a deep CNN networks with limited trained dataset will correctly classify the remote sensed image into respective annotations with high accuracy in less time consumption. The Deep CNN dominated for past two decades owing to the aid of the Graphical Processing Units (GPU) for the extraction of salient edges and borders [8]. In order to effectively run the CNN network, the characteristics based on architectures like Spatial Exploitation, depth, multipath, width, feature map and channel exploitation have to be conditioned properly. Although recent techniques like Auto Encoders (AE), Generative adversarial Networks(GAN) have been successful in the remote sensing classification for large dataset, the pre trained CNN models renders less training consumption with greater accuracy and almost negligible losses for emergent applications using real time images [3].

With this as base, this study analyses the different state of the art CNN deep learning models which categorizes unknown remote sensing images with two different datasets UC Merced (400 samples without categorical labels) and Eurosat database (10935 samples with categorical labels) with different imaging conditions (Image orientation and spatial resolution). The purpose of this study is to effectively classify the agricultural region in the urban and semi urban area. The performances of Alexnet and VGG (better in Spatial Exploitation), Resnet and Densenet (Depth and Multipath based CNN) are analysed for remote sensing applications. The reason for particularly choosing these categories is that remote sensing applications require spatial exploitation and depth while extracting essential feature objects in the image. Eight Pretrained networks Alexnet [8], Resnet34 [9], Resnet 50 [9], Resnet-101 [9], Resnet-152 [9], VGG-16 [10], VGG-19 [10] and Densenet-121 [11] are tested for the dataset mentioned in Sect. 2. The results in terms of accuracy, precision, recall and F-Score are quantified and the closer accuracy to unity is recorded for superior performance of the CNN architectures.

The paper is organized as follows: Sect. 2 concentrates on the satellite data considered for testing performance analysis. Section 3 concentrates on the networks that are considered for the performance evaluation. The result of the analysis is presented in Sect. 4 and conclusion is provided in Sect. 5.

## 2 Satellite Data

Two state of the art databases, UC Merced Landuse dataset and Eurosat Dataset, are used for testing. The reason for choosing particularly these datasets are (i) Both the datasets comes under the category of landuse with the common signatures like Agriculture, Residential, River and Salt Lake. These signatures are considered for the scarch of agriculture area in a given remote sensed image by training the other signatures, (ii) UC Merced has no labeled categories whereas the Eurosat has labeled categories, (iii) UC Merced dataset is captured at predefined zoomed region of interest whereas the Eurosat Dataset does not have zoomed region of interest. This analysis will give insight to the network model that trains the signature and save time in search of the particular object.

UC Merced dataset is taken from [12] that composed of 2100 overhead scene with 21 land use scene classes. Figure 1 shows the sample of UC Merced dataset. It is seen that the dense depth of extracting the features renders better precision and accuracy as the images are zoomed at 150% level. This is because each class consists of 100 aerial images with spatial resolution of 0.3 m per pixel in RGB color space measuring 256 * 256 pixels which renders better search object without any label. Moreover, the visibility of the features/objects is seen clearly without further zooming of the region of interest.

|  a)Agriculture | b) Residential | c) River | d) Salt Lake |

**Fig. 1.** Sample signatures from the UC Merced Dataset

Eurosat dataset [13] consist of 27000 geo referenced and labeled images with 10 different land use and land cover classes. Each class consists of more than 2000 aerial images with spatial resolution of 10 m per pixel in RGB color space measuring 64 * 64 pixels. Both datasets are having different spatial resolution and large number of training samples per class and provide large training samples for a pre trained model which improves accuracy of the classification. Therefore, they are selected in this paper for the analysis. Figure 2 shows the sample signatures from the Eurosat dataset. For training the network model, two parameters define the testing of similarity features of training and test data. One is the training samples which are used to fit the model with appropriate bias and weight. Training data contains the input data with annotated labels and techniques which improves the accuracy with prediction through learning. Second is the testing sample. Testing is an unbiased evaluation of the model that fits the training dataset while tuning hyper parameters of the network. The difference between the training and testing is training informs the model to make decisions, while the testing will give information on the classifier performance.

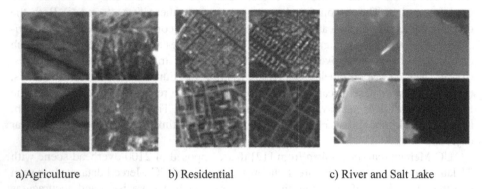

a)Agriculture                    b) Residential                    c) River and Salt Lake

**Fig. 2.** Sample signatures from the EUROSAT Dataset

Training Data output will be available to the model whereas predictions have to be made to the testing data. In general, training sample will be larger than test data. However, this is attributed by the level of the zooming of region of interest, clarity in the feature representation, spatial resolution from which the data is being captured and image patch size.

**Table 1.** Details on the number of samples considered for testing and training the network

| Signature | UC Merced Dataset | | | EUROSAT Dataset | | |
|---|---|---|---|---|---|---|
| | Trained samples | Tested samples | Total number of samples | Trained samples | Tested samples | Total number of samples |
| Agriculture | 80 | 20 | 100 | 1944 | 486 | 2430 |
| Residential | 68 | 17 | 85 | 2412 | 603 | 3015 |
| River | 84 | 21 | 105 | 2140 | 535 | 2675 |
| Beach/Salt Lake | 88 | 22 | 110 | 2252 | 563 | 2815 |
| Total | 320 | 80 | 400 | 8748 | 2187 | 10935 |

The variations in the training and testing samples can be customized based on the need and has a significant impact on the accuracy. In general, the more the training dataset and less the testing dataset would define possible patterns for the classification problem with accuracy in modeling domain. It is seen from the Table 1 that the training dataset is more as compared to the testing for both the datasets. Conventionally, Training - Testing ratios 60:40, 70:30, 80:20, 90:10 are used. For this experiment, it is inferred that 80:20 (Pareto principle) renders better accuracy. This ratio is decided based on the two facts - Firstly, the quantum of dataset-UC Merced and Eurosat. Second is the problem statement - Search Automation of particular remote sensed scene. The datasets considered for the experiment has the small dataset samples (UC Merced Dataset-400 samples) measuring 256 * 256 pixel image patches of clear zoomed visual representation without any categorical labels and a large dataset samples (EUROSAT dataset-10,935 samples) uses categorical labels are included in its datasets measuring 64 * 64 pixel image patches without zooming of region of interest. It is also found from the literatures that this ratio has the potential to describe the accurate number of points to be represented in feature space for defining object patterns which is essential for any remote sensed scene classification. Hence, 80:20 ratio of the samples is considered for testing and training the samples which is shown in Table 1. The tradeoff between the small and large dataset with proportion variation in training and testing of this 4 class problem helps to decide the appropriate network for automating the search of particular remote sensing object with accuracy.

## 3   Related Works - CNN Architectures

The technological advancement with high performance computing resources is the key success of Deep CNN over shallow and conventional vision based models. The utility of the Convolutional operation in neural networks extracts both low and high level of features to generic recognition task by exploiting the concept of Transfer Learning. Deep CNN have showed potential to learn useful representation from a spectrum of unlabeled data. CNN uses multiple mapping functions to extract the invariant representations and recognition tasks of large categories of data.

First ever, CNN architecture exploiting the depth at multiple levels of transformation with regularization term and parameter optimization strategies is Alexnet [6]. Alexnet works on two NVIDIA GTX 580 GPUs to overcome the hardware requirements. Figure 3.a shows the basic block diagram of the Alexnet. Alexnet uses 8 layers with five convolution layers and three fully connected layers. This architecture overcomes over fitting problems by data augmentation and drop out. The automation for the object scene detection and classification is achieved using this network. Inspired by the alexnet, VGG [8] network is used as effective receptive field by utilizing small filter size for feature visualization. The two variants of the network VGG-16 (Fig. 3.b) and VGG-19 (Fig. 3.f) indicates the weight layers (16 and 19) in the network. The VGG network convergence pretraining the smaller networks initialized for larger and deeper networks. Although this network finds itself prominent for the object search, the time taken for pretraining is more with large updation of weights for the network architecture. Similar to VGG variants, feature visualisation through larger depth and introduction of skip connection was visible in Resnet. The variants of the weight updation are Resnet 34, 50, 101 and 152. The Resnet uses micro architecture module (network in network) which is visible from Fig. 3 (c–e). ResNet showed 20 and 8 times

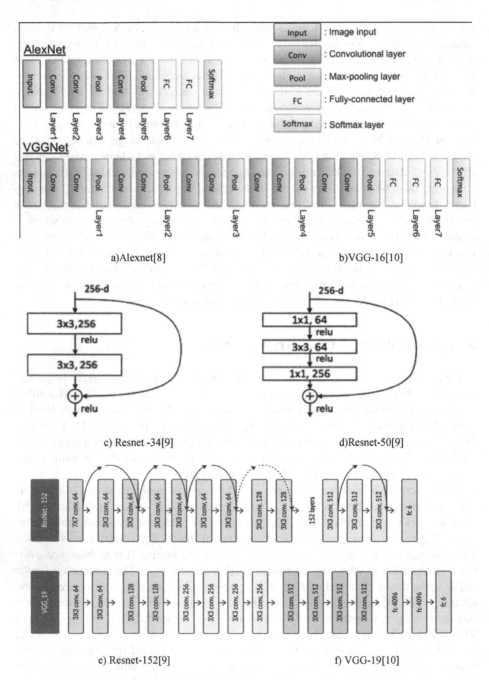

a)Alexnet[8]

b)VGG-16[10]

c) Resnet -34[9]

d)Resnet-50[9]

e) Resnet-152[9]

f) VGG-19[10]

**Fig. 3.** Pretrained CNN architectural models considered in this paper

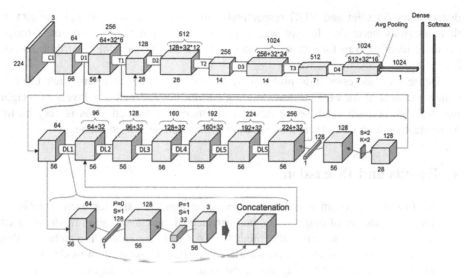

g) Densenet 121[11]

**Fig. 3.** (*continued*)

**Table 2.** Summary on the Existing Architecture categories and descriptions used in this paper

| Architecture | Contribution | Parameter | Error rate | Depth | Lacunae |
|---|---|---|---|---|---|
| Alexnet (2012) | Deeper and wider CNN tested in GPUs NVIDIA GTX 580 **Advantage:** Introduction of regularization concept in CNN | 60M | UC Merced: 5.49 WhuRS: 5.43 Brazzilian coffee: 14.86 ImageNet: 16.4 | 8 | Aliasing artifact in learned feature map due to large filter size |
| VGG (2014) | Utility of Small kernel for deeper structure **Advantage:** Homogenous topology with effective receptive field | 138M | UC Merced: 5.47 WhuRS: 5.33 Brazzilian coffee: 15.88 ImageNet: 11.7 | 19 | Complex fully connected layers |
| ResNet (2015) | Residual learning with Identity map based skip connection **Advantage:** Decreased error rate for deeper network owing to residual learning and vanishing gradient problem | 6.8M 1.7M | UC Merced: 25.86 WhuRS: 5.33 Brazzilian coffee: 15.88 ImageNet: 3.6 CIFAR-10: 6.43 | 152 110 | Degrades information in feature map in feed forwarding Conditioning of hyper parameters is required |
| Densenet (2018) | Cross layer information flow with deeper feature extraction **Advantage:** Depth ensures maximum data flow between the layers and avoids relearning redundant feature maps | 25.6M 25.6M 15.3M 15.3M | CIFAR-10:3.46 CIFAR-100-17.18 CIFAR-10-5.19 CIFAR-100:19.64 | 190 190 250 250 | Increased number of feature map at each layers |
| In this paper | Alexnet, Resnet34, Resnet 50, Resnet-152, VGG-16, VGG-19 and Densenet-121 are tested for the state of the art database **Advantage:** Tradeoff between the labeled and Nonlabeled categories is analyzed. More number of labeled categories will improve the accuracy | 60M 138M 6.8M 1.7M 15.3M | UC Merced-1.07 (Average) Eurosat-0.95 (Average) | 8 19 152 190 250 | Tradeoff between labeled categories and non-labeled on the accuracy |

deeper than AlexNet and VGG respectively, showed less computational complexity than previous networks. Resnet was explicitly preserving the information through additive identity transformation as many of the layers do not contribute much information.

Dense Net addressed this problem by utilizing cross layer where each layer is connected in feed forward fashion (Fig. 3.g). Densenet-121 has 121 layers of weight updation where each small set of new feature maps are learned. This is very useful while dealing with categorical classification of the remote sensed scenes.

## 4  Results and Discussion

A classification algorithm is one that takes some input set and for each member, it classifies the fixed set of outputs. The performance of the classification model on a set of test data depends on the true value prediction. A Confusion matrix is a technique that summarizes the performance of classification algorithm. Classification model gives the correct classification by breaking down the count values into respective labels with types of errors. The outcome of confusion matrix is the number of correct predictions for each class (Actual class) and number of incorrect predictions for each class (Predicted class).

Between the actual and predicted class, four parameters that discriminate between the observations with specific outcome from normal observations are "True Positive (TP)" for correctly predicted event values, "False Positive (FP)" for incorrectly predicted event values, "True Negative (TN)" for correctly predicted no-event values and "False Negative (FN)" for incorrectly predicted no-event values. The diagonal of the confusion matrix is the correctly predicted TP values of respective categories.

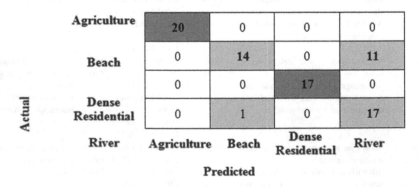

**Fig. 4.** A sample confusion matrix for Alexnet for UC Merced Dataset

Figure 4 shows the sample confusion matrix for the Alexnet network of UC Merced data. It is seen that correctly predicted classes are Agriculture, dense residential area. Since there is similarity in the features between the river and beach, there was a 1 sample count contributed towards beach while seeing the river which is negligible. The confusion matrix is plotted for all datasets and networks and results are summarized in Table 3.

**Table 3.** Summary on the Quantitative analysis of Deep CNN networks

| Model and signature | | UC Merced Dataset | | | | EUROSAT Dataset | | | |
|---|---|---|---|---|---|---|---|---|---|
| Pretrained model | Signature | Precision | Recall | F₁ Score | Accuracy | Precision | Recall | F₁ Score | Accuracy |
| Alexnet | Agriculture | 1 | 1 | 1 | 1 | 0.93 | 1 | 0.93 | 0.95 |
| | Residential | 0.912 | 1 | 0.9539 | 0.912 | 1 | 1 | 1 | 1 |
| | River | 1 | 1 | 1 | 1 | 1 | 1 | 1 | 1 |
| | Salt Lake | 0.9444 | 1 | 0.9714 | 0.9444 | 0.93 | 1 | 0.9186 | 0.92 |
| | **Average** | **0.9641** | **1** | **0.9813** | **0.9641** | **0.965** | **1** | **0.9621** | **0.9675** |
| Resnet 34 | Agriculture | 0.8421 | 1 | 0.9142 | 0.8421 | 0.9634 | 1 | 0.9674 | 0.9537 |
| | Residential | 1 | 1 | 1 | 1 | 0.9766 | 1 | 0.8966 | 1 |
| | River | 1 | 1 | 1 | 1 | 0.9962 | 1 | 0.8971 | 1 |
| | Salt Lake | 0.9047 | 1 | 0.95 | 0.9047 | 1 | 1 | 0.8871 | 0.9886 |
| | **Average** | **0.9367** | **1** | **0.9660** | **0.9367** | **0.9840** | **1** | **0.9120** | **0.9855** |
| Resnet 50 | Agriculture | 0.8888 | 1 | 0.9411 | 0.8888 | 0.9854 | 1 | 0.9874 | 0.9753 |
| | Residential | 0.9473 | 1 | 0.9729 | 0.95 | 0.9966 | 1 | 0.9966 | 0.9933 |
| | River | 1 | 1 | 1 | 1 | 0.9962 | 1 | 0.9971 | 0.9869 |
| | Salt Lake | 1 | 1 | 1 | 1 | 0.9786 | 1 | 0.9871 | 0.9786 |
| | **Average** | **0.9590** | **1** | **0.9785** | **0.9597** | **0.9892** | **1** | **0.9925** | **0.9835** |
| Resnet 101 | Agriculture | 0.85 | 1 | 0.9189 | 0.85 | 1 | 1 | 1 | 1 |
| | Residential | 1 | 1 | 1 | 1 | 1 | 1 | 1 | 1 |
| | River | 1 | 1 | 1 | 1 | 1 | 1 | 1 | 1 |
| | Salt Lake | 0.6111 | 1 | 0.7586 | 0.6111 | 0.95 | 1 | 0.9494 | 0.9095 |
| | **Average** | **0.8652** | **1** | **0.9193** | **0.8652** | **0.9875** | **1** | **0.9873** | **0.9773** |
| Resnet 152 | Agriculture | 0.95 | 1 | 0.9743 | 0.95 | 1 | 1 | 1 | 1 |
| | Residential | 0.96 | 1 | 0.9795 | 0.96 | 1 | 1 | 0.9539 | 0.912 |
| | River | 1 | 1 | 1 | 1 | 1 | 1 | 1 | 1 |
| | Salt Lake | 0.9444 | 1 | 0.9714 | 0.9444 | 0.9444 | 1 | 0.9714 | 0.9444 |
| | **Average** | **0.9636** | **1** | **0.9813** | **0.9636** | **0.9861** | **1** | **0.9813** | **0.9641** |
| VGG-16 | Agriculture | 1 | 1 | 1 | 1 | 1 | 1 | 1 | 1 |
| | Residential | 1 | 1 | 1 | 1 | 1 | 1 | 1 | 1 |
| | River | 1 | 1 | 1 | 1 | 1 | 1 | 1 | 1 |
| | Salt Lake | 0.8095 | 1 | 0.8947 | 0.8095 | 0.96 | 1 | 0.987 | 0.9823 |
| | **Average** | **0.9523** | **1** | **0.9736** | **0.9523** | **0.99** | **1** | **0.9967** | **0.9955** |
| VGG-19 | Agriculture | 0.9473 | 1 | 0.9729 | 0.9473 | 1 | 1 | 1 | 1 |
| | Residential | 0.95 | 1 | 0.9743 | 0.95 | 0.9966 | 1 | 1 | 1 |
| | River | 1 | 1 | 1 | 1 | 1 | 1 | 1 | 1 |
| | Salt Lake | 0.6923 | 0.6923 | 0.6923 | 0.68 | 0.9786 | 1 | 0.9871 | 1 |
| | **Average** | **0.8974** | **0.9230** | **0.9098** | **0.8943** | **0.9938** | **1** | **0.9967** | **1** |
| Densenet-121 | Agriculture | 1 | 1 | 1 | 1 | 1 | 1 | 1 | 1 |
| | Residential | 1 | 1 | 1 | 1 | 1 | 1 | 0.9966 | 1 |
| | River | 1 | 1 | 1 | 1 | 1 | 1 | 1 | 1 |
| | Salt Lake | 0.883 | 1 | 0.935 | 0.88 | 0.97 | 1 | 0.99 | 0.98 |
| | **Average** | **0.9705** | **1** | **0.9843** | **0.9705** | **0.9946** | **1** | **0.9984** | **0.9967** |

The metrics that define correct classification of the respective labels are Precision, Recall, Accuracy and $F_1$ Score.

i) **Precision** - Measure of correctly identified positive cases from all the predicted positive cases.

$$precision = \frac{TP}{(TP+FP)} \tag{1}$$

ii) **Recall** - Measure of correctly identified positive cases from all the actual positive cases

$$Recall = \frac{TP}{(TP+FN)} \tag{2}$$

iii) **Accuracy** - Measure of correctly identified cases

$$Accuracy = \frac{(TP+TN)}{(TP+FP+TN+FN)} \tag{3}$$

iv) **$F_1$ Score** - Harmonic mean of precision and recall gives the measure of incorrectly classified cases than the Accuracy metric.

$$F_1 Score = 2 * \frac{(\text{Pr } ecision * \text{Re} call)}{(\text{Pr } ecision + \text{Re} call)} \tag{4}$$

Table 3 shows the summary of metrics calculated for eight deep CNN networks versus the datasets (UC Merced and Eurosat Dataset). On average, the Precision difference (%) between UC Merced and Eurosat dataset starting from Alexnet, Resnet-34, Resnet-50, Resnet-101, Resnet-152, VGG-16 and VGG-19 for UC Merced data and Densenet-121 are 0.09, 5.12, 3.14, 14.13, 2.34, 3.95, 10.72 and 2.84 respectively. It is clear from results that network is robust enough to identify the positive cases from all the predicted positive cases correctly, irrespective of the dataset complexity. On average, the recall difference (%) between UC Merced and Eurosat dataset for the above mentioned networks is nil which shows the correct identification of positive cases from all the actual positive cases. This shows that irrespective of the dataset, the deep CNN network is able to categorize the remote sensed scenes into respective labels. This shows the robustness of the network. On average, the accuracy difference (%) between UC Merced and Eurosat dataset for the above mentioned networks are 1.95, 5.20, 2.47, 12.95, 2.24, 11.81, 10.57 and 2.59 which shows the measure of correctly identified cases. This shows the effectiveness of the network model susceptible to the dataset. It is also seen for precision difference percentage and accuracy difference percentage is large for Resnet 152 and VGG-19. This is because these networks are able to classify the labels accurately. If there is more number of trained labeled data, the classification accuracy is higher. On average, the $F_1$ score difference (%) between UC Merced and Eurosat dataset for the above mentioned networks are

1.93, 8.43, 1.41, 7.42, 0, 2.37, 9.55 and 1.43 which shows the harmonic incorrectly classified cases than the Accuracy metric. This reflects on requirement of clear definition of the image patch labeling. On average for all the cases irrespective of the dataset, Densenet-121 outperforms others in all the metrics.

To show the conformity of the state of the art model with latest emergent technique, Densenet-121 is tested with the database mentioned in [14]. The method in [14] was proposed for crowd detection of drone safe landing. Although, there is dissimilarity in the objectives between [14] and this paper, the attempt of testing the performance of nine layer designed CNN model for real time images as compared to pre trained model (Densenet-121) is performed. This attempt will render insight on designing an efficient CNN model for particular application superseding the performance of pre trained models. Table 4 shows the testing of the state of the art model with latest drone based application.

**Table 4.** Comparison of obtained results with works in the literature using databases [11, 12, 14]

| Model | Database | Accuracy |
|---|---|---|
| CNN model for crowd detection [14] | [14] | 86.80% |
| | UC Merced [11] | 89.20% |
| | Eurosat Dataset [12] | 93.90% |
| Densenet-121 | [14] | 96.22% |

The database in [14] is simulated with the model in [14] and compared with densenet-121. It is found from the Table 4 that there is improvement in the accuracy for the nine layer CNN model for UC Merced and Eurosat Dataset by 3.5% and 8.19% respectively as compared to nine layer CNN model. This is due to the fact that the images in the training data [14] are having noisy and irrelevant patterns in the training data [14]. Since UC Merced and Eurosat have enough dataset to define the patterns, there is improvement in their performance. Similarly, the Densenet-121 is tested with database given in [14]. It is seen that there is improvement of 9.79% for Densenet 121 as compared the CNN model in [14]. This is due to the fact that the input image is parsed through 121 layers of CNN layers in dense network that rendered fine details of feature for classifying to respective labels. Designing an appropriate dense layer with more depth would improve the accuracy to greater extent. Hence, it is concluded that Dense networks with more number of depth penetrating layers is recommended where real time applications are prevailing and if new network has to be designed, the network should be robust enough to extract minute details without any loss.

# 5 Conclusion

In this paper, eight deep CNN networks are tested with the UC Merced (400 samples without categorical labels) and Eurosat database (10935 samples with categorical labels). The tradeoff analysis between with and without categorical labels for the dataset is analyzed. It is concluded that the lesser training samples with more testing categorical labels increases the accuracy. Further, the more number of labeled samples, the more accurate is the classification into respective labels. From results, it is concluded that Densenet-121 layers has accuracy of 99.67% which renders correct classification of signatures into the respective labels. The depth of the labeled signature categories enhances the search of the particular object signature. Hence, Densenet -121 is recommended for automating the process of object identification without any manual search of remote sensing scene.

# References

1. Luo, C., et al.: Utilisation of deep convolutional neural networks for remote sensing scenes classification. In: Advanced Remote Sensing Technology for Synthetic Aperture Radar Applications, Tsunami Disasters and Infrastructure. Intech Open, London (2018). Intech open-open access peer reviewed chapter
2. Vakalopoulou, M., et al.: Building detection in a very high resolution multispectral data with deep learning features. In: IEEE international Geoscience and Remote sensing Symposium, IGARSS 2015, pp. 1873–1876 (2015)
3. Zhao, L., Zhang, W., Tang, P.: Analysis of the inter-dataset representation ability of deep features for high spatial resolution remote sensing image scene classification. Multimed. Tools Appl. **78**, 9667–9689 (2019). https://doi.org/10.1007/s11042-018-6548-6
4. Gong, W., Wang, Z., Liang, Y., Fan, X., Hao, J.: Research on high resolution remote sensing image classification based on convolution neural network. In: Li, D., Zhao, C. (eds.) CCTA 2017. IAICT, vol. 545, pp. 87–97. Springer, Cham (2019). https://doi.org/10.1007/978-3-030-06137-1_9
5. Negrel, R., Picard, D., Gosselin, P.H.: Evaluation of second-order visual features for land-use classification. In: 12th International Workshop on Content-Based Multimedia Indexing, CBMI 2014, Austria, pp. 1–5. IEEE Xplore (2014)
6. Castelluccio, M., Poggi, G., Sansone, C., et al.: Land use classification in remote sensing images by convolutional neural networks. arXiv preprint arXiv:1508.00092 (2015)
7. Pritt, M., et al.: Satellite image classification with deep learning. In: 2017 IEEE Applied Imagery Pattern Recognition Workshop (AIPR), USA. IEEE Xplore (2017)
8. Krizhevsky, A., Sutskever, I., Hinton, G.E.: ImageNet classification with deep convolutional neural networks. In: Advances in Neural Information Processing Systems 25, NIPS 2012, Canada, NIPS Proceedings (2012)
9. He, K., Zhang, X., Ren, S., Sun, J.: Deep residual learning for image recognition. In: 2016 IEEE Conference on Computer Vision and Pattern Recognition (CVPR), USA. IEEE Xplore (2016)
10. Simonyan, K., Zisserman, A.: Very deep convolutional networks for large-scale image recognition, computer vision and pattern recognition. arXiv:1409.1556 (2015)

11. Huang, G., Liu, Z., van der Maaten, L., Weinberger, K.Q.: Densely connected convolutional networks. In: 2017 IEEE Conference on Computer Vision and Pattern Recognition (CVPR), USA. IEEE Xplore (2018)
12. UC Merced Database. http://weegee.vision.ucmerced.edu/datasets/landuse.html
13. Eurosat Database. https://unilnet.github.io/datasets.html
14. Castellano, G., Castiello, C., Mencar, C., Vessio, G.: Crowd detection for drone safe landing through fully-convolutional neural networks. In: Chatzigeorgiou, A., et al. (eds.) SOFSEM 2020. LNCS, vol. 12011, pp. 301–312. Springer, Cham (2020). https://doi.org/10.1007/978-3-030-38919-2_25

# Buddhist Hasta Mudra Recognition Using Morphological Features

Gopa Bhaumik$^{(\boxtimes)}$ and Mahesh Chandra Govil

National Institute of Technology Sikkim, Ravangla, India
gopa.bhaumik09@nitsikkim.ac.in, govilmc@gmail.com

**Abstract.** Mudras are considered as spiritual gestures in the religious sense and hold a very important place in the cultural and spiritual space in India. Images are the symbolic representations of divinity in religious artwork and their origins are conveyed through the religions and spiritual beliefs. Such gestures also have some specific meaning in the Buddhist religion. It refers to some of the events in the life of Buddha or denotes special characteristics of the Buddha deities. In recent years, automatic identification of these gestures has gained a greater interest from the machine learning community. This would help to identify the various deities that exist in the Buddhist religion, leading to digital preservation of cultural heritage art. This paper provides a framework that recognizes the Buddhist hand gesture or Hasta Mudra. The morphological features are extracted from the gesture employing geometric parameters. The experimental results show that utilising geometric features and using k-Nearest Neighbor (kNN) as a classifier, an approximately 70% recognition rate is achieved.

**Keywords:** Buddhist culture · Hasta Mudra · Thangka · Morphological features · K-Nearest Neighbour

## 1 Introduction

The characteristic features of the Buddha images in Thangka, a painted scroll serve a very important function in the study of Buddhist history and art these unique features identify the figures as different derived forms of the Buddha. Each figure in these images, particularly the hand gestures or Mudras indicate the nature and function of these aforesaid Buddha deities. Historians and Buddhist subject matter experts decode these images, mudras and other unique features to classify these deities leading to the decode and dissemination of rich Buddhist culture and heritage. But most of these study and identification right now is happening manually where numerous diligent man-hours are put in to decode these intricate pieces of art. A very long and rather tedious process. This presents a two pronged problem first as all of the aforesaid is manually done a lot of dissemination is subject to individual biases of the decoder as to the meaning of the Mudras and images and second as manual work is time consuming there is a genuine risk of these rich historical artefacts being lost in time

© Springer Nature Singapore Pte Ltd. 2020
A. Bhattacharjee et al. (Eds.): MIND 2020, CCIS 1240, pp. 356–364, 2020.
https://doi.org/10.1007/978-981-15-6315-7_29

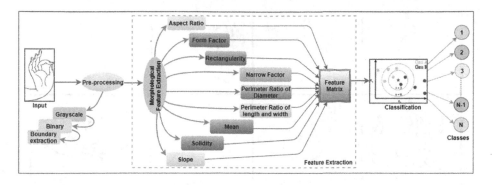

**Fig. 1.** The overview of the Buddhist Hasta Mudra Recognition System

if not preserved and decoded. This paper explores automating this said process - automatic identification of the hand gestures will lead to the recognition of different deities existing in the Buddhism as well as their functionalities within a very short period of time. This automation would also help in removing the inaccuracies and inconsistencies that are typically associated with the manual process of painting Thangka.

Buddhist culture and heritage is preserved through art. The authenticity of this art is maintained by following the iconometric measurement specified for each deity [8]. This paper aims to equip historians and Buddhist subject matter experts with tools, so that representation of this art may be restored digitally using computer vision and pattern recognition techniques. This would be an exercise in decoding this great heritage so that future generations may bask in its immense glory.

Recently, the researchers of machine learning community are focusing on this area and much work has been carried out in Tibetan Thangka painting. Liu et al. has proposed an algorithm for Thangka image in painting using the adjacent information of the broken area [1]. The image in painting method based on Morphological component analysis is used by Hu et al. in [2]. Several interesting methods have been proposed for analysis and detection of headdress area of Buddha, lotus seat in the Buddha images, classification of Thangka and non-Thangka images [3–6]. Fei et al. have introduced a technique for retrieval of Thangka image using Multi granular method [7]. Hand gestures are very useful in expressing thoughts. Several researches are being done on the recognition of hand gesture for humans. Now a days people are also interested in analyzing and retrieving useful information from various Mudras of Indian classical dance form by making use of computer vision and image processing techniques [9, 10,15]. In Buddhist culture also, the Mudras performed by the deities convey meaningful information. These Mudras express the functionalities and different form of Buddha. The automatic identification and recognition of these Mudras would further help in identifying and analyzing the characteristics of different Buddhist deities [16].

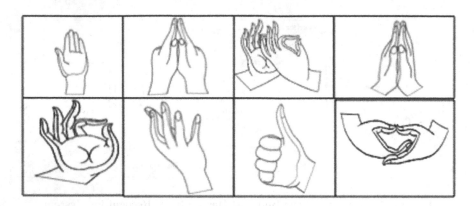

**Fig. 2.** Sample images in the dataset considered

This paper describes an approach for automatic identification of Buddhist Hasta Mudra. We have considered in this paper 25 different types of Buddhist Mudra. Our system is able to detect all the Mudras that are most commonly found in the statues of Buddha. However, the accuracy of recognition may be improved by increasing the training dataset. The task of recognizing the Buddhist Hasta Mudra is more challenging due to the difficulty in collecting the authentic dataset because of its non-availability.

To the best of our knowledge, this is the first attempt to automate the recognition of Buddhist Hasta Mudra for the preservation of Buddhist cultural heritage. The contributions of this paper are summarized as follows:

- The image is preprocessed such that the region of interest must have a clear background. The boundary of the hand gesture is then extracted from the image using erosion and dilation.
- The morphological features are extracted from the gesture using geometric parameters.
- The experimental results show that the kNearest Neighbour classifier achieve better recognition rate as compared to other classifiers.

## 2    Hasta Mudra Recognition System

The work flow of the proposed system is presented in details in the Fig. 1. Firstly, the preprocessing techniques are discussed followed by the description of the features used and concluded with classifier selection.

### 2.1    Preprocessing of the Image

A dataset consisting of 54 samples of 25 different Mudras as presented in Fig. 2 are created. The images are collected from the ancient textbook as well as from Internet [12]. The images considered for training are the line drawing of Buddhist

Hasta Mudra. The input image is preprocessed and the background of the object is removed. The image is converted in to gray scale and then binarized. The boundary of the object is extracted using morphological operations like erosion and dilation as shown in Fig. 3 [11]. Morphological operations are performed to remove the distortion that are caused by noise and textures. The dilation adds pixel to the boundaries of the region of interest where as erosion removes pixel from the boundaries. The structuring element determines the number of pixels to add or remove from the image. Let $f(x, y)$ be a binary image and $s$ be the structuring element. The dilation and erosion operation can be represented by the following equations.

$$f \oplus s = \left\{ z | [(\hat{s})z \cap f] \in f \right\} \tag{1}$$

$$f \ominus s = \left\{ z | (\hat{s})z \in f \right\} \tag{2}$$

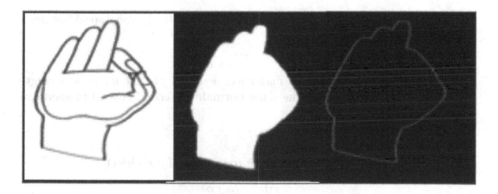

**Fig. 3.** Boundary extraction process of Gyan Mudra taken as example

## 2.2 Morphological Features

The pre-processing step results in a Hasta Mudra image with smooth boundary. There are many variations in the shape of different Hasta Mudras and there is no symmetry among them. Such variations are captured geometrically making use of the following 9 morphological features. Features are useful in identification as it make the best representation of the objects. Like other features such as color, texture etc, shape can also be used as feature. The use of shape or morphological features can make a much better representation of an object. Morphology represents and describes the shape of the region in object such as boundaries, skeletons, convex hull. The geometric components are computed from the image to extract the shape of the hand gesture region [13,14].

There are many shape features that can be computed such as area, which is calculated based on the number of pixels that occupies the object, perimeter is calculated based on the number of pixels on the boundary of object. The other morphological features such as rectangularity, solidity, roundness, aspect ratio, slope etc. are computed using the area, perimeter, major axis and minor axis features as shown in Fig. 4. These features are then fed into the classifier for classification.

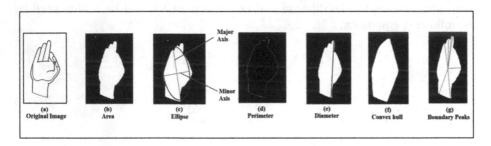

**Fig. 4.** The geometric parameters used for calculating the Morphological features

- Aspect Ratio: It is the ratio of major axis length(L) to the minor axis length (W) of the ellipse that has the same normalized second central moments as the object.

$$AR = \frac{L}{W} \tag{3}$$

- Form Factor: It is the measure of the roundness of the object.

$$FF = 4\pi A P^2 \tag{4}$$

where A is the area of contour and P is the perimeter.
- Rectangularity: It measures the rectangularity of the object.

$$R = L.\frac{W}{A} \tag{5}$$

- Narrow Factor: It is the measure of the narrowness of the object.

$$NF = \frac{D}{L} \tag{6}$$

where D is the diameter i.e the largest distance between two extreme points on contour.
- Perimeter Ratio of Diameter: It is defined as the ratio of perimeter to its diameter.

$$PRD = \frac{P}{D} \tag{7}$$

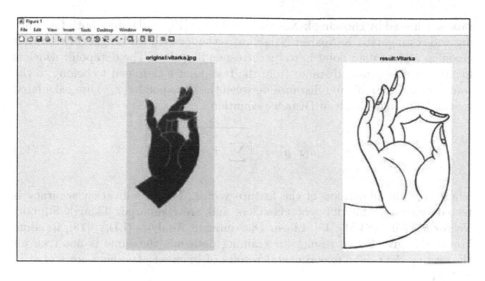

**Fig. 5.** Recognition of Vitarka Mudra

– Perimeter ratio of length and width: It is defined as the ratio of perimeter to the sum of length and width.

$$PRP = \frac{P}{L + W} \tag{8}$$

– Solidity: It is the measure of the portion that are in the convex hull as well as the region of the object.

$$S = \frac{A}{CA} \tag{9}$$

where CA is the convex area of the object.

– Mean: It is the measure of mean of the distance of boundary peak from the centroid.

$$M(d_i) = \frac{1}{n} \sum d_i \tag{10}$$

where n is the number of peak considered.

– Slope: It is the measure of angle $(\Theta)$ that the line joining the peak $(x_i, y_i)$ makes with the centroid $(C_x, C_y)$.

$$\Theta = \sum_i tan^{-1} \frac{(C_y - y_i)}{(C_x - x_i)} \tag{11}$$

## 2.3  Feature Extraction and Classification

Extensive experimentations are carried out with many classifiers using the morphological features computed in feature extraction phase. The effective accuracy rate is achieved by choosing k-Nearest Neighbour [19] as classifier both for training and testing data. K-Nearest Neighbor is a supervised learning algorithm that classifies a given data point in to its corresponding class. The datapoint which is located at a minimum distance from the test point is assumed to belong to the same class. The minimum distance between the data points $(x, y)$ are calculated by the following Euclidean Distance equation

$$d(x, y) = \sqrt{\sum_{i=1}^{n} (x_i - y_i)^2} \tag{12}$$

where $n$ is the dimension of the feature vector. The classification accuracy is tested separately for different classifiers and are compared. Though Support Vector Machine (SVM) [15], Linear Discriminant Analysis (LDA) [18], Random Forest [17] give better results for training data but the same is not true for the testing data. The experimental results of different classifiers are stated in Table 1.

**Table 1.** The accuracy rate (%) of recognition by different classifiers on the training and testing data

| Classifier | Training data | Testing data |
| --- | --- | --- |
| SVM [15] | 98.1 | 38.5 |
| Random Forest [17] | 100 | 38.5 |
| LDA [18] | 85.2 | 46.1 |
| k-NN [19] | 100 | 70 |

## 3   Results Analysis

It has been observed that 100% of the training data are correctly classified using KNN based on the morphological features as computed in Sect. 2.2. The screenshot of the identification system is presented in Fig. 5 and Fig. 6. In testing phase also, the most commonly found Mudras both in line art and colored image format are classified correctly. The limitation is that the system is not able to identify some of the Mudras that have similar shape and structure, for example, Anjali Mudra and Namaskara Mudra as presented in Fig. 7. However, this limitation can be overcome by training the system with a large number of samples. Recently, deep learning has achieved great success in the field of image processing. A large number of training samples are required to train a network of deep learning. Since these paintings belong to a period of ancient era and are very expensive, it is difficult to collect authentic dataset for training and testing.

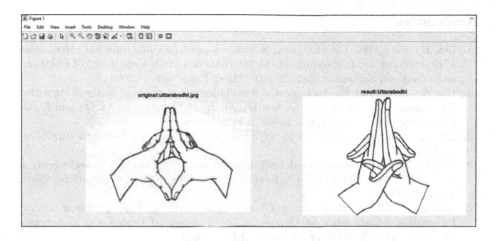

**Fig. 6.** Recognition of Uttarabodhi Mudra

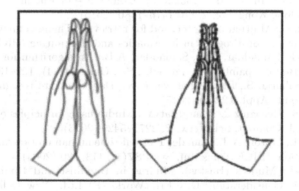

**Fig. 7.** (i) Anjali Mudra (ii) Namaskara Mudra

## 4    Conclusions

In this paper, an attempt has been made to develop a system that will automatically identify the Hasta Mudra from the images of Buddha. The present system uses geometric parameters to compute the morphological features. The experiment shows that the effective recognition using these features is achieved by k-NN. The objective of this research is to contribute to the preservation of Buddhist culture. The result obtained in this paper can further be extended to the identification of different deities and their functionalities. This work is just an initiation. In future, an authentic database of these images may be generated and various other feature extraction and classification algorithms may also be applied to achieve more accurate results. The extension of database may also overcome the limitations mentioned in this paper.

# References

1. Liu, H., Wang, W., Xie, H.: Thangka image inpainting using adjacent information of broken area. In: Proceedings of the International Multi Conference of Engineers and Computer Scientists, IMECS 2008, Hong Kong, vol. 1 (2008)
2. Hu, W., Li, Z., Liu, Z.: An improved morphological component analysis algorithm for tangka image inpainting. In: 6th International Congress on Image and Signal Processing (CISP), vol. 1, pp. 346–351. IEEE (2013)
3. Liu, X.: A survey on thangka image inpainting method based on structure-borne (2015)
4. Yin, L., Wang, W.: Headdress detection based on saliency map for thangka portrait image. In: MVA2011 IAPR Conference on Machine Vision Applications, Nara, Japan (2011)
5. Zhang, W., Lin, S.: Research on Tibet Tangka based on shape grammar. In: 9th International Conference on Computer-Aided Industrial Design and Conceptual Design, CAID/CD 2008, pp. 373–376. IEEE (2008)
6. Yin, L., Wang, W., Yang, D.: Study on how to distinguish Thangka and non-Thangka image. In: International Multi Conference of Engineers and Computer Scientists, Hong Kong, vol. 2, pp. 1476–1480 (2010)
7. Fei, X., Liu, C.: Multi-granular method for retrieving Thangka images. In: International Conference on Progress in Informatics and Computing (PIC). IEEE (2014)
8. Bhaumik, G., Samaddar, S.G., Samaddar, A.B.: An algorithm for digital authentication of Buddha painting on Thangka. Sci. Cult. 84(34), 129–133 (2018)
9. Devi, M., Saharia, S., Bhattacharyya, D.K.: Dance gesture recognition: a survey. Int. J. Comput. Appl. 122(5) (2015)
10. Mozarkar, S.: Recognizing Bharatnatyam Mudra using principles of gesture recognition. Int. J. Comput. Sci. Netw. 2, 2277–5420 (2013)
11. Fujiyoshi, H., Lipton, A.J., Kanade, T.: Real-time human motion analysis by image skeletonization. IEICE Trans. Inf. Syst. 87(1), 113–120 (2004)
12. Bunce, F.W.: Mudras (Hastas). Mudras in Buddhist and Hindu Practices-An Iconographic Consideration. D.K PrintWorld (P) Ltd., New Delhi (2017) ISBN 9788124603123
13. Arora, A., Gupta, A., Bagmar, N., Mishra, S., Bhattacharya, A.: A plant identification system using shape and morphological features on segmented leaflets. In: CLEF. Team IITK (2012)
14. Manik, F.Y., Herdiyeni, Y., Herliyana, E.N.: Leaf morphological feature extraction of digital image anthocephalus cadamba. Telkomnika (Telecommun. Comput. Electron. Control) 14(2), 630–637 (2016)
15. Kumar, K.V.V., Kishore, P.V.V.: Indian classical dance mudra classification using HOG features and SVM classifier. In: Satapathy, S.C., Bhateja, V., Das, S. (eds.) Smart Computing and Informatics. SIST, vol. 77, pp. 659–668. Springer, Singapore (2018). https://doi.org/10.1007/978-981-10-5544-7_65
16. Futane, P.R., Dharaskar, R.V.: Hasta Mudra: an interpretation of Indian sign hand gestures. In: Electronics Computer Technology (ICECT), Vol. 2, pp. 377–380. IEEE (2011)
17. Liaw, A., Wiener, M.: Classification and regression by randomForest. R News 2(3), 18–22 (2002)
18. Ye, J., Janardan, R., Li, Q.: Two-dimensional linear discriminant analysis. In: Advances in Neural Information Processing Systems, pp. 1569–1576 (2005)
19. Cover, T., Hart, P.: Nearest neighbor pattern classification. IEEE Trans. Inf. Theory 13(1), 21–27 (1967)

# Image Compression Using Deep Learning Based Multi-structure Feature Map and K-Means Clustering

Gyanendra Verma$^{(\boxtimes)}$ and Anant Kumar$^{(\boxtimes)}$

National Institute of Technology, Kurukshetra, Kurukshetra, India
{gyanendra,anant_31803107}@nitkkr.ac.in

**Abstract.** Image compression play significant role in the data transfer and storage. Recently, deep learning has achieved tremendous success in various domain of image processing. In this paper, we propose a multi-structure Feature map-based Deep Learning approach with K-means Clustering for image compression. We first use a modified CNN to select a multi-structured region of interest MS-ROI feature map by using several stacked of convolution layers then compress the image by integrating MS-ROI map with K-means. We can establish through experimental results that the proposed approach perform better compared to traditional K-means clustering approach.

**Keywords:** K-Means · Image compression · Deep learning

## 1 Introduction

These days, data is increasing at an exponential rate, so to handle the data and to extract meaningful information from it, clustering is one of the methods that is widely used. Clustering is a technique to class raw data into different clusters based on various properties or features of data. Clustering divides raw data into different groups so that data in the same cluster have some standard features. There are so many methods for clustering the data like K-Means, DBSCAN [1] in which k-means is the one that we are using to compress the image.

Image compression is a type of data compression which is applied to images to reduce the memory taken by that image in the hard disk and also to reduce the transmission cost of that so that image can be transferred easily and quickly from one device to another. We can compress the image by reducing the redundancy in the image. In lossless compression, we maintain the same quality of the image as it is before applying the image compression. Examples of lossless image compression formats are PNG, BMP, etc. In lossy compression, we achieve a significant amount of compression but with the cost of quality. Examples of lossy compression formats are JPG, GIF, etc.

To refer code https://github.com/anant95/K_means-image-compression.

© Springer Nature Singapore Pte Ltd. 2020
A. Bhattacharjee et al. (Eds.): MIND 2020, CCIS 1240, pp. 365–374, 2020.
https://doi.org/10.1007/978-981-15-6315-7_30

K-Means is an unsupervised, numerical, easiest, and fast method to compute cluster from given data. For the implementation of K-Means, we need to decide the required number of clusters for the given data, or we can say that how many clusters are enough for our data? The elbow method is probably one of the most popular methods to determine the required number of clusters. We can detect peoples and objects in images and videos by using deep learning models, we compress the region of interest in such a way so that visual quality of this region of interest found by deep learning models does not reduce to too much extent while remaining region we can compress it to greater extent. This paper is divided into four parts: The second part gives the detail of K-means clustering algorithm and show how this data clustering algorithm can be used in compressing the image. The third part presents how we are using deep learning and integrating deep learning with K-Means. Experimental results and discussions are given in the last section.

## 2   The K-Means Clustering Algorithm

### 2.1   The Process of K-Means Algorithm

The K-Means clustering algorithm is the most straight forward clustering algorithm used in recommendation system and data mining, this algorithm is extensively used to cluster an extensive data set to some number of clusters based on the features of that data set. MacQueen in 1967, firstly proposed the k-means clustering algorithm; it is a non-supervised algorithm and easy to implement [2].

The implementation of the K-means clustering algorithm includes three separate phases. The first phase of algorithm is to select k cluster centre randomly, where we have to fix the value of k in advance. We can use the elbow method to find out the number of clusters(k) that best suited for our data. In the second phase, take each data point to its nearest centroid. There are various methods to calculate the distance from a point to the centroid. Euclidean distance is a classical method for the same. We choose centroid for a data point that has a minimum distance from that data point. In the last phase for each centroid, compute the mean of every data point. Make the mean, the centroid of that cluster. Repeat this step to some number of iteration or until no centroid is changed. The Euclidean distance $d(x_i, y_i)$ between two points $x_i$ and $y_i$ can be calculated as follows:

$$d(X_i, Y_i) = \left[ \sum_{i=1}^{n} (X_i - Y_i)^2 \right]^{1/2} \tag{1}$$

Input to K-Means algorithm:

– Number of cluster (K)
– Data set containing n data objects

Output of K-Means algorithm:

– A set of K clusters

## 2.2  Image Compression Through K-Means

Firstly, let's see how the images are stored in the memory of the computer. An image is made up of minimal intensity values or dots known as pixels. In a coloured image, each pixel has 24 bits, i.e., 3 Byte containing Red-Blue-Green (RGB) values having Red, Blue, and Green intensity values. Each colour from Red, Blue, and green can take 8 bits, which means each pixel can have 0 to 255 different intensity values of each colour. Since 24 bits required to represent an RGB(8 bits for each colour) pixel so from one pixel we can represent one of the 16777216 colours

$$256 * 256 * 256 = 16777216$$

For example if we have an image of 200*200 resolution then memory needed for this is 118 KB

$$24 * 200 * 200 = 960000 \; bits \; (118 \; KB)$$

But every image does not have 16777216 or $2^{24}$ colors so we can do color quantization. if we divide our image into 64 cluster i.e. 64 or $(2^6)$ colours then we require only 6 bit for a single pixel [3]

$$6 * 200 * 200 = 240000 \; bits \; (30 \; KB)$$

So, by reducing colour from $16777216(2^{24})$ to $64(2^6)$we can reduce the size of the image up to 70%.

With K-Means clustering, we grouped similar colors in the image into a cluster, we take a particular value of K and then consolidate all the pixel values into K clusters. Therefore, each centroid of a cluster is a representative of all the pixels in that cluster. These centroids of K clusters that formed replace all the color vector in their respective clusters. Now we only need to store the label of the cluster for each pixel. It tells the cluster to which this pixel belongs, and besides that, we need to keep the record, which determines the color vector for each cluster centroid.

## 3  Deep Learning Based Approach for Image Compression

### 3.1  Introduction to Deep Learning and CNN

Artificial intelligence has been witnessing tremendous growth in bridging the gap between human and machine intelligence. There are numerous aspects in the field of artificial intelligence, and one of them is computer vision which helps the machine to see the world as a human saw, discern it similarly, extract information from what it sees and use that information for an abundance of tasks such as image analysis and classification, Natural language processing, Recommendation system, etc. The evolution in deep learning and computer vision has been constructed and perfected with time basically over one particular algorithm CNN or Convolutional Neural network.

The convolutional neural network is the regularized version of a multilayer perceptron; we can say that a convolutional neural network is an algorithm of deep learning which takes an input image, assign weights, and biased to various objects and aspects of an image. It can differentiate one object from the other in the image. Fully connected networks is a network in which each neuron in one layer is connected to every neuron in the next layer. CNN differs from a fully connected network as the dimension of the learned filter in CNN is much smaller as compared to the dimension of the given input image. And also, while using convolutional operation, we use the same kernel weight at every image position of kernel size. CNN generally contains a convolution layer, pooling layer, and fully connected layer.

Given an image x, weight matrix W and a convolutional filter of size $m \times m$, then the convolutional layer operates as shown in the below equation.

$$y_{ij} = \left[ \sum_{a=0}^{m} \sum_{b=0}^{m} W_{ab} x_{(i+a)(j+b)} \right] \tag{2}$$

CNN includes a pooling layer after every convolutional operation in which the width and height of the generated feature map are make smaller by restoring several neighbouring activation values generally within square window. There are three types of Pooling operations -

– Max pooling [4]: In this, we take the maximum value from the square window of the feature map and then shift this window according to the stride decided. If the stride is one, then we shift pooling window one step left in the feature map and then again choose maximum from that window. The $k^{th}$ component of the obtained map(M) from the feature map window which contains n activation values is

$$M_k = max(u_{1k}, u_{2k}, u_{3k}, .........u_{nk}) \tag{3}$$

– Average pooling: Calculate the average of all the activation values present in the feature map that comes in the window
– Sum pooling [4] : Calculate the sum of every activation values that come in the window of the feature map. The $k_{th}$ component of the obtained map from the feature map window which contains N activation values is

$$M_k = \sum_{n=1}^{N} u_{nk} \tag{4}$$

In all the above ways of pooling, the most commonly used method is max pooling. In practice, the pooling window is generally of size $4 \times 4$and $2 \times 2$, with stride value of 2. It decreases the number of activation values by 75%. CNN applies some form of non-linear activation function on the output of the convolution layer, such as Rectified Linear Unit (Relu) $max(0, x)$, sigmoid $(1-e^{-x})^{-1}$. These types of CNN help to learn the feature map from the image.

## 3.2   Modification in CNN

We are using a non-uniform image compression, in which a region of interest to be find out within the image and compress only that region of interest to some extent. In contrast to other region of the image that is compressed as usual. Therefore, a search model is required to find out region of interest within the image. As can be seen in Fig. 1, there are two feature maps for the same image. The first one (Fig. 1) identifies only face in a girl image. Whereas, second feature map (Fig. 2) identifies face along with hands. Therefore, we are targeting a model that generates the second type of feature map.

**Fig. 1.** CAM feature maps                          **Fig. 2.** MS-ROI

A typical CNN network contains convolutional layers, maxout layer, ReLU layer and a fully connected layer as prefinal layer followed by softmax layer as final layer. The softmax layer is act as classification layer. The model requires a large size of database for effective training of the network. These models are useful for object detection in autonomous cars but not for us as we need a model that highlights all the objects present in the image. Since images of real-world typically contain multiple object of interest, and we want to find all the objects present in the image and compress them accordingly.

# 4   Multi-Structure Region of Interest (MS-ROI)

## 4.1   Generation of MS-ROI

Class Activation Mapping (CAM) [5] highlights the most enlightening image region relevant to the predicted class which is one of the classes for which model is trained like, Imagenet dataset contains 1000 classes, Caltech-256 is a dataset, which has images of natural and human-made objects, buildings, animals and plants. As we don't want to highlight only the most informative image region relevant to only one class in the image however we want is to highlight all relevant objects in the image, so we MS-ROI. We can find out MS-ROI [6] with a set of feature map that contain a feature map of every class. However the problem is for L layers, where each layer $l$ contain $d_l$ features, $C$ classes and an image of size $n \times n$, this result in total activation size of

$$\sum_{l \in L} d_l \times C \times \frac{n}{k^l} \times \frac{n}{k^l} \tag{5}$$

where k is stride size for max pooling, this needs high computational power and also not practicable for real-world data. For our requirements, we do not care about the difference between a labra dog and rottweiler or between Rose and Arabian jasmine. We combined similar classes by increasing the inter-class variance to reduce the total number of classes, which reduces the total activation size. For classes that are not present in the given image we remove the effects of activations for them to reduce the computational complexity for learning the model. This process can be accomplished by introducing a threshold operation that discards those class whose learned feature maps do not have that much large activation than a hyper-parameter T(threshold). Let $Z_l^c$ is the total sum of activation's for layer $l$ for all feature maps of a given class $c$; $Z_l^c$ can be obtained by summation of all the feature maps of class $c$.

$$Z_l^c = \sum_{d \in D} \sum_{x,y} f_d^c(x,y) \tag{6}$$

Now we use this $Z_l^c$ to filter classes. Calculation of MS-ROI is as shown below

$$M(x,y) = \begin{cases} \sum_d f_d^c(x,y), & if \, Z_l^c > T \\ 0 & \text{otherwise} \end{cases} \tag{7}$$

M denotes the generated multi-structure feature map; T is a hyper-parameter for learning hyper-parameter are the constant that is defined before training. The sigmoid function is used to maximize the discovery of all objects in the image as a substitute of softmax function, as softmax function gives a probabilistic output.

## 4.2   Integrating MS-ROI Map with K-Means

For finding MS-ROI in an image we generate feature map by using several stack of convolution layer with max pooling repeating these layer five times and at last we add fully connected layer like VGG16 [7] model as shown below:

$$IMAGE \mapsto \left[ \left[ CONV \rightarrow RELU \right]^2 \rightarrow MAXPOOL \right]^5 \mapsto MS-ROI \mapsto MAP$$

MS-ROI feature map give us the saliency value for each pixel in the range [0,1], where 0 represents no saliency, and 1 represents maximum saliency. Divide these saliency values into m levels, where m is an adjustable hyperparameter. The first

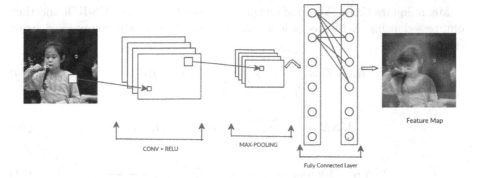

**Fig. 3.** Generation of feature Map

level contains the pixel whose saliency value is in the range $[0, 1/m]$, second level contains pixels whose saliency value in the range $(1/m, 2/m]$ and so on. Now we select the value of K (Number of clusters for K-Means) from $k_l$ to $k_h$ for every saliency level defined above. Each saliency level is compressed by taking the different value of K, correspond to that level.Or we can say that saliency level n with range $[n/k, (n+1)/k]$ is compressed with K value calculated as follows:

$$K_n = K_l + \frac{n*(K_h - K_l)}{m} \tag{8}$$

For each saliency level n, where $l \leq n \leq h$ we obtained a compressed image with $K_n$ number of clusters. For each $8*8$ chunk of our final output image, we select the chunk of color pixel value collected from the compressed image correlate with that chunk of saliency value.

## 5    Experimental Results and Analysis

Model is trained with the Caltech - 256 dataset [8], which contain 256 different classes of natural and human-made object, common animals and plants, buildings, etc because it contains a medium number of classes to distinguish objects from background, i.e. neither too many classes like ImageNet with 1000 classes [9] which identifies every other object uniquely and nor too less classes like CIFAR-100 [10] which has only 100 classes, so that we miss some of the objects.

We can use our personal computer with general configuration to compress the image with some of the module installed like tensorflow, conda etc, all other requirements are mentioned in the requirement.txt file on github. And also we added README file on github which describes how we can use this code.

### 5.1    Evaluation Measures

We have used four evaluation matrices namely PSNR (Peak Signal to Noise Ratio), MSE (Mean Square Error), RMSE (Root mean square error) and SSIM (Structure Similarity Index Method) value with the original image.

Mean Square Error (MSE) of image compressed by finding MS-ROI and then compressed using K-Means is less than the image directly compressed using K-Means

$$RMSE = \sqrt{\frac{1}{mn} \sum_{i=0}^{m-1} \sum_{j=0}^{n-1} ||f(i,j) - g(i,j)||^2} \qquad (9)$$

$$MSE = \frac{1}{mn} \sum_{i=0}^{m-1} \sum_{j=0}^{n-1} ||f(i,j) - g(i,j)||^2 \qquad (10)$$

$$PSNR = 10log_{10} \frac{L-1}{\frac{1}{mn} \sum_{i=0}^{m-1} \sum_{j=0}^{n-1} ||f(i,j) - g(i,j)||^2} \qquad (11)$$

**Table 1.** Performance comparison with PSNR and SSIM for Deep learning based K-means with K-means method

| Image name | PSNR | | SSIM | |
|---|---|---|---|---|
| | K-Means | K-Means DL | K-Means | K-Means DL |
| kodim01 | 35.4470 | 35.8744 | 0.9203 | 0.9319 |
| kodim02 | 33.8289 | 34.0235 | 0.6968 | 0.6991 |
| kodim03 | 31.6219 | 33.0705 | 0.5110 | 0.5806 |
| kodim04 | 32.0489 | 32.1359 | 0.7085 | 0.7139 |
| kodim05 | 29.3661 | 29.7043 | 0.8821 | 0.8861 |
| kodim06 | 34.2914 | 35.2984 | 0.8024 | 0.8097 |
| kodim08 | 30.2153 | 30.3559 | 0.8677 | 0.8715 |
| kodim09 | 33.8275 | 34.3958 | 0.5765 | 0.5832 |
| kodim10 | 33.5142 | 34.1738 | 0.6751 | 0.6863 |

**Table 2.** Performance comparison with MSE and RMSE for Deep learning based K-means with K-means method

| Image name | MSE | | RMSE | |
|---|---|---|---|---|
| | K-Means | K-Means DL | K-Means | K-Means DL |
| kodim01 | 55.6542 | 50.4388 | 7.4601 | 7.1021 |
| kodim02 | 80.7819 | 77.2414 | 8.9878 | 8.7887 |
| kodim03 | 134.2810 | 96.1939 | 11.5879 | 9.8078 |
| kodim04 | 121.7061 | 119.2935 | 11.0321 | 10.9221 |
| kodim05 | 225.7273 | 208.8230 | 15.0242 | 14.4507 |
| kodim06 | 72.6211 | 57.5924 | 8.5218 | 7.5889 |
| kodim08 | 185.6395 | 179.7273 | 13.6249 | 13.4062 |
| kodim09 | 80.8062 | 70.8954 | 8.9892 | 8.4199 |
| kodim10 | 86.8506 | 74.6136 | 9.3193 | 8.6379 |

We can see from the result that PSNR and SSIM [11] value is increased when we do non uniform compression using deep learning so higher the PSNR value good is the quality of image, So we can conclude that by using deep learning quality of the compressed image is slightly improved. We can use this approach of compressing images with different lossy image compression methods like JPEG [12], JPEG 2000 [13], etc (Tables 1 and 2).

## 6 Conclusion and Future Work

We have used a model like VGG16 that identifies multiple objects in an image and then generates a map that highlights multiple-region of interest in that image. This map provides sufficient information to perform non-uniform image compression. We use K-Means Clustering algorithm to compress the image, the goal of this scheme is to use a simple algorithm to compress image and to improve the visual quality of the image. So, with the help of K-Means, we compress the image in different qualities, i.e., different values of K, then we use these different compressed images to perform non-uniform image compression. This variable compression improves visual quality. In future, we will try to implement our proposed approach to other applications based on lossy compression.

## References

1. Schubert, E., Sander, J., Ester, M., Kriegel, H.-P., Xu, X.: DBSCAN revisited, revisited: why and how you should (still) use DBSCAN. ACM Trans. Database Syst. **42**(3), 21 (2017). Article 19
2. Na, S., Xumin, L., Yong, G.: An improved k-means clustering algorithm. In: Third International Symposium on Intelligent Information Technology and Security Informatics. IEEE (2010)
3. Paek, J., Ko, J.: K-means clustering-based data compression scheme for wireless imaging sensor networks. IEEE Syst. J. **11**(4) (2017)
4. Wang, X., Wang, L.M., Qiao, Y.: A comparative study of encoding, pooling and normalization methods for action recognition. In: Lee, K.M., Matsushita, Y., Rehg, J.M., Hu, Z. (eds.) ACCV 2012. LNCS, vol. 7726, pp. 572–585. Springer, Heidelberg (2013). https://doi.org/10.1007/978-3-642-37431-9_44
5. Zhou, B., Khosla, A., Lapedriza, A., Oliva, A., Torralba, A.: Learning Deep Features for Discriminative Localization, arXiv:1512.04150v1 [cs.CV], 14 Dec 2015
6. Prakash, A., Moran, N., Garber, S., DiLillo, A., Storer, J.: Semantic Perceptual Image Compression using Deep Convolution Networks, arXiv:1612.08712v2 [cs.MM], 29 Mar 2017
7. Qassim, H., Verma, A., Feinzimer, D.: Compressed residual-VGG16 CNN model for big data places image recognition. IEEE (2018)
8. Griffin, G., Holub, A., Perona, P.: Caltech-256 object category dataset (2007)
9. Deng, J., Dong, W., Socher, R., Li, L.-J., Li, K., Fei-Fei, L.: Imagenet: a large-scale hierarchical image database. In: IEEE Conference on Computer Vision and Pattern Recognition, CVPR 2009, pp. 248–255. IEEE (2009)
10. Chrabaszcz, P., Loshchilov, I., Frank, H.: A downsampled variant of ImageNet as an alternative to the CIFAR datasets. arXiv preprint arXiv:1707.08819 (2017)

11. Horé, A., Ziou, D.: Image quality metrics: PSNR vs. SSIM. In: 2010 International Conference on Pattern Recognition (2010)
12. Raid, A.M., Khedr, W.M., El-dosuky, M.A., Ahmed, W.: Jpeg image compression using discrete cosine transform - a survey. Int. J. Comput. Sci. Eng. Surv. (IJCSES) **5**(2) (2014)
13. Rabbani, M., Joshi, R.: An overview of the JPEG 2000 still image compression standard. Sig. Process.: Image Commun. **17**, 73–84 (2002)

# Building Detection from Satellite Aerial Images Using Morphological Operations

Gunjan Paul[1], Saravanan Chandran[2(✉)], and Jose Hormese[2]

[1] University of Engineering & Management, Jaipur, India
gunjan.mtbpaul@gmail.com
[2] National Institute of Technology Durgapur, Durgapur, India
cs@ieee.org, josehormese@gmail.com

**Abstract.** The satellite image is a picture taken from a satellite in the form of a photograph of the earth and other planet. Building detection from satellite image is an important research work to study changes in a particular region of the city. Identifying the structure of the different shape of the rooftop in rustic regions are difficult to process and scientists deal with various technologies for detecting or segmenting buildings. In this research article, we described a model, which segments building images from high-resolution satellite images by image processing and object segmentation algorithm. The visual highlights incorporate shading, surface, smallness, differentiate, and the nearness of the rooftop corner and intelligent activity are the outcome. With the assistance of this model, we are getting a careful consequence of 7% of all structures bigger than 70 m$^2$ could be identified and 85% of every single distinguished structure bigger than 70 m$^2$ were right in the two cases. Structures littler than 30 m$^2$ are not identified.

**Keywords:** Building detection · Rooftop segmentation · Rooftop extraction · Building segmentation

## 1 Introduction

Building detection requires a characterization of input information that separates objects based on structures such as road, buildings, vehicles, trees and others. Several issues to be addressed in this research work for detecting buildings and the extraction of topographic items in urban regions [6]. The issues are interrelated. The high-caliber advanced digital terrain models (DTMs) are used in various research works. The LIDAR focuses on the highest points of structures and trees must be eliminated [4]. Thus, data about the positions of such objects is required. DTM is computed if structures or trees are to be distinguished. These works are carried out as preprocessing at the initial stage. In the preprocessing stage several objects are enhanced, eliminated, segmented, edges are detected, to achieve the objective. During this preprocessing stage the building edges may damage and create further issues for identifying the building.

At present, there are several numbers of building detection and building segmentation techniques available in the literature. These building detection models achieved higher accuracy. These conventional, variation, bend proliferation techniques uses

A. Bhattacharjee et al. (Eds.): MIND 2020, CCIS 1240, pp. 375–383, 2020.
https://doi.org/10.1007/978-981-15-6315-7_31

snakes, dynamic forms, and deformable models. Set have been utilized to represent the general errand of sectioning satellite pictures for streets and for programmed location of structures which is the thoroughly picture-based system and it causes deluding in low-level picture information [3]. In this research article, we addressed these issues with a better picture preparing strategy for better detection of low-level information. To overcome these circumstance, we propose picture thresholding strategy for programmed detection of building shape. The rest of this research article is sectioned as follows: Sect. 2 discusses the latest two research works. Section 3 discusses about the methodology of building recognition. In Sect. 4, Experimental Results are discussed. Section 5 concludes the present research work with a description of future perspectives.

We considered satellite aerial pictures for this research work and convert into a grayscale picture [8]. Further, we apply thresholding with different range and apply XOR coherent activity with particular range. Moreover, we apply the logical function to summarize the XOR esteem. Besides, we fill up all the holes in the binary image. Further, we organize the components of different ranges of the picture. Finally, the accurate house structure is produced and marked with a bounding box (Fig. 1).

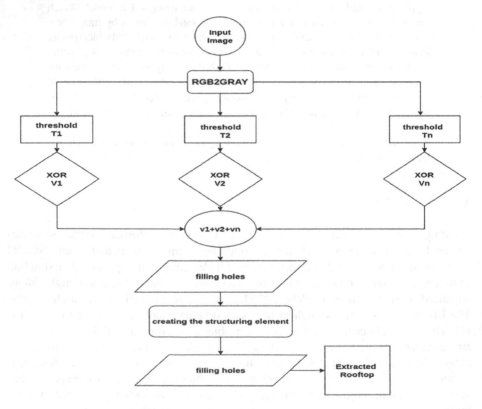

**Fig. 1.** Flowchart of the proposed model

## 2 Related Woks

Shunping Ji et al. proposed a scale robust FCN (SR-FCN) network to enhance accuracy of the building segmentation [13]. They used WHU building dataset has a collection of aerial and satellite images for the research work. They used Keras and Tensorflow platform for implementing the algorithms. They used VGG-16 encoder. Two Atrous convolutions are introduced in the first two lowest-scale layers. Further, they applied a multi-scale aggregation approach. The building labels were predicted using the last feature maps at each scale. Further, features were up-sampled to the original scale and concatenated for the final prediction. Furthermore, they introduced a joined data augmentation and relative radiometric calibration technique for multi-source building identification. They validated the new model using an aerial dataset consists of 180,000 buildings of different architectural types, and a satellite image dataset having 29,000 buildings. Their model achieved 0.944 precision.

David Griffths et al. improved public data for building segmentation [14]. They addressed the major issue in the deep learning models which require large quantity of data for training. They improved public GIS building footprint labels by using Morphological Geodesic Active Contours (MorphGACs). They collected aerial data of UK using an automated script. They evaluated the models using a large UK-based dataset of 24,556 images comprising 169,835 building images. They achieved by training several Mask/Faster R-CNN and RetinaNet deep convolutional neural networks. They achieved an accuracy of 0.92.

## 3 Methodology

In this model, we are considering a RGB picture that has three matrices a Red, a Green and a Blue stacked over each other.

The algorithm for transformation:

1. Read the source RGB image
2. Convert the RGB image into 3 distinctive Red, Blue, and Green 2-D grids
3. Make a lattice with similar number of lines and segments as an RGB image, containing zeros.
4. Convert RGB pixels at the coordinates $A(i, j)$ to grayscale values $G(i, j)$ by framing a weighted aggregate of the Red $R(i, j)$, Green $G(i, j)$, and Blue $B(i, j)$ segments

$$G(i, j) = 0.2989 \times R(i, j) + 0.587 \times G(i, j) + 0.114 \times B(i, j) \tag{1}$$

The following Fig. 2 displays the source RGB image and the converted Gray image.

**Fig. 2.** Source Image and converted Grey Image

## 3.1 Image Thresholding and XOR Operation

Image thresholding is one of the image segmentation method. This method makes two images from the source grayscale image. This method is performed to isolate objects or foreground pixels from the background pixels [1]. The objects are identified based on the pixel values of the boundary of the object and neighborhood pixel values. The image contrast plays important role and higher contrast image is separated foreground and background better. The threshold value T is calculated using the maximum pixel value *max* and minimum pixel value *min* of the image.

$$T = (max + min)/2 \tag{2}$$

The XOR function outputs true if one of the value is true otherwise false. XOR represents selective OR. The XNOR is the opposite of the XOR. The XOR process two images and produces output image whose pixel values are only those of the first image, XORed with the second image pixels. It is significant that all the pixel being worked on having a similar number of bits in them. The pixel values in the images are in bits and the XOR activity is completed on comparing each bit [14].

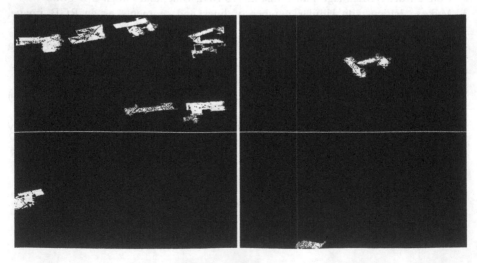

**Fig. 3.** Image Thresholding and XOR operation

## 3.2 Logical Sum and Fillup

Logical (A) changes over A into an array of logical values [2, 5]. Any nonzero component of A is changed over to 1 (true) and zeros are retained as 0 (false).

$$L = logical(V1 + V2 + V3 + \ldots + V_n) \tag{3}$$

A few openings are recognizable in the image and have to fill up each of those openings. The fill work plays out a flood-fill activity on twofold and grayscale images. Fill changes background pixels (0s) to foreground pixels (1s), halting when it arrives at object limits. For grayscale images, fill brings the force esteems of dull territories that are encompassed by lighter regions up to a similar force level as encompassing pixels. As a result, fill expels provincial minima that are most certainly not associated with the picture outskirt. Observe the finding areas of High-or Low-Intensity for more data. This activity is helpful in expelling unimportant ancient rarities from images [9, 10]. The following Fig. 4 shows the images after logical sum and fillup operation, which identifies more objects than in Fig. 3.

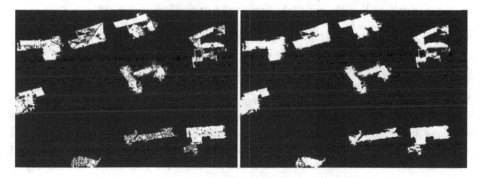

**Fig. 4.** Logical sum and fillup

## 3.3 Erosion of the Binary

In double morphology, an image is considered as a subset of a Euclidean space $R^d$ *or* on the other hand the number framework $Z^d$, for some measurement $d$. The essential thought is twofold morphology is to test an image with a basic, pre-characterized shape, making determinations on how this shape fits or misses the shapes in the image. This straightforward "test" is called an organizing component and is itself a double picture (i.e., a subset of the space or matrix) [12]. Let E be a Euclidean space or an integer grid, and A a binary image in E. The erosion of the binary image A by the structuring element B is defined by:

$$A\theta B = \{z \in E | B_z \subseteq A\} \tag{4}$$

An object represents a flat morphological organizing component, which is a basic piece of morphological enlargement and disintegration tasks [11]. An organizing component is a paired esteemed neighborhood, either 2-D or multidimensional, in which the true pixels are remembered for the morphological calculation and the false pixels are definitely not. The inside pixel of the organizing component called the beginning, distinguishes the pixel in the picture being handled. Utilize the work portrayed beneath to make a level organizing component. We can utilize level structuring components with both double and grayscale pictures. The accompanying figure outlines a level organizing component. J = erode (I, shape) dissolves the grayscale, double, or pressed twofold image I, restoring the disintegrated image, J and determines the size of the yield image. After we process expansion on J with organizing component S. The expansion of J by S is characterized by

$$[J \oplus S = \bigcup_{b \in s} J_b] \tag{5}$$

### 3.4 Morphologically Close and Fillup

Morphological closing is obtained from the key operations of disintegration and expansion. In scientific morphology, the closing of a set binary image A by an organizing component B is the disintegration of the expansion of that set,

$$A \cdot B = (A \oplus B) \ominus B \tag{6}$$

where, $\oplus$ $\ominus$ denote the dilation and erosion, respectively.

Closing is opening acted backward. It is characterized just as an expansion followed by a disintegration utilizing the equivalent organizing component for the two tasks. The end administrator in this manner requires two sources of info: an image to be shut and an organizing component. Grey level shutting comprises direct of a grey level enlargement followed by a grey level disintegration. After that we apply gap top off procedure to top off every one of the holes in image [7, 10]. The following Fig. 5 shows the segmented buildings.

**Fig. 5.** Segmented buildings

## 4   Experimental Results and Discussions

The images utilized here is acquired from Massachusetts Buildings Data comprising of Satellite images data set. Here, subsequent to accepting the first image as RGB from this information set and we converted the image to a grayscale image and afterward applied to sift thresholding to segment frontal area and foundation and afterward we use XOR function with explicit range. Then we summarize all the values and fill the holes in the paired image. Then, we applied distinctive Morphological activities like opening, closing, and so forth for the expulsion of noise and in the wake of obtaining the resultant image out of it. Further, we applied Erosion procedures for the expulsion of the pixels from the object limits.

Subsequent to applying every one of the means referenced in the strategy, we obtained the resultant image, it identifies, OST of the building shape and concentrate from other objects. However, since each approach has limitations and at the same time, the proposed new model unable to distinguish all structures in the pictures with extremely little structure shape.

Furthermore, the accuracy of the detection is calculated. The pace of recognition rightness (RoD), the false-negative rate (FNR), exactness, review, f - score and in general precision are worked out (Table 1). Also noted the number items of effectively identified as building ($N_{TP}$), the number of different objects delegated as building ($N_{FP}$), and the number of building delegated another item ($N_{FN}$),

$$N_{TP} = 8$$

$$N_{FP} = 1$$

$$N_{FN} = 0$$

Accuracy $= \frac{N_{TP}}{N_{TP} + N_{FP} + N_{FN}} \times 100\%$

Accuracy = 88.8%

Rate of detection correctness (RoD) $= \frac{N_{TP}}{N_{TP} + N_{FP}} \times 100\%$

RoD = 88.8%

**Table 1.** The accuracy assessment of the proposed framework in the set of images

| Total no. of buildings | No. of TP | No. of FP | No. of FN | RoD | Accuracy |
|---|---|---|---|---|---|
| 12 | 8 | 1 | 0 | 88.8% | 88.8% |

Notes: TP = True Positive, FP = False Positive, RoD = Rate of detection, FNR = False negative rate.

## 5  Conclusion

A model for segmenting buildings from satellite image is proposed in this research article. The research work used standard data set obtained from MIT. The RGB image is converted to grayscale further threshold values are calculated. The XOR operation is performed. Moreover, the holes are filled to create the structuring the element. Further, holes are filled to extract rooftop. Low-level processing is utilized here to identify buildings which are tedious process. The proposed model is increasingly productive and faster. The methodology doesn't require any height or other extra information. The new model is developed such that with few image parameters the building is identified. The calculation is sensitive to certain parameters, for example, the shadow power limit, and vegetation coefficient which are set precisely for best identification. These are effectively calculated and there are regions where we noticed an additional improvement. The proposed model achieved 88.8% accuracy.

## References

1. Bradley, D., Roth, G.: Adaptive thresholding using the integral image. J. Graph. Tools 12(2), 13–21 (2007)
2. Fukui, M., Kitayama, K.-i.: Image logic algebra and its optical implementations. Appl. Opt. 31(5), 581–591 (1992)
3. Karantzalos, K., Paragios, N.: Automatic model-based building detection from single panchromatic high resolution images. In: The International Archives of the Photogrammetry, Remote Sensing and Spatial Information Sciences, vol. XXXVII. Part B3a, pp. 127–132 (2008)
4. Verma, V., Kumar, R., Hsu, S.: 3D building detection and modeling from aerial LIDAR data. In: IEEE Computer Society Conference on Computer Vision and Pattern Recognition (CVPR 2006) (2006)
5. Huang, K.S., Jenkins, B.K., Sawchuk, A.A.: Binary image algebra and optical cellular logic processor design. 45(3), 295–345 (1989)
6. Rottensteiner, F., Trinder, J., Clode, S., Kubik, K.: Using the Dempster-Shafer method for the fusion of LIDAR data and multi-spectral images for building detection. Inf. Fusion 6(4), 283–300 (2005)
7. Rane, S.D., Sapiro, G., Bertalmio, M.: Structure and texture filling-in of missing image blocks in wireless transmission and compression applications. IEEE Trans. Image Process. 12(3), 296–303 (2003)
8. Smith, K., Landes, P.-E., Thollot, J., Myszkowski, K.: Apparent greyscale: a simple and fast conversion to perceptually accurate images and video. Comput. Graph. 27(2), 193–200 (2008)
9. Chen, J., Zhu, X., Volgelmann, J.E., Gao, F., Jin, S.: A simple and effective method for filling gaps in Landsat ETM + SLC-off images. Remote Sens. Environ. 115(4), 1053–1064 (2011)
10. Criminisi, A., P´erez, P., Toyama, K.: Region filling and object removal by exemplar-based image inpainting. IEEE Trans. Image Process. 13(9), 1–13 (2004)
11. Hedberg, H., Kristensen, F., Nilsson, P., Owall, V.: A low complexity architecture for binary image erosion and dilation using structuring element decomposition. In: IEEE International Symposium on Circuits and Systems, pp. 3431–3434 (2005)

12. Liang, J.I., Piper, J., Tang, J.-Y.: Erosion and dilation of binary images by arbitrary structuring elements using interval coding. Pattern Recogn. Lett. **9**(3), 201–209 (1989)
13. Ji, S., Wei, S., Meng, L.: A scale robust convolutional neural network for automatic building extraction from aerial and satellite imagery. Int. J. Remote Sens. **40**(9), 3308–3322 (2019)
14. Griffiths, D., Boehm, J.: Improving public data for building segmentation from convolutional neural networks (CNNs) for fused airborne lidar and image data using active contours. ISPRS J. Photogram. Remote Sens. **154**, 70–8371 (2019)

# Performance Analysis of Feature Detection and Description (FDD) Methods on Accident Images

P. Joyce Beryl Princess⬛, Salaja Silas$^{(\boxtimes)}$⬛,
and Elijah Blessing Rajsingh⬛

Karunya Institute of Technology and Sciences, Coimbatore, India
joeprincess84@gmail.com, blessingsalaja@gmail.com,
elijahblessing@gmail.com

**Abstract.** Feature detection and description is a significant process in several computer vision tasks such as object recognition, detection, image classification and registration. The challenge relies on choosing appropriate feature detector and descriptor, concerning an application, regardless of the appearance and the content of an image. The objective of the performance analysis is to identify the suitable FDD method, in order to extract distinct and robust features from the accident images, possess crucial information for the analysis of accident severity. In this paper, the feature detection and description methods from the literature is applied to the accident images. However, the accident images captured in real-time through mobile cameras confronts motion blur, illumination, rotation and scale variations. Therefore, the robustness of the feature detectors and descriptors are evaluated under various image transformations and the results are compared and analyzed. The result shows, under feature detectors, CenSurE and SIFT performs better with reference to repeatability and matching score. SIFT and ORB are better in the category of feature descriptors for the analysis of accident images.

**Keywords:** Feature detector · Feature descriptor · Repeatability · Matching score · SIFT · MSER · SURF · FAST · CenSurE · AGAST · ORB · BRISK · BRIEF · FREAK

## 1 Introduction

In the recent past, automobiles have been increased enormously, leading to approximately 400 deaths and 1374 road accidents every day in India [1]. As a consequence, the casualty is either dead or injured presumably with incurable disabilities. Analyzing the severity of the accident and providing on-time emergency rescue services is a significant research challenge. Hence, predicting the severity of the accident in real-time is remarkably important to help the survivors with suitable emergency services. For real-time severity analysis, accident image is identified as the significant data. In this regard, to interpret the raw captured image it is essential to extract salient features, which can be accomplished through FDD methods. The schematic representation of accident severity analysis is illustrated in Fig. 1. The outcomes from these methods

© Springer Nature Singapore Pte Ltd. 2020
A. Bhattacharjee et al. (Eds.): MIND 2020, CCIS 1240, pp. 384–396, 2020.
https://doi.org/10.1007/978-981-15-6315-7_32

enclose the information for the analysis of accident severity and availed for further processes such as recognition, detection and classification.

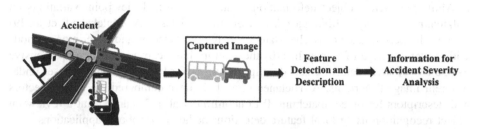

**Fig. 1.** Schematic representation of accident severity analysis

FDD is an essential component for image processing and various computer vision tasks such as object recognition, detection, and tracking [2, 3]. The FDD methods interpret and describe the content of the image concerning specific applications [4, 5]. The features obtained from an image can be categorized as global and local features. The features such as shape, texture and color are the global features that illustrate the entire image as a feature vector constituting every pixel. On the other hand, the local features are edge, corner and blob, which are also named as key or interest points [6]. The feature detectors enable to extract the aforementioned local features, on the other hand, the feature descriptors impart these features in the form of a vector, utilized for further processing namely, image matching, registration and classification.

In this paper, the feature detector and descriptor methods are applied to the accident images with a purpose to identify a suitable technique for the analysis of accident severity. The performance analysis includes comparing the correspondences, identifying the correct and false matches between the set of images subjected to geometric and appearance variations such as motion blur, scale, illumination and rotation. The feature detectors were compared using repeatability and matching score. The recall vs 1-precision curve was used to compare the performance of the feature descriptor.

The remaining paper is organized as follows: the related work on performance analysis of FDD methods applied in different applications is discussed in Sect. 2. Section 3 illustrates an overview of the reviewed feature detector and descriptor methods. Section 4 explains the experimental setup. The evaluation metrics discussed in Sect. 5. The results are shown in Sect. 6 and concluded in Sect. 7.

## 2   Related Work

FDD is used as a preliminary step for most of the computer vision tasks. Hence, a vast number of methods have emerged. The following is a brief discussion on the performance comparison of the developed feature detectors and descriptors studied under different image variations for effective usability in distinctive applications.

Tarek Moutas et al. [7] carried out performance evaluation with six feature detectors, descriptors and its combinations under camera panning, rotation, scale, non-uniformity noise, motion blur variations, applied for far-infrared imagery. In [8] M. Lee and I. Park evaluated the performance of ten feature descriptors for Maximally Stable Extremal Regions (MSER) feature detector under various transformations such as Multiview stereo, object deformation, scale, rotation and viewpoint variations on Salzmann's, Heninly's, Mikolajczyk and Schmid's dataset. A. Malekabadi et al. [9] studied the performance of twelve state-of-art feature detector and descriptor methods with a stereo image of a tree. In [10] the authors have carried out a comprehensive evaluation of local detectors and descriptors for Oxford and Fischer's dataset under different image distortions. A. Hietanen et al. [11] have compared the local detectors and descriptors for object matching. P Loncomilla et al. [12] carried out a review on object recognition using local feature detection methods for robotic applications.

However, a plethora of feature detectors and descriptors have been developed, the challenge relies on identifying suitable feature detectors and descriptors effectively utilized for the relevant applications. In this context, the feature detector and descriptor methods from the literature are studied and applied to accident images for severity analysis.

## 3 Overview of FDD Methods

In this section, the overview of the FDD methods from the literature, considered for the performance evaluation is discussed. Table 1 summarizes the feature detector and descriptor methods chosen from the literature for the performance study on accident images.

**Table 1.** Summary on feature detectors and descriptors methods

| S. No | Name | Abbreviation | Type | Remarks [13] |
|---|---|---|---|---|
| Feature Detectors | | | | |
| 1 | Harris [14] | – | Corner | Scale and rotation invariant. Also, robust to illumination |
| 2 | Shi and Tomasi [15] | GFTT | Corner | Scale, rotation invariant and robust to illumination |
| 3 | Features from Accelerated Segment Test [16] | FAST | Corner | Invariant to rotation. Fast feature detector |
| 4 | Adaptive and Generic Acceleration Segment Test [18] | AGAST | Corner | Robust to blur and noise and invariant to scale and rotation |

*(continued)*

**Table 1.** (*continued*)

| S. No | Name | Abbreviation | Type | Remarks [13] |
|---|---|---|---|---|
| 5 | Maximally Stable Extremal Regions [19] | MSER | Blob | Invariant to scale, rotation, affine and robust to blur |
| 6 | Center Surrounded Extrema Feature [20] | CenSurE | Blob | Robust to rotation, illumination, view point and scale variation |
| Feature Descriptor | | | | |
| 7 | Binary Robust Invariant Scalable Keypoints [21] | BRISK | Binary detector and descriptor, Blob | Invariant to scale and affine transformations |
| 8 | Oriented FAST and Rotated BRIEF [22] | ORB | Binary detector and descriptor, Corner | Invariant to rotation, illumination, noise and blur |
| 9 | Fast Retina Keypoints [23] | FREAK | Binary descriptor, Blob | Robust to blur and rotation variation |
| 10 | Binary Robust Independent Elementary Features [24] | BRIEF | Binary descriptor, Intensity | Robust to illumination, blur and perspective transformations |
| 11 | Scale Invariant Feature Transform [25] | SIFT | Floating-point detector and descriptor, Blob | Robust to rotation and scale |
| 12 | Speeded-Up Robust Feature [26] | SURF | Floating-point detector and descriptor, Blob | Invariant to scale, rotation and affine transformations |

However, the behavior of the methods varies based on the applications and with the appearance of the images. Finding an optimal method, irrespective of image content is still an open research challenge.

## 3.1 Feature Detector

The subsection is an overview of the feature detectors used for the performance analysis, grouped with respect to the type and discussed in terms of methodology.

**Corner Based Detector.** Harris corner [14] is an intensity-based, computes the intensity difference between an image area and window that shift with a displacement in all directions (horizontal, vertical and diagonal). The corners are detected from the Harris score, using two eigenvalues $\lambda 1$ and $\lambda 2$ deduced from the intensity matrix. Shi & Tomasi corner detector [15] otherwise Good Feature To Track (GFTT), differs from Harris corner in corner selection criteria. The candidate feature is said to be corner if the least of the two eigenvalues (i.e., min ($\lambda 1 \lambda 2$)) is larger than a predefined threshold.

FAST the corner detector [16], is computed using Accelerated Segment Test (AST) considering 16 pixels in the form of a circle around the candidate pixel p. The test categorizes the pixels as darker, brighter and similar. FAST uses ID3 a tree-based decision learning algorithm [17] which forms a ternary tree for the pixel states (brighter, darker, and similar). The pixel that yields high information gain is identified as a corner. AGAST [18] is a corner detector that uses AST and non-maximum suppression as FAST. However, for decision making, AGAST builds a binary tree considering computation efficiency. The decision tree by AGAST adapts automatically to the changes providing most efficient corner detection, unlike FAST, it does not learn from scratch for every new pixel added to the training set.

**Blob Based Feature Detector.** MSER [19] is a blob detector capable of detecting regions, such are invariant towards rotations, scale, perspective and illumination transformations. MSER extracts the regions that are stable for a wide range of thresholds. The extracted regions that are above or equal to the threshold and below the threshold are considered as darker and brighter regions respectively. The blob region is computed by connecting the maximal and minimal regions. CenSurE [20] detects the blob by locating the peaks in an image I at different scales using the Hessian and Laplacian method. It uses square, hexagon, and octagons shape bi-level filters, multiplying the image pixel value with either +1 or −1. Then non-maximum suppression is implemented at entire scale spaces, eliminating the weak points that are lesser than the filter threshold response. Finally, line suppression is done using the ration of principal curvature to remove unstable features.

### 3.2 Feature Descriptor

The feature descriptor methods were discussed in this subsection. The descriptors are categorized as floating-point and binary descriptors. The binary descriptors developed lately concerns real-time applications with limited storage and computation speed [10].

**Binary Descriptor.** BRISK [21] is a binary detector and descriptor, detects the key point from the image pyramid constructed at different scale space. To locate the key points, it employs AGAST, the fastest version of the FAST feature detector. BRISK introduces a novel sampling pattern to construct the descriptor for the detected keypoints. The sampling pattern in which the samples are distributed in the form of a concentric circle. The weights of the sample points are categorized as shortest-distance pair and longest-distance pair using the defined threshold. The local gradient is computed from the long-distance pairs. The gradients are summed up to find the direction of the key points. The obtained directions are used to rotate the shortest-distance pairs and the BRISK descriptor is constructed. ORB [22], binary detector and descriptor is developed at OpenCV lab as a workable alternative for SIFT and SURF. Since SIFT and SURF are patent algorithms. ORB utilizes the FAST feature detector and BRIEF descriptor.

FREAK [23] a binary descriptor uses the human retina pattern as a sampling pattern. The density of key points is maximum at the center and decreases towards the borders. To select the appropriate features for the descriptor, the saccadic search is used which mimics the search of human vision. The descriptor is constructed same as the BRISK by computing the sum of the gradients at the rotation of the key points. BRIEF [24] the binary descriptor, enables fast image matching at low computation cost. In BRIEF, each keypoint is described in 128–512 bits string. The descriptor is constructed by considering image at each pixel from an image patch p and to avoid noise the patch is smoothed using Gaussian kernel. Moreover, this makes the descriptor, increasing the recognition rate. For constructing binary feature vector, binary test ($\tau$) is performed at every image patch of size $P \times P$. The test point (a, b) in a patch is selected at random. Blob based feature detector and descriptor.

**Floating-Point Descriptor.** SIFT [25] detects the keypoints computing the maxima and minima from the image at different scale spaces. The unstable points are removed using keypoint localization. The gradient and magnitude are calculated for $4 \times 4$ neighboring pixels around every key point. The peak orientations are identified and described in a set of 8 bins histograms. Therefore, the SIFT feature descriptor has features of size 128 that are distinct and robust. SURF [26] employs box filters and determinant of Hessian for detecting the key points for fast computation. The descriptor is constructed by finding the orientation using Haar wavelet in a circular fashion around the keypoints detected at scale space s. The integral image is employed again for filtering the orientations since the wavelet is huge at larger scale spaces. The orientations which have the largest sum value are identified as predominant orientation resulting as SURF descriptor of length 64 (Harr wavelet response in $4 \times 4$ subregions $\times$ 4 values).

In summary, it is important to highlight that the performance of the feature detector and descriptor methods will be influenced by the number of features detected and the length of the descriptors. This variation is due to the dissimilarity in the implementation of each method. For instance, corner features are not the same as blob regions and the size of the floating-point descriptors is not the same as binary descriptors. Hence, the performance will vary apparently.

## 4 Experimental Setup

The experiment is carried out with the dataset created containing accident images collected from the public domain. The dataset includes 1112 fatal and 1072 non-fatal accident images. The sample images from the dataset are presented in Fig. 2.

**Fig. 2.** Sample accident images from the dataset

The reference images are randomly chosen from the collected accident images. The query images are generated by applying four image transformations such as motion blurring, varying scale, rotation and illumination using OpenCV. The features are detected from the set of reference and query images. Feature matching is performed between the features detected from both the images and they are evaluated using the metrics discussed in Sect. 5. The implementation of the feature detector, descriptors and image matching are performed using the OpenCV library in Python.

## 5   Evaluation Metrics

The feature detector and descriptor are evaluated using the standard metric described in the literature [27, 28]. It defines repeatability, matching score as metric for evaluating feature detectors and recall vs 1-precision curve, as performance comparison metric for feature descriptors.

Repeatability is used to measure the invariability of the features obtained from the different feature detectors under different image transformations. Repeatability is defined as given in Eq. 1, the proposition of correspondences to the minimum number of features in reference and query image. The correspondences are computed by using ground truth homography as given in [28].

$$Repeatability = \frac{Number\ of\ Correspondence}{\min(reference\ image\ features,\ query\ image\ features)} \quad (1)$$

The matching score discloses the algorithm's distinctiveness and is computed using Eq. 2. It is defined as the ratio between the number of correct matches to the total number of matches between the reference and query image.

$$Matching\ Score = \frac{Number\ of\ correct\ matches}{Total\ number\ of\ matches} \tag{2}$$

The common strategy to measure the feature descriptor is applying a matching strategy to the feature vectors obtained from the reference and query image and plotted as recall vs 1-precision curve. The recall and 1-precision are calculated from Eq. 3 and 4 respectively. The number of correct and false matches is identified using the Nearest Neighbor Distance Ratio matching strategy. The match is declared as correct when the distance between the first and second nearest neighbor is less than a threshold. The distance measure used for floating-point descriptors is L2-Norm (Euclidean distance) and Hamming distance for binary descriptors.

$$Recall = \frac{Number\ of\ correct\ matches}{Total\ number\ of\ correspondences} \tag{3}$$

$$1 - Precision = \frac{Number\ of\ false\ matches}{Total\ number\ of\ matches} \tag{4}$$

## 6  Results and Discussion

The performance analysis of feature detectors and descriptor methods on accident images is discussed in this section. Figure 3 shows sample feature detection and matching.

**Fig. 3.** Sample feature detection and matching

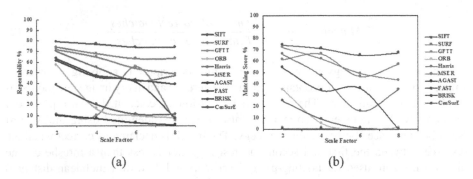

**Fig. 4.** Performance analysis of detectors in repeatability % (a) and matching score (b) under scale variations

Figure 4 illustrates the performance analysis of feature detectors about scale variations. The size of the image varies with the camera of the smartphone in terms of dimension, while capturing the accident image in real-time. Therefore, a series of images are generated by varying the size of the reference image in terms of width and height. The performance of the feature detector is evaluated for the images at various sizes to identify the suitable image scale for processing the real-time accident image. The repeatability and matching score from the result proves SIFT detector performs better in terms of various scales, as the method is invariant to scale variations.

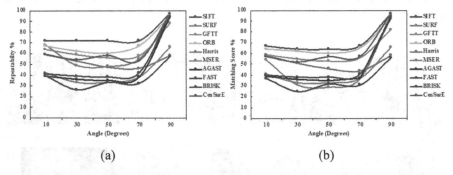

**Fig. 5.** Performance comparison of detectors with respect to repeatability score (a) and matching score (b) under rotation variations

Generally, the smartphone adjusts the orientation of the camera to detect the face on the screen. It rotates from 0° to 90° on the optical axis. Therefore, the original images in the dataset are transformed from angle 0° to 90° and the performance of the feature detectors is evaluated to understand the invariance towards rotation. Figure 5 illustrates the robustness of SIFT towards the rotation variation from the repeatability and matching score.

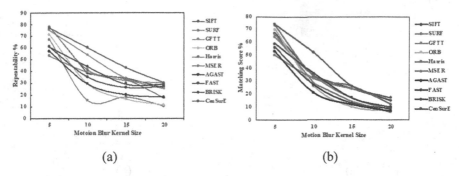

(a)                                              (b)

**Fig. 6.** Performance comparison of detectors with respect to repeatability score (a) and matching score (b) under motion blur

Figure 6 demonstrates the performance analysis of feature detectors through motion blur. When a person captures an accident scene from a moving vehicle using the mobile camera, the captured image may be distorted due to motion. Therefore, for the experimental purpose, the reference images are subjected to motion blur effect by convoluting image with the filter of size n × n. As the size of n increases, the effect of the motion blur also increases. The feature detectors are evaluated in this context. However, the performance of the detectors degrades as the motion blur increases. But the CenSurE detector performs better compared to other detectors.

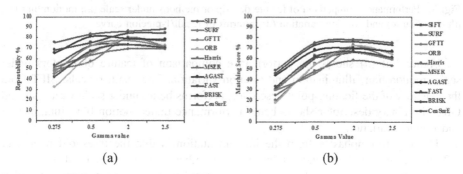

(a)                                              (b)

**Fig. 7.** Performance comparison of detectors with respect to repeatability score (a) and matching score (b) under illumination variation

It is observed that the accidents occur during dawn, day, noon, dusk or night and besides it is recorded, most of the accidents occur during the dawn time [29]. In this context, the ability of the invariance towards light conditions of the feature detectors are tested and evaluated by transforming the original images under various illumination variation. The performance comparison of feature detectors shown in Fig. 7 reveals, CenSurE feature detector performs better in dark (0.25 Gamma value) and brighter (2.5 Gamma value). The FAST detector is close to CenSurE concerning matching score.

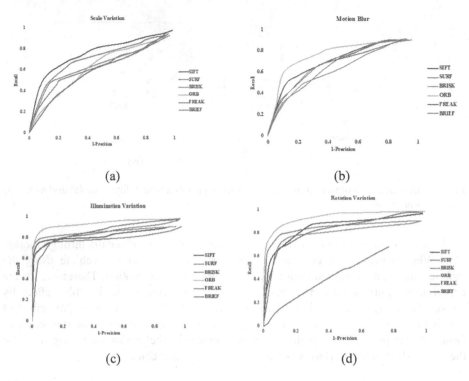

**Fig. 8.** Performance comparison of feature descriptor methods under scale (a), motion blur (b), illumination (c) and rotation variation (d) in terms of recall/1-precion curve.

Figure 8(a)–(d) shows the performance comparison of feature descriptors under scale, motion blur, illumination and rotation variation. The result reveals, SIFT from the category of the floating-point descriptor, performs better under scale variations and ORB the binary descriptor shows better performance under motion blur, illumination and rotation variation.

The fact to emphasize from the implementation is that the threshold parameter differs with the methods and influences the number of features to be detected. For instance, FAST and AGAST extract a large number of features compared to other detectors, but has lesser repeatability and matching score. Fine-tuning of the threshold parameter was challenging against the geometric variations and the content of an image. The increase in the number of features and size of the descriptors influences the computation time. On the other hand, limiting the features in the number and dimension of the descriptors leads to the loss of essential information. This trade-off is another challenge in the evaluation of the performance of FDD methods with the accident images.

# 7 Conclusion

Features such as edge, corner and blob define the object instances in an image. These image features can be detected and described using feature detector and descriptor methods, which play a major role in machine learning, computer vision-based applications. Due to the deepened research on feature detection and description and emerge of computer vision, various methods were proposed eventually. In this regard, methods from the literature were experimented, analyzed and applied for the accident images with various image transformations. For accident images, the result reveals, the performance of the feature detector SIFT and CenSurE are better in performance compared to other detectors. The former is better under scale and rotation variation, whereas the latter shows better performance under motion blur and illumination variation. The SIFT and ORB are better under the category of feature descriptors. As a future scope, this investigation intends to extend for classification of accident severity applying learning algorithms.

# References

1. Mahata, D., Narzary, P.K., Govil, D.: Spatio-temporal analysis of road traffic accidents in Indian large cities. Clin. Epidemiol. Glob. Health 7(4), 586–591 (2019)
2. Cadoni, M., Lagorio, A., Grosso, E.: Incremental models based on feature persistence for object recognition. Pattern Recognit. Lett. **122**, 38–44 (2019)
3. Bhuvaneswari, R., Subban, R.: Novel object detection and recognition system based on points of interest selection and SVM classification. Cogn. Syst. Res. **52**, 985–994 (2018)
4. Xu, W., Zhong, S., Yan, L., Wu, F., Zhang, W.: Moving object detection in aerial infrared images with registration accuracy prediction and feature points selection. Infrared Phys. Technol. **92**, 318–326 (2018)
5. Vinay, A., Aklecha, N., Meghana, Murthy, K.N.B., Natarajan, S.: On detectors and descriptors based techniques for face recognition. Procedia Comput. Sci. **132**, 908–917 (2018)
6. Awad, A.I., Hassaballah, M.: Image feature detectors and descriptors: foundations and applications. Stud. Comput. Intell. **630**, 11–46 (2016)
7. Mouats, T., Aouf, N., Nam, D., Vidas, S.: Performance evaluation of feature detectors and descriptors beyond visible. J. Intell. Robot. Syst. **92**, 33–63 (2018). https://doi.org/10.1007/s10846-017-0762-8
8. Lee, M., Park, I.: Performance evaluation of local descriptors for maximally stable extremal regions. J. Vis. Commun. Image Represent. **47**, 62–72 (2017)
9. Malekabadi, A., Khojastehpour, M., Emadi, B.: A comparative evaluation of combined feature detectors and descriptors in different color spaces for stereo image matching of tree. Scientia Horticulturae **228**, 187–195 (2018)
10. Wu, S., Oerlemans, A., Bakker, E.M., Lew, S.: A comprehensive evaluation of local detectors and descriptors. Sig. Process. Image Commun. **59**, 150–167 (2017)
11. Hietanen, A., Lankinen, J., Kristian, J., Glent, A., Krüger, N.: A comparison of feature detectors and descriptors for object class matching. Neurocomputing **184**, 3–12 (2016)
12. Loncomilla, P., Ruiz-del-Solar, J.: Object recognition using local invariant features for robotic applications: a survey. Pattern Recogn. **60**, 499–514 (2016)

13. Johansson, J.: Interest point detectors and descriptors for IR images: an evaluation of common detectors and descriptors on IR images, Dissertation (2015)
14. Harris, C., Stephens, M.: A combined corner and edge detector. In: Proceedings of Alvey Vision Conference, pp. 147–151 (1988)
15. Shi, J., Tomasi, C.: Good features to track. In: Proceedings of International Conference on Computer Vision and Pattern Recognition (CVPR), pp. 593–600 (1994)
16. Rosten, E., Drummond, T.: Fusing points and lines for high performance real-time tracking. In: Proceedings of the Tenth IEEE International Conference on Computer Vision (ICCV 2005) (2005)
17. Rosten, E., Drummond, T.: Machine learning for high-speed corner detection. In: Leonardis, A., Bischof, H., Pinz, A. (eds.) ECCV 2006. LNCS, vol. 3951, pp. 430–443. Springer, Heidelberg (2006). https://doi.org/10.1007/11744023_34
18. Mair, E., Hager, G.D., Burschka, D., Suppa, M., Hirzinger, G.: Adaptive and generic corner detection based on the accelerated segment test. In: Daniilidis, K., Maragos, P., Paragios, N. (eds.) ECCV 2010. LNCS, vol. 6312, pp. 183–196. Springer, Heidelberg (2010). https://doi.org/10.1007/978-3-642-15552-9_14
19. Matas, J., Chum, O., Urban, M., Pajdla, T.: Robust wide-baseline stereo from maximally stable extremal regions. Image Vis. Comput. **22**(10), 761–767 (2004)
20. Agrawal, M., Konolige, K., Blas, M.R.: CenSurE: Center surround extremas for realtime feature detection and matching. In: Forsyth, D., Torr, P., Zisserman, A. (eds.) ECCV 2008. LNCS, vol. 5305, pp. 102–115. Springer, Heidelberg (2008). https://doi.org/10.1007/978-3-540-88693-8_8
21. Brisk, B., Card, O.R.B.: BRISK: binary robust invariant scalable keypoints. In: IEEE International Conference on Computer Vision (ICCV), pp. 1–8 (2011)
22. Rublee, E., Rabaud, V., Konolige, K., Bradski, G.: ORB: an efficient alternative to SIFT or SURF. In: Proceedings of IEEE International Conference on Computer Vision, pp. 2564–2571 (2011)
23. Alahi, A., Ortiz, R., Vandergheynst P.: FREAK: fast retina keypoint. In: IEEE Computer Society Conference on Computer Vision and Pattern Recognition, pp. 510–517 (2012)
24. Zhang, F., Ye, F., Su, Z.: A modified feature point descriptor based on binary robust independent elementary features. In: Proceedings of 2014 7th International Congress on Image and Signal Processing, CISP 2014, pp. 258–263(2014)
25. Lowe, D.G.: Distinctive image features from sclae-invariant keypoints. Int. J. Comput. Vis. **60**(2), 91–110 (2004). https://doi.org/10.1023/B:VISI.0000029664.99615.94
26. Bay, H., Ess, A., Tuytelaars, T., Van Gool, L.: Speeded-Up robust features (SURF)". Comput. Vis. Image Underst. **110**(3), 346–359 (2008)
27. Mikolajczyk, K., Schmid, C.: A performance evaluation of local descriptors. IEEE Trans. Pattern Anal. Mach. Intell. **27**(10), 1615–1630 (2005)
28. Schmid, C., Mohr, R., Bauckhage, C.: Evaluation of interest point detectors. Int. J. Comput. Vis. **37**(2), 151–172 (2000). https://doi.org/10.1023/A:1008199403446
29. Road Accident Data – India. https://data.gov.in

# Image Authentication Using Tensor Decomposition and Local Features with Geometric Correction

Madhumita Paul$^{(\boxtimes)}$, Ram Kumar Karsh, and F. A. Talukdar

National Institute of Technology Silchar, Silchar 788010, Assam, India
mita6paul@gmail.com

**Abstract.** In this paper, we proposed an image hashing using both global and local features. Global features are determined using tensor decomposition and local features are takeout from salient regions. SLIC algorithm are used to find out the salient area. The hash are constructed from global and local features. The test results on large dataset specify that the suggested method is vigorous to content-preserving operations (CPOs) and has good distinction. In addition, the method can also localize the tampering reigns. In this method, there are two phase. In the first phase," the different image pairs" and "similar and tampered pairs" are segregated using threshold T1. In second phase, tampering localization and separation of. "the similar (authentic) image pairs" and "tampered image pairs" are carried out with another threshold T2. The receiver operating characteristics (ROC) indicate that this technique is superior than others.

**Keywords:** Image hashing · Image authentication · Tensor decomposition · Tucker decomposition · Tampering localization

## 1 Introduction

With the advancement in technologies, digital images can be stored and shared via various multimedia devices such as smart phones, digital cameras and scanners. Digital images can be easily manipulated due to openness of networks. This can be done using many sophisticated editing tools and software such as Adobe Photoshop, Corel Paint Shop etc. The reliability of the image content has happen to an urgent concern because of its widespread use in courtroom evidences, scientific scams, insurance claims, crime investigation, medical fields, entertainment and education etc. [1]. These manipulations affect the opinions and decisions based on the images. In recent years, there have been many issues like journalists have tampered images to create fake news events and gain attention. These are used in the field of research and development. Also, the crime investigators, lawyers, employ the images to manipulate the opinion of others.

Image tampering is defined as "adding or removing important features from an image without leaving any obvious traces of tampering." A number of the familiar image tampering techniques are copy-move, image splicing, resize, cropping, noise or blurring etc. As tampering of digital images has become so convenient, authenticity of images has become a question. So, there is a requirement of a robust and reliable

© Springer Nature Singapore Pte Ltd. 2020
A. Bhattacharjee et al. (Eds.): MIND 2020, CCIS 1240, pp. 397–411, 2020.
https://doi.org/10.1007/978-981-15-6315-7_33

tamper detection method. There are two types of Image tampering detection techniques. One of them uses prior information that is available to tell us whether the image is digitally altered or not, known as Active forgery detection whereas it has become seemingly more important to do this without any prior information available, giving rise to Passive forgery detection.

Active forgery includes: Watermarking – Process of embedding information into a digital image so that it is difficult to remove [2]. Digital Signature- Used for converting of the information in encryption and decryption [3].

Image hashing is a process which takes out a brief unique sequence from the image so as to resolve the difficulties of image verification and content-based image retrieval [4]. Perfect image hash should have the following. Robustness-Visibly Similar images contain the identical hash irrespective of their digital portrayal [5]. Thus, digital operations require vigorous image hashing. Discrimination- Images having different contents should have variable hashes. Security-The image hash must be created with the help of a cryptic key, so that estimation of the hash becomes tricky and complicated on not knowing the appropriate key. The literature survey on hashing is discussed in next section.

## 2 Literature Survey

Hashing of image is a method of mapping an image to a small sequence known as image hash quantity. It has significant importance in many applications [6–11], like digital watermarking, approximate nearest neighbor search, image retrieval and authentication, quality assessment of image and multimedia forensics. As per literature, robust image hashing is first introduced in [12]. In this algorithm, binary hash has been constructed via randomized signal processing. The method is robust against compression and geometric distortions. In another work, a DCT-based features approach was used by Fredrich et al. [13] so as to find out region copying. This system although being useful, the fallacy lies that presence of large variations in copied regions lead to the failure of the method.

The earlier works are discrete wavelet transform (DWT) given in [14]. It uses a safe image hashing technique for tamper localization but is flimsy to certain digital manipulating operations. Image hashing can also be done using Discrete Fourier transforms (DFT) as developed by Swaminathan et al. [15] which produced image hashes using the DFT coefficients. This is flexible to operations like rotation within 20. Creation of robust image hashes against perceptually acceptable modifications was done by Monga et al. [16] using the properties prevailing in the non-negative matrix factorization (NMF). Examples - Gaussian filtering, JPEG compression and are too sensitive to image rotation. NMF has great performance when compared to that of SVDs (singular value decomposition). Further, NMF approach was improved by Tang et al. [17].

Lv et al. [18] planned a SIFT-Harris detector to detect a large number of stable SIFT key points for rotation operations. This approach can identify tampered image and is robust against geometric attacks. But the performance be deteriorated if there is non-matching of perceived key points between the test images and the original one.

Method [19] includes principal component analysis (PCA) along with Radon transform used to extract characteristics which is robust against geometrical modifications which includes scaling and rotation and normal image transformations like compression, filtering, and blurring.

Schneider and Chang [20] constructed image hash by extracting histogram of block pixels. In a further study, Xiang et al. [21] formed image hash using invariance of histogram. This is strong to large angle rotation. Lei et al. [22] developed a good process with rotation robustness where important moments of the DFT coefficients are used to compute hash. Fan-beam transform based hashing was proposed by Tang et al. [23]. Its performance is better in classification and running speed than conventional RT based hashing [22] and thus computational cost was reduced.

A singular value decomposition (SVD) twice is exploited in [24]. It has effective rotation robustness although lack discrimination. The performance of [24] has been improved in [25] using DWT-SVD. Davarzani et al. [26] proposed a technique using SVD and local binary patterns. It prevents brightness, JPEG compression, and blurring change, but has weak ability of discrimination. In [27] speeded up robust feature (SURF) has been used to create hash. This method is strong to some digital operation, however tampering localization is not discussed. From above survey it is found that hashes generated only from global feature provide poor discrimination property.

Present work is generating the desired hash function by combining both local and global features to generate Global features is obtained using the entire image using tensor decomposition while the local features is created only from salient area. To discriminate "the different image pairs" and "similar and tampered pairs" global feature are used. Whereas local features segregates "the similar (authentic) image pairs" and "tampered image pairs". In addition, it has been also used for localization of tampering area.

The rest of the paper is structured as follows. The proposed method for hashing the image has been included in Sect. 3. The implementation of hashing for content authentication is represented in Sect. 4. Section 5 addresses experimental findings. Section 6 narrates the findings and possible scopes.

## 3   Proposed Image Hashing

Proposed hashing strategy flow map is sketched in Fig. 1. In the subsequent subsections the details of techniques have been discussed.

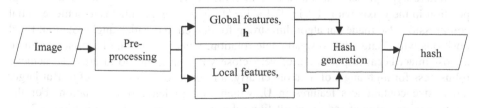

**Fig. 1.** Proposed image hashing

The received input image is initially pre-processed by method as mentioned in reference [35]. Image is preprocessed for reducing the influences of content preserving operations. Then third order tensor is generated from normalized image. Later, a compact hash is generated by tensor decomposition (TD) [12, 13]. TD uses a very well-known algorithm known as Tucker Decomposition [28]. Core tensor and three orthogonal matrices are prepared from three-order tensor which are exploited to construct a compact image hash. The following subsections describe the stages of our hashing method.

### 3.1  Pre-processing

Initially, the input image is pre-processed by bi-cubic interpolation. An iterative multi-scale bicubic interpolation method resizes the input image to a $M \times M$. Thus, a constant size hash which is robust against image rescaling is obtained. Next, convert an RGB image into CIE $\mathbf{L}^*\mathbf{a}^*\mathbf{b}^*$ model and intensity component, $\mathbf{L}^*$, has been used for further analysis due to perceptually uniform [41]. Further, reduction of the effect of minor changes, such as filtering and noise is done by the Gaussian low-pass filtering yields preprocessed image.

### 3.2  Global Features

The global features have been extracted using tensor construction and tensor decomposition, discussed in next subsections.

**Tensor Construction.** The pre-processed image produced tri-order tensor in order to generate a hash with tensor decomposition. For this, the preprocessed image is split into blocks of size $S \times S$ without overlapping. Let $M$ be an integral multiple of $S$. As a result, there are $D = M/S$ blocks along x-axis and y-axis directions. For making an early compression the mean value of individually block is estimated, and a feature matrix $\mathbf{U}$ is attained below.

$$\mathbf{U} = \begin{bmatrix} U_{1,1}U_{1,2} & \cdots & U_{1,D} \\ U_{2,1} & U_{2,2} & U_{2,D} \\ \vdots & \cdots & \vdots \\ U_{D,1}U_{D,1} & \cdots & U_{D,D} \end{bmatrix} \qquad (1)$$

Where $U_{i,j}$ represents the block's mean value in the $i-$ th position in x-axis and j-th position in the y-axis with $(1 \leq i \leq D, 1 \leq j \geq D)$. This operation helps to achieve initial compression also made our algorithm strong for detection of small angle rotation. Pixel positions will change due to small angle rotation, where the mean of the block remain almost intact because pixels are of very close value in a tiny local area. To achieve robustness for high angle of rotation, clearly, a large size of block is useful. But larger block size contain less features in $\mathbf{U}$, which in turn harm discrimination. For the purpose of experiment and to get rotation robustness as well as discrimination, a $2 \times 2$ block size is chosen. $\mathbf{U}$ is than further separated into un-overlapped blocks of $Q \times Q$

dimension. For easiness, let $D$ is integral multiple of yields $n = (D/Q)^2$ blocks. Hash is secure using key $k1$, in this respect generate $n$ block sized $Q \times Q$. The overlapping region between random blocks that occur during the selection but cannot be selected again for the same block. Hence, $L = 2n$ diverse blocks designated. To raise the security of algorithm, one more secret key $k2$ is opted to stack these $L$ block arbitrarily. A three-order tensor $\mathbf{X}$ of dimension $Q \times Q \times L$ is thus generated. Hence random block selection and random block stacking ensure security.

**Tensor Decomposition.** Tucker decomposition is a method of higher-order analysis of principal component. Computer vision, data mining, graph analysis, signal processing etc. use this [28, 29]. Here, Tucker Decomposition [29] was used to decompose a tensor X into a core tensor G multiplied by a matrix in each direction. For instance, a tensor $X \in R_{i \times j \times k}$ of third-order is decomposed as [29].

$$\mathbf{X} \approx \mathbf{G} \times \mathbf{U}_1 \times \mathbf{U}_2 \times \mathbf{U}_3 \tag{1}$$

Where $\mathbf{G} \in R_{P \times Q \times R}$ is the core tensor, and $\mathbf{U}_1 \in R_{i \times p}, \mathbf{U}_2 \in R_{j \times Q}, \mathbf{U}_3 \in R_{k \times R}$ are the orthogonal factor matrices. As Tucker Decomposition's orthogonal factor matrices can represent the original tensor's intrinsic structure, we are exploiting that to generate an image hash. For $\mathbf{U}_1$, we measure the mean of each row and then get a vector function as follows:

$$P^{(U_1)} = \left[ P_1^{(U_1)}, P_2^{(U_1)}, \cdots P_Q^{(U_1)} \right]^T \tag{2}$$

here $P_i^{(U_1)}$ represents mean for $i$–th row of $U_1 (1 \leq i \leq Q)$). Further, $P^{(U_1)}$ is translated into a binary sequence as

$$h_i^{(U_1)} = \begin{cases} 0 & P^{(U_1)} < m^{(U_1)} \\ 1 & \text{Elsewhere} \end{cases} \tag{3}$$

where $m^{(U_1)}$ depicts mean of all $P^{(U_1)}$ elements. Likewise, the feature vector for $\mathbf{U}_2$ generated as

$$P^{(U_2)} = \left[ P_1^{(U_2)}, P_2^{(U_2)}, \cdots P_Q^{(U_2)} \right]^T \tag{4}$$

here $P_i^{(U_2)}$ represents mean for $i$–th row of $U_2 (1 \leq i \leq Q)$). Further, $P^{(U_2)}$ is translated into a binary sequence as

$$h_i^{(U_2)} = \begin{cases} 0 & P^{(U_2)} < m^{(U_2)} \\ 1 & \text{Elsewhere} \end{cases} \tag{5}$$

where $m^{(U_2)}$ depicts mean of all $P^{(U_2)}$ elements. Likewise, the feature vector for $U_3$ generated as

$$P^{(U_3)} = \left[ P_1^{(U_3)}, P_2^{(U_3)}, \cdots P_Q^{(U_3)} \right]^T \tag{6}$$

here $P_i^{(U_3)}$ represents mean for $i$-th row of $U_3 (1 \leq i \leq Q))$. Further, $P^{(U_3)}$ is translated to a binary sequence as

$$h_i^{(U_3)} = \begin{cases} 0 & P^{(U_3)} < m^{(U_3)} \\ 1 & \text{Otherwise} \end{cases} \tag{7}$$

where $m^{(U_3)}$ depicts mean of all $P^{(U_3)}$ elements. Now, the first intermediate hash is represented as

$$\mathbf{h} = \left[ h_1^{(U_1)}, h_2^{(U_1)}, \ldots, h_Q^{(U_1)}, h_1^{(U_2)}, h_2^{(U_2)}, \ldots, h_Q^{(U_2)}, h_1^{(U_3)}, h_2^{(U_3)}, \ldots, h_L^{(U_3)} \right] \tag{8}$$

The length of first intermedia hash is $2Q + L$ bits.

### 3.3 Local Features

The salient area is a visual perceive of an image. Here, we have explored a recent technique for saliency detection which is composed of both super pixel segmentation and objectness estimation method [30]. According to [31] the binarized normed gradients (BING) is used to find out relevant objects in the original image. Its disadvantage is that some parts of the salient objects are missed out so there has to be a combination of BING method with super-pixel segmentation technique. The method [30] is discussed briefly as follows:

**Object Estimation by BING.** According to the method proposed by Alexe et al. [32], homogeneity is exhibited by the background regions of the image while heterogeneity is exhibited by the object regions. Thus there exists a strong correlation between the generic objects with well-defined closed boundaries. This occurs after rescaling of the corresponding image windows considering the norm of the gradient to a small fixed size [31]. Several windows on the preprocessed image were initially selected and multiscale transformations were performed on the entire image. The gradient map was then calculated by normalizing the windows to $8 \times 8$ and normed gradients (NG) features were further derived. A $8 \times 8$ classification matrix is opted to see if the NG feature map was an object. There is then a separation of the original image from all NG feature maps categorized as an object.

**Saliency Map Calculation.** The saliency map is calculated using regional feature methods [33]. In order to divide the image into small regions, a graph-based image segmentation was used, and a color histogram is created for each area. Finally, the salience value $S(r_k)$ for each region $r_k$ was calculated by the following equation:

$$S(r_k) = \sum_{r_k \neq r_i} w(r_k) D_{r(r_k, r_i)} \tag{9}$$

where $w(r_k)$ denotes the weight of region $r_k$ and $D_r(\cdot, \cdot)$ depicts the color distance metric among two regions.

**Super-Pixel Segmentation.** This method has split the image into different sub-regions and will have the same saliency value. For this reason the simple linear iterative clustering (SLIC) method [34] is employed.

**Image Fusion.** To cover for the missing salient areas an image fusion approach was used between the salience map and the sub-regions. It can be described as follows: The average saliency value $(A_k)$ for each sub region $(k)$ obtained from super pixel segmentation was calculated as:

$$A_k - \sum_{i=1}^{N} n_i / N \tag{10}$$

where N represents is the total count of pixels in the sub region. The saliency value of each pixel in the sub region is $n_i$. The succeeding equation enhances average saliency value.

$$E_k = \begin{cases} 0; A_k < 6 \\ 255 \times lg(A_K + 1)/lg256 \end{cases}; A_k \geq 6 \tag{11}$$

All pixels in sub-region $k$ were ensured to have the same saliency value as $E_k$. From each salient regions coordinates of the upper left corner $(x_k, y_k)$, height $(ht_k)$ and width $(wd_k)$ are considered as local features, $\mathbf{p}_k = [x_k, y_k, ht_k, wd_k]$, where $k = 1, 2, \ldots, \delta$. Experimental results on 2500 images have shown that in 96.4% images the number of salient regions is up to six. If the number of salient regions increases, the length of hash increases and if number of salient regions decreases, hash length decreases. The hash length and number of salient regions are therefore a tradeoff between them. Hence, we have considered 6 salient regions as optimum value for local feature construction. Finally, the second intermediary hash is as follows

$$\mathbf{p} = [\mathbf{p}_1, \mathbf{p}_2, \ldots, \mathbf{p}_6] \tag{12}$$

The length of second intermediate hash is $4 \times 6 \times 8 = 192$ bits.

### 3.4    Hash Generation

Final hash are created from both global and local features based intermediate hashes as follows

$$\mathbf{h}_f = [\mathbf{h}, \mathbf{p}] \tag{13}$$

Final hash consist $2Q + L + 192$ bits.

### 3.5   Performance Measuring Parameters

The efficacy of the proposed method is discussed based on L2 norm (Euclidean distance or hash distance). Let the hash values of the source and query image are $\mathbf{h}_f = [\mathbf{h}, \mathbf{p}]$ and $\mathbf{h}'_f = [\mathbf{h}', \mathbf{p}']$. Then the hash distance (only global features are used) between $\mathbf{h}$ and $\mathbf{h}'$ is obtained as

$$\text{Hash distances } d, = \sqrt{\sum_{i=1}^{n} |h(i) - h'(i)|^2} \tag{14}$$

where $h(i)$ and $h'(i)$ represents $i$−th element of $\mathbf{h}$ and $\mathbf{h}'$. There is comparison between the obtained hash, $\mathbf{h}'$, with the original image hash, $\mathbf{h}$, using Euclidean distance. While Euclidean distance is larger than the selected threshold $T1$ (where $T1$ is selected threshold, discussed in Sect. 5.1), we analyze that the images given are different. When the images aren't different, we detect the salient regions. The image is said to be an 'authentic one' when the hash distance of all the salient regions match, else it is a 'tampered one'. The FPR and TPR are defined as follows via hash distances:

$$P_{FPR}(d \leq T) = \frac{Number\ of\ different\ images\ judged\ as\ similar\ image}{Total\ Pair\ of\ different\ image} \tag{15}$$

$$P_{TPR}(d \leq T) = \frac{Number\ of\ pair\ of\ similar\ image\ judgedas\ similar}{Total\ number\ of\ similar\ image} \tag{16}$$

FPR and TPR are the measure of discrimination and robustness, respectively. The visualization of the algorithm's classification accuracy is interpreted by the receiver operating characteristic curve (ROC) for fair comparisons. The curve is formed by taking parameters of true positive rate (TPR) on the abscissa and false positive rate (FPR) as ordinate respectively. The larger the area under the ROC curve, the higher the performance of classification.

## 4   Application of Proposed Hashing in Image Authentication

The image validation using our suggested hashing system is shown in Fig. 2. The particulars are discussed in the subsequent subsections.

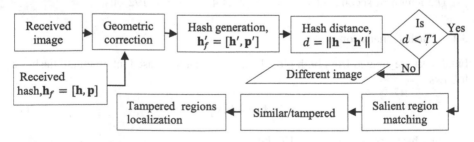

**Fig. 2.** Proposed image authentication system

## 4.1 Geometric Correction

For authentication or tampering localization, geometric transformation influences of the received image is eliminated at first. In order to accomplish this, we have used the method proposed in [35]. Here initially rotation angle is obtained from following geometric transformation as:

$$\theta = \arctan(\Delta Y / \Delta X); \quad \theta' = \arctan(\Delta Y' / \Delta X') \quad (17)$$

Where, the non-zero pixel coordinates for the extreme left, right, top and bot-tom pixels are defined by $(X_l, Y_l)$, $(X_r, Y_r)$, $(X_t, Y_t)$, and $(X_b, Y_b)$ respectively. Here, $\Delta x = X_r - X_b, \Delta y = Y_r - Y_b, \Delta x' = X_t - X_l, \Delta y' = Y_t - Y$. A received image is said to be rotated by an angle $\theta'$, if $\theta \cong \theta$. This distortion is corrected by anti-rotation of the image by $\theta'$. Eventually, area of interest is cropped to obtain the desired image.

## 4.2 Image Authentication

The reference hash, $\mathbf{h}_f = [\mathbf{h}, \mathbf{p}]$, is sent by a protected network and the image of the same hash is sent through the internet (unsecure channel). The received image is corrected using geometric method, discussed in Sect. 4.1. Next, generate the hash of the corrected image, $\mathbf{h}'_f = [\mathbf{h}', \mathbf{p}']$. The Euclidean distance, $d$, is determined between $\mathbf{h}$ and $\mathbf{h}'$. The received image is considered as distinct image, in case $d$ is greater than the threshold $T1$, else it is manipulated. The segregation between the tampered and similar images, also localization of tampered regions are discussed in next subsections.

## 4.3 Localization of Tampered Regions

In order to distinguish the similar image from a manipulated image and to find the manipulated regions in case of manipulated image, we use information about saliency regions made up of local features, discussed in Sect. 4.3. If the image obtained is changed, the salient regions in the image transmitted and received will be different. For salient region matching, we initially find mean value of local features corresponding to each regions, $mean(\mathbf{p}_k)$ and $mean(\mathbf{p}'_k)$ for reference and query image, respectively. If $dmin = mean(\mathbf{p}_k) - mean(\mathbf{p}'_k)$ is less than $T2$, the query image is considered similar one (authentic), otherwise maliciously tampered. Experiment carried out on 800 tampered image pair and selected $T2 = 1.7$. Further, the mismatch regions are highlighted in the received image called tampered regions. Let us study a reference image by four salient regions and two in case of received, then the position vectors for each image are $p = [p_1 p_2 p_3 p_4 00]$ and $p' = [p'_1 p'_2 0000]$ respectively. Here, regions 1 and 2 may be exactly matching regions between the reference and the received image. Within the received image the regions 3 and 4 could have been deleted (i.e., p03 and p04 respectively). The image receiving these two deleted regions will be highlighted. Similarly, in case salient regions in the reference image is smaller than the one received, it could be a case of insertion and the area inserted in the image received will be highlighted. Moreover, if number of salient regions in reference as well as received images are same and *dmin* is greater than $T2$, then the received image consists replaced objects.

## 5   Experimental Results

The optimal values of parameters of our TD hashing are considered as: The reference image is rescaled to size $M \times M$; a Gaussian low-pass $3 \times 3$ filter having unit standard deviation and mean zero is used; $S \times S$ non-overlapping blocks are formed on dividing the $L^*$ component and thus the matrix $U$ of the size $D \times D$ is formed which is again separated into non-overlapping parts of size $Q \times Q$. Let $n$ equal to random blocks number, $I, J, K$ of Tucker decomposition is designated as 1. For the calculation of global hash, we have $n = 16, M = 256, D = 128, S = 2 \, and \, Q = 32$. As a result, the tensor construction requires $L = 2n = 32$ the number of blocks used. Hence, the generated global hash length is $N = 2Q + L = 96$ bits. For calculation of local hash, we have: six salient regions, each regions needs four parameters. Therefore, it require $4 \times 6 = 24 \, integers$. Experimentally find that the value of integers not exceed with 256, hence each integer may be denoted by 8 bits. Hence, length of local hash is $4 \times 6 \times 8 = 192 \, bits$. Therefore, total hash length is $96 + 192 = 288 \, bits$.

### 5.1   Robustness and Discrimination Performance

To classify the test images as, forged, different or similar to input images, threshold value is determined by the following method. We have used the USC-SIPI database [36], which is a collection of digitized images. There are different images sizes like $256 \times 256, 512 \times 512, \, or \, 1024 \times 1024$. We consider 38 aerial images and 39 miscellaneous images from this database and create a database of $(38 + 39) \times 76 = 5852$ visually similar image pairs via Stir Mark 4.0 [37], MATLAB 2018a, and Photoshop with distinctive CPOs along with specific constraints reveals in Table 1. The proposed technique is used to calculate the Euclidean distances between the reference and the digitally transformed images, Fig. 3 (blue line) shows histogram of the hash distances.

From a set of 200 different images out of which 70 from the database [38] and 130 from the internet which forming $200 \times (200 - 1)/2 = 19900$ image pairs. The proposed techniques are used for calculating the hash distances for all the image pairs. Figure 3 represent histogram of hash distances (red line). Table 2 is numerical calculation of TPR and FPR of Fig. 3. From Table 2, the optimal value of threshold is selected as $T1 = 2.4$, which provides high value of TPR as well as low value of FPR. It is observed (Fig. 3) that maximum hash distances for similar image pairs are below the threshold, consequently, the proposed approach is efficient for CPOs. It also has very good capability for discrimination, as FPR is 0.000201.

**Table 1.** CPOs

| Software | Manipulations | Parameter values | Number of images |
|---|---|---|---|
| Photoshop | Brightness changes | ±10, ±20 | 4 |
| Photoshop | Contrast changes | ±10, ±20 | 4 |
| StirMark | JPEG contraction | 30–100 | 8 |
| StirMark | Watermark embedding | 10–100 | 10 |
| StirMark | Scaling | 0.5,0.75,0.9,1.1,1.5,2.0 | 6 |
| StirMark | Rotation | ±5, ±10, ±15, ±30, ±45, ±90 | 12 |
| MATLAB | Gamma correction | 0.75, 0.9, 1.1, 1.5 | 4 |
| MATLAB | Gaussian low pass filtering | 0.3–1 | 8 |
| MATLAB | Salt and pepper noise | 0.001–0.01 | 10 |
| MATLAB | Speckle noise | 0.001–0.01 | 10 |
| | | Total | 76 |

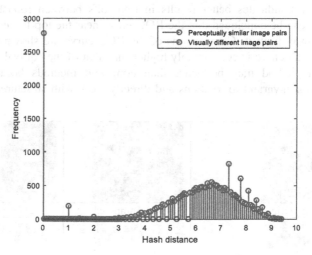

**Fig. 3.** Distribution of hash distances (Color figure online)

**Table 2.** Threshold detection

| Threshold value | TPR | FPR |
|---|---|---|
| 2.3 | 0.9970 | $1.010 \times 10^{-4}$ |
| **2.4** | **0.9980** | **$2.010 \times 10^{-4}$** |
| 2.5 | 0.9990 | $5.025 \times 10^{-4}$ |

## 5.2    Localization of Tampered Regions

In this experiment, 400 tampered images are selected from CASIA tampered database [39]. The proposed algorithm is used in above the selected image pairs to identify the forgery. Approximately 94% of the forged images are found to be correctly identified and the forgery is localized. Figure 4 presents some examples of the forged images. The original pictures, the corresponding forged image and the position of the forgery are depicted in the Fig. 4. Here the rectangle regions represent the tampered region.

## 5.3    Performance Comparison

The proposed technique is compared with different standard hashing algorithm for robustness and discrimination. The algorithms listed include Fourier transform based hashing [15], randomized signal processing based hashing [12], image authentication using Zernike moments and local feature [40], and ring partition hashing and invariant vector distance [41]. The classification performance is described by ROC curve for fair comparisons. The FPR and TPR are the measure of discrimination and robustness. The suggested solution has greater area under the curve (AUC) compared to other algorithms. This thus indicates better results in trade-offs between robustness and discrimination. It can be concluded that the ROC curve near the top-left corner is higher than that far away from it. Comparisons of the ROC curve are shown at Fig. 5. The suggested hashing curve is considerably higher than that of the equivalent algorithms. The proposed method may be better than compared methods because of tensor decomposition is invariant to rotations and directly work with structure.

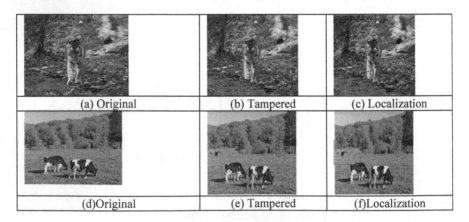

**Fig. 4.** Localization of tampered regions

From Table 3, the developed technique has TPR (0.9980 with optimal FPR) and FPR (0.0002 with optimal TPR) which is superior in comparison to other methods. All algorithms are implemented with MATLAB 2018a. The configurations of the used computer are as follows: the CPU is Intel Core i5 7th Gen with capacity of RAM 8.0 GB. The computation time by proposed idea to develop the image hash is less than the methods in [12, 15, 40], but greater than the method in [41]. However, some other performance of the proposed method is better than [41].

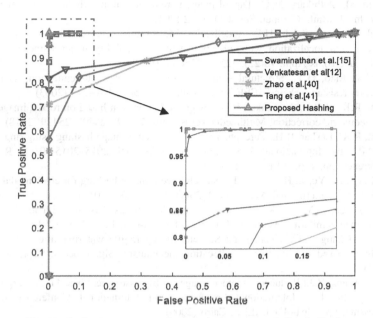

**Fig. 5.** Performance comparison for robustness and discrimination

**Table 3.** Performance comparison for robustness and discrimination

| Comparison parameters | Zhao [40] | Tang [41] | Venkatesan [12] | Swaminathan [15] | Proposed method |
|---|---|---|---|---|---|
| TPR with optimal FPR | 0.9157 | 0.8101 | 0.6374 | 0.8162 | 0.9980 |
| FPR with optimal TPR | 0.2187 | 0.4972 | 0.6271 | 0.3891 | 0.0002 |
| Average time (s) | 2.4 | 0.9 | 2.4 | 2.3 | 2.2 |
| Hash length (bits) | 560 | 320 | 400 | 7168 | 288 |

# 6 Conclusions and Future Works

In this paper, a hashing approach has been designed via local features (positions from salient regions) and global features (tensors) for content authentication. Experimental results depicts that the proposed approach truly recognition of image content is better than many existing method, shown by ROC curve. This may be due to the robustness properties of global as well as local features against many CPOs. Further, the proposed approach achieves good discrimination and is secure. In addition, it can locate forged areas in the images with high accuracy. In future work, the proposed method may be extend to video frame authentication.

# References

1. Mishra, M., Adhikary, M.C.: Digital image tamper detection techniques: a comprehensive study. Int. J. Math. Comput. Sci. **2**(1), 1–12 (2013)
2. Abdelhakim, A., Saleh, H.I., Abdelhakim, M.: Fragile watermarking for image tamper detection and localization with effective recovery capability using K-means clustering. Multimedia Tools Appl. **78**(22), 32523–32563 (2019)
3. Lu, C.S., Liao, H.Y.: Structural digital signature for image authentication: an incidental distortion resistant scheme. IEEE Trans. Multimedia **5**(2), 161–173 (2003)
4. Karsh, R.K., Saikia, A., Laskar, R.H.: Image authentication based on robust image hashing with geometric correction. Multimedia Tools Appl. **77**(19), 25409–25429 (2018)
5. Karsh, R.K., Laskar, R.H.: Perceptual robust and secure image hashing using ring partition-PGNMF. In: International Proceedings on TENCON 2015–2015 IEEE Region 10 Conference, pp. 1–6. IEEE, Macao (2015)
6. Li, K., Qi, G., Ye, J., Hua, K.A.: Linear subspace ranking hashing for cross-modal retrieval. IEEE Trans. Pattern Anal. Mach. Intell. **39**(9), 1825–1838 (2017)
7. Song, J., Yang, Y., Li, X., Huang, Z., Yang, Y.: Robust hashing with local models for approximate similarity search. IEEE trans. cybern. **44**(7), 1225–1236 (2014)
8. Qin, C., Chang, C.C., Chen, P.Y.: Self-embedding fragile watermarking with restoration capability based on adaptive bit allocation mechanism. Sig. Process. **92**(4), 1137–1150 (2012)
9. Lv, X., Wang, Z.J.: Reduced-reference image quality assessment based on perceptual image hashing. In: 16th International Proceedings on International Conference on Image Processing, pp. 4361–4364. IEEE, Cairo (2009)
10. Karsh, R.K., Laskar, R.H., Richhariya, B.B.: Robust image hashing using ring partition-PGNMF and local features. Springer Plus **5**(1), 1995 (2016)
11. Lu, W., Wu, M.: Multimedia forensic hash based on visual words. In: International Proceedings on International Conference on Image Processing, pp. 989–992. IEEE, Hong Kong (2010)
12. Venkatesan, R., Koon, S.M., Jakubowski, M.H., Moulin, P.: Robust image hashing. In: International Proceedings on International Conference on Image Processing, pp. 664–666. IEEE, Vancouver, BC (2000)
13. Fridrich, J., Goljan, M.: Robust hash functions for digital watermarking. In: International Proceedings on International Conference on Information Technology: Coding and Computing, pp. 178–183. IEEE, Las Vegas (2000)
14. Ahmed, F., Siyal, M.Y., Abbas, V.U.: A secure and robust hash-based scheme for image authentication. Sig. Process. **90**(5), 1456–1470 (2010)
15. Swaminathan, A., Mao, Y., Wu, M.: Robust and secure image hashing. IEEE Trans. Inf. Forensics Secur. **1**(2), 215–230 (2006)
16. Monga, V., Mihcak, M.K.: Robust and secure image hashing via non-negative matrix factorizations. IEEE Trans. Inf. Forensics Secur. **2**(3), 376–390 (2007)
17. Tang, Z., Wang, S., Zhang, X., Wei, W., Su, S.: Robust image hashing for tamper detection using non-negative matrix factorization. J. Ubiquitous Convergence Technol. **2**(1), 18 (2008)
18. Lv, X., Wang, Z.J.: Perceptual image hashing based on shape contexts and local feature points. IEEE Trans. Inf. Forensics Secur. **7**(3), 1081–1093 (2012)
19. Lefebvre, F., Macq, B., Legat, J.D.: RASH: radon soft hash algorithm. In: 11th International Proceedings on European Signal Processing Conference, pp. 299–302. IEEE, Toulouse (2002)

20. Schneider, M., Chang, S.F.: A robust content based digital signature for image authentication. In: 3rd International Proceedings on International Conference on Image Processing, pp. 227–230. IEEE, Lausanne (1996)
21. Xiang, S., Kim, H.J., Huang, J.: Histogram-based image hashing scheme robust against geometric deformations. In: 9th International Proceedings on ACM Multimedia Security Workshop, pp. 121–128. ACM (2007)
22. Lei, Y., Wang, Y., Huang, J.: Robust image hash in radon transform domain for authentication. Sig. Process. Image Commun. 26(6), 280–288 (2011)
23. Tang, Z., Huang, L., Yang, F., Zhang, X.: Robust image hashing based on fan-beam transform. ICIC Express Lett. 8(8), 2365–2372 (2014)
24. Kozat, S.S., Mihcak, K., Venkatesan, R.: Robust perceptual image hashing via matrix invariants. In: International Proceedings on International Conference on Image Processing, pp. 3443–3446. IEEE, Singapore (2004)
25. Karsh, R.K., Laskar, R.H.: Robust image hashing through DWT-SVD and spectral residual method. EURASIP J. Image Video Process. 2017(1), 31 (2017)
26. Davarzani, R., Mozaffari, S., Yaghmaie, K.: Perceptual image hashing using center-symmetric local binary patterns. Multimedia Tools Appl. 75(8), 4639–4667 (2016)
27. Paul, M., Karsh, R.K., Talukdar, F.A.: Image hashing based on shape context and speeded up robust features (SURF). In: International Proceedings on International Conference on Automation, Computational and Technology Management, pp. 464–468. IEEE, London (2019)
28. Karami, A., Yazdi, M., Mercier, G.: Compression of hyperspectral images using discrete wavelet transform and tucker decomposition. IEEE J. Sel. Topics Appl. Earth Observ. Remote Sens. 5(2), 444–450 (2012)
29. Kolda, T.G., Bader, B.W.: Tensor decompositions and applications. SIAM Rev. 51(3), 455–500 (2009)
30. Wang, B., Meng, L., Song, J.: Image saliency detection for multiple objects. Multimedia Tools Appl. 78(5), 5329–5343 (2019)
31. Cheng, M.M., Zhang, Z.M., Lin, W.Y., Torr, P.: BING: binarized normed gradients for objectness estimation at 300 fps. In: International Proceedings on Computer Vision and Pattern Recognition, pp. 3286–3293. Columbus, OH, USA (2014)
32. Alexe, B., Deselaers, T., Ferrari, V.: What is an object?. In: International Proceedings on Computer Vision and Pattern Recognition, pp. 73–80. IEEE, San Francisco (2010)
33. Cheng, M.M., Zhang, G.X., Mitra, N.J., Huang, X., Hu, S.M.J.: Global contrast based salient region detection. IEEE Trans. Pattern Anal. Mach. Intell. 37(3), 569–582 (2015)
34. Achanta, R., Shaji, A., Smith, K., Lucchi, A., Fua, P., Süsstrunk, S.: SLIC superpixels compared to state-of-the-art superpixel methods. IEEE Trans. Pattern Anal. Mach. Intell 34(11), 2274–2282 (2012)
35. Saikia, A., Karsh, R.K., Lashkar, R.H.: Image authentication under geometric attacks via concentric square partition based image hashing. In: International Proceedings on TENCON 2017–2017 IEEE Region 10 Conference, pp. 2214–2219. IEEE, Penang (2017)
36. USC-SIPI Image database (2007). http://sipi.usc.edu/database/
37. Petitcolas, F.A.P.: Watermarking schemes evaluation. IEEE Sig. Process. Mag. 17(5), 1–4 (2000)
38. Ground Truth Database. http://imagedatabase.cs.washington.edu/groundtruth/
39. CASIATampered image detection evaluation database. http://forensics.idealtest.org/
40. Zhao, Y., Wang, S., Zhang, X., Yao, H.: Robust hashing for image authentication using Zernike moments and local features. IEEE Trans. Inf. Forensics Secur. 8(1), 55–63 (2012)
41. Tang, Z., Zhang, X., Li, X., Zhang, S.: Robust image hashing with ring partition and invariant vector distance. IEEE Trans. Inf. Forensics Secur. 11(1), 200–214 (2015)

# Author Index

Printed in the United States
By Bookmasters